Morning Glory

MORNING GLORY

A Biography of

MARY LOU WILLIAMS

Linda Dahl

UNIVERSITY OF CALIFORNIA PRESS
Berkeley · Los Angeles · London

University of California Press
Berkeley and Los Angeles, California

University of California Press, Ltd.
London, England

First Paperback Printing 2001

Illustration credits appear on page 465.

Library of Congress Cataloging-in-Publication Data
Dahl, Linda, 1949–
Morning glory : a biography of Mary Lou Williams / Linda Dahl.
p. cm.
Includes bibliographical references, discography, and index.
ISBN 0-520-22872-3 (alk. paper)
1. Williams, Mary Lou, 1910–2. 2. Pianists—United States—
Biography. I. Title.
ML417.W515 D34 2001
786.2'165'092—DC21
[B]
00-064849

Book design by Fritz Metsch

Printed in the United States of America

08 07 06 05 04 03 02 01 00
9 8 7 6 5 4 3 2 1

For A. J. Vogl

Contents

Morning Glory

Introduction

She sits a bit forward on the piano bench, her feet away from the pedals marking off tempo while she nods to that sense of balance that combines drive and relaxation. A half smile lights up the high cheekbone nearest the listener. If she is playing with a band there is sometimes a slight inclination of the head in awareness. But the concentration is in the hands; slender, strong fingers reaching unerringly for the note, the chord, the mood.

— CHARLES EDWARD SMITH
(his liner notes to *Mary Lou Williams and Her All Star Five*)

MARY LOU WILLIAMS's childhood, like that of Ethel Waters and Billie Holiday, two other great black female musicians of her era, was rough and short. Like Waters and Holiday, she had to earn her own livelihood while still a child, and became a woman before she was ready. Also like them, Mary succeeded against forbidding odds. Yet no matter how much she accomplished, she could not crack the carapace of her parents' fundamental indifference to the fact of her existence. It was musicians, not family, who nurtured her talent, who shared her life of poor-boy sandwiches, broken-down cars and rooming houses, the many stretches with no pay. But more than anything else, it was Mary's own innate vision of possibilities, her tremendous grit and empathy, that molded her musical gift. That and later her religious faith kept her going through many hard years—what she called the "muck and the mud" of American show business.

From the time she was a child, Mary (the name she was born with, the name her family and close friends used) had an innate sense both of the depth of her own talent and of the significance of the African-American musical heritage. Throughout a career that lasted more than half a century, she was careful to save the piles of her reviews and notices, telegrams, photographs, and other memorabilia, all of which found their way into scrapbooks that tell nearly as much about the twentieth century as they do about her own career. And there was the music, of course; she wrote stacks of it. Though a good deal of it was never commercially recorded, she saved some on a collection of private tapes.

Mary had a funny, even jolly side, but she was an intensely private person, difficult to know well, and she was highly protective of her own (and others') pain. Seldom did she discuss the hurtful events in her life, and never publicly. Yet she revealed a good deal of her life story in letters and in the small spiral notebooks where she made an attempt at an autobiography. At the bottom of a dusty box of her effects, I found a piece of paper with just these four lines jotted down:

> *Jazz created for all people.*
> *Jazz created through suffering.*
> *Got beaten everyday.*
> *And school—Amy Frank.*

Cryptic and clipped—a kind of Rosetta stone to her life—these lines are emblematic of the distinctive, triumphant personal philosophy that Mary forged out of a difficult existence. They contain, I think, the essence of her personal struggle.

Jazz [was] created for all people.

With this simple, deeply felt declaration, Mary reveals her instinct and her yearning for universal acceptance and harmony. Moreover, she refuses to bow to any ethnocentrism, any limitations, from any side. Like Duke Ellington—who said that there was good music and there was bad music—she only reluctantly accepted the designation "jazz" for the music that was born of African-Americans.

Mary sought and fought all her life for equal acceptance of this uniquely American art form within the musical power structure, the European-derived canon of symphonic music. And when in the sixties, after she had been playing professionally for more than forty years, some African-Americans criticized her when she did not jump on the Black Nationalist bandwagon, Mary replied that she did not want to go back to Africa. Yet when she started tapping her foot and bore down on the piano, there was no doubt about Mary's roots. She was, as Ellington's oft-quoted assessment of her put it, like "soul on soul." She and her music were undeniably *African-*American.

She also saw jazz as a world music, universally accessible. Jazz would be her bridge, her passport, to other people's worlds. It was African-American music that moved her white teachers and principal to take her from her poor neighborhood to play in Pittsburgh's citadels of wealth, as later it carried her around the country, around the world. And everywhere she went, she found an audience that responded to the music she played.

Jazz [was] created through suffering.

When Mary discovered as a little girl, as gifted children do, that she could live in her head, she found in the world of her people's music what she could not find in her family: order, grace, a meaning beyond daily struggle. Moreover, she built up a richly mystical interior life (if at times out of balance) through her music. Gaining meaning through suffering was, indeed, a major motif for Mary. It gave incalculable emotional heft and resonance to her playing, especially after her conversion to Catholicism in the mid-1950s, when the Christian tenet of redemption alleviated her own emotional pain and answered a lifetime of searching for meaning. But Mary's concern was not so much with her own suffering; rather, she focused on the historical impact of suffering on a people—black people in America. As a little girl, she would eavesdrop on conversations of her elders about the cruelties of slavery, the wickedness of racism. She came to understand how the slaves, out of their anguished condition, developed a vital musical communication, combining spirituals and work songs with rhythms that, in Mary's words, "reached deep into the inner self, giving expression of sincere joy." This was her definition of jazz, and she played it that way.

But even as Mary became convinced from her own experience that one's "crosses," as she liked to call her sufferings, can deepen and even ennoble a person's character, she grew aware that for many people, suffering merely degrades and deadens hope. She became a rescuer, trying to help many desperate people, most of them musicians. At times she was abused for her kindness, and seldom was she able to rehabilitate others. After some years of this, she noted, sadly, that some people were too weak to withstand suffering and come out the other side to redemption. But she never stopped caring.

Continually tested in the tempering fire, Mary played the strongest music of her life when she was old and in great physical pain. She had mastered the blues, alchemizing the form into boiling restiveness or tender lyricism or resolute triumph. If she had any one message, it was that jazz meant very little indeed if it lacked the emotional resonance that comes from understanding not only the *form* of the music but where the blues came from. "You ain't said nothin'," she played in a song, "'til you play the blues."

Got beaten everyday.

Mary left few clues about the cruelty she knew as a child, none so stark as this: *Got beaten everyday.* Nearly everything worked against her as a young person—her place and time, her class, her race, and her sex. During her early years, child labor was common, often necessary, to feed a family, and many of the harsh childrearing dictates of the brutal slave era had survived. Mary's was an impoverished southern family, struggling in the cold, smoke-choked air of Pittsburgh, where the family defenses—the demons of drink and indifference—flourished. Mary and her older sister both left home when they were barely in their teens, but their ties to the family remained steadfast and they continued to feel responsible for their younger brothers and sisters. If music became Mary's refuge, her castle, her life, conditions on the road in the 1920s were often as meager, mean, and violent as at home. Mary wrote only peripherally about beatings and neglect from her mother and from the flawed musician lovers who attracted her with their highly intelligent, sensitive playing, but who could become violent when they drank. But clues are scattered in her diaries and in snapshots where her shy, beautiful, smiling face is shadowed by pain. Though she accepted it, kept quiet about it, physical violence cast a long shadow across her life.

And school—Amy Frank.

A careful separation, this, between the private violence of family, and the public. Mary's family, one of thousands of southern black families that poured into the industrial North seeking a better life, were feared and resented by other recent poor immigrants. In Germantown, where Mary's family, the Risers, moved, the neighborhood was composed mostly of Poles, Italians, and Germans. Amy Frank was a white youngster from Germantown, a schoolmate at the red-brick Lincoln School who bullied eight-year-old Mary, just arrived in a cheap cotton shift and her mother's narrow black Oxfords. Rocks were thrown, followed by taunts, hair-pulling, shoving, slaps. As if that were not enough, the light-skinned blacks who lived nearby ostracized her: with her satiny dark brown skin color, Mary was judged too dark for the café au lait children to play with.

But Mary had a special gift. A child prodigy, she could play back by ear on the piano nearly anything she heard and obligingly performed the pop tunes of the day whenever she was asked. Soon, she was welcome as the "little piano girl of East Liberty" at the parlor pianos in all the houses around the neighborhood, taming Amy Frank and the rest as she took requests, and climbing into chauffeured cars to be taken to entertain the wealthy at bridge parties in their hillside mansions above the smoke and slums of the city. It was the first of many dragons she would slay in her life with her beautiful music.

Chapter One
My Mama Pinned a Rose on Me
1910–1916

My mama pinned a rose on me,
She pinned it where everybody could see . . .
Everybody is talking about the way I do.
I'm gonna leave this hard-luck town,
I'm gonna leave before the sun goes down,
Everybody is talking about the way I do.

MARY WAS MARKED from birth with a sign of significance in African-American culture, a sign that indicated special powers, especially a tendency toward "second sight." She writes in her memoir, "The midwife told my mother that I was born with a veil over my eyes and for her to save this veil and dry it out and she could tell when I was sick and all that." (This is the caul, a portion of the membrane that sometimes covers a fetus's head at birth.) "My mother," Mary concludes, "was frightened." Yet Mary did fulfill the omen of the "veil": she soon was drawn to the supernatural, seeing ghosts and having visions and premonitions. As a girl, and even as a young woman, she would sometimes become so agitated at her fearful hallucinations (of cows and dogs) that those around her would resort to tying her to the bed.

Displaying psychic powers was not seen as deviant behavior in African-American folk culture, at home with root doctors and conjure men, but it did set her apart. Combined with her natural nervousness and supersensitivity as a child prodigy—she began playing the piano at about the age of four—it helped to stamp her as something of an outsider. "Everybody was afraid to be around me because I was seeing so many weird things," Mary said. "My mother said at an early age I was seeing spirits. I used to hear so many stories about spooks and ghosts. Seemed like I picked up on that when I was about two or three years old because my mother was afraid to take me out anywhere with us. She said that one day we were walking in a field and I saw a little white dog which grew into a cow. I often wondered about other kids, their imagination," Mary continued. "Because I've gone through life like that, seeing various things."

Jazz musicians, who must be incredibly focused to improvise, are, as a group, highly intuitive and what Mary called her "seeing" was to become very useful to her as a player. "At one time I could hear a musician playing and could hear the note he was going to make next," she said. "It was just that fast, just like telling someone's fortune; it may have something to do with the fastness of the mind and hearing. Some people lose their minds," she cautioned of this ability. "But I think it's useful in your music. You can't control it. You see these things when you're not even expecting them."

———

MARY WAS BORN in Atlanta, Georgia, and spent approximately the first five years of her life there before moving to Pittsburgh—no one in her family can now recall the exact date, but she probably emigrated by train with her mother, sister, and possibly other relatives in 1915. She wrote a good deal about her childhood and her mother, Virginia Burley, much of it after she had come to terms with that problematic figure. But the loneliness of the neglected child and her repressed needs manage to seep through the narrative.

I was born during a superstitious era. Some say our house was built on top of a sunken cemetery in Atlanta. But the house looked more sunken than the cemetery. It was a wooden frame house near swampy woods, one of the most cheerful and charitable houses, 'cept for the regular weekend drinking sprees and even this was not harmful. My mother and my grandmother were the only drinkers. Their drinking was understandable, due to the fact all week long they were washing and ironing for white people. My poor mother was known for her beauty and her tiny little feet, almost became a hunchback carrying their clothes on her back. So when the weekend came they lost themselves in drink, inviting their friends to the house. The only drag to them was my grandfather.

Family history was vague even in Mary's day, although the mixing of races—African, Caucasian, Native American—could be clearly seen in the skin tones, features, and hair of generations of Parkers and Risers, Mary's maternal elders. Indeed, the blending of black, white, and red was the first thing Mary wrote about in describing her relatives. "My great-grandparents' complexions were very fair. My great-grandfather's hair was blond. He wore it down to his shoulders like a pioneer. My great-grandmother was part Indian (Cherokee, I think), and she had straight black hair." Her sister Mamie, four years her elder, told her daughter Helen that she could recall a tepee in the backyard of her Georgia home, set up by Matilda Parker, their great-grandmother.

The light-skinned, straight-haired Matilda Parker had been raised as a black slave, and the cruelties of slavery scarred her memories. "As a young kid, I'd sneak under the bed," Mary wrote, "and listen to their conversation and I learned a great deal about the past. They never allowed the kids to sit in on conversations when they had company. I used to hear them tell stories about how badly they were treated," she added in an interview. "Both my great-grandparents told stories about how the slave-owners on the two different farms on which they were raised used to put them in the sun to parch their skin black to escape guilt and the neighbors' talk. It was a question of easing guilty consciences."

Matilda Parker, called "Mama" by all, was the family matriarch. Widowed soon after the family arrived in Pittsburgh in the second decade of the twentieth century, she moved among the homes of her children up north like visiting royalty. She had a regally irascible temper, stoked by the homebrew she liked to drink. "She was spoiled by all her daughters in Pittsburgh and Philadelphia," says a grandchild, Geraldine Stokes. She would stay with one until a fight erupted, then sweep off to the train station, a sign around her neck to ensure that she got off at the right stop, for as was not uncommon in that age, Matilda was illiterate. "She was a very prejudiced woman: if you were light, you were all right. But if you were dark-skinned, she tended to beat you far more often," adds Geraldine Stokes, herself a dark-skinned woman.

Many of Mary's male ancestors were either unknown, unacknowledged, or simply untraceable, their identities supplied by family gossip. Matilda Parker, for example, took her name from the people who owned her, and was supposed to have been fathered by one of the males in that family. But it was Mary's grandmother, Anna Jane, light-skinned like her mother though she was, who married the mixed-race Andrew Riser, in vehement reaction against what she viewed as the enforced miscegenation of her elders. It was Anna Jane also who agitated to get the family out of Georgia, clean away from the painful past.

Of the paternal side of Mary's family almost nothing is known. It was hardly an exaggeration when Mary wrote, "I never knew my father." In fact, she did meet her father, but till then nothing was ever told her about him. Mary wrote flatly, "I was born out of wedlock, a common thing not only for black people but also for whites in the South." It was not until she was well out of her teens and a renowned soloist with Andy Kirk's Clouds of Joy that Mary learned his identity.

Mary's half-brother in Atlanta, Willis Scruggs, later vividly recalled introducing his famous half-sister to their father in the late 1930's; Mary, whose memory for dates was sometimes hazy, was to remember meeting her dad, Joseph Scruggs, much later—in 1953, when she was in Atlanta to get a birth certificate, which she needed in order to obtain a passport so she could work abroad. "We didn't know anything about what Mary had become," says Willis Scruggs. "We just thought she was playing piano; but we had no notion she had gone with the big bands. Then an uncle of mine had gone to Pittsburgh and came back to Atlanta in about 1936 or so, and he told us what Mary was doing. And then one day in the summer, there were posters out telling you who's coming to town among the bands and I saw that Andy Kirk's band was going to play at a new amusement park just for blacks, on Magnolia and Sunset, an enclosed park with a roller-coaster and Ferris wheel, because otherwise blacks in those days could only go to the big amusement park, Lakewood Fairground, on Labor Day. Well, after I saw this poster of Andy Kirk's band and Mary's picture on it, I asked my uncle, 'Is this the Mary Lou Williams who's my sister?' And when he told me it was, I said I was going to see her perform. I remember she was beautifully dressed. The piano was up front and the spotlight was put on her when she was playing solo.

"There were no hotels in those days for blacks and I knew where she'd be: at Scott Sutton's, which had a restaurant with excellent, home-style food and rooms upstairs. It was considered expensive, it cost $1.50 to $2.00 for a meal. I knew Miss Sutton and she told me Mary was staying there. John Williams, her husband who was with the band, was on the bed asleep when I knocked on the door and introduced myself. He said, 'She isn't here; she went downtown to get something at the drugstore.' I said, 'I'll just stand here and wait on her.' I saw her walk up the street very slowly, very dignified. She was dressed in a little jacket and a dress, and some little heels and she was bareheaded, with her hair parted in a page-boy. She had a neat-looking figure. She always looked good. I said, 'Mary Lou Williams? Do you remember me? I'm your brother.' 'I don't have a brother,' she said. 'Oh, yes, you do. Your daddy is the same man as mine. His name is Joe Scruggs.' She said, 'My daddy's name is Fletcher Burley.' 'No, that's your mother's husband. That's not your father. When you get back to Pittsburgh, you ask them about it.' She said, 'Where does he live?' I said, 'In Edgewood.' Just then my cousin with a car came by. 'Come on, I'm going to show you where you were born.' She said, 'This I gotta see.' A smile on her face, in amazement.

"We went out to Edgewood, parked the car by his store and we got out," continues Willis Scruggs. "He was sitting on the porch area in front with his pants pulled up to his knees cuz it was hot. And we got out the car and walked up toward him. He stood up. I said, 'Do you know who this is?' He said no. 'This is your daughter—Ginny Riser's daughter, your daughter. This is Mary Lou Williams.' He said, 'My daughter?'

"He looked at Mary, and asked her, 'What did you bring me?' He thought he was being funny. And she said, 'Not a goddamn thing, you son-of-a-bitch. What did you bring me, what have you given me all these years?' That was it. Just like that. The expression on his face! My cousin John Scruggs and I, we just cracked up. That was around 1937 or 1938."

Then Willis Scruggs took a stunned Mary away from the equally startled Joseph Scruggs and gave her a tour of her childhood neighborhood. "The house was still there where she was born and reared and I showed her the house where I was born. I could stand on my front porch and see into her porch. In those early days, I was in and out of that house; we'd go from house to house. I showed her where her mother and aunts grew up. Then she began to ask questions. She didn't know about any of this. She went back to Pittsburgh and she questioned her mother and her grandmother and they told her the truth. I imagine she wanted to know why they hadn't told her before."

Of the several males Mary remembered with affection from her childhood, her grandfather Riser was the first, a quiet, sober man who liked to build things. Had he been born white, he might have been an engineer; he had the rather dry, sober personality, intelligence and love of tinkering suited to such a profession. As it was, he worked as a laborer. Although at times he was overwhelmed by the carryings-on of his womenfolk, it was he who "kept them in line," as his granddaughter Mamie told her own children later. He also was the only grown-up who seemed to pay any attention to the children in the household. "He built a train for the neighborhood kids, with a real boiler," wrote Mary. Sometimes he took Mary on walks; they'd go watch the trains and talk. He gave her her first nickname, "Messy," which she used in the title of her first composition, "Messa Stomp," and he liked to hand out candy to the neighborhood children. Andrew Riser also tried to save money, for he dreamed of owning real estate, but his wife and daughters would invariably find the box where he hid it and take what they wanted.

After the family finally settled in one house in Pittsburgh, Mary recalled that her grandfather, defeated in his plans to acquire real estate, simply withdrew from the cacophony around him. He "built himself a little apartment in the basement, where he lived," she wrote.

————

THERE WAS A song from Mary's childhood, a pretty little old-fashioned blues called "My Mama Pinned a Rose on Me," that Mary loved to play, infusing it with the luminous mystery of early memory, that "light" from the mind that makes ordinary little houses seem like great mansions, a stand of trees a deep, dark forest. "Mama Pinned a Rose" is a modest song, but to Mary it was one of the most beautiful she'd ever heard, and she played it (and occasionally sang the lyric) tenderly, all her life. Yet it had nothing to do with her mother, but rather her stepfather Fletcher Burley, a feckless, life-loving man who did his little stepdaughter the great and rare service of paying her serious attention. It was he who taught her the value of the blues, she said.

It was fortunate Mary had him to listen to her, because she got precious little attention from her mother. Virginia Burley, *née* Riser, and often called "Miss Ginnie" or "Miss Jenny" for short, was to have eight children by several different fathers. "You grew up like a weed. We don't know where you came from or who you are," Mary recalled a cruel relative telling her after the family had moved to Pittsburgh. "Those children raised themselves," confirms Mary's closest niece, Helen Floyd. All the more reason that Mary clung to the few golden moments of her childhood, polishing and embellishing them in the telling and retelling. Hers was a childhood shorn of innocence and freedom from care. "When you're poor, you grow up fast," she said simply.

The hard facts about her first years are scarce, and the family history, compiled orally—largely by Mary's cousin Geraldine Stokes Williams—remains incomplete. Even Mary's surname changed with a casualness conferred by the often makeshift quality of a family that had to struggle to stitch together a life. "I've had a lot of names," she said once in her matter-of-fact way. "I was born Mary Elfrieda Scruggs, and later I was Mary Lou Winn and Mary Lou Burley, after stepfathers. I don't know where the Lou came from."

She added, "As I went along, I guess if one father made me angry, I'd switch to another's name. Joe Scruggs was my real father, from Atlanta. But I loved [Fletcher] Burley. Anyway, everybody knew me as 'the little piano girl.' The names didn't matter."

Mary always gave her birthday as May 8, 1910, but no doctor attended her birth at home in Edgewood, and there was no birth certificate, so that the actual date remains—as with many rural blacks and whites of that era—an approximation. Also, according to Willis Scruggs, who remained in Atlanta and became a schoolteacher, many poor people "fudged" birth dates of children because of the high infant mortality rates. "I think her birthday may have been a few years earlier. You see, in the early days in the black community, blacks were not permitted to get life insurance until the child was at least three years old. When a child was born the insurance agent would come around and write a life insurance policy and change the age, make it age three or four, because the insurance company would not pay if it wasn't that way. The only real way that our parents kept up with dates was to write it in the Bible. When the child was born, they'd write it in the front of the Bible." No Bible with family records has survived, and even if one did, people have been known to fudge birthday entries in the Good Book too.

The house in Atlanta where Mary Scruggs was born, with the assistance of a local midwife, was a "shotgun" cottage, that ubiquitous, simple, long and narrow timberframe dwelling in the South. "If you fired through the front door," Mary explained, "the shot passed through all the rooms and out into the backyard, likely ending up in the privy."

She lived her very first years on a dirt lane the people of Edgewood called Gotsipling Street. So separate was this black pocket of Atlanta that to Franklin Garrett, Atlanta's preeminent historian, the name must have been "Gospero," rather than the unfamiliar (to him) Gotsipling. Edgewood was essentially a dirt track lined with wooden shotgun cottages and shacks. But it was also a real village.

Mary was teenaged Ginnie Riser's second child to be born in Atlanta. Her first, Mamie Winn, was about four years older than Mary, and her closest companion all through her life. The two girls grew up together, shifting about with various relatives, first in Georgia, later in Pennsylvania. Willis Scruggs supplies a clear picture of the childhood neighborhood. "Mary lived in a house that was about four or five rooms. They washed clothes for a living. People who didn't work in private homes or factories, they washed and ironed in their backyard. They'd pick up the dirty clothes from the homes of the whites, bring 'em back to the house, and wash them and scrub them and drop them into a big black pot that was setting on a fire. Where Mary lived, it was built like a barbecue and they'd boil the clothes, then take them and rinse them, hang them on the clothesline."

Mary's parents were probably both born in the little community of Edgewood in the generation after slavery. Virginia Riser, who died in the early 1970s, was probably born in the early 1890s, to Anna Jane and Andrew Riser ("Nanny" and "Grandpa" to Mary), both light-skinned people. Anna Jane had a half-white mother and a white father, and Andrew was, Mary wrote, "short and whitish looking." But Virginia, like Mary after her, was a warm brown, which lowered her status somewhat in the family; nevertheless, she had dainty little feet and a pretty, heart-shaped face, which Mary inherited. Indeed, she was something of a local belle, or at least a fun-loving girl who attracted men, with her love of music (she played the organ a bit), and willingness to loosen up with a few drinks. In old family snapshots there is a pettish set to Miss Ginnie's mouth, and her small hands are crossed tensely on her lap. With only drudgery to look forward to, Miss Ginnie rebelled by becoming what Mary called "a party girl." When she and Anna Jane brought out the jugs on a Friday afternoon, after the washing was done for the week, Grandpa Riser, a teetotaler, seethed on the sidelines. Family members concur that Virginia was not much good at the physical or emotional side of mothering. (Vain about her looks, Virginia later insisted that her grandchildren call her Miss Ginnie rather than Grandma.)

————

EVEN SO, MISS GINNIE became for Mary a mythic first influence at the keyboard. As poor as she was, Mary's mother had access to a reed organ (also called a harmonium) at the storefront Beulah Baptist Church nearby, where her father held the respected post of deacon. Playing an instrument was a hugely important source of pleasure and entertainment at a time when not even Victrolas were widespread, and Virginia often played and danced for donations—after church, a cloth draped over the altar. Music lessons were inexpensive, and, according to both Mary and Willis Scruggs, Virginia took some instruction. But not surprisingly, given her indifference to her children, she never taught them to read even a note of music. Instead, Mary relied solely on her ear. Later, she came to place enormous importance on her ear training and it became part of her credo that real jazz—improvisation with feeling—could not be systematically taught. Nor is it too much to say that in Mary's mind, at a fundamental level, playing music and improvising were synonymous.

Later in her life Mary had a strong tendency to burnish her mother's memory. She certainly seems to have done so when it came to Virginia's musical ability, often saying that "books" (by which she meant the rote learning of exercises such as those from Czerny's popular series) had "destroyed" her mother's ear so that Virginia couldn't improvise. "My mother wouldn't allow a teacher near me," Mary would go on. "She played by ear [at first], then went to a teacher, and ended up not playing at all, just reading music." Except for Miss Ginnie, hardly anybody in Mary's immediate family seems to have played a musical instrument. The one exception was Mamie's husband, Hugh Floyd, who played the popular music of the day on the saxophone. But they all enjoyed listening. Grandpa Riser was partial to the classics, Fletcher Burley to ragtime and the blues. Noticeably absent was church music—hymns, spirituals, gospel. But Mary did learn about the importance of music in the slaves' hard lives when she listened to the grown-ups talk at night. "The old folks said that the slaves were taken to church on Sundays by their owners and were taught the psalms from which they began creating their own sounds, leading to the creation of spirituals, the base of black music. Whenever a slave was abused or beaten, he'd return to the cotton field or his work, creating a new song and the others would join in singing together." In Edgewood, Mary may have heard some hymns at the tiny storefront Baptist church, but once the Riser clan moved to Pittsburgh, they seem to have fallen away from churchgoing.

What *is* clear is that Mary was able to teach herself an astonishing amount of musical technique by watching and listening, and the fact that her mother was the first person to hear her play the piano was crucial. Mary's most cherished memory was of Virginia's discovery of her daughter's incredible talent. In a scene that Mary described many times with obvious relish (and embellishment), Mary is sitting on her mother's lap at the little harmonium (sometimes she is age three, sometimes four) while Virginia is playing. Without warning, Mary reaches up to the keys with her baby hands and plays back, note for note, what she has just heard her mother play. "I must have frightened her so that she dropped me then and there, and I started to cry," Mary wrote. "It must have really shaken my mother. She actually dropped me and ran out to get the neighbors to listen to me."

Again, as with the birth sign of the caul, Mary was marked as different. "I never left the piano after that. Always played. Nothing else interested me." "My half-brother would come over to play with me," she added in another reminiscence, "but I'd be busy at the piano. Sometimes I'd stop and go out and play with him a little while, and then come back in to the piano, getting my own sounds, and I've been doing that all my life. . . . I didn't know what I was doing . . . but the piano played for my fingers. If somebody hummed something, I played it." Today, Willis Scruggs remembers: "It was an organ you pump with two big pedals"—for despite Mary's reference to a piano, it was the organ-like harmonium—"but because Mary was so short, her legs didn't reach the pedals. So she'd say to me, 'Willis, pump the organ,' and I'd get down there two or three minutes with my hands, and I'd pump those two big pedals with my hands on my knees until I said I was tired. I was just a little kid of about three or four, so Mary had to be four or five. She was old enough to be playing."

Even when Mary became a star player in a popular black swing band in the thirties, no one in the family can remember Ginnie ever going to hear her play. Nor did her mother come to New York to hear her daughter play after Mary had established herself there in the forties. The estrangement between daughter and mother cut deep, recall many friends, and Mary was to struggle for many years to forgive her mother. "What did Mary and I have in common?" muses Gray Weingarten, a well-to-do white woman who became a close friend of Mary's in the 1940s. "Well, for one thing we both hated our mothers." Says Bernice Daniels, another longtime close friend, "You ask about her mother. Well, I don't like to say. Well, she called her mother names, bad names. 'Dirty old whore,' things like that. And she hated her father too." Only rarely did Mary choose to get down to specifics. At the end of her life, when she was terminally ill and bedridden, she had long conversations with a new friend, Marsha Vick, who kept a diary. When Vick remarked, "Your family must have loved you when you were little," Mary, she remembers, responded bluntly, "No, they didn't give me any space. They used to spit in my mouth when I was sick, paid no attention to me." "To make ends meet," Mary adds in her memoir, "along with taking in laundry, Mom would also work for a few private families, leaving me in the care of a baby-sitter. Thank God when Mamie was old enough to look out for me. My baby-sitter, as I remember, was young but not very nice. She never fed me, made me chew tobacco and swallow the juice and got great kicks out of tickling me until I almost had a spasm. This impaired my speech and for years I stuttered very badly."

"The kids," Mary's niece Helen recalls her mother, Mamie, telling her, "had to fend for themselves." Mary wrote, "I was trying to help with the housework, washing and ironing, just a busy little body and a nose picker from birth. Once while trying to iron, I burnt my arm very badly and the scar is still with me." It was one of several accidents she suffered while unsupervised.

As other children came along, her mother's drinking got worse. In 1927, well after Mary had left home to work in vaudeville, she paid a visit to her mother's Pittsburgh home during a layover, with her new husband, John Williams. "She was kind of an alcoholic," Williams recalled of Ginnie, who lived at that time in a rundown house in an alley reminiscent of Edgewood, in Atlanta. "They had music on and Fletcher [Mary's stepfather] was dancing around in his bare feet, drinking. Sort of a rough gambling kind of guy. Well, Miss Ginnie was nice to me, but they were always tippling, you know. I wasn't brought up in that atmosphere where your parents were drinking and you might walk in the room and they're knocked out, but Mary was practically raised up in that. The drinking went on all day. Mary told me that they weren't hungry or nothing when they were kids, but her mother didn't pay much attention."

Virginia's situation grew even worse during the Depression. By then a widow who still had young children to raise, she was so poor that, as Mary told a friend, her half-sisters had to go search for coal along the railroad tracks for fuel in the winter. Mary, who often suffered severe financial constraints of her own, sent home money, clothes, whatever she could, for years and years.

Chapter Two
The Little Piano Girl of East Liberty
1915–1924

WHEN MARY'S FAMILY decided to move from Atlanta up to Pittsburgh toward the end of World War I, they were among many thousands who made similar plans. War was a boon for the industrial North, and for the unskilled, it seemed to offer a limitless supply of jobs. Like other migrant groups, African-Americans were determined to get some of those jobs.

But they faced stiff competition from the many recent European immigrants, as well as native-born whites. Blacks often discovered that, while there was work to be had, the better jobs were out of bounds for them. "Almost everywhere white labor tended to exclude Negro workers from the unions," states historian John Hope Franklin flatly. And it would take decades to change that. In the teens of the century, "Smoketown" gave them the dirtiest, hardest work for the least pay.

Grandpa Andrew Riser found work as a common laborer, as did Mary's stepfather when he came north a bit later. He had been reluctant to leave Atlanta; a fortune-teller, Mary wrote, warned him to stay put, predicting that he would die up North "smothered by sand." Years later he perished at a construction site when a dump truck unloaded a ton of gravel on him, burying him alive.

"On the train to Pittsburgh, we must have looked just awful with all the luggage tied with rope, our phonograph player with the megaphone and all the trunks, etc.," Mary reminisced. But she found her first train trip thrilling, especially "the noise of the engine and cross ties, like music to my ears."

One can only imagine the family's culture shock at arriving in cold, smoggy Pittsburgh after the hot, small-town ways of Edgewood. An army of smokestacks lined up along the Allegheny and Monongahela rivers, belching coal and steel fumes. By noon the sun would have dimmed to premature night, blotted out by thick black smoke. Air pollution was not curbed until the 1960s, and Pittsburgh had one of the highest tuberculosis rates in the nation.

At first the Risers lived with relatives who had preceded them, Aunt Hattie and her husband, Uncle Joe. Mary was terribly homesick for the Georgia woods where she had played. "There were 11 or 12 of us in the house with no more than four bedrooms," Mary wrote. Mary remembered a string of addresses for her struggling family: Broad Street and Lemington; Euclid, Wilmington, and Larimer avenues. Eventually, they moved to 6211 Hamilton Avenue, on the cusp of Homewood and East Liberty townships, where they were joined by Fletcher Burley, soon Mary's stepfather.

Today the area where Mary grew up is bleak, a typical product of urban renewal, its heart bisected by a highway that slices through what had been a bustling shopping district. Back then, however, East Liberty was a new, vibrant neighborhood, full of woodframe and brick houses, many of them quite commodious. It had shops of every kind, as well as numerous churches, taverns, gambling dens—and brothels. Yet by comparison, Edgewood, with its rigid racial segregation, was stable, while the ethnically fragmented townships and burgs that made up Pittsburgh felt themselves to be under siege. Competition for housing and jobs was so fierce that newcomers sometimes were forced to live in boxcars with breathing holes cut out of the sides, where they paid a nickel a night. Crime flourished, and both whites and established black Pittsburghers blamed it on the surge of black newcomers from the South. Earl Hines, who was five years Mary's senior and one of her first musical idols, was a Pittsburgher from a solidly working-class family. He recalled that the northern African-Americans complained that southern blacks were disrupting the delicate balance between the races.

For the first time in her short life, Mary had direct experience with racism. "My new home," she wrote, "was in a section called

East Liberty, at least six miles from the downtown section. We lived . . . between two white families on both sides of us, in fact they were all around us. This was my first encounter with hate and prejudice. Bricks came our way several times. Two blocks from where we lived was Germantown and this was really murder. Playing on the sidewalk in front of the house, with other kids, we'd have to run for our lives when a couple of German 'gentlemen' passed, because they always tried to kick the kids in the mouth or beat them up. . . ." She remembered being chased by a white kid's mother with a butcher knife, and being snubbed by black neighbors, who "belonged to the Amphibian Society, for Negroes with light skin only. Our neighbor next door had a beautiful little girl with long hair and curls. She was not allowed to play with me and other dark-skinned kids, but my sister whose skin was light could play with her." Decades later she added drily, "Now, black is beautiful!" And if she also recalled good neighbors, such as an Italian family who gave the Risers gifts of macaroni, olive oil, and the like, racism still cut deep. " 'Nigger'? 'Snowball'? What did these names mean?" she wondered, recalling the taunts. "And, why would a family of blacks discriminate against another because of the color of his skin?" Mary never felt really at home with the caste of lighter-skinned blacks who reigned socially in the cities where she lived and worked later in her life, such as Kansas City, Washington, D.C., New York, and Durham. And even after she became famous and had offers to play in Europe, Mary hesitated—as she confided to her friend Joyce Breach in a letter decades later—reluctant because of her childhood experiences of racial prejudice. She was genuinely surprised, she wrote, at the warm hospitality shown her by whites when she did go overseas.

It wasn't long, however, before Mary found she had a way to escape the poverty and ill-feeling in Smoketown: "I began building up a defense against prejudice and hatred and so many other miserable blocks by taking my aching heart away from bad sounds and working hard at music. Looking back, I see that my music acted as a shield, preventing me from being aware of many of the prejudices that must have existed. I was completely wrapped up in my music. Little else mattered to me." Nearby was a Catholic girls' school where she often lingered to listen as the girls' choir practiced. To Mary, their singing was "angelic" and had a deep influence that revealed itself years later when she began to write choral jazz and sacred works.

Without a piano at home as yet, Mary still found plenty of instruments to play in the homes of neighbors. And once she played for them—waltzes, marches, sentimental ballads, ragtime—she began to make money, as much as fifty cents for requests at the age of seven or eight, very good money indeed at a time when a laborer earned between twelve and fifteen dollars a week. Mary promoted her new career on her own, and on the sly. "None of my family," she wrote, "knew what I was doing—until I broke my arm." She had jumped over a box on a dare and fallen heavily on her left arm, and although she was in great pain, she hid for the rest of the day under a bed, afraid (without reason, it turned out) of her mother's wrath. Her accident, however, had some interesting consequences: "Not seeing me, the neighbors came to our house and asked why I hadn't been around to play for them. Not realizing it, my little visits had changed the entire scene."

After her arm healed, Mary's family saw that she could contribute to their income as an entertainer. (If it had not healed, she would have had to end her career as a pianist then and there.) Her very first professional gig was for an undertaker, "a very popular mortician called Peyton Rose, in East Liberty," as Mary described him. "He didn't live very far from us. After my first job for him, he would have me back often to play for his guests." Word of mouth built her reputation quickly. "Offers for me to play dances, society parties, even churches, were now coming in regularly. For most dates I was paid the sum of $1 per hour and they always tipped me at the end of the night." Handsome wages for a preteen.

Occasionally, Mary got work as an accompanist for silent movies at a theater on Broad Street, or filled in at a dance hall for a few dollars. She also found work in more sordid surroundings, as did many another black entertainer who went on to later fame. "The whores in her neighborhood liked her and she said she would play for pay—not much—in the whorehouse," said her friend Joyce Breach. Added Father Peter O'Brien, "She said there used to be this keyhole or viewing hole or something. She was supposed to play for the 'duration,' and one time she got mad—her hands got tired—because the duration went on and on."

Mary was running wild. "I was out booking my gigs—my mother didn't know where I was," she explained. It is tempting to lay all the blame for the deprivations of Mary's childhood on her mother.

Yet Ginnie Riser was herself consumed by the scramble for survival in an era where charity of any kind scarcely existed, where daily life unfolded in a culture of improvisation, and where middle-class notions—saving for a rainy day, or postponing gratification—made little sense. Children were expected to learn to both fend for themselves and contribute to the family, and Ginnie's method of ensuring their obedience was old-fashioned and harsh. "Before going to work, she'd say if we got into any mischief, she'd kill us," Mary wrote. "When a child misbehaved, she got a whuppin'."

Yet Ginnie had gotten a break. Mary's great-uncle by marriage, a "sportsman" named Max Sloane, had staked the Risers to a laundry business. Running it out of their home, they were soon successful enough to employ a half-dozen or so women, supplying local businesses with clean linen. But the business was short-lived, as partying took precedence. Before long, Ginnie was working freelance as a maid and laundress in the white middle-class Squirrel Hill district, work that she did off and on until she became old and ill. (Max Sloane came to a grisly end soon after: when he failed to pay a bad debt, he was drugged, tied to railroad tracks, and run over by a train.)

There were good times in the family, too. Mamie and Anna Mae (Mary's aunt, but close enough in age to be like a sister) would put up a sheet for a stage curtain and perform skits and plays, with Mary providing the music. "Anna Mae and Mamie always kept me with them, even when they had their little 'puppy love' dates," wrote Mary of the years when she was seven and eight. "They would take me along, buying me ice cream, cookies and candy and leaving me on the steps of the church to enjoy myself. They'd go away with their friends but I'd still be sitting on the church steps when they returned. And later, when Anna became old enough to work—she was a skilled dressmaker—she'd buy me beautiful dresses and gifts to get me to play for her friends on Sunday, as there was nowhere to go on Sundays in Pittsburgh. If I refused to play she'd whisper in my ear, 'Take off that dress I bought you.'" A few years later, when Mary began to get occasional jobs performing for bridge and tea parties at the homes of wealthy whites, Mamie and Anna Mae "would beg me out of my tips. I would give it to them freely until I needed money for myself to buy a dress or a pair of shoes, then I would hide tips."

At the same time, Mary was handing over most of her pay to Ginnie, to feed the growing family. "I was holding down three jobs," Mary remembered of her preteen years. "I was booked playing churches throughout Pennsylvania and I had other jobs—as a maid, and performing at afternoon teas at $1 an hour, and as helper to a woman who made wigs—that paid $2 per week." Miss Ginnie apparently needed her financial help despite having remarried again in late 1916. Fletcher Burley was, in Mary's embellished portrait, "a professional gambler, but a man who worked hard every day and brought his pay packet home to Mom every week. He never gambled with the money he earned. He'd go out then, to Frankstown Avenue to his favorite joint and have a friend put him in the game. He always came home loaded with money and kept cigar boxes full of change—he had a thing about saving change. Fletcher had a very strenuous job, lifting cement blocks. But he was never too tired to help me."

Clearly, Mary adored this "light tannish man with sandy brown hair, what one would call a Georgia brown during those days," Mary wrote. He was the first man who gave her the attention she had long craved. He prized Mary's ability as a pianist and treated her as *his* little girl. She had found, she felt, a father at last, and a romantic one at that, a bon vivant—but a man with a dangerous temper when crossed. "When angered, he had a habit of spitting just once. When this happened, everybody moved out." Once, family legend has it, Fletcher Burley stopped off for a drink at a nearby tavern, and was called "a name" by the white bartender who refused to serve him. Enraged, he ran home for his gun. Ginnie and Nanny begged him not to go back. But he did, and shot the man in the arm. Somehow, he managed to get off in court. "His kind heart must have saved him," Mary reasoned. At night, Fletcher Burley would trade his laborer's overalls for the fine suit and vest he wore when he conducted his real business: gambling. "And he sometimes took me with him at nights—to bring him luck, he said. He bought himself an extra large coat and would put me underneath and sneak me into one of his gambling joints, most of which had an upright piano against one wall. The game was generally 'skin'—the Georgia skin game—and the players would all be men, for women weren't allowed in these places. I was kind of smuggled in and before the cards began I used to play a few things on the piano. Inside he'd stop the game, throw a dollar in his hat and say, 'I want everybody to put some money in this hat for my little girl to play for you.' The money would roll in." The take would be substantial in an era when fifty cents would buy you a place to sleep or food for a day: twenty or thirty dollars! "Outside again, he'd say 'Give me the dollar back I put into the hat to start your tips.' "

Burley went to the great expense of buying a player piano (Mary thought he'd paid $1,000, which seems improbable) and gave it "pride of place," in Mary's phrase, in their parlor. The player piano was a clever machine. It could function like a regular piano, but also, in that era before Victrolas—the first record players—were widely available, allowed people to "hear" the work of well-known pianists by "playing" their piano rolls. Such an addition to the modest Burley home drew neighbors—one could hear Jelly Roll Morton or James P. Johnson right there in the parlor.

Not yet in her teens, Mary fell under the influence of both those masters and especially loved Morton's "The Pearls." (Interestingly, Duke Ellington said he learned the work of the great early masters the same way, by slowing down the piano rolls and committing them to memory; and Fats Waller studied James P. Johnson's piano-roll solos.) But she listened in person to another Atlanta emigré, hard-stomping Jack Howard, who "ragged." It was from him that Mary discovered "broken tenths," a two-key reach beyond the octave especially useful for the small span of a little girl's hands. Howard took Mary under his wing, coaching her in various tricks of the trade, emphasizing the importance of a strong left hand and showing her how to stretch the web between her fingers. He was a loud and a "full" player, Mary said, playing so heavy he "smashed" the keys. "He told me always to play the left hand louder than the right because that's where the beat and the feeling was," Mary recalled. "It's just like a drum keeping a steady beat. I think," she added, "I got the masculine quality of playing from him."

As ragtime experts David Jasen and Trebor Jay Tichenor point out, "None of the original pianists played ragtime the way it was written. They played their own style. . . . No two pianists ever played syncopated numbers alike." From the teens of the century, brilliant black pianists were playing popular rags, putting their inimitable stamp on them and often committing them to piano rolls: Luckey Roberts in Philadelphia, James P. Johnson in New Jersey, Eubie Blake in Baltimore, Willie "The Lion" Smith in New York, and players like Jack

Howard, who never became known beyond their hometowns; and they all emphasized syncopation and speed of execution. Their compositions were written for professional pianists to play, but quite different from the ragtime of Scott Joplin, which Mary viewed as a type of European music that precluded improvisation, explaining, "You don't get the feeling and the sounds when everything's on paper." So when Mary recorded Joplin in her prime years, she did it her way.

As a precocious player who at first relied completely on her ear, Mary learned mostly by imitating—Jack Howard at first, and then the masterful Fats Waller. But above all, she learned by playing. Late in life, when her friend Marsha Vick asked her who had taught her to play, she could honestly answer, "Nobody." She just "never left the piano."

———

BUT RAGTIME WAS not the only style she was acquiring. "I learned to play a few classical tunes, by pressing my fingers down with the keys of the player piano. My grandfather always wanted to hear the classics, and he gave me money to play them." There were Irish ballads, waltzes, light opera, too. And then there was the foundation: the blues. "Fletcher taught me the first blues I ever knew by singing them over to me," Mary wrote. When he was flush, she could remember him paying her as much as "$15 and $20 to play the blues and boogie-woogie."

This accumulation of musical styles was casual, often indirect, yet Mary had a very orderly, highly analytic mind. "I had to see things for myself," she said. "I wouldn't ask questions. I'd take a clock or something apart and put it back together again; I wanted to see how it worked." Perhaps she inherited this trait from her engineer grandfather. She was blessed with perfect pitch and an unshakeable sense of time, combined with sensitivity, intelligence, and a fierce will to achieve.

While Mary ran free, playing and hearing music, Virginia Burley had her hands full, bearing children. There were six more between 1916 and 1928: Grace, Howard, the twins Geraldine and Gerald, Marge, and Josephine. But Grandpa Riser died in 1920, when Mary was ten. His death and the heart condition that afflicted Fletcher Burley shortly after, curtailing his job as a laborer, drastically reduced the family income. Burley's gambling take and Miss Ginnie's laundry work could not meet the demands of this growing family. "That's the time when Mary would come home with money and her mama and papa would get that to buy food and drink with it. *She was half-supporting the family at that young age,*" emphasized her husband, John Williams.

After Grandpa Riser died, Mary's life changed drastically: she left her mother's house. Decades later, in a letter to Robbie Mickles, a nephew she regarded as a son, Mary explained, "I had to leave home as a child to get away from fear, alcoholism, fights. And I left when I was 12, then again when I was 16. And I thank God for leaving when I did." Her half-sister Grace, who grew up in those impoverished years, echoed those feelings when she wrote years later: "I was born from a nervous, alcoholic mother. Our mother never gave us a decent home life. We had to go out into the world and live the best we can." Mary sought to do this by taking shelter with her older sister Mamie, who that year married Hugh Floyd and persuaded him that they should get their own place, which they did, in nearby Winfield Street. By all accounts, they were remarkably mature. Though Mamie was only fourteen or fifteen, she was pregnant with her first child, but she ran her household firmly and steadily. From the age of twelve Mary never again lived *full-time* with her mother, although the boundaries separating the family households were porous and Virginia Burley continued to assert her authority at times—and not only need but *expect* Mary's financial help. In later years, when Mary was a mature woman and an established presence in the music world, she would pay her mother a courtesy call on visits home; but then "it was on to Mamie's," as Mary's niece Helen Floyd recalls. Mamie was the true matriarch, and Mamie brooked no nonsense. Years later, Mary's then-lover, the great tenor saxophonist Don Byas (who had a drinking problem), was staying with Mary at Mamie's. He got drunk and, in Helen's words, "got rough with Mary while drinking. Mom threw him not just out of the house, but *down* the stairs." It was Mamie, the sister who remained in Pittsburgh, who hosted family gatherings and fielded the many family crises, and it was she who kept Mary in school in the 1920s. Although Mary's attendance was haphazard, she worked at her piano playing with discipline and drive while living with the Floyds. "This period of my life was hard work for me," she wrote. "My brother-in-law Hugh said I'd sit at the piano for hours and hours without food, just drank water, and would practice all day. All the other children would be outside playing hopscotch or something but I'd be sitting at the piano." Hugh Floyd, who played sax and had his sons play in a marching band, was the second important man in Mary's life. A lover of music, he enthusiastically supported Mary and escorted her to concerts when she was much too young to go by herself. One was particularly memorable, at a theater on Frankstown Avenue that booked the best black acts. It was there, Mary thought, that she saw the well-known Lovie Austin, a veteran pianist and arranger from Chicago who wrote and conducted music for shows, and backed many artists on early Paramount records. Mary certainly saw Austin—she recalled the event in loving detail—though it was probably a bit later in Chicago, when she was fourteen or fifteen and traveling with various bands, for Austin never left Chicago. "You can imagine my surprise and thrill to see a woman sitting in the pit with four or five other male musicians, with her legs crossed, cigarette in her mouth, playing the show with her left hand and writing music with her right hand for the next act to come on the stage. And was she a master of conducting the music. This scene I never forgot. And later on, when I was with Andy Kirk's orchestra, I remembered this woman in the pit in Pittsburgh and began imitating her on one-nighters. I thought, 'I'm going to do that one day,' and I did." Shortly before she died, in 1981, in Durham, North Carolina, Mary told Marsha Vick that "being able to write and play at the same time is my proudest accomplishment."

At the Floyds', Mary listened to Fats Waller and James P. Johnson discs on the brand-new Victrola that Hugh bought on time. And as she woodshedded, honing her technique, she remembered how "During the summer when I practiced, people would stop by and listen. Everyone would stop on their porch, and truck drivers would stop." She began to get more and more gigs—graduation parties, teas, summer picnics. "I began playing little church gigs. And a friend of my mother's would take me to Castle Shannon and other small cities near Pittsburgh. I was all over the city playing. I became," she added, "the little piano girl of East Liberty and anytime anybody was having a party or anything they'd say 'Well, let's get the little piano girl.' "

But despite the fact that the local police, whose station was near her home, were friendly, often walking her home from the streetcar when she returned late at night, they couldn't solve other problems. Sometimes she wasn't paid. Another time, "I had to walk home from a

Saturday night date in Homestead, Pennsylvania. The manager of the place had run out on the quartet he'd hired, and there was nothing to do but walk. I started about midnight and arrived home, I think, between 10 and 11 on Sunday morning.

"It wasn't wise for a girl to go out alone at night, and in fact my step-father took me to most of my gigs after the time I played at a rich man's house, when that affair turned out to be a stag party with the parents away in Europe and the boys tried to move in on me. They were upstairs getting drunk and I just left. I wouldn't tell my stepfather because he would have gone back and killed everybody because he was very mean about things like that." And she remembered a series of other problems with "a very good alto player called Matt Adison who bilked me on all his jobs."

————

MARY BEGAN HER schooling at the Lincoln School, now replaced but still boasting the original giant cast-iron bell that summoned the children to class. Nearby is Westinghouse High School, larger now and adorned with bars and locks, which Mary—and later Erroll Garner, Billy Strayhorn, and Ahmad Jamal—attended. A decade and a half after her death, a portrait of Mary was hung inside Westinghouse and a historical marker placed in front of Lincoln in her honor. All this for an alumna who completed only the first term of her sophomore year of high school, a fact Mary was apt to fudge, as when she told *Seventeen* magazine rather grandly in the late 1940s that after she graduated she "took a position with a dance orchestra."

When she entered school, at seven or eight, Mary's musical ability immediately set her apart. As perhaps also did her neglect and poverty. "I went barefooted until I was three or four," Mary wrote. "In grade school I'd sneak out a pair of Mom's oxfords and wear them to school with half of my heels sticking out the back. I'd hobble through classes and before going home I'd have to take the shoes off and go home barefooted." (Later in life, she developed a passion for expensive shoes.) Two young teachers, Miss Itzel and Miss Milholland, took her under their wings. "I was only good in music, mathematics, and maybe one or two other subjects," Mary recalled, "and most of the time I was found playing the piano, or playing for the kids. Miss Milholland hummed her favorite marches for me to play for the kids to march up long winding stairs to the second floor. I'd improvise too, playing a boogie beat, and the kids would stop and dance on the landing, holding up the first floor line. So Miss Milholland would come to the top and discover the hold-up and I was in trouble. She wouldn't allow me to play until I promised to play it as a march. But she still got me gigs. Miss Milholland did special things for talented black kids. I received instruments from several music stores, and took lessons on violin but was sent home because I played 'The Sheik of Araby' on one string. The teacher said I shouldn't be tampered with, I should teach myself."

School was Mary's first contact with the white world—there were no black teachers at Lincoln or Westinghouse then—and she reacted instinctively, lashing out against these representatives of what the adults around her painted as an unjust society. She often told the following story—which varied only in its details: "One day I went to school and grabbed a long ruler and hit my teacher who had always been very nice to me. I distressed her. I said, 'You white people made slaves out of us.' She was very upset. She said, 'Oh, you poor child. I wonder who's been telling you all these things.' From that day on she brought me presents every day—little things I liked. She must have told the other teachers because they started to have me to come to their boardinghouse to play for them. I used to return home with a lot of money tied up in my handkerchief."

After graduating from eighth grade at Lincoln in December of 1923, Mary enrolled at Westinghouse High for the winter term of 1924. Her school entrance certificate is the first official document attesting to her existence, although it has Mary's name and birthday slightly in error: she is called Mary Lou Freda Burley instead of Mary Lou Elfrieda, and her birth date is listed as June 8, 1909. Again at Westinghouse, Mary's musical talent caught the attention of her teachers, and the principal, a Mrs. Leopole, took her to hear new kinds of music, such as opera, and gave her opportunities to test herself against new audiences (at the University of Pittsburgh she played for professors and students, as Earl Hines had done). And it was probably through her teachers that Mary began to play at afternoon teas for the Mellons and the Olivers, two of the wealthiest families not just in Pittsburgh but in the nation. (Mary's aunts from the Riser side, Mamie and Minnie, were domestic servants to the Andrew Mellons.)

Mary was suitably impressed by the grandeur, recalling one such event: "A very rich lady who was a relative of the Mellons sent her chauffeur looking for colored talent to entertain at a dinner party. I picked up a girlfriend of mine who did the Charleston very well and Sonny who was featured with the 'Three Cobs.' He drove us to this wealthy lady's house and told us to wait at the entrance. Inside, I was led to a piano, where a beautiful, silver-haired lady asked what I charged. 'Dollar an hour,' I replied, 'my standard fee.' " How the lady must have smiled at that as she withdrew to an adjacent room to play bridge, drink tea, and listen as Mary entertained from her repertoire of pop tunes "for an hour or two." She was given an envelope with a check, thanked, then driven home by the chauffeur. When she opened the envelope at home, Mary found a check for a hundred dollars. "I earned $100! My mother almost fainted. She wanted to know if the lady drank. She called the people to see if they had made a mistake. The entire household stayed up until the bank opened the next morning."

If Mary had completed high school, she would have had Mrs. Jane Patton Alexander as her music teacher—the same Mrs. Alexander who drilled Billy Strayhorn in music theory and harmony like a sergeant a decade and a half later. But she left after only a term and a half to go out on the road with a show, and so she never really got a musical foundation; indeed, she never learned to read a note of music. "I couldn't play Rachmaninoff and those things. I had to improvise on it. I couldn't play it the way the music was," Mary later explained. It was a limitation she struggled with. "I always felt I'd never be a great reader because of my ear sounds," she wrote. "Even then I knew if someone made a mistake in a composition I didn't know, and I was able to call chords as fast as they were played." She had to call on her "ear sounds" at her first really important job between freshman and sophomore years, when she was hired to play a picnic dance with the local musicians' union for the Amphibians, "a big local society of class-conscious half-whites who would engage the best entertainment they could find. I was too young to be in the musicians' union, but the president of the colored subsidiary local insisted on taking me along to play with his twelve-piece band. We played such songs as 'Dardanella,' 'Royal Garden Blues,' and an orchestration of the popular tune, the 'Doll Dance.' " The problem was, Mary didn't know the tune. "That is when I really learned how to use my ears. I probably was a fraction behind each note they played, and after the first chorus, I knew the melody and what notes would follow. When the leader called other arrangements, I would get the piano part and would play and look as if I was reading. I think my ESP carried me through a great deal. I was pretending I could read." In fact, it would be about five more years before Mary finally learned how to read music—because she wanted to write it.

Mary's autodidactic approach to music study led her at times to stereotype both jazz and classical music. Because it was already written down, she at times implied that classical music simply had to be mechanically mastered, while jazz, on the other hand, had to be constantly created. But this view merely compared jazz at its best with classical music at its worst. In fact, a true artist works for freshness and immediacy at every performance, and what passes for improvisation in jazz is very often a skillful reworking of familiar riffs and patterns, while the classical musician mines known works for hidden technical and emotional nuggets—not so very different in the end, perhaps. And for all Mary's later ardent defense of jazz over classical music—"Why would I want to play something somebody else has written?"—she benefited by listening closely to such modern composers as Gershwin, Hindemith, and Schoenberg. Even in jazz, her first role model when it came to writing was the conservatory-trained big-band arranger Don Redman.

What she did shun instinctively was the sometimes drily analytical approach of the Academy in Western classical music, its distrust of intuition, and, especially, and deeply, its refusal largely to take seriously African-American music-making. She knew, perhaps from the very beginning, that the Academy was an arena where she would never be accepted. There was, of course, very little future for black pianists in traditional white Western classical venues. Earl Hines had begun classical training and gave concerts to Pittsburgh's elite in 1916. But as Hines observed, "They gave me $10 and a box of handkerchiefs for a concert and said, 'He's great.' I had to learn 60 or 70 pages of music for a concert and work like a dog for 10 bucks, some linen and a few kind words. It didn't look like a hell of a living, so at 16 I cut out."

———

MARY CONTINUED TO pursue her musical education in her own way. When she was eleven and twelve, she went to Saturday afternoon dances at the Arcadia Ballroom in East Liberty, where singer Lois

Deppe appeared with his band, which included the young Earl Hines. Despite the gang fights that cleared the place, Mary had a fine time, absorbing both the pop tunes the band played, like "Milenberg Joys," "Congaine," and "Isabelle" (which she later recorded), and Hines's sensational piano style, in particular his way of playing octaves so as to be heard above the band.

Mary herself was gaining a reputation among musicians. "Bands coming into Pittsburgh for one-nighters would drive to my house and take me on their gigs. If I was playing wrong, they'd show me. I was just like one of the boys," she wrote. She heard tunes arranged then by Don Redman, a major influence. Redman was known for his economy of ideas and his writing of "choirs" for the reed and brass sections of Fletcher Henderson's orchestra. Todd Rhodes, the pianist with the Synco Jazz Band/Cottonpickers, "used to take me out jamming and on one date let me sit in with the band. Some nights we jammed all the way from East Liberty down to Wylie Avenue, then a notorious section of town held in dread by so-called decent people. We always wound up in the Subway on Wylie—where Louise Mann and Baby Hines, Earl's first wife, sang—a hole in the ground to which the cream of the crop came to enjoy the finest in the way of entertainment. For me it was a paradise."

The district known as the Hill, which black Pittsburghers called with pride "Little Harlem," was an important stop on the vaudeville circuit. Pittsburgh itself became an important town for the black community nation-wide, with a powerful newspaper, the *Courier*. (Excluded from the normal white distribution systems, the *Courier* organized a network of black railroad porters to get the paper out all over the country, thus keeping Pittsburgh in the forefront of news about black America.) Like East Liberty, several miles away, the Hill had changed dramatically in the course of a few years, shifting from a patchwork of Jewish, Italian, Polish, and Hungarian enclaves to a flourishing black community where whites came mostly to purchase vice and entertainment. The center of things was thriving Wylie Avenue.

Pittsburgh proved a fertile ground for musicians. Among pianists, besides Mary and Hines, the city produced Billy Strayhorn, Erroll Garner, Ahmad Jamal, Horace Parlan, and Shirley Scott. Young Maxine Sullivan got her start as a singer there, as did Billy Eckstine and Dakota Staton (and for a time, Lena Horne lived on the Hill), as well as players

such as Art Blakey, Kenny Clarke, Ray Brown, Stanley and Tommy Tur-
rentine, Roy Eldridge, George Benson, and Jimmy Ponder. But black
musicians are seldom cited in histories of Pittsburgh; in one serious
work, there's not a single mention, while, on the other hand, Stephen
Foster's birthplace is a Pittsburgh landmark.

———————

AROUND THE HILL and East Liberty dancehalls, Mary was squired at
times by her third important father-figure, whose involvement in her
life is a bit more shadowy than Fletcher Burley's or Hugh Floyd's.
Roland Mayfield, a sporting man with a stake in a gambling club, was
"the Black prince of East Liberty," wrote Mary, adding that her mother
"trusted" him to squire her daughter around at night. "In order to
hear Earl Hines often I formed the friendship of Roland Mayfield,"
Mary explained, adding perhaps disingenuously, "I would introduce
him to girls who were beautiful; they had to have long hair. Mayfield
was fearless; he would stop brawls at the dances. I met him when I was
12. He was so rich that my girlfriends from Westinghouse and I would
sit on the floor and count his money. He never thought of putting his
money in the bank. He always carried it and many diamond rings in his
pockets. He taught me to drive a car. And I'd go out by myself a lot and
he'd get in his car and pick me up and bring me home. He would
always pick me up or give me anything that I needed.

"He would come out to Westinghouse school and pick up 4 or 5
girls, driving us at breakneck speed downtown to a famous restaurant
called Dearings during our lunch period and get us back to school in
time to make our classes, then he'd leave the keys in his car on the
street for whoever reached the car first to drive. After school there was
always a mad rush trying to get to his specially made car before any of
the other girls. Once when I returned Roland's car, it was really a
wreck. He looked at me and said, 'Don't worry kid, we'll get another
car.' Roland and I became quite chummy."

Mary's portrait of Mayfield as having an air of sexy but rich-uncle
indulgence about him—cigar-smoking, laconic and wise, with pockets
full of money—squares with the opinions of others who knew him:
Mary's niece Helen, who knew them both all her life, is positive Mary
and Roland's was a father-daughter relationship. "Maybe it's Mary
needing a father, and he was in fact a father—he had two daughters of

his own. I could see Roland becoming Father and Uncle very quickly," adds Peter O'Brien. "When I knew him in the '60s and '70s, he was still very strong and barrel-chested and Mary told me that Roland would say, 'Nobody touches the kid.' That's what he called her, 'the kid.'" Mary and her protector remained friends for life, with Mayfield later coming to visit Mary in her New York apartment, and indulging the quiet passion of his sunset years: fishing. All through her career, he bailed her out when she was stranded on the road (as happened fairly often) and supplied her with cars. "There was repeatedly a new Cadillac during the years I knew her," recalls Peter O'Brien.

————

AS MARY APPROACHED her teenage years, she was, in her own words, a "daredevil and a gypsy. And at the age of 12 I looked like 18." No longer the little piano girl, she sped into adolescence, like her mother and sister before her, with a woman's rounded body. At the same time she was shy and introverted, intimidated by the wild antics of some of her friends, who were already sexually active. She fell in love. "My first love affair was my cousin Max Sloane [son of the unfortunate man who died on the railroad tracks], who was so very kind to me that I fell in love with him at twelve. He'd often take me on his bike and bring me the nicest gifts. In the summer whenever I'd see him riding towards my house, my little heart would skip a beat. This little puppy love was cut short before anything detrimental could happen. His mother moved her family to Philadelphia." But a greater danger for her was at the clubs and dancehalls she haunted, and where she became a target of predators. Mary's description of one foiled rape fails to amuse: "I begged a friend of my stepfather to teach me to drive his very old Cadillac. One day he consented, driving me to an isolated place in Highland Park and tried to attack me. I fought like a wild cat and said, 'I'll tell my stepfather!' which made him come to his senses knowing that my stepfather was very kind, yet vicious about something like that. Being stubborn, I kept going with him to learn to drive, yelling 'stepfather!' as a threat until I learned to shift gears and start in first." Yet his unspecified sexual advances continued. "They became so annoying," Mary admitted, "that I really wanted to leave home."

Chapter Three
Hits 'n Bits
1924–1929

"WHEN DID I leave Pittsburgh? Soon as I could," Mary told Marsha Vick. "My aunt and sister Mamie were the only ones I missed. And when we got stranded on the road, I was afraid to write home for loot—afraid my mother would make me return to Pittsburgh and stay there." Mary was probably thirteen when she ran away from home to join a "home talent show" that, according to John Williams, went by the name Boise De Legg and His Hottentots. It was one of dozens of such groups, descendants of the tent shows that had traveled rural America since the 1800s, and was just about the meanest employment for an entertainer next to carny shows, their income being nothing more than pickup change.

It was a rude start, a troupe filled with raw beginners, black teenagers eager for the glamour and, they hoped, the fame of show business. About the only good thing that came out of Mary's time with the Hottentots was a lifelong friendship she formed with dancer Margaret Warren. At eighteen, the more seasoned Warren acted as a kind of surrogate mother to Mary and the other younger girls. They needed it. "The manager of this show gave us something out of a Coke bottle which tasted quite good to me," wrote Mary. "I began to feel very giggly and drank more of the sweet tasting stuff—I had a complete blackout. I woke up later in Margaret Warren's room. She was very angry and told me what happened. She had discovered I wasn't in my room and returned to the theatre with one of the band boys and they caught the manager in the act of misusing one of the girls—and on his way to doing the same to me. He was beaten badly by the musician."

For once, Ginnie Riser was concerned enough to go after her daughter. "Mother had everybody looking for me. After about two weeks, she found me in Washington, Pennsylvania, about 50 miles from home, and came there, dragging me out by my ear to the train."

Mary, fearful of the sexual predator who had pursued her in East Liberty, and restless to get back on the road, rebelled against returning home. "I threatened to run away, commit suicide, anything to frighten her and Aunt Anna, who'd come with her. Well, a slap across the face really cooled me. But back home again, I was bored to tears living with Mamie, going to school and playing gigs for afternoon teas and social functions." In the fall of 1923, she dutifully went back to school, but she had caught the show-business bug.

After school let out for the summer in 1924, though, she got her first real break with a professional show playing a Pittsburgh theater on the black vaudeville circuit, called the Theatre Owners' Booking Association, or TOBA ("Tough on Black Asses" was what the performers called it). Buzzin' Harris and His Hits 'n Bits was a raggedy show, to be sure, but a definite step up from the Hottentots. And when, just as in a B movie, the show's pianist got drunk and took off a few hours before curtain time, the desperate leader of the troupe was ready to grab at any straw. There was no show without a pianist, the glue that held the acts together. So when someone told Harris about Mary, he raced across town to hear her. "Was he ever surprised," Mary said, "when he drove up in front of my house and the guy with him pointed at *me*. I was playing a game with the kids on the sidewalk. Buzz was so upset, he almost returned to town, saying, 'What is this, a joke?' But he decided to come in the house and listen to me. I began playing and he became so elated that he began humming the entire show to me, which took no time for me to memorize. With my mother's permission, he took me downtown and once again we rehearsed the show. I played the entire show later that evening from memory, and broke it up. And since it was during the summer vacation, I was able to work the entire week with the show in Pittsburgh. Then he pleaded with my mother to allow me to travel with them for the rest of the summer. A notary was called in and papers were signed because I was underage."

When she returned to school that September, after playing the small towns around Pittsburgh, Mary was more confused than ever about her future. The summer with Buzzin' Harris had shown her that the shows were "an animal life. And I liked going back to school very much because I enjoyed my music classes, my loads of friends. But still I was lonely and miserable to travel." Then, in early December, a crisis at home resolved the question. Suddenly, Fletcher Burley was bedridden, unable to work. The family turned to Mary in earnest now; they were destitute. Her mother wanted her to stay and work in Pittsburgh; her brother-in-law, Hugh Floyd, always conservative, urged her to finish her education and even offered to help support her in college, so that she could become a music teacher—a good, steady job. But Mary had a standing offer to join Harris and his Hits 'n Bits. She'd send home money from the road, she promised, and dangled the wondrous figure of $30 a week in front of Virginia's eyes. (She seldom if ever came close to that amount, for in the winter of 1925, "cancellation and starvation set in.") She also recalled making a "hysterical scene" with her mother to get her way. By then, Mary had completed the first term of her second year at Westinghouse. It was to be the end of her formal education.

Now she joined the "animal life" of the TOBA in earnest, as the Hits 'n Bits traveled a circuit of the smaller cities around Pennsylvania and Ohio, occasionally getting bookings in big cities like Pittsburgh and Detroit. The TOBA had been formed under tough conditions after the turn of the century and endured well into the Depression. Headliners like Bessie Smith, Ethel Waters, and Ma Rainey received respectable salaries, but even the stars had to put up with poor conditions. "You could go into a theatre and not have a bathroom or anything," recalled Mary. "It was terrible—you should have seen the dressing rooms." Yet there was no shortage of would-be entertainers. Very few black acts got jobs on the better-paid, larger, white vaudeville circuits, which maintained strict racial quotas. Mary was one of scores of young black women around the country who avidly competed for jobs on the TOBA—jobs that at least held out the promise of a better life than washing white folks' laundry or cleaning their houses. But there was one major difference between Mary and the other naïve young girls: her goal was to become a pianist, when most girls with talent dreamed of becoming dancers, actresses, or singers. She was lucky also in that the public accepted female piano players—not the case with most other instruments. (If Mary had been a saxophonist, for instance, she would either have changed the course of jazz history, making it far more open to women players, or she would have become one more footnote.)

With Hits 'n Bits, Mary learned performance lessons that would last a lifetime. "I was trained to play with everyone and play everything," she said, and she learned humor, timing, instant recovery, and how to play under all conditions. She was, then, an *entertainer,* and she was proud to be. It was still an age of blackface comedy, of gags and pratfalls. Popular musicians performed tricks: they played instruments behind their backs, or with their feet. They crossed their eyes and mugged for the audience, as in Josephine Baker's pre-Paris routine. Mary joined in with gusto. As she described her act: "Spreading a sheet over the keys, I did a version of 'Milenberg Joys' mostly with my elbows, winding up by taking a break while spinning around on the piano stool." And, she added, she did "many comical things with my toes, fists and elbows." Her clowning, her versatility and fast ear, her strong touch and rhythmic ability, made her a crowd-pleaser right away.

Yet even then, she felt the pull to put aside gimmicky antics and play good music. Hits 'n Bits was in Chicago in the winter of 1925. There Mary ran into Earl Hines, whom she knew from Pittsburgh and who had joined Louis Armstrong in Chicago. He squired her to the Sunset cabaret to hear King Oliver, and at the Vendome Theater introduced Mary to Armstrong and pianist Ford "Buck" Washington. Armstrong, of course, was a sensation, but being a pianist, Mary was also fascinated by Washington, a terrific stride player who recorded with Armstrong in 1927 and on into the mid-thirties (though now he is remembered as half of the famous vaudeville team of Buck and Bubbles). Washington was to show her some great runs, including his own most prized one, which he warned her to play backwards so that Art Tatum, when he heard it, would not be able to "steal" it. (Tatum, Mary added, quickly figured out "Buck's run" and used it thereafter in his repertoire.) Everything Washington played, said Mary, was "unusual," a compliment.

Aside from such high spots as meeting Armstrong and Washington, life on the road was as rough as ever. Even though Mary's friend Margaret Warren had also joined the troupe of Hits 'n Bits, she could protect her only so far. Men and women often paired, as John Williams later explained it, for reasons that were as much practical as romantic: salaries were small and erratic, and sharing expenses became a necessity. And for a single woman, finding a steady man helped protect her from constant advances by others. Mary quickly formed a liaison with the leader of the combo that played for Hits 'n Bits, trumpeter Shirley Clay.

Violence was commonplace, and Mary's sometimes curiously offhand remarks reflect the attitude that violence between men and women was inevitable. When, for example, Buzzin' Harris developed "big eyes" for Mary's Aunt Anna Mae, his wife, Arletta, found out and pulled a knife on him, Mary wrote. She added, "He had to give his wife two black eyes, to straighten her out. It was certainly comical seeing him following a cow trying to get some manure to put on her eyes to clear them," she finished merrily.

––––––––

MARY HAD BEEN with Hits 'n Bits for only a few weeks when John Overton Williams, the man who would become her first husband, joined the troupe in Ohio, near Christmastime. Williams told his story at the age of ninety, one year before he died in Columbus, Ohio; his memories of his beginnings as a young vaudeville musician were crystal clear:

"I was born in Memphis, Tennessee, on April 13, 1905. I went to school with W. C. Handy's son—he lived down the street, on Saxon Street. My father, Thomas Williams, was a deacon in the church and sang in the choir, so they had me baptized at 10. But kids almost had to do that at that time. They had the moaners' bench where they had revivals, a week or two weeks, and different kids would come up and confess that they had religion. I was the last one, 'cause I didn't have no religion. But I didn't want my parents to look bad.

"But it was okay with them when I went out on the road. I'd been making gigs when I'd go back to Memphis each summer from Kansas City, where I was going to school. My father never made over $11 a week. He was a porter in a small printing office. That was his highest salary. When I would make $2 or $3 a night on these gigs of mine, well, that set alright with them. Now, in order to get a C-melody horn I wanted, I had to promise my mother, Parthenia—Polly, as she was

called—that I was going to play in church, because by playing for dancing, we were supposed to be doing the devil's work. But when I started
making that $2 and $3 and bringing it home, they forgot about that
religion. I was putting more food on the table.

"I failed in school in the eighth grade. I got in with the bad boys
and I would be at the Palace Theater in Memphis—I would play
hookey and slip and go to the show every day. I wanted to see William
S. Hart and Mary Pickford and all. This made my mother cry and cry
and I felt so bad. So my mother said I could go to Kansas City and live
with a favorite aunt, Aunt Eliza Marshall, who people called 'Babe,'
and my cousin Mabel and go to school. This was 1920, and Ben Webster was a classmate there. I wasn't thinking about music. But in 1921, I
heard one of my friend's brothers play a baritone sax. I'd had about
eight piano lessons when I was younger, till my friends kidded me that
I was a sissy and I quit. But I could read music. And I heard it. Radio
was the new thing, you could make you a crystal set real easily. I heard
the Coon Sanders band then [a popular white dance band] there in
Kansas City, that was about 1920. I liked that band.

"I never had a music teacher. In elementary school, they taught us
a little. Then, in Kansas City, when I was going to school and living with
my aunt, I told my mother I wanted a saxophone for Christmas. It
arrived early in January of 1922 and then I taught myself. I asked questions after I found out where to put my fingers for C and D, and I went
down to the music store and bought a beginner's book. I would ask different saxophone players like Jack Washington in Kansas City, the baritone player that ended up playing with Count Basie's band. And a guy
that lived down the street from me that was playing professionally
would show me different things. My aunt in Kansas City had a player
piano. I used to pump it and play by ear with some of those songs. I
started gigging in Kansas City with Paul Banks's band, in 1922. I substituted for a guy and Banks put me in the union right away. I played C-
melody sax at that time, but I liked the sound of the baritone, and I
happened to see an ad in the paper in Memphis that summer that they
had this baritone in some little town in Tennessee. I think they wanted
$50 or $60 for it. And I sent him the money and he sent me the baritone. I think I was the first to play baritone on the stage at the time.
(Later I found out in order to play with the big bands, I'd have to get
an alto, so late in '22, I got one.) There was something you called slap-

tongue and flutter-tongue that was popular in the twenties, where you make it pop, and of course the baritone would pop louder. I caused a couple of guys to buy baritones later, in around '24 and '25, after that. But the baritone was just a little novelty on the side, 'cause there wasn't no special part for it. I just had it along. They hadn't added baritone to bands at that time—they didn't *have* big bands. Well, baritone is now in all big bands. My last six years of playing, I played only baritone in Earl Hines's band.

"Joining Harris's Hits 'n Bits was the first time I started traveling, at age nineteen. I was recommended by a saxophone player that was from St. Joe, Missouri, who was already with the show, so they sent me a wire to Memphis and asked me if I would join the show. And I said yes. It was on a Sunday I went to join the Hits 'n Bits. My mother put me on the train in Memphis. We were right up next to the engines—the trains were segregated, of course, then—and she gave me $6. 'Course that was a lot of money then. Well, they used to have guys they called 'butch': the butch sold magazines and fruit and stuff on the trains. Here I was, a young kid, and the butch introduced me to a blackjack game, and by the time we got to Cincinnati, a twelve-hour trip—we arrived at nine at night—he'd taken all of my money. Here I am, flat. All I got is the address where I'm going, so he gave me a nickel since at that time, transportation was a nickel. And he told me what streetcar to catch and that's how I arrived in Cincinnati on that Sunday night. There was an act that was closing that night and one of the guys, a comic named Sidney, asked, 'Kid, you're joining the show that opens tomorrow?' I said 'Yeah.' 'Have you had anything to eat?' And he fed me. The next morning before they left they showed me where the theater was and that's when I first met Buzzin' Harris and Mary and everybody. That was around the middle of December of 1924. I remember because we played that one week there and the second week we played in Columbus and it was Christmas week.

"This was on the TOBA. The TOBA was just comedy and chorus girls and your blues singers, with anywhere from fifteen to twenty people in the show. You'd have week stands, and you'd go from one city to another.

"Buzzin' Harris did this funny kind of step. It wasn't nothing, just buzzin' off the stage. He'd be in a crouch and do this dance where he made his exit. Well, it really wasn't no dance at all—it wasn't no *act* at all. You came out and did a number, a feature, and then the band did some music and he'd buzz off the stage. Nothing.

"There wasn't no band pianists that were women. I'd made this trip and here was this little girl—she was only fourteen at the time—playing piano. When they had the first rehearsal, I was very disgusted when I saw it was a girl. I'd played with women piano players and they'd be just tinkling. Women really couldn't handle it at the time—I'm not lying. And it wasn't popular for them to be doing it in the first place. Because at that time, in the teens and twenties, musicians were kind of ruffians—drinking and hanging out and staying out all night. Society people called them hired hands. We'd go to entertain the society people, but they'd look down on us. There was no thought of a girl like Mary ever playing with a band.

"But there she was and I said, 'Oh my goodness, I come up here and I got to be fooling with this little girl.' Mary was already playing for this show when I joined. Well, then she hit on the piano and I'd never heard nothing like that in my life. Terrific. She outplayed any piano player I'd ever played with. She played note for note anything that she heard, Earl Hines, Jelly Roll Morton, and heavy like a man, not light piano. At fourteen."

It was not love at first sight for these two. Mary was involved with Clay, and John quickly hooked up with Margaret Warren. But when Clay left the band soon after the New Year, Harris appointed John Williams leader. "I had the qualities needed. I was playing a lot of horn for the time, baritone and alto saxophones, and I kind of excited them. And, they didn't have no better with nobody else.

"I quit Margaret and started going with Mary in a month or two. But Margaret was so crazy about Mary and admired me and my playing and all, so that it was all right, because I'm a take-charge person and she knew that Mary really needed to have a male to take care of her, look out for her. It was never no deep love or nothing like that. It was always like baby sister–big brother. That's the way it was."

"John had eyes for me," Mary wrote in her version, "but I was too busy with my music to pay attention to him or anyone. Love was secondary to me. My music was always first. I didn't love him," she said. "He'd get in the bed and I'd get up and go play music. Margaret liked John very much and she told me so. I said it was okay by me, but when he began showering her with nice gifts, I changed my mind. That was his psychology, to try and make me look his way. He never gave up. My mother and relatives trusted me with him and I finally turned to him. Then, too, I felt I would not be made to return home. So, latching on to John helped me to continue with the show." The shapely dancer Margaret Warren, who eventually returned to Pittsburgh, where she settled down to have a family, remained a firm friend to both Mary and John.

"Mary and I started a romance pretty soon," affirmed John. "It was around about February or March in 1925 that she and I started shacking together to cut expenses and we did that until we married in '26. You'd pick your favorite and shack up. By us being in music and me being the leader and the glamour boy and the new one, well, it threw us together. It really wasn't no love, but I was lucky enough to have a real good brain and I was a father image to her. How much does a girl know, traveling around at fourteen, fifteen years old? And she was awful quiet, didn't smoke at that time, or drink. She was never a drinker.

"Mary had ideas even then, but she wasn't writing yet. We used to copy stuff off of records—like Red Nichols and His Five Pennies. But it was hard to survive. There were twelve to fifteen of us in the show, and sometimes the whole take wasn't but $500, and there was no pay when you didn't work." The troupe became desperate for bookings. "We even worked with a carnival," Mary wrote, "the lowest of the low. These roustabouts, they are terrible. Our group stayed more or less to themselves. No one ever molested the girls or me except if they wanted to be molested. I learned about a 'poor boy' sandwich: sardines and onion inside of a loaf of bread. You allow this to soak a couple of hours and it would be good for all day. But most of the time we just did not eat." Although she always referred to this period as a "terrible life," she would add that, "nothing bothered me because music was my food. And there was so much love among musicians in those days."

Among those musicians was the late trumpeter Adolphus "Doc" Cheatham, who joined the Syncopators in Nashville in the spring of 1925 for a brief spell and became a friend. Cheatham was in the pit band of the Bijou Theatre where Hits 'n Bits was booked for a week. "I was playing saxophone at that time," Cheatham recalled. "John Williams needed another horn and approached me, and I joined that band as a saxophone player. From Nashville, we went to St. Louis, Chicago, Newark. All black audiences. All the owners were white.

"Mary was very good-looking," continued Cheatham. "I was

attracted to her. Everybody in that band was attracted to Mary Lou. Mary wasn't yet married to John, but her relationship with John was very obvious; they were always together. John was slender, tall, very dark-complexioned. A good player. Leader of the group. He was protective of her. Like her guardian or something. She and John were very close for quite a while and no one could get between them. I think that kind of got on her nerves after a while—like training her, always right there. She wasn't ready for marriage. Music—that was her life. She was happy, lived a great life.

"Then, we were playing in the pit in St. Louis, where I had an uncle, and he came down and took me out of the show, took me back to Nashville. So I was just there with that Buzzin' Harris troupe for about six or eight weeks."

"Doc Cheatham left the show," Mary confirmed in her memoir, "but the rest of us stuck it out until the show broke up."

———

"EVERYBODY LIKED JOHN WILLIAMS," wrote Mary of the man who would be her husband for the next decade and a half. "He was a very sensible young man. He knew how to maneuver out of trouble with his glib tongue. A real born leader and a controller of dissension. He would have made a great psychiatrist." In early band pictures his gaze is level, staring the world straight in the eye, with a slightly brash but charming smile but without pugnacity—the look of a shrewd conciliator. From Mary's point of view he was an invaluable buffer, practical where she was off in the clouds. And he was a good promoter for Mary, who was shy and usually hung back. John, like her later manager, Father Peter O'Brien, pushed her—sometimes literally—into the limelight, knowing that once she was parked at the piano bench and her fingers hit those keys, she would be transformed. "He seemed so proud of me musically and kept me on the scene, showing me off to other musicians the way my stepfather and brother-in-law did," she wrote.

But he was also tough on her, as O'Brien also would be, in a different way. "My husband would say, 'If you don't play you're going to get a beating.' He used to take me around and he'd make me play with all of the top musicians. I think that each time he had to threaten to hit me. I was scared each time. 'Get up and play,' he said. I said, 'Oh no,' and I started crying. He says, 'You'd *better* play.' So I sat down and played with them." When Marsha Vick asked her at the end of her life if it was true that her husband really had knocked her off the piano bench once when he was annoyed with her playing, Mary readily confirmed it. "Yes. I've been beat up. And they used to take food from me because they knew I played better on an empty stomach." "You certainly didn't enjoy that!" her friend responded, appalled. But Mary answered, "No, but it was good for me. I played better." Although John Williams, it should be said, adamantly denied striking her, Mary elsewhere repeated her accusation that he did so.

———

IT WAS AN era when not only children were spanked and routinely beaten, but the "childlike" female as well. As part of their "training," Mary said, chorus girls often were beaten. "You come out with a black eye if you don't do it right," Mary recalled of her first years with the Clouds of Joy after 1929. But it was worth it, she added: "I could expand with that band."

It will come as no surprise, then, to learn that Mary was later involved with a number of men who were physically abusive: often brilliant, sensitive musicians who were known as "bad drinkers"—including long-time lovers Ben Webster and Don Byas, and her second husband, Shorty Baker. This was the dark side of the romance of the jazz life.

Mary was not an easy young woman to be around, always off in her own world and painfully shy. She stuttered, sometimes so badly that musicians told her "not to talk, just play." And she continued to have what she called "nervous fits" where she saw ghosts and spirits—just as she had done as a small child. "Someone was always with me at night," she wrote, "not only because of strange people, but because they knew I could still see spirits and they were afraid I'd panic."

Her "nervousness" wasn't helped by her constant worry about the small brothers and sisters she had left behind and whom she'd pledged to support, but could not. That her failure to do so consumed her with guilt is clear from her letters to friends later. But she was the typical child of an alcoholic, carrying her burdens in secret. John knew little of her private worries, and as the paymaster as well as the band's leader, kept a tight rein on the small income they made. So Mary turned deeper into her music. "There was always music in my head," she wrote. "Half the time I could not hear a conversation. There was no room for vicious or bad sounds. Music compensated for all bad sounds." This pattern continued into her later life. Whenever reality became too much for her, Peter O'Brien asserts about the Mary he knew from the 1960s on, "she would become dysfunctional and have to escape into her music."

————

IN 1925, UNDER John's leadership, the band—usually called the Syncopators, or sometimes the Syncojazzers—contained six members. As Mary remembered, they were: "A tenor player called Martin, who was a friend and schoolmate of Coleman Hawkins from St. Joseph, Missouri [replaced first by Sylvester Briscoe, a trombonist, then Bradley Bullet]; Shirley Clay, from St. Louis, who was already blowing good trumpet— we used to call him 'Hoggy' [replaced by Doc Cheatham, then Henry McCoy]; drummer Edward Temple, a showman, but also a solid, subtle rhythm player; and Jo Williams, out of Kansas City, a banjoist and guitarist. He played none of the minstrel kind of music but crazy guitar chords," Mary emphasized of this player who became a very close friend. (Jo and John Williams between them covered the then common tuba part.)

During her tenure with the Syncopators, Mary had an epiphany crucial to her future as a musician. Her idol as a performer in the troupe was the trombonist Sylvester Briscoe. "He did a feature on 'Tiger Rag,' " Mary reminisced, "playing with his foot, and the last chorus he'd put both hands in back of him, his mouth on the mouthpiece with his head bobbing up and down, and the slide on the floor, doing a Charleston—and he was so sensational they had to take his act out, because no one could follow him." He inspired Mary to work harder on perfecting her act of playing with her elbows and feet. It won her raves. "Then one night, as I was leaving the stage, an older musician grabbed me and said, 'Hey, little girl, I heard some good chords in about two things you played. You should stick to playing good music and cut out the clowning.' " Immediately, she understood the truth of what he said, and she dropped the gimmicks. In fact, she became known as a "plain" performer, who spoke little and gave her attention to her instrument on stage. She may have begun as a flat-out entertainer, but even in the twenties Mary was on her way to becoming a serious musician.

————

"HITS 'N BITS folded in late 1925," recalled John Williams. "We were in Kansas City, the last date we played. We couldn't get any more bookings. Our show wasn't all that good, anyway." In fact, the era of the old-fashioned traveling shows, with what Mary called its bandanna music, was drawing to a close. Vaudeville, black and white, appealed increasingly to urban tastes.

Out of work, most of the Syncopators hung around Kansas City. John and Mary found a room with his Aunt Babe, but it wasn't long before they got the kind of break they dreamed of. "Seymour and Jeanette was an act in vaudeville, and they were playing Kansas City at the Pantages Theater for a week, during this time," recalled John. "We heard that Seymour and Jeanette were in the market for a jazz band. It had become popular then to get you a five- or six-piece jazz band with your act. That meant something flashy—like a drummer who could throw his sticks around."

But the top-ranked dancing duo, one of a few dozen black acts playing big-time white vaudeville, didn't want a band just for the sake of prestige. Though he was only twenty-seven and at the top of his career, Seymour James was plagued by increasing shortness of breath and pain due to an enlarged heart. Told by doctors to quit dancing, he chose instead to shorten his own performance, thus making room in the act for a band.

"My drummer," continued John, "told them, 'We got a band, and the show is breaking up. I'll find John and we'll make an audition for you.' " "Before the band played," Mary wrote, "Seymour and Jeanette came on the stage and greeted us. I was sitting at the piano quietly. Seymour said to John, 'Get that girl off the stand and let's start the rehearsal.' John's answer was "Okay," and he stomped off the tempo we were going to play. Was Seymour surprised to hear me play! Now, I was playing a real Fats Waller style. He began to say how great I was, but what will our manager say about a girl being with the act? We'll have to put pants on her.' During this period a woman was not really allowed to be in with a group of men or anything." In fact, Seymour's wife, the other half of the team, often wore top hat and tails (as did, a bit later,

Josephine Baker and Marlene Dietrich). At the audition, John Williams, to his credit, insisted they let Mary dress as a woman, arguing that having a female musician would be a big draw—and he was proved right. The ensemble of musicians was dressed impeccably, like collegians from the era, with Mary for all the world a sweet-faced coed in matching cardigan and skirt.

After the audition in Kansas City, the dancers told John they'd send for the Syncopators once they got to Chicago. "We thought they were kidding," John recalled, "but in no time, less than a month, they sent us tickets! We went to Chicago and played around the area for a few months, to break in the act. They were on big-time vaudeville, the Keith and Orpheum, so we had to be polished, get the rusty parts out. They uniformed us, they taught us stage manners, how to bow and smile and act onstage. We had the talent. They didn't have to do nothing to our music. They were crazy about our sound."

The Syncopators had arrived in Chicago broke, but anticipating good times. "I was supposed to get $50 or $75 a week—this was like $500 in those days. I just couldn't believe my ears," Mary reminisced.

She was right to doubt her good fortune. "John loved gambling, shooting craps. He kept my $75 a week and gave me a dollar a day to eat with," wrote Mary. "That was not enough during that era. Seymour and Jeanette were disturbed about it all because at times I didn't have proper clothing and food. Jeanette spoke to me about my appearance and told me I looked like a ragamuffin." She began to hide her earnings from John, often to send money home to Pittsburgh.

From Chicago, the troupe went by train to the promised land: New York. If they were a hit there, they could count on good bookings all over the country. "It was in 1926 on Easter Sunday when they brought us into New York," John recounted. "I remember Seymour and Jeanette had a Packard car and a chauffeur and drove us all around. The first place they took us after they got us a room and we rested and all, was down to Fifth Avenue so we could see the parade—those guys with the pinstripe pants. That was the first time we were in New York, both me and Mary. And she didn't go out much; she was a little homebody, liked to stay in most of the time. We stayed in private homes. The act played Yonkers, and Loew's Eighty-first Street Theater, and Hackensack, and all over. We used to get the ferry over to New Jersey. Atlantic City. They were slipping us into big-time."

At Loew's Theater, Mary got her first big-time review, which she pasted into the first of the many scrapbooks that preserve her notices. "Special mention," read the unsigned clip, "to the young lady pianist with the band." Seymour and Jeanette and their Syncopators were on the same bill with Fanny Brice, famous for her Baby Snooks act.

Living in Harlem that summer of 1926, Mary had great music practically at her doorstep and plenty of time on her hands to enjoy it. "All the big vaudeville acts at that time worked forty-two weeks a year, but summertime you didn't work," explained John Williams. "And we had forty-two weeks fixed on the Pantages and Keith circuit starting that fall. We didn't have no steady salary during the summer. We would play a week or a split week somewhere—three or four days on. But then, we didn't need much."

Seymour and Jeanette, who had appeared on Broadway in the hit show *Plantation Days,* knew all the entertainers who counted. "They introduced us to all the big players—James P. Johnson and Jelly Roll Morton, Fats Waller," John recalled. They met the young comedienne Jackie "Moms" Mabley and her partner, John Mason, and Bill "Bojangles" Robinson, whom Mary recalled as a great pool player and a terrific runner, able to race backwards and still beat the *forward* competition—and stars like Nina Mae McKinney, Adelaide Hall, and especially beautiful Florence Mills, who would die the following year. The Rhythm Club, where *all* the musicians went to jam, was close by. There Mary heard Willie "The Lion" Smith hold forth at the piano, and Benny Carter; and there she got reacquainted with Louis Armstrong. "People," she wrote, "treated him like a god." Seymour and Jeanette played the Lafayette Theater, and next door was Connie's Inn, where Fats Waller played and wrote music for the shows at the club. Waller's "Handful of Keys" was among Mary's favorites then, and meeting the composer was one of her cherished memories. Although Waller was only six years older than Mary, he was already a recognized genius. "There was a musician friend of Fats Waller in Connie's Inn, playing for the chorus girls, and this musician put me over in a corner and I just sat there," Mary remembered. "Fats was a fabulous composer. He'd wait until the chorus had gotten set up, then the conductor would say to him, 'Okay, Fats, compose a tune for this.' Right away, he'd sing it off and play it. Later on, the musician said to Fats, 'You see that little girl?' Now, I used to weigh like ninety pounds, and I looked," she added with characteristic poetic license, "like I was nine or ten years old. 'She can play everything you composed today.' Waller said, 'She can't.' He put me on a stool and I played that tune and the other things he'd composed and he went simply mad, he threw me up to the ceiling—I thought he was going to kill me, he was so happy about it. And during that period I could play anything, even the classics if I heard them, you know."

She added, "The owner, Leonard Harper, must have caught me playing, for I received an offer to play intermission piano in Connie's Inn for two weeks while the band was doubling in the Lafayette Theater, making about $60 a week for about an hour. But my pay was swindled by my greedy husband, who taught me how to play blackjack and won all my money, keeping it. And then, Leonard Harper used me for his Brooklyn shows and several things in Newark to help out. I actually made enough to share with our group until we decided to go back to Chicago."

Mary met the great Jelly Roll Morton, another major influence, around the same time, but she got a very different reception from him. Though reluctant, she was persuaded to go to Morton's office, where she played her favorite of his pieces, "The Pearls." "Almost immediately I was stopped and reprimanded, told the right way to phrase it. I played it the way Jelly told me, and when I had it to his satisfaction, I slipped in one of my own tunes. This made no difference. I was soon stopped and told, 'Now that passage should be phrased like this.' " (Eleven years later, she had her chance to play "The Pearls" as she wanted on a record.)

———

THOUGH JOHN LIKED to maintain that Mary stayed quietly at home at the rooming house while he, to use her pungent phrase, was roaming "up and down the chorus line," this was not altogether true. She was hardly living it up, but she had fallen in love: with the band's banjo player, Jo Williams (no relation to John). "I remember taking long walks [with him] on Seventh Avenue, saving just enough money to eat one meal. We had such great times together. He never left my side." They would stop at a landmark uptown, long since vanished: the famous wishing tree. It was a gathering place for out-of-work entertainers. "We'd find so many happy people there, including musicians and performers, all looking for work. There was always laughter there and fabulous jokes. Sadness and worry never stayed long." Holding hands, she and Jo Williams would keep on walking. "It was just the most beautiful friendship anyone could wish for," she wrote. They were both sixteen, and their closeness bothered John not a bit. "In love?" he scoffed. "I'd go out at night and leave them playing cards together. They were like two kids."

Yet it was to Jo, not John, that Mary turned for protection from her landlord, an elderly man who was constantly on the prowl—"scaring me almost to death," she wrote. "And I used to have awful nightmares. One night, I jumped out of bed and almost fell out of the window. After I told Jo about the landlord and my nightmares, he used to come to my room and sit in a chair, sleeping until dawn. In fact, he stayed with me both day and night. He was my best friend, who had tried so hard to protect me from harm. To tell the truth, we had fallen in love, being thrown together so much, but he was such a fine young man and respected John so very much that he'd never get out of line in any way. He would never attempt to hug or kiss me. And I was very much in love with him. We never mentioned my troubles to John. He probably would have said, 'Oh she can take care of herself.' For some reason I felt kind of loyal to John, who was never around. His slogan was, 'Don't worry about what your wife or girlfriend is doing.' "

———

AS FALL APPROACHED, life looked rosy. A year's worth of work was lined up, at far better theaters than on the TOBA circuit. Indeed, Seymour and Jeanette were in the inner circle, as a list of black acts working in the white theaters in 1926 makes clear. There was a total of only twenty-one on all of the white vaudeville circuits—ten of them with Keith Albee and two with Pantages—and one of those acts was Seymour and Jeanette. Seymour James was a fabulous strut dancer; Jeanette's specialty was "eccentric dancing" and rhythmic slapstick, as well as belting pop tunes. Both had elegant stage presence. "On opening night Seymour and Jeanette were just beautiful when they stepped out on the stage in their white clothes," recalled Mary. "Jeanette had on a white dress and hat, the dress with fur on the bottom of it, and Seymour was in his white suit and straw hat." Everything pointed to a fine future for Seymour and Jeanette—and the Syncopators. "The tour began on the Pantages circuit," recalled John Williams. "Our first week was in St. Paul, and the next week we played the World Theater in Omaha. And the third week we were in Kansas City. All this time Seymour was really a sick man. He told us he ate soap to make his heart bad to stay out of the army. After he would do his little dance and come off the stage, they'd have a chair for him. He'd have to sit for maybe twenty minutes before he could go to his dressing room to get ready for the next show, and our whole show wasn't but seventeen minutes. Anyway, he made it that week but he was too sick for us to go any farther. He wired New York and told them to set our route back, because we'd just played three weeks of our forty-two. Jeanette said we're going to sit for a month and let Seymie recuperate and feel better."

John sent Mary back to Pittsburgh and, with no prospects for work in sight, soon followed her there. They hung around for a month or so, but they could find no steady work together. John spent time gambling with Fletcher Burley while Mary, the native daughter, found intermittent work as a single. "Then we decided to go down to Memphis until Seymour got better; then we'd continue on those other thirty-nine weeks we had coming. I was always a mama's boy, so I'd go to see my mother and father. Mary said, 'I'm going too,' and I told Mary, 'You do, you pay your own fare,' and she said, 'I don't care.'

"In Memphis, we had a six-room house, and Mama gave her a room in the front and me one in the back. Although Mama was there and we were in separate rooms," John recalled, "Mama said, 'People are talking, and Mary said she loves you and she wants to get married.' I said, 'I don't want to get married,' but she said, 'Son, I think that's the thing you oughta do.' I said I hadn't got any money—I did—and then she said, 'Here's five dollars, go down to the Justice of the Peace.' So, November the tenth, 1926, we got married. No cake, no ceremony. No nothing. Just a marriage certificate. And we were young, and sowing our wild oats! Well, I wanted to sow *mine*." Their open relationship became, if anything, even more relaxed after the marriage; they were both free to come and go as they pleased, in John's phrase, but had to be "home" by 3 A.M. to sleep in the same bed (although this rule appears to have been bent or broken quite a few times).

"There was very little love left on either side," Mary wrote flatly. Despite this, they were more comfortable in Memphis than either had been in years, with a neatly kept house and a large backyard with a garden and chickens. "I was happy to be back where there were flowers and plenty of grass," wrote Mary, who always took pleasure in nature.

Within weeks, Seymour James was dead. End of the act, but Jeanette wired them to hold on. Soon, she sent them train tickets to join her in Chicago to hone a new act; and in the winter of 1927, they did go north, hoping to get back into the big-time. As they worked on the act, Jeanette James persuaded "Ink" Williams, a talent scout for Paramount, to let Mary accompany her on a record date. It was Mary's first time on record, and although she dismissed the date as "bandana days music"—the musicians all sound as if they were inside a tin drum, and they even misspelled her name Mary *Leo* Burley—her short solos on "Midnight Stomp," "The Bumps," and "Now Cut Loose" were, in the words of a reviewer many decades later, "strikingly precocious." Conductor and music historian Gunther Schuller agrees, characterizing her solos on "Midnight Stomp" and "Now Cut Loose" as "notable for both their advanced conception and virtuosic execution, second only to Hines and Johnson." To be sure, Mary's technical arsenal at seventeen was precocious. Schuller enumerates: "Broken 'walking' tenths, right-hand octaves and tremolos (à la Hines), stomping shifted rhythmic accents, fleet hand crossing over-hand cascade figures, and other surprises—but in each instance shuffled around in different sequences." For all her brilliant harmonic explorations and refinements over the next half a century, Mary's approach to craft as an improviser, her rhythmic security, seem to have been clearly decided before she was even in her late teens. It is as fellow pianist Billy Taylor put it: she was "a natural metronome," if at times she pulls the time a tad too breathlessly.

Making a record then was apparently no big deal. "We didn't care about those records or the names they put on them," said John Williams. "All we cared about was traveling. We were kids and were making more money than the average black person, who was working for $10 a week, and we were seeing all the big cities, so we didn't care. And all through all the recordings, including the ones with Andy Kirk and the Twelve Clouds of Joy, not a dime royalty to me or Mary. Not a dime."

The Syncopators followed Jeanette James to New York, but the unit broke up soon after when she quarreled with her new partner over money. "And that," said John, "was the end of the band." "Stranded again," Mary wrote. "I couldn't cook but I would try, like some spaghetti in a cheap dish that we all could share. One day I had only enough money to buy rice, and I remember cooking rice pudding for the guys in the combo, and I put it out on the window to cool. Half an hour later, I looked outside and saw a cat eating like mad. I said nothing to the boys, just raked off the top where paw tracks were and no one knew."

While John hustled blackjack, poker, and crap games, Mary tried to get work as a single, and Jeanette James, also struggling to make it on her own, hired her again when she got work. The stage star Nina Mae McKinney heard Mary and offered her a job as her accompanist, but John was opposed to her going out on the road without him. She had offers to make piano rolls for a few dollars, but they fell through. "By now," Mary wrote, "I was quite used to starvation." When she got a job with a pit band backing the beautiful dancer Fredi Washington, who became a well-known actress, the star bought her a dress and shoes for the stage. "I've never forgotten her kindness," Mary recalled. "She went to the I. Miller shoe store and bought me the most beautiful pair of shoes, silver evening slippers for $25, to open the show."

She met Duke Ellington and his Washingtonians—not yet a full band—when she was backing Jeanette James at the now-vanished Lincoln Theater off Lenox Avenue, and played with several of the Washingtonians in the pit before they went on stage with Ellington. As John Williams explained, "The union had a rule all over the United States that when a traveling act like Jeanette James came in, they would make you hire two or three musicians who were in that local even if they didn't do anything but stand by. They had to be there. So Tricky Sam and Bubber Miley sat in the pit and helped play the show."

"I played the entire show in the pit, then went on stage to accompany her act," Mary recollected. "That week was the most exciting of my life thus far. I was working with some of Duke Ellington's boys: Sonny Greer, Bubber Miley and Tricky Sam Nanton. Never had I heard such music before." Elsewhere she added, "If they were telling jokes that I should not hear, I heard them say, 'Cool it, here comes the kid.' Tricky Sam Nanton had a jug of whiskey—it seemed that this was the style—and he would throw his jug over his shoulder and take a big drink, but he was a great trombonist and guy. He helped me quite a bit with my music."

These were the highlights in an otherwise grim existence, and in the spring, Mary and John, accompanied by Jo Williams, gave up on New York, limping back to Pittsburgh again to wait for the fall vaudeville season. They patched together work in Pittsburgh that summer of 1927 at a place called the Liberty Gardens. Then John's luck picked up, as they thought, when a telegram came, asking if he'd back singer Mamie Smith. He and Mary went back to New York for a fresh start. "They gave the trumpet player from the Syncopators, a trombone player, and myself a job," said John. "But there was nothing for Mary there in New York, and no way to make a living, so I sent Mary home.

"In 1920, Mamie Smith was the queen with the 'Crazy Blues,' " John continued. "But by the fall of 1927, when I joined her, there was Bessie Smith, Ma Rainey, Ida Cox; so many blues singers that Mamie Smith couldn't make a comeback. Well, the show broke up in about six weeks. Then the Musicians Union gave me my fare back to Pittsburgh. But Mary and I decided to go back to Memphis in time for Christmas of 1927." Remaining in Pittsburgh, Jo Williams snowed Mary under with letters. What a contrast between Jo's beautiful handwriting—the penmanship that all schoolchildren used to learn—and the descriptions he relayed of his mean existence. Jo attempted to sound jocular about his bouts of drinking. He was trying to quit, he reported, but sometimes got home too late for dinner. "I always keep a hot coal fire in my room and I was going to fry eggs in the hearth grate, but Ginnie, and Mrs. Riser and Anna Mae throwed water on my fire and put it out, so I went out and got me a big hunk of pork and onion and coffee. Then they said they were going to treat me like *you* did that time you cracked me when I was drunk. So they beat me with player rolls."

Music was the basis of Jo's passionate bond with Mary. He was searching for the sheet music to "Rhapsody in Blue" that she'd asked for, and in his letters mentioned arrangements by Fletcher Henderson, Duke Ellington and Red Nichols. Gaunt and wracked by coughs, the seventeen-year-old was fatally ill (and probably knew it)—with tuberculosis. By the following year, he'd be dead, only the first of a number of dear friends to die at a cruelly young age.

IN MEMPHIS, MARY soon started getting work on her own. "A dancehall promoter billed her as 'Memphis Mary,' but "she didn't like that," said John. "We didn't go for all that clowning and stuff." She worked on Beale Street at the TOBA theater. She was backing blues singers like Ida Cox and Alberta Hunter, who became legends in their own right, but what she remembered most vividly were the particularly filthy conditions of the theater and the abysmal wages. Musicians had to depend on tips to survive. John, however, brought about improvements. "There was no real union for black musicians then, and he got a union going," Mary wrote. "One thing I have to say for John: he knew how to talk up salaries. Memphis musicians were getting $1.50 or $2.00 a night when we were there. John kept working on it and by the time we left they were making five and seven bucks, and I was making ten."

By January of 1928, John had taken over leadership of a band that became very popular locally. "Everybody wanted me, so I could do what I wanted. I took over this band and had it for about eight months. We had eight pieces: two trumpets, two saxophones, a banjo, bass, drums, and Mary on piano." (Among the players they recalled were Charlie Robinson and Clarence Davis on trumpet; Dickie Mullen on tenor sax; Harry Rooks on bass; Morris Mill on drums; and sometimes "the other" John Williams on bass or tuba.) "John maneuvered the new combo into clubs and hotels that ordinarily never employed a colored outfit," Mary wrote. "Yes," John responded, "but they only paid $5 for the guys in the band, and $8 for me, and that's all."

By springtime, John's band, still called the Syncopators, was working steadily in a dance hall with the lovely name of the Pink Rose Ballroom, for which the band was redubbed the Pink Rose Orchestra. "There were tales that a very rich ofay had purchased this estate for his mistress, a black woman, years before, and it was considered very modern then," Mary wrote. But John, ever the realist of the two, called it "just a barn built in back of this guy's house right in the neighborhood, about two or three blocks from my house. It *was* a big backyard." Today the site of the Pink Rose is a grassy slope, in an area dotted with abandoned buildings and drug dealing. "You could crowd maybe a thousand doing that close dancing they did in that time," John went on. "But no Lindy hopping. Robert Henry did the bookings. His father was a white man, and you couldn't tell Robert Henry from white. But he was a black man. We played about twice a week there, and then I would get other gigs with people. We did a lot of house parties, Mary and me," said John.

Right about the time John and Mary moved back to Memphis and

started the band, a shabbily dressed young man named Jimmie Lunceford also arrived in town to be the music teacher at one of the two
black high schools in town. Lunceford, who was to become a well-
known bandleader in the Swing Era, was soon a friendly rival of John's:
both had ambitions beyond the sleepy southern town, and John's
success at the Pink Rose fueled Lunceford's ambition to put his own
group together. He started the Chickasaw Syncopators, using high
school talent and a good local pianist, Bobbie Jones, before casting his
net beyond Memphis for players. "They were very good friends," wrote
Mary. "Everything that John did, Jimmie would try to do better. He and
John used to play checkers and John would beat him. Jimmie'd say,
'That's all right; I'm going to get a band better than you.' " A decade
later, Mary's composition "What's Your Story, Morning Glory?" became
a hit in a new arrangement by Lunceford's orchestra.

————

IT WAS ON August 25th of 1928, remembered John with his precise
recall, that he accepted an offer to join a band called the Dark Clouds
of Joy, led by trumpet player Terrence "T" Holder. Dance bands were
growing in popularity all around the Southwest and Midwest, and
especially in the oil-boom Oklahoma territories, where the Dark
Clouds were based.

"Another band, led by Alphonse Trent, came through town, and
his men recommended me for Fats Walls's job—he was lead alto—
after Walls had handed in his resignation to Holder," remembered
John. "Then I bargained up my pay to $60 a week," he added proudly.
"I said to friends, 'That's more than both me and Mary are making
here in Memphis.' At that time, Andy Kirk, the oldest guy in the band,
was the tuba player and *he* was earning $55; the rest of the guys, $40. I
told Mary, 'I'll go out for a month and see if I like it. If I don't, I'll come
on back.'

"I caught the train from Memphis to Oklahoma City. The band was
playing at the amusement park, their summer gig. I was so enthused;
that was the first big band I'd ever been in and I liked it so much and I
fit in so well. And they were paying me the highest. After I saw I was
really set with "T" Holder's band and they were satisfied with my playing, I wired Mary and told her drive the car, come on up to Oklahoma
City. The band was traveling as a stage attraction in Indiana, Ohio, and

Pennsylvania, with a TOBA show, and after that, we were based in Oklahoma for about a year."

During John's trial period with the Dark Clouds, Mary fulfilled the bookings made for the Memphis band, some of them with Jimmie Lunceford taking John's place as lead alto. She also took whatever other engagements she could get on her own, jobs that she never told John about so she could salt away her own "loot." "I had begun to keep my money," Mary wrote, adding meaningfully, "This John did not like too much and was not always too nice about."

On her own, she was again at the mercy of the unsavory, and even dangerous, individuals who have always peopled nightlife. "If you've never met a tough southern underworld character, just thank God," she wrote, recalling one racist club owner who refused to pay her and her band when they filled in for another group who couldn't make it. "He refused to honor our contract, saying, 'I can get all the niggers I want on Beale Street for two dollars a dozen.' I couldn't talk, I was so angry, but when I returned to the boys and told them, they told *me* to forget it, that we were in Mississippi. I refused to listen and they split, leaving me there alone. But I wouldn't leave until I had collected our loot. His wife, who already had a black eye, pleaded with me to leave, saying he'd kill me. But I guess a little of my stepfather had rubbed off on me. I began to cry, jumping up and down, almost screaming. 'He's gonna give me my money!' He finally gave in and paid most of what he owed."

Then there was what Mary politely called a "bad night club," a roadhouse-brothel on the outskirts of Memphis where Mary was hired to play piano in the parlor. To get there, she had to ride to the end of the city's trolley line, then wait for a car to take her the rest of the way, driven by a young man—a "Jack Dempsey look-alike," as Mary put it— who worked for Mrs. Singleton, the owner of the joint.

"Never in my life had I ever heard so many 'nigger, nigger, niggers.' No one had explained the conditions in the South to me. On our way to the club in the car, we passed an old Negro man on a bridge and someone yelled, 'There's a nigger, run over him, he's too old to live anyway!' I was with too many people and too far out in the woods, so kept quiet, counted to ten very fast, and thought of a beautiful composition.

"Of course I had to eat in the kitchen at the gig, with the colored help. I didn't mind, they'd cooked my favorite dish of yams and marsh-mallows. I waited until I was back home and let loose on the white driver, who told me then, 'The South always holds neck parties when your kind gets out of line.' And I wouldn't go back to work until Mrs. Singleton called my mother-in-law and said, 'Polly, make Mary come back to work, they like her out here.' I was a big hit. I suggested getting a male pianist, but Singleton let me know immediately that a young female pianist appealed to her customers most. Well, I went back to the job after I got a raise and presents. But what I hated about that job was, I was expected to entertain in more ways than one. I still have cards with the addresses on them, for dates. They were laid nicely on the piano.

"Well, I still didn't get it. The clientele consisted of barrel-bellied, loud-mouthed, third-grade readers whose preoccupation was gambling and girls. A rich, big fat redheaded, freckle-faced plantation owner came up to Memphis from Mississippi with this little nurse. Every night he'd give me $5 each time I played his requests. Around the third night his girlfriend tried to take him away, saying, 'You like nigger girls?' And Singleton came up, very excited, telling me to go home at once and stay home a couple of days. When I returned to the job, she told me that this sick man had paid the cook $50 to kidnap me and bring me to his farm in Mississippi. After this, I did not stay on the job very long, because I had heard many tales about black women being kidnapped and taken to Mississippi across state lines, out of the reach of Tennessee authorities. And when their parents had gone to get them, they were shot at the gate."

In fact, as preposterous as that might sound to today's more gently raised generation, "white" slavery was every bit as real as the lynch mob, or "necktie party," as the driver of the car had warned Mary.

It surely must have come as a relief when John wired Mary to come out to Oklahoma that fall of 1928. Mary packed up the car, their aging Chevy that looked like "a red bathtub," with her possessions, her mother-in-law Polly Williams, and a friend of Polly's, Mrs. Buchanan. It can be blazingly hot in the Panhandle during Indian summer. "We left at four in the morning, since there was not much traffic on the road until around eight or nine. The roads were gravel, turtleback, and there were holes everywhere. I must have had over ten flats, the carbu-retor was not working, and I don't know what-all wasn't wrong with this old Chevy. We stopped so many times. It's a good thing that Roland and a mechanic friend taught me how to fix cars. I'd drive twenty-five or fifty miles and would have to stop to let the car cool off. We were just miserable—the sun, the sand in our eyes and shoes and mouth when another car passed us. But I made Oklahoma. John sent his mother back to Memphis and I guess the other lady went to the hospital."

Exhausted as she was, Mary made sure to be at the band rehearsal the very next morning. "Holder's boys rehearsed two days a week, beginning at 11 A.M. I was in the hall by nine. I thought them the handsomest bunch of intellectuals I had seen so far. They looked like collegians—all had beautiful brown complexions and wore sharp beige suits to match. Going out, they sported yellow raincoats with the instrument each man played illustrated on the back. Most came from good families and their manners were perfect. As I suspected, the music was out of the ordinary. They were all reading like mad. It was smooth showmanship coupled with musical ability."

Not that she saw a future for herself with the band: they had a pianist. Perhaps she thought of starting her own little combo, or working as a single around Memphis. For the time being, she may have thought she could be content with being the wife of the highest-paid member of the band, and with hovering in the background.

Chapter Four
Nite Life
1929–1931

THE DARK CLOUDS of Joy liked Terrence "T" Holder—he was said to have been an excellent musician. But when he either gambled away the payroll at Christmastime of 1928 or absconded with it to Texas to woo back his estranged wife (depending on whom you talked to), the band revolted. Being left flat broke was particularly galling to the band because they were doing well, booked into long engagements in Oklahoma City and Tulsa dancehalls by the biggest promoter in those parts, a man named Falkenberg. The band members got together and on New Year's Day 1929 voted "T" Holder out.

That they were able to fire their leader was, of course, highly unusual. But this band was a rarity, what John Williams and Claude "Fiddler" Williams, both Clouds veterans, called a commonwealth band, or, in Gunther Schuller's term, a cooperative. Interestingly, the popular white band called the Casa Loma Orchestra was organized along similar lines, although with more sophistication. (One of its saxophone players, Glen Gray, was its president, and the rest of the band served as board of directors and stockholders.) "I remember reading that with the Casa Lomas, they would share out the money, a salary, and put aside something in the bank every week," said John, who soon became the road manager, responsible for overseeing finances, among other jobs. "So this one guy when he leaves the band after years, he has $10,000 savings. Now our band couldn't do like that—save money. But we played percentage dances where we'd get, say, 10% of the take, and we automatically split up the money except for a little more for Andy and so on."

For its new leader the band voted in Andy Kirk, a handsome light-skinned musician whose wife, Mary, was also a pianist in the stride style. Kirk was seven years older than John Williams and had been with the Clouds since '26. Like Jimmie Lunceford, Kirk had gotten his musical education in Denver from Wilberforce J. Whiteman, the city's superintendent of schools and the father of Paul Whiteman, the most famous bandleader of the twenties. As leader, Andy Kirk was the man who became well-known to the public and later to interviewers, and deservedly so. But his second-in-command, road manager John Williams, also had an important role: "*I* would call the four numbers to a set, *I* stomped all the tempos. Andy stood out there and watched my foot come down. Say we were going to play 4/4 time, he's watching my foot and when I come down on four, he come down with his baton. He wasn't even leading the band. *I* led the band."

But never openly. Although Kirk, Williams, and Mary pointedly avoided the question of color, all were aware that one's skin shade held enormous importance in black society. Mary, who had felt the sting of prejudice from her light-skinned, "blue-veined" neighbors as a little girl, observes this when she mentions casually, "Most all the boys were the same complexion 'cept John Williams and Marion Jackson, the dark-skinned brothers." "Well, John was black as you could get," notes Peter O'Brien. "Very dark. And that would be a real no-no then. Look at Lunceford, cherubic and light. Duke Ellington's light. And Andy was light-skinned and had high polish." Of course color consciousness mattered in other realms as well, notably on the stage. And the few "black" actresses to secure glamorous roles in Hollywood—Fredi Washington, Lena Horne, Dorothy Dandridge—were all pale, although, to their credit, they fought the caste system. Darker-skinned beauties had virtually no place on the screen except as maids and "mammy" character actresses. But John Williams, who grew up when Jim Crow was the norm, sidestepped the issue of color when explaining why he was passed over as leader of the band. "They voted in Andy because he was a gentleman," he insisted. "Andy didn't drink, he didn't smoke, he was well liked. I hadn't been there hardly no time at all and the guys were just learning me. They didn't know

what kind of disposition I had, and I didn't want to become leader."
Fair enough.

"Later, guys wanted me to take over the band, because I was good
about keeping guys together, whether they were making money or
not," John went on. "I was always the type of guy that had connections.
People liked me and would help me do things."

One of the first things Andy Kirk did was change the name of the
band. At first he wanted it to be "Andy Kirk's Orchestra," but the band
nixed that. They wanted to retain the "Clouds of Joy." "But Andy didn't
like the 'Dark,' and he took it out—they could see we were dark anyway," John said drily. The band played as it had under Holder. "We had
that easy-going Western swing and we played mostly for whites. Now
when you played for blacks, it didn't make no difference what the tune
was, as long as you had the tempo there. But while we were playing for
whites, they wanted all the latest numbers. The hit numbers from all
the Broadway shows—*No, No, Nanette* was a popular one then. Every
month, we would go to the music store and buy the stock orchestrations for 50 cents, usually by a popular orchestrator of the day named
Archie Bleyer."

Dancehalls like the Winter Garden in Oklahoma City and the Crystal Palace in Tulsa, where the band played for the winter and summer
seasons respectively, had an oil-boom, movie-Western flavor, featuring
what they called "jitney" dances, with "ten-cents-a-dance girls" waiting
behind ropes to be picked by paying partners. The customer got a very
short whirl of a two-step or waltz or foxtrot for his money. "The idea,"
Mary wrote, "was to get the dancers off the floor as quickly as possible.
Two 32-bar choruses was an arrangement." Andy Kirk elaborated: "To
get around that, we'd make up an introduction that served as a bridge
for the next chorus following, and we'd always make up a different
ending for the same number. These things helped make it more interesting." This was basic training for many bands, where the rudiments,
primitive though they were, were established for arranging early
jazz music: solo space was sparse, leading to a compact, compressed
approach to playing. And when such bands made records, they were all
too familiar with the time constraint of three minutes for 78-rpm discs.

Mary listened to the band avidly, inspired rather than intimidated
by the fact that the musicians were well trained while she could barely
read a note of music. "This was the most exciting thing in my life, seeing

the guys get together, making up their arrangements and novelties. They'd call a rehearsal and nobody would prepare an arrangement. They'd do it while they were there. In one corner somebody would be playing cards or talking and Andy would say 'Okay, rhythm section first.' And after that the trumpets and the saxophones. . . . They could play like Guy Lombardo and they could swing like Count Basie. It was the most amazing band I've ever been with in my life. They could play so many different styles. They could play for proms and then go on to an all-black dance and be just as good, swinging."

With solid bookings and a stable new leader, the future looked promising for the Clouds of Joy. But Mary became restive with little to do in the raw and ugly boom towns. Only the year before, a huge gusher had erupted in the middle of a backyard. Now, as everyone in Oklahoma City tried to cash in, a forest of derricks and pumps was installed without regard for safety. Gigantic fires fed by underground pools of oil often burned out of control, filling the air with the stench of oil and devastating entire streets, and when it rained, the unpaved roads became seas of red mud. Mary developed a lifelong habit of driving off by herself in the car to some pretty spot where she would be alone, just looking, dozing, and thinking about music.

Despite the rawness and pollution, there was money and vitality in Oklahoma, plenty of work for everyone, including musicians. This combination of full pockets and a frontier mentality fostered an easing of racial segregation—looser than in places like Memphis and the East—that made it easier for black and white musicians to mix. Trombonist Jack Teagarden, who would become a lifelong friend a bit later, was playing opposite the Clouds of Joy at the Winter Garden; and his sister Norma, who, Mary said, "played piano crazy for a woman," was also gigging in Oklahoma.

Mary settled uneasily into the role of a band wife. When they weren't playing the cities, the Clouds traveled the circuit of small towns from Little Rock to Dallas, which the musicians called "Indian Territory." Mary traveled with the band, but as John's spouse; John had talked her up to Andy Kirk, but Kirk was satisfied with Marion "Jack" Jackson, especially his ability to read music, and had no plans of replacing him with a female ear pianist. When the band settled in Tulsa in the summer of '29, she and John got a room above an undertaker. Sometimes she cut hair or did manicures to make a little money, but she preferred being a chauffeur. "To break the monotony," Mary wrote, "I got permission to drive for the undertaker. Apart from driving the car, I had no way of passing the time. I couldn't see myself getting ahead in music and the life was getting me down fast." She was, however, beginning to pinch-hit for the Clouds—when Jackson was late, or "if they got stuck and weren't going over big, I'd sit in and play. This was very exciting for me."

But it was not enough, clearly. She hated having to live in what she called "bombed out Negro areas," stuck in a loveless marriage. John was out every night, rolling dice and hanging with his friends, especially with his lifelong buddy, clarinetist Johnny Harrington; yet he warned Mary to stay away from some of the hard-partying band wives she'd been going out with. "My friend Mabel Durham, the trombonist Allen Durham's wife, asked why I didn't go out with the wives anymore. I told her that my husband John did not want me around because of their heavy drinking. A couple of the wives got together with me and told me the real reason. He didn't want me to know that he was jiving around with a secretary and had promised to marry her due to the fact that she was giving him money. He stood her off for quite awhile and finally said I wouldn't give him a divorce. Being a hot-tempered native, she thought that if she got rid of me, she'd have more of a chance with John as far as marriage. So she was stalking me to catch up and do me in." Nothing came of that, except to drive a greater wedge between Mary and John. "I couldn't have cared less about what he was doing. I feared John more than I loved him and had begun to dislike him intensely." He still kept her to a budget of a dollar a day, and she now had no work of her own to supplement an allowance she considered "ridiculous. I went on with the dull life of being a housewife with no money."

But, she added casually, "I was seeking thrills here and there, which was unknown to my husband. My friends and I were daredevils. Mabel Durham and I were quite wild together. John and Allen would say, 'Please don't go out tonight, trouble is expected,' but we'd wait until the guys had gone to work, and down we'd go to the main Negro street to watch the fights and shooting, especially Saturday. This was fun to me. We never realized we could have gotten shot. Once when John came home, he said that quite a few people were killed."

With so much time on her hands, Mary soon knew the individual strengths and weaknesses of the players in the band. With her quick ear, Claude Williams recalls, she had begun fashioning solos for non-improvising players like tenor saxophonist Lawrence "Slim" Freeman and trumpeter Harry "Big Jim" Lawson. Another musician, probably Andy Kirk, wrote down the ideas she demonstrated on the piano—an approach similar to what Duke Ellington later made famous in big-band jazz.

As the summer dragged on, Mary had a premonition of bad news while making pastries with Mabel Durham in their landlady's kitchen. "I began crying. Tears fell into the bowl of flour, I was crying so. When John and Mabel and the landlady asked what was troubling me, I just said I wanted to go home to Pittsburgh. They thought this was strange, but a few hours later I received a wire that my stepfather had passed away. Well, John sent me to Pittsburgh."

Back in East Liberty, a griefstricken Mary rolled up her sleeves, got down on her hands and knees, and cleaned her mother's dirty house in preparation for the wake. In a diary, she added details about her unhappy relationship with her mother that she later excised from her planned autobiography:

I was very unhappy staying with my mother and family. I had taken care of the family since Stepfather was unable to do work. I stayed there for about a month or so, my mother never thanking me, but always asking for more money.

I was very unhappy staying with her. I wanted to put the smaller kids in private school, away from her. This she wouldn't listen to. In her warped way of thinking, she felt I was trying to take her kids from her. There were unpleasant scenes and we never got along after this.

I decided to secure work to once again support them. I got a job at the Subway Club for $20 a night—with tips it was sometimes up to $50. Baby Hines was there with her wonderful voice. And I moved in with Mamie, who was very kind and understanding. Hugh and Mamie weren't doing too good, due to the fact my brother-in-law had spent just about all his money to try and cure his father, who was paralyzed on one side. I bought a new rug, stove, divan, and other things they needed, and everyone was happy.

Then, the Andy Kirk band passed through Pittsburgh on a one-nighter and John insisted I leave with him, which I did, this time graduating to the chauffeur job, often driving 12 hours without resting. The Pla-Mor in Kansas City had decided to bring in a black band as something new, to boost sagging admissions. So we headed to Kansas City.

———————

"WE'D HAD IT real good in Oklahoma," John Williams explained, "but we ran into trouble with the white union there, a man named Fox, I remember. He tricked us. A lot of the black bands were getting most all the work because they were the jazz bands and could play the music and they were putting the white musicians out of work. The Clouds of Joy had the best jobs—ballroom in the winter, amusement park in the summer—and the white union wanted them. We played for white dances, but one night a week, usually Monday, would be for blacks at the dancehalls. They raised the scale—minimum you had to pay the musicians—but didn't tell Kirk. Well, that was the night they came afterward to where we were playing and said Kirk had underpaid. We were fined about $1,500 total. We didn't have that kind of money. No way. And this was segregation days; you didn't protest. So we had to leave Oklahoma."

Luckily, the popular Kansas City bandleader George E. Lee had become a good friend of Andy Kirk's and helped the Clouds put together a string of engagements in Kansas and Missouri to pay off their fine. And a lavish new ballroom had just opened in Kansas City. Called the Pla-Mor, it had a swimming pool that converted to an ice hockey rink in the winter, a bowling alley, a restaurant, and a huge dancehall. Lee thought the Clouds of Joy would go over well there, where there was plenty of work and an appetite for fresh-sounding bands.

"We didn't even know what a plum we'd picked off the 1929 Boom Tree when we rolled into Kansas City on that hot June day, the first out-of-town colored band to play the Pla-Mor," wrote Andy Kirk. The city had a border-state mentality, not quite northern, nor quite southern. Mary was pleased that she could again sit wherever she wanted on the bus, but segregation still marked most aspects of daily life. The separate black and white musicians' unions, for example, were not to merge until 1970. (The black musicians' union hall, a brick building at 1823 Highland Avenue, still stands.)

What pleased Mary most was the music, which had evolved a great deal since her interlude a few years before. "Music everywhere in the Negro section of town," she exulted, "and 50 or more cabarets rocking on 12th and 18th Streets" (though others, such as Claude Williams, reckoned there were at most a dozen). There were certainly scores of fine players in Kansas City. Some, like George and his sister Julia Lee, remained local stars, while others, like Charlie Parker and Ben Webster, achieved jazz immortality. The rich musical flavor of the era is reflected in a newspaper ad from December 1929 promoting a veritable banquet of bands in a "battle" sponsored by Local 627— bands led by Bennie Moten, Andy Kirk, George Lee, Walter Page, George Williams, and Paul Banks.

John and Mary stayed at first again with his hospitable Aunt Babe and Uncle Quincy Williams. Mary earned some change playing for their daughter Mabel's dancing classes. "I also taught her routines I knew, for I was a pretty good tap dancer myself," she added. But a great deal of her time was spent out on the town, soaking up "Kansas City Swing," which had a profound impact on her playing and writing. She admired Julia Lee, one of several excellent women pianists based in Kansas City. And she loved the Blue Devils, who would provide the nucleus for the Count Basie Orchestra, observing that "They were sensational with Page doubling on bass and bass saxophone. Page's group had great men like Jimmy Rushing, 'Hot Lips' Page, Buster Smith on clarinet. These three later joined Bennie Moten's band. A show had come to K.C. and Count Basie was with the show. He liked K.C. so much he decided to stay." She further recalled: "There was Harlan Leonard with crazy Herman Walder on tenor, and Jay McShann, a real crazy stylist on piano, and his orchestra. Jay McShann took on an alto player, young Charlie Parker. Charlie Parker in knee pants, too young to play with a band. Often musicians would catch him peeping in the door of dates. When he was a little older, he and beautiful Mary Kirk, a pianist, had a gig together with a very good drummer whose name I've forgotten. The boys and I would stop by to hear them play and we never knew what Charlie was saying, it was so way out. But it sounded good. Also, there was Jap Allen with young Ben Webster. Pete Johnson and Joe Turner were shouting the blues at the Sunset, on 12th Street. Alphonse Trent's band was often in town." Even the school bands were great, she added. "Maybe they played out of tune but they could really swing."

There was lots of work but not much money for the musicians; bands at the black clubs often got paid in sandwiches and beer, and counted themselves lucky at that. But the relaxed atmosphere gave musicians the time to work out ideas. "Nobody ever got homesick for New York when they visited K.C. Kansas City boasted of everything New York had, including the best musicians. And their famous barbecue, chili and crawdads were the end. There were the races, and swimming, and beautiful Swope Park and the zoo, jam sessions all the time and big dances such as the annual union dance. If you were without funds, people would make you a loan without you asking for it, would look at you and tell if you were hungry and put things right."

Meanwhile, Mary was still on her dollar-a-day budget, supplemented by pickup work at parties, accompanying dance classes, and teaching piano lessons. But she made the rounds, with her pals Mabel Durham and Othie Harrington. "I remember once that I did not even have a dress to wear and the woman where I was living took the curtains off her window—a pongee material—and made me a dress. Whenever I did receive money, I'd share it with Mabel and Othie."

What she liked best was going to the jam sessions after the paying gigs ended, around midnight. Neither the ensuing Great Depression nor Prohibition kept those good times from rolling. "No other city in the world was quite like Kansas City," says journalist and record producer Dave Dexter, a native. "Musicians and singers came into the Jackson County town of 400,000 like cattle—in droves. For under the wide-open yet iron rule of Democratic political czar Thomas J. Pendergast there were no closing hours for saloons and nightclubs. Prostitution flourished day and night in the open. There were jobs available for entertainers of every type." As for the stock market crash? Said Andy Kirk, "In Kansas City it was like a pin dropping; the blast of jazz and blues drowned it out. People were crowding the clubs and ballrooms as usual."

––––––––––

MARY SOON BECAME a player to watch on the after-hours scene, and what a formidable school that must have been in classrooms like Piney Brown's and the Sunset. Instead of having to contend with highly compressed solos and arrangements of the "10 cents a dance" format, musicians had the luxury of time to "tell a story" on their instruments. And with her terrific musical memory, acute harmonic sense, perfect pitch, assured rhythmic sense, and abundance of ideas, Mary flourished. "It was the first time we had ever seen a girl cat who could carve the local boys," remarked Harlan Leonard, an excellent local bandleader.

Kansas City was Mary's coming of age as a musician and as a woman. She had found her intellectual peers and was challenged and stimulated to develop a formidable technique in the inherent lyricism of the blues form that shaped the sessions. Kansas City in the thirties was her Paris, her Harvard, her Haight-Ashbury, a free and easy communal atmosphere. As Mary put it, "If you don't play well, then all of them will sound bad." Everybody's art bloomed under these conditions.

"In K.C. there was so much love around. . . . There was never that distinction between classes or that complexion madness I had found in Pittsburgh. The elite socialized with the middle class. They would attend our dances and any of the other dances if the music was good, yet they had their sorority things going also. But among musicians especially, there was no throat cutting or deceit. Those who were not making it always got help from capable musicians. Count Basie and I had a thing going, teaching young kids music. Often he'd send me pupils and vice versa. At one time we must have had over 30 kids between the two of us, teaching them."

Although she socialized from time to time with white musicians— Jack Teagarden, in town with Ben Pollack's band, squired her to his gig at the Muehlebach, *the* big white hotel in downtown Kansas City, "an exclusive white spot where Negroes weren't ordinarily allowed," as Mary put it—the creative center of jazz was uptown. "My attention was focused where the giants were, and that was 18th and Vine or 12th Street," she said firmly.

———

IN THE FALL of 1929, producer Jack Kapp of Brunswick/Vocalion Records came to Kansas City from Chicago. Victor, its rival, had signed Bennie Moten's band, and Kapp wanted to sign on the best of the rest of the jumping bands in town. With him was Dick Voynow, a former pianist with the Wolverines and now his recording engineer.

Serendipity gave Mary the piano chair for the date. Wrote Andy Kirk, "They auditioned us at the Pla-Mor and four other bands at other spots. That audition turned out to be a real 'sleeper.' We were all set up and ready except for Marion Jackson, our pianist. Nobody seemed to know where he was. Things were getting tense," Kirk went on. "We'd have to start soon or blow it. John Williams said, 'How about getting Prelude?' Prelude was our name for his wife, Mary Lou.

"When John first came on the band he had asked me to hear Mary play. . . . I did and agreed that she was a fine pianist, but we already had one that met our requirements. And we were making a lot of road trips and I always thought doing one-nighters would be hard on a woman. But this was an emergency. I told John, okay. When Mary Lou came in and sat down at the piano to audition with us, no one had the wildest idea she'd be a big factor in our landing an excellent two-year recording contract, or wilder yet, that she would make jazz history."

"When I arrived at the audition," Mary wrote, "I played everything the band played as if I had been with them all along, this surprising them greatly. They gave me solos to play and Kapp must have liked them because he set a date to record the band the following week at radio station KMBC in Kansas City. . . . Andy said later because I made the audition he thought it no more than fair that I record with them."

On the strength, then, of a last-minute, ad-lib performance, Mary was included in the Clouds of Joy recording debut over several days in November of 1929. And Kapp liked what he heard at that recording session so much that he signed an exclusive contract with the band. This was Mary's doing. As soon as the record date had been set—for a week from the audition—she approached Kirk. "Andy knew that I had ideas," she wrote. "I was writing all along but I couldn't write it down. I'd give them ideas during rehearsal. Maybe they wanted to play a song like 'Singing in the Rain' and I'd say, 'Well, listen to this.' Andy would take it down real fast." For the recording date, she dictated at a furious pace. "Never have I written so many things so quickly in my entire career, about 20 things, including 'Cloudy' and 'Corky.' " (Although Kirk maintained that he wrote part of "Corky," most sources give sole composer credit to Mary.)

Harmonically and rhythmically, she was way ahead of the pack, just as she'd been in her tiny solos two years before with the Syncopators.

But she still had much to learn. When she dictated her first composition to Kirk, for instance, called "Messa Stomp," it was carefully plotted, building from a cheerful stroll to a jaunty strut, with the approach to horn voicings she'd admired in Don Redman's work. But much of it, initially, was unplayable—beyond the range of half the instruments. "But the boys," Mary wrote, "gave me a chance and each time I did better, until I found myself doing five and six arrangements per week. Later on, I learned more theory from people like the great Don Redman, Edgar Sampson, Milton Orent and Will Bradley."

Between November 7 and 11, 1929, the band recorded eight tunes, five of them written by Mary or originating with her: "Messa Stomp," "Corky Stomp," "Cloudy," "Froggy Bottom," and "Lotta Sax Appeal." When Mary collaborated—with John or Andy at that time— she contributed the creative meat of the voicings for the reeds and brass, as in "Cloudy" and "Froggy Bottom." It is impossible to disentangle claims of authorship for many past jazz compositions; jazz was such a collaborative and informally processed music. Though internal evidence strongly suggests that the works cited are Mary's, she sometimes ceded co-composer credit, often only to keep the peace. One example: on the second, much-reworked "Froggy Bottom," recorded in the late 1930s, John Williams received co-composer credit, though Mary—who had conceived and worked out the new arrangement—maintained later that the song was "hers." She almost certainly wrote the majority, if not all, of the voicings for the band's tunes at that time. Of the remaining three tunes, the uncredited "Somepin' Slow & Low" may well be Mary's arrangement. "Somepin'" has a rather ambitious, long, lilting melody line and 4-bar solos, including a good one for trombonist Durham, and one for Mary, whose sophisticated rhythmic breaks and harmonic innovations distinguish her. On "Lotta Sax Appeal," a sprightly, upbeat blues, John Williams sometimes took full composer credit, but at times shared it with Mary.

As for her playing, it was supple and dazzling, "richly chordal" and "astonishingly self-assured," to use Gunther Schuller's phrase. Along with drummer Crack McNeil, she helped to balance the rather heavy, plodding effect of Kirk's tuba. She had a sparkling and confident, still Hinesian manner, but, as tunes like "Cloudy" show, she was already heading into the early swing era. (Confusingly, as with "Froggy Bottom," the "Cloudy" recorded a few years later was quite a different piece.) On November 11, when the band recorded her co-credited "Froggy Bottom" and "Corky Stomp," Mary gets into one of her most pleasing grooves, a relaxed, lilting blues. She got the idea for "Froggy Bottom" when she passed through a little town in her travels, a town where, she said fancifully, folks "just sank down to the bottom of things, like frogs in a pool, leading a carefree life, just eating ham 'n cabbage." There is a gracefulness to her playing of this, one of her all-time favorites, that is a hallmark of Mary's style.

But despite Mary's appeal to Kapp and the musicians in the band, despite her astonishing output for the recordings, and despite her own efforts—"She was so determined to play that piano, I began calling her 'the pest,' " said Andy Kirk—Mary was replaced again by Marion Jackson as the band pianist.

Again, it was Jack Kapp who gave her a chance to record with the Clouds. In the spring of 1930, he telegraphed them to come up to Chicago, where Brunswick was located, to make more records, and they left Mary behind. But Kapp didn't want them without Mary. "He told Andy that the band didn't sound the same and he didn't want to record it without me," wrote Mary. Send for her, he told Kirk.

But in the meantime, while she was home on her own, she was undergoing some sordid and brutal experiences, as Mary detailed in a diary entry. It speaks volumes about both her marriage and her habitual secretiveness that she wrote with such detailed candor, while never revealing to anyone else what had happened to her:

Mabel and I were out being daredevils and met a man. He was abnormal sexually. He expressed a desire to do something abnormal to the both of us. I took Mabel aside and told her that this would be good to experience, and we agreed. Not saying anything to anyone, we went to his room and after having some wine to give ourselves courage (neither one of us drank!) we relaxed with our clothes on, except for our panties which we later took off. Well, I've never been so frightened in all my life. The guy was a maniac and we couldn't stop him. He held us and the only way I could get rid of him was to kick him in the head. After this ordeal, we could barely walk. I began thinking of all the tales people had told us about other women who ended up in a hospital after being chewed up. We ran home.

Sadly, as Mary's medical records reported many years later, her body bore evidence of "trauma to the uterus"—an abdominal scar—that Mary dated to 1930, when she had this unsavory and violent encounter. Permanent damage to the uterus due to rough sex, or hard blows or kicks, is not, doctors say, terribly uncommon.

But there was more to come. When, the following day, Mary received the telegram from Kirk, summoning her to Chicago right away to record with the band, she continued her chilling narrative.

> The next night I caught a train, sitting most of the time on one hip. Before the train reached St. Louis, where I had to change trains, I was awakened by someone doing the same thing. I screamed and looked around, but it was the conductor. I was the only passenger on the train and the lights were very dim. I had to fight like mad. I wasn't fit for anything when I arrived in Chicago that morning, but I went straight to the studio to record.

It is truly incredible that, despite what sounds like two episodes of sexual brutality in two days, coupled with the aftermath of emotional distress, fatigue, and physical pain, Mary was able to produce two shining solos. But she did. The band was not ready to start when she arrived, so Kapp decided to start the tape rolling with a piano feature. Apparently Mary did not even know she was being recorded; she simply followed Kapp's instructions to play something. "So I sat down and played," wrote Mary. "I had been in the habit of making up my own things when asked to play. Out of this training and the way I was feeling the beat, came the two originals, 'Nite Life' and 'Drag 'Em.' " Both were very good three-minute blues that established her as a musician worthy of serious attention among discerning critics. (Despite reissues through the years, Mary fought unsuccessfully for royalties for decades.)

The slow "Drag 'Em" has a lot of the flavor of Earl Hines—octaves and tremolos in the right hand, melodic fragments and rhythmic devices in the left. The delightful ending is a favorite musical "upset" of Mary's in which she shifts from a minor key to the relative major. But it is "Nite Life," a faster blues, that especially demonstrates her unforced but crisp and authoritative command of the piano. The

French jazz critic Hugues Panassié, who was one of the first to understand the *passion* in Mary's playing, paid special attention to her performance of "Nite Life" in his (somewhat overwrought) *Guide to Swing Music*. While her style was clearly derivative of James P. Johnson and Fats Waller, Mary, says Panassié, "is much more fantastic and ardent. On 'Nite Life' she has made one of the most beautiful hot piano solos we have. Her hot, panting right hand phrases, and the swing she gets by the accentuation in the bass by the left hand, must both be admired." Sometimes, Mary's playing spilled over into a kind of nervous passion that would lead her to play at the very brink of rushing the time. This gave her music an edginess and lent a certain abruptness to her endings. But it also fueled the sense of excitement that is one of the prize elements of good jazz.

Panassié adds, almost as a throwaway, "Mary Lou Williams' playing is like that of a man; one would never guess that it was a woman playing." Thus he laid bare (though presumably unintentionally) the whole dilemma for women artists who must perform not as women but as men in order to be taken seriously. Mary, a product of her era, often said proudly that she "played heavy like a man"; though it would be more to the point to say that she was playing heavy *like herself*. Sharon Pease, a musician who sometimes collaborated with Mary, thought she achieved her strong touch by "proper relaxation, thus getting the weight of her arms and body onto the keyboard much in the same manner as a prizefighter gets the weight of his body into a punch. This relaxation not only improves tone quality, but makes for faster and smoother execution." Where Panassié and many others thought in terms of brute strength, Pease thought of balance points.

Almost a week after Mary had recorded "Nite Life" and "Drag 'Em," the band as a whole went into the studio, recording six tunes, enough material for three 78s. The band recorded mostly pedestrian material of limited musical interest, with a few notable exceptions. Her "Mary's Idea," (a title she used again later) has a striking, spiky melody line and is intelligently plotted. She makes good use of Kirk's tuba, having him sign off the tune with deeply dipped grace notes, and she deftly incorporates her main influences of the time: the introduction is melodically beholden to Redman's introduction in "Cotton Pickers' Scat" and his "singing" arrangements for reed and brass, as well as the strutty, bright, short piano bits he liked to insert. "Don Redman was my model," she declared about such early arranging efforts. "I could hear my chords in my head but didn't know how to write them." She also paid homage to Redman in the opening chorus for saxophones on "Travelin' That Rocky Road."

Then, working with a combo called the Seven Little Clouds of Joy, with John Williams as the leader, Mary wrote her most ambitious tune to date. "Gettin' Off a Mess" has the kind of sinewy, odd melody line that she would so often write, and the centerpiece is her solo, with a ravishing interlude of Gershwinesque harmonies. Along with "Mary's Idea," "Gettin' Off a Mess" demonstrates unequivocally that here was an original thinker.

Shortly before Christmas of 1930, the Clouds went to New York, where they recorded more tracks for Brunswick, including a Rudy Vallee-ish selection called "Saturday" that Jack Kapp may have hoped would be a crossover hit—from the "race" records section to the larger white market. It wasn't. On "Sophomore," another unabashedly commercial tune with vocals, Mary had her first 32-bar solo and used it to brilliant advantage. A reviewer lauds her playing as a "masterpiece with its aggressive percussive quality, broken tenths and quick runs. One of her tricks is a device used to build and release tension. This is heard in the third eight-bar set. Moving into the chorus, she upsets the rhythmic flow by holding a chord in the left hand for the first measure. The right returns to prance lightly through the rest, ending the whole matter with a surprise—a flurry of notes in the higher octaves."

As usual, she and the band were paid peanuts for their work, "Maybe $4 or $5 for recording," said John. "That was it. And never saw one penny from royalties, none of us. They'd take a number and then the engineer or someone would put any name on it—that's why it's hard to remember what tune someone's talking about now. We just played them and didn't think about it." As for Mary's arrangements, John thought she got $5 or $10 tops. No salary. Not that it mattered. Even John, the highest-paid member of the band, wasn't being paid much, because it wasn't there to give.

Money troubles exacerbated the problems in their marriage when they got back to Kansas City. "I left town to go play with the band for several days and didn't leave her nothing. It was the one time she got me really angry." All over a pair of shoes. "I asked my husband for money to buy a pair of good, I. Miller shoes," said Mary, "and he blew his stack, saying I should be happy to get $2 for shoes. I never forgave John. He knew I had holes in my shoes and no winter coat, yet refused to give me money. And *I* knew he had over $300 in his pocket. Well, I wired home for money and I moved in with Mary Kirk, who was very kind to me. She fed me and gave me a short suit coat to wear underneath my little spring coat." Mary added meaningfully, "After this, he looked ugly to me and I'd sit up all night writing to keep from being in bed with him."

The country was plummeting into deep economic depression. People couldn't afford to buy records, and Brunswick dropped the band from its roster. But Kirk, hoping to record with Brunswick again when the economy bettered, took care to have the band use the pseudonym "The Joy Boys" when the rival company, Victor, recorded the Clouds that year behind vaudevillian Blanche Calloway, sister of Cab. But the Clouds were to make no more records for five years, a period during which some of the finest talent passed through the band—Ben Webster, Lester Young, Buddy Tate—and also when the band's attractive brand of swing matured.

They were still riding fairly high, despite Black Tuesday and a worsening economy. Between the first recording session in Chicago and the next in New York, the band got a break: two weeks in the spring of 1930 at the famous Roseland Ballroom in New York, where Fletcher Henderson had the house band. "He liked the band," recalled John Williams, "and he said, 'I can give you a break, I'll put you in there while I'm out on tour with my band.'" But the band arrived at Roseland exhausted and broke, having had a car accident on the way that made them miss a gig and run out of money. Both John and Claude Williams emphasized that the Clouds were no match then for the established bands they played opposite—the white bands of Gene Goldkette and his Vagabonds, and Glen Gray and the Casa Loma Orchestra, with their bigger sections and better arrangements. But the Clouds' sound was still a success with audiences, and their engagement was extended. Mary sat in once or twice a night to do specialty numbers like "Froggy Bottom" and "Mary's Idea," during which, she remembered, the kids would stop dancing to crowd around the piano.

While in New York, they accumulated good new arrangements (new for them). The Casa Loma Orchestra was cleaning out their band book, recalled John Williams. "Glen Gray gave us about 12 to 15 charts. This was good stuff," John emphasized. "Glen Gray was one of your greatest bands back at that time. Before Tommy Dorsey and Benny Goodman made it, Glen Gray was it." Among the new music was a discarded chart of the lovely Bix Beiderbecke piece "In a Mist." Mary, though still not able to read music, learned the piano part perfectly and played it with the band. And John Williams's friend Benny Carter copied some charts that the terrific drummer Chick Webb's band was currently playing—"Ol' Man River" and "Liza"—for five dollars apiece. John recalled that the Clouds went on to play the Savoy Ballroom after their Roseland stint, opposite Webb. "He would always let the other band play their best arrangements, then come out after and get 'em. But now we sounded like a new band." They sounded so good not the least because Andy Kirk had asked Mary to custom-tailor the new arrangements for the Clouds of Joy, providing high polish and pointing up individual players' strengths.

By 1931 there wasn't much lucrative work for the Clouds (or any band). They put together strings of one-nighters, and played the Grand Terrace Ballroom in Chicago, but entertainment was becoming a luxury fewer and fewer people could afford. Everyone was "at liberty" a lot, and Mary filled her time by becoming an avid card player, a lifelong passion. Never good at holding her liquor, she avoided drinking; instead, she went bowling, hung out with her girlfriends, and filled in on piano whenever she could for "Jack," which troubled Kirk. "She was very attractive and very talented, but you know how they were on women in those days," he explained to friend Delilah Jackson. "They didn't want women to be in the band and the musicians would really get upset; seemed like the musicians were jealous. But she was just so determined to play that piano." For her part, Mary never acknowledged having been aware of any conflict in the band because of her gender. "No one ever rejected me or my music," she was wont to say. True, and not true. While she did win over the crowd and her fellow musicians with her music, the fact remained that there *was* a lot of winning over to do.

———

ANDY KIRK AND Mary Lou Williams were oil and water, developing an adversarial relationship that got worse over time. Hardly surprising: as Mary put it, Kirk wanted to be the black Guy Lombardo, while she was all about jazz. Still, they were adversaries who realized fully that each had ambitions beyond the ordinary and was bound to attain them. Though Kirk made it seem in his autobiography that he "decided" to make Mary the band's regular pianist eventually, by all accounts he resisted as long as he could. "I told her," Kirk said, 'I didn't want you to get a head. Hot-headed. You are a pest.' " Then the Clouds ended up in Philadelphia, scuffling, after working in Chicago in the winter of 1931, and counted themselves lucky to put together a week at a theater called the Pearl. It was run by a man named Sam Steiffle, who by a lucky coincidence was looking for a house band to back his headliner Blanche Calloway, whom he was trying to promote as a rival to her brother Cab. The Clouds grabbed Steiffle's offer.

Mary wrote tactfully, "Sam Steiffle had the idea of putting Blanche in front of the band because Andy played tuba in the band and the only front man we had was Billy Massey, our vocalist; but Steiffle's idea didn't work out too well." Though Blanche was tall, vivacious, and seasoned, the records she made with the Clouds of Joy—with Mary on piano—make clear that she was not particularly musical. (Nevertheless, Miss Calloway, who failed in her attempt to "steal" the Clouds away from Kirk for a road show, did put together another band in the teeth of the Depression, and pieced together a living as a bandleader until the end of the thirties.)

At first, Mary was hired as a second piano attraction with the band. "Steiffle got a great idea: put two pianos on the stage, a baby grand for Marion Jackson and a Tom Thumb for me. I made people scream and carry on, because they saw a woman that weighed around 90 pounds. To hear me play so heavy, like a man, that was something else.

"Over the two pianos, Kirk had a shed-like enclosure built," she continued. "On top of the shed stood the drums. Ben Thigpen had joined the band, replacing Crack McNeil. It was tough going; I was used to a large piano, but . . . I was doing my best. And I could hear practically nothing but the thunder of drums overhead.

"This went on for some time, when Marion Jackson began not showing up on time. One day, when Jack didn't show up at all, I jumped on the baby grand and played, surprising everyone in the theatre. When Jack came in he seemed to be loaded. This did it. Steiffle went over Andy's head and fired Marion, saying, 'You don't need him. Keep her—she's great!' " Jack was given two weeks' pay and a ticket back home. I stayed on as the orchestra pianist, composer and arranger."

Other now legendary talents came to play at the Pearl, and Mary met seasoned pianists who gave her tips. Eddie Heywood, Sr., was a conservatory-trained veteran who was accompanying the famous act of Butterbeans and Susie. (Mary and Heywood's son, Eddie, Jr., were featured pianists at Cafe Society in the forties.) The second was Pearl Wright, longtime accompanist to the great Ethel Waters, headlining that year in the show *Blackbirds*. "Pearl had to go away and sat with me for at least a week teaching me how to accompany Ethel Waters, because I'd have to play for her while she was absent." Evidently it went very well. Five years later (in December 1936), Ethel Waters pleaded with Mary by telegram to drop everything and come with her on tour. "What a beautiful, tall woman, and so kind," Mary wrote of that complex personality. "I used to hear how Ethel would take her big car and chauffeur to a very poor Negro section, fill her car with poor kids and take them downtown to buy them clothing."

Meanwhile, John Williams had come down with diphtheria, for which there was then no effective treatment, and lay in a hospital until he was released at Eastertime, fully recovered. During his convalescence, Bennie Moten, passing through Philadelphia, told Andy Kirk to contact the union back in Kansas City. "A couple places that had never hired Negroes had an opening: exclusive Winnwood Beach and Fairyland Park," Mary wrote. In May, the Clouds, broke again, got a job in Baltimore that funded their return to Kansas City.

"This," Mary said, "was the beginning of my career as the pianist, arranger and composer with the Andy Kirk band." By now Kirk had changed his tune, confiding after her death, "She had a set of ears you wouldn't believe. I used to say that if you dropped a dishpan on the floor, she'd tell you what key it was ringing in." To a friend he added, "She was so smart, plus she could arrange and was very attractive."

Chapter Five
Walkin' and Swingin'
1931–1935

ALTHOUGH THE CLOUDS made no known records from 1931 until 1936, it was a fecund period for jazz in general, for the band itself, and for Mary. In the intensely creative atmosphere of the homely, homey clubs in black Kansas City, a music at once handcrafted and sophisticated evolved. And Mary was in the thick of it.

While economic despair was new to many formerly comfortable whites in the 1930s, for many blacks the widespread poverty produced by the Great Depression was just another step or two down the American ladder that they never seemed able to climb. A piquant comment summarized their situation: "It's hard to jump out the window and kill yourself when you're living in the basement." John Williams expressed a commonly held view among black musicians: "White musicians— they worked all the time, 'cause they had those white bands in every leading hotel with their ballrooms, all over the United States. Dancing was the big thing. But we had to get what we could. We couldn't play in those white hotel ballrooms regular, so we were playing for a night or a week. Sometimes we were the house band for a month. But then after that, you're on your own."

Road life was gritty, and more so as the thirties wore on. Black musicians in Kansas City had little choice but to go on the road, though. Despite the occasional solid engagements in town—a summer at the popular white resort Winwood Beach and a tour at Fairyland Park, a run at the elegant Vanity Fair club—the town simply couldn't support them full-time. The Clouds' bread-and-butter dancehall jobs dried up and, as with other bands, their stories of those years traveling the "territory" are filled with tales of being left without money or prospects. "In 1933, when President Roosevelt closed all the banks—they called it the banking holiday—we played a theatre in Little Rock, Arkansas, and there weren't but 20 people in there for a show," recalls John Williams. "Well, we were stranded in Little Rock. So was Bennie Moten's band, which had Basie in it.

"We went to Memphis, got a little work at the Pink Rose and then we were stranded for about six weeks and my mother fed the entire band," Williams continued. "To get back to Kansas City we only got one booking, in Hannibal, Missouri—400 miles for a one-night gig! It took us eight hours to drive that and we get into town about two, three in the afternoon. The dance usually started at nine o'clock, and we're tired. Mary and I are going to lay down and get a little rest. We went to this rooming house where a woman had musicians to stay—in all those towns they had places where show people and bands could stop overnight. No sooner did we get undressed than the landlady comes knocking on the door. 'Okay, y'all can pay me now.' Well, I didn't have nothing to pay her with because we'd been stranded. Except what I called mad money—$2 that I kept in my watch pocket for when things were real desperate. I said, 'I'll pay you after the dance tonight.' And *she* said, 'No, I want my money now.' We're going back and forth, I'm telling her we're going to play the dance. She said, 'You're going to play the dance but you ain't going to make no money. Ain't nobody coming to the dance.' She made us put on our clothes and get up! I went and got Mary and me some hamburgers with that mad money, then we nodded in the car in front of the place where we were going to play at nine that night. And the rooming-house lady knew what she was talking about: wasn't but three people at the dance. Every time our promoter hired a band, this other promoter would give a free dance to whites, so there wasn't no need to come hear us. We didn't have no money, and for about an hour Andy begged the promoter of our dance to lend us enough money to buy gas so we could drive our cars to Kansas City. He finally lent us enough to fill our tanks."

It went on like this, off and on, for years. The band would be paid in fried chicken or frogs' legs instead of cash, or had enough for only one meal a day, often a cheap bowl of stew or soup. They picked the corn out of farmers' fields at night and roasted it. They even tried to play softball for money (but once only: they weren't very good). Sometimes they had to push their cars when they ran out of gas. "When Kirk came backstage after a job with his head down," Mary said, "we'd know he hadn't been paid. Instead of gettin' angry or quittin' or running off, we'd just laugh. I made a little extra money by manicuring the boys' nails. They paid me a nickel, and I'd take it out of the money they made from cards, which I held for them."

After a job fell through in Cincinnati late in '33, players took whatever work they could get on their own. Mary found a job in a roadhouse playing with drummer Ben Thigpen and trumpeter Earl Thompson. And she told John she was really going to quit the band this time: she saw no future for the Clouds. But John talked her out of it. "I'd tell the musicians, 'One day we'll make it big.' "

The worst was yet to come. Buffalo, New York, 1935: five years into the Depression and no end in sight. Joe Glaser, the agent who represented Louis Armstrong, booked the band into the Vendome Hotel Nightclub, promising to follow up with a date at the Apollo in New York. "But," said John, "he couldn't do it, so he dropped us there in Buffalo, in the coldest part of the winter. Andy would give us each 50 cents every day, to eat. His coat was so ragged that the elbows were out. It was hard times, though some people don't like to remember the bad days. Andy didn't put no bad things in that book of his he wrote [*Twenty Years on Wheels*]. Finally we played one dance at a black dancehall, nothing fancy, so we could get enough money together to get out of town."

Back in Kansas City, Mary and John boarded with his relatives again, while she picked up a bit of work playing for dancing classes again and sharing from the musicians' humble but communal pot. Despite the continual money problems, Mary said over and over that it was the high point of her life. "I just loved it. I could live that life over once again. Because those that were playing were great musicians."

And compared to many other cities, Kansas City was in relatively good shape. "Any musician that was broke, there was places you automatically had a job, $2 a night and all you could drink," John recalled. "You could get a steak dinner for 35 cents, a room for 75 cents a night. So you could live. And you could pick a good woman out of that and they would take care of you all night for sure." There were dances at the many social clubs, 25-cent music lessons, and places like Piney Brown's with pots of food and liberal glasses of whatever the musician was drinking.

———

AFTER MIDNIGHT ON nights when they were lucky enough to have had a paying gig, the band stashed their uniforms—worsted knickers for the men, a skirt for Mary—and headed off to jam. "We played from 9 to 12 and afterwards all the guys would rush to get to Piney Brown's club on Twelfth Street. John would drop our carload off and take me home to bathe and put on a cool dress," she wrote. The session, when she got there, might continue until well after dawn. Tenor saxophonist Coleman Hawkins was starring in Fletcher Henderson's band in 1934, while Lester Young and Ben Webster, still unknown, were local heroes. One night, after playing a job with the Clouds, Mary was tired and went home to bed. "The word went round that Hawkins was in the Cherry Blossom"—a Japanese-decorated club "with beautiful little brown-skinned waitresses in kimonos" where high-rollers liked to hang out— she wrote, "and within about half an hour there were Lester Young, Ben Webster, Herschel Evans, Herman Walder, and one or two unknown tenors piling in the club to blow. Hawk [Coleman Hawkins] didn't know the Kaycee tenormen were so terrific, and he couldn't get himself together though he played all morning. I happened to be nodding that night, and around 4 A.M., I awoke to hear someone pecking on my screen. I opened the window on Ben Webster. He was saying, 'Get up, pussycat, we're jammin' and all the pianists are tired out now. Hawkins has got his shirt off and is still blowing. You got to come down.' Sure enough, when we got there Hawkins was in his singlet taking turns with the Kaycee men. It seems he had run into something he didn't expect. Lester's style was light and it took him maybe five choruses to warm up. But then he would really blow; then you couldn't handle him on a cutting session. That was how Hawkins got cut up. The Henderson band was playing in St. Louis that evening, and Ben knew he ought to be on the way. But he kept trying to blow something to beat Ben and Herschel and Lester. When at last he gave up, he got straight in his car and drove to St. Louis. I heard he'd just bought a new Cadillac and that he burnt it out trying to make the job on time."

Earliest known photograph of Mary, probably taken between
1921 and 1922, when she was eleven or twelve and at the height of her
local fame as "the little piano girl of East Liberty" in Pittsburgh.

Mary's beloved stepfather, Fletcher Burley, is on the left, with his half-brother Julius Burley. A laborer by day, Fletcher Burley cut a dashing figure as a gambler at night, often sneaking Mary into taverns to play for tips.

The redoubtable Anna Jane "Nanny" Riser, Mary's maternal grandmother.

Mary's mother, "Miss Ginnie," holding an unidentified infant, probably one of her many grandchildren, circa 1950.

Mary, at right, with her favorite sister, Mamie Floyd, center,
and Mamie's children, Alvin and Helen, in the 1940s. Mary often went
back to Pittsburgh to stay with Mamie, her version of a vacation.

Mary with Robbie Mickles, the nephew she part-raised,
probably in 1957 or 1958, at Birdland.

Mary, at bottom right, with Buzzin' Harris
and His Hits 'n Bits, her first job as
a traveling professional pianist, in 1925.

Saxophonist John Williams in 1926.
He was Mary's first husband.

Mary in 1926 with the band that backed the dance team Seymour
and Jeanette on big-time vaudeville. Usually called the Syncopators,
the group was here billed as the Midnite Strutters' Band.

Left to right: Mary, dancer
Margaret Warren, and
Arletta Harris in 1925, with the
Hits 'n Bits. Finery aside, the
troupe could barely feed itself.

Mary, right, and Mabel Durham, trombonist Allen Durham's wife,
kicking up their heels, probably in Oklahoma in 1929, just before the
Clouds of Joy moved to Kansas City.

The Clouds of Joy, 1933. Bandleader Andy Kirk, in the white coat, is next to
Mary, the band's featured soloist, arranger, and composer. Fourth from the
left is saxophonist Ben Webster, with whom Mary had fallen in love.

Mary, third from the left, looking bored, between Andy Kirk on her right and vocalist Pha Terrell on her left, others unknown, circa 1937 or 1938. The Clouds of Joy was then enjoying its biggest success.

Mary in the mid-1930s.

Mary hung out at other clubs on Twelfth Street, too. One of her favorites was the Subway, where she'd go to listen to Bill Basie's rocking, crisply aphoristic piano. "I listened to how a pianist pushed, like Count Basie, and *I* pushed." Basie's witty and thrifty swing style, along with Art Tatum's, was one more coat of veneer carefully applied to the base coats of James P. Johnson, Earl Hines, Fats Waller. But Basie was also listening to her: "I didn't hang around [the Subway Club] too often," he said, "because the Subway also used to be one of Mary Lou Williams's stopping-off places. . . . Anytime she was in the neighborhood, I used to find myself another little territory, because Mary Lou was tearing everybody up." Kansas City pianist Pete Johnson, a great blues-based pianist to whom Mary pays tribute in her "Roll 'Em," told the story of meeting Mary in about 1930 in Kansas City, when a friend took him over to the rooming house where Mary was living. "When we arrived no one was stirring, so we sat in the living room and my pal suggested that I play a little something on the piano, which I did. This started the roomers to getting up and coming in to listen. I felt pretty good with that audience because I had the reputation of being the best pianist in K.C. then. When I had finished, my friend said: 'Mary Lou, why don't you play a little something?' So a girl sat down at the piano and I thought to myself that it would not be much. Well, when I heard her I told everybody that I had never heard so much piano played by a woman and *very few* men! I did not feel so big after that. You see, my friend knew just how great Mary Lou was but he wanted to see my reactions under these particular circumstances!" Johnson chose Mary's 1930 recording of "Nite Life" as one of his three favorites.

Visiting the old sites of such memorable music is now a pretty melancholy business, but in the thirties, Piney Brown's, the Sunset, the Reno, the Subway, and similar clubs were a kind of after-hours jazz Juilliard. Mary gathered heaps of raw material and began weaving them into new works for the Clouds of Joy. Riffs at late-night jam sessions were generated seemingly without effort or end, spearheaded by greats like the outstanding trumpeter Hot Lips Page, a mellow, supportive ensemble following right along. "An arranger in a band would never be able to write such great arrangements as you'd hear on these sessions," Mary declared. "We'd jam until the wee hours of the morning, often ending up in somebody's house and the boys having me play some of my weird harmonies which they called 'zombie music.' " But such experiments were only for the insiders, principally other musicians, not for the paying public.

Already a veteran in her mid-twenties, she'd learned to "play with everybody and everything," and to transpose to any key, depending on other players' preferences or limitations. "If they were looking for somebody who could play in all of them badass keys Hawk was calling for," said Basie, "Mary Lou was the one to get."

Not last came the soulfulness of her playing when she was "bearing down," as essential to the music as the notes themselves in an atmosphere where, as writer Whitney Balliett puts it, "the blues was never tongue in cheek." But if Mary was consistently capable of tearing it up at the piano, *away* from that piano she remained shy and retiring. Producer Dave Dexter, who was a teenager when Mary played with the Clouds at Fairyland Park (admission, fifty cents), recalled, "At set's end Mary Lou quickly retreats to backstage. She's too shy, too modest, to rap with the dancers jammed around the bandstand."

After she became an official member of the band in '31, Andy Kirk continued to transfer Mary's ideas to paper, a tedious process for both. "In Kansas City, Andy'd come to the house like at 10 in the morning and sit there till 12 at night," Mary wrote. "I said, 'I can't go through this!' " But he also had the patience to start from scratch in teaching her the rudiments of music theory. "His simplified version of teaching enabled me to learn fast. He taught me in a way I've never forgotten: telling me that there were only three diminished chords, with examples. Lower your third a half tone, he'd say, and this is your minor; raise your fifth a half tone, and this is your augmented chord. This was good for my ear and I watched him with the band. So I learned the key transpositions for the instruments and then I could do it myself."

"She had a good ear and tried to write down what she heard," acknowledged Kirk. "If she wasn't out all night at the jazz clubs in Kansas City, listening and getting ideas, she'd be sitting up at the foot of the bed, legs crossed like an Indian, just writing and writing, while John was sleeping. Sometimes she'd stay up all night working at her arrangements. She'd try one thing, then another, get mad, and start over. As time went on she learned voicing for the different horns from things I showed her from some arrangements I'd bought."

Mary was never a consistently prolific composer, but had periods of high creativity, including the unrecorded period in the thirties when the band spent so much time hanging out in Kansas City. Claude "Fiddler" Williams, no longer in the band but still living in Kansas City, recalls watching Mary at work on arrangements at Local 627 Musicians Union Hall. She wrote her ideas out on paper without playing them on the piano, which she said slowed her down, and then took the arrangement into rehearsal. There, she said, "I always experimented quite a bit, which caused me to rearrange, because you don't know what it's going to sound like." She could write anywhere—dressing rooms, bathrooms, park benches, the back seats of cars—a useful knack for a traveling composer. "I always liked lying flat on my back on the grass in Paseo Park in Kansas City, looking up at the stars, composing, late at night." But most of all, she liked to write in bed. Living in cramped quarters, her bed became her desk, indeed her office, containing her sheet music, her sharpened pencils, her ashtray, lighter, and cigarettes, perhaps a plate of food and drink.

In Kansas City, as Andy Kirk pointed out, blacks had their own "everything," including a well-run union with its good-sized building and a dynamic leader in their president, William Shaw. "We were just about the only Negro union with a charter," Mary stated. "In other cities the Negro unions were subsidiaries. He [Shaw] always gave fabulous dances at the Paseo Ballroom every year to raise money for the union. It held at least 1,000 people and usually everybody in K.C., Missouri, turned up at the dances at the Paseo. It booked big-name bands: Fletcher Henderson, Cab Calloway, Fats Waller, Earl Hines. Even the elite was found at many of the public dances, seated upstairs," she added, referring to the light-skinned caste, among whom Andy and Mary Kirk socialized. The "elite" was from Kansas City, *Missouri.* Across the Missouri River in *Kansas,* Mary noted, the comparable set "was much stricter. *They* would not go a public dance—only their private dances that our band played for." Nor would most whites, for if Kansas City was not as rigidly segregated as the South, it was still on the border of North and South.

———————

WHITE MUSICIANS, THROUGH their own subculture, tried to circumvent segregation. Mary recalled that in the twenties in Pittsburgh,

"Actor Dick Powell, who led a band before getting beat up in the movies, sent taxis for me so that I could play for his band during their breaks at the Inwright Theatre." In Kansas City, "Jack Teagarden and Paul Whiteman used to drop down to hear me. Glen Gray's musicians never seemed to miss us when they were in town and they made something of a point of getting me to play for them and with them."

Mary's relationships with white musicians were not only friendly, they could become quite intimate, and sometimes romantic, as apparently happened with Jack Teagarden, who was in and out of Kansas City with Ben Pollack's band. Mary had become friendly with three light-skinned "glamour girls" with money to spend, who were crazy about jazz—and jazz musicians, like the tall, good-looking, sexy Teagarden. But *he* had eyes for Mary. "Right away we felt like friends. We visited most of the speaks downtown. One in particular fascinated me. It was decorated to resemble the inside of a penitentiary, even with bars all over the place. The waiters wore striped uniforms like the convicts down south. Later on that evening, I played for the boys, after which they focused their attention on me (being musicians), forgetting about the glamour girls. Jack, not having his trombone, got up and sang 'I gotta right to sing the blues,' which was the end. He never got fresh or embarrassing, he was the nicest. I think we were in love yet afraid to say or do anything about it. Just felt good being together. Of course it was all very flattering, especially when he asked if I'd marry him, but we dismissed that very lightly. What my girlfriends didn't know was how easy it was for two musicians to fall in love: music has its own charm. I think of Jack as a charming fine person. And I didn't hear of the glamour girls after that."

––––––––––––

MARY HAD LEARNED very early in her life to compartmentalize her personal life. Even music, the essence of her being, she kept to herself unless she was around musicians. Her niece Helen Floyd recalls of Mary's visits to her house, "If you didn't know she was a musician, you'd never suspect it. She didn't sit down and play, even if there was a piano. She'd do crossword puzzles, play games, cards. . . . She'd lay up in the bed and think. Sometimes she'd write music in the bed. But she'd never talk about it, play it."

Family was in a box of its own. During the scuffling years of the mid-1930s, she didn't have money to wire home to the children, and her correspondence clearly shows the guilt she felt for "abandoning" them to stay on the road instead of settling in Pittsburgh and working, say, as a music teacher or local performer. (How illogical is guilt to the one not suffering it!) But few people knew the concerns she had for the children, the depth of the problems at home.

Her marriage was boxed separately from love, and neither was a very tidy bin. She and John fought as usual about money. But Mary also badly wanted children. "She pleaded with me, but I said no. Not the kind of life we had, traveling every day and we were so young," recalled John Williams. "My mother would be raising up my child and I would hardly know it? No. I didn't want that." But without his knowledge, Mary stopped using protection; though when time had passed and she had failed to get pregnant, she went to a clinic in the neighborhood, where, John said (for she tearfully confessed the whole thing to him later), she was told she had "some kind of female problem, like a tipped womb and had to be 'fixed up' to have a baby." (A tipped, or retroverted, womb in and of itself need not be an impediment to pregnancy or delivery, however. And years later, Mary did in fact get pregnant.)

By 1933 Mary no longer troubled to disguise her liaisons from her husband. John Williams, sounding amused (at a remove of more than fifty years), recalled, "I caught Mary in bed three times with men." She countered, "I never kept anything from John. He knew everything anyway. I had told him I didn't love him. In fact I didn't love anyone for long." She shied away from the ultra-casual sex scenes easily available to musicians, but she got around. "I did the pickin' and I only had one boyfriend at a time," she said meaningfully. Not quite true that John knew everything: he did not know about a heated clandestine affair she was conducting with a married bandmate, Johnny Harrington— John's best friend and the husband of Mary's girlfriend, Othie.

Another breach between Mary and John was the taste she had acquired for marijuana, or "reefer," as musicians used to call it. Kansas City was a major railroad hub of the nation, distributing drugs along with corn and wheat, so it was easily available in the nightclubs there. "You know, Mary tried to drink to keep up with the crowd but she could *not* drink," emphasized Henrietta Randolph, wife of trumpeter Irving "Mouse" Randolph, who was in the band in the mid-thirties. "We'd get together on Mondays, the day off, to play cards and drink hot corn liquor and doctor it with Coca-Cola. Others could drink it, but Mary would fall out. I remember once she fell off a stool."

Pot, on the other hand, agreed with her. "Pha Terrell [the smooth vocalist with the Clouds] joined the group then and he turned her on to reefer," said John Williams. "I became one of the squares as far as she was concerned," he added, grinning. (The band even recorded a song by Earl Thompson about reefer, or "jive," in 1936 titled "All the Jive Is Gone.") "I liked a taste of whiskey and she liked her little thing, and we went off our separate ways."

Mary told a couple of stories about her experiences with reefer, recalling how once in about 1937 she, Pha Terrell, and saxophonist Dick Wilson smoked some very strong pot when they were on the road in Texas and ended up sitting on tombstones all night, too high to move. Another time, she and Terrell went with Jack Teagarden to meet his mother, stopping first to smoke some "jive." When Mrs. Teagarden started singing opera, they could not contain themselves. Giggling and falling over with laughter, the three dashed outside and ran around the house, angering Jack's disapproving sister, Norma, who was also there.

WHEN BEN WEBSTER, who was to become Mary's great early love, joined the Clouds (in the summer of 1932, according to band member Mouse Randolph, but a little later according to others), Mary was involved with Johnny Harrington. But Webster's great talent replaced him in her affections. "My weakness in life was my loving someone whom I thought great on his instrument," she wrote. "When Ben played I loved him so much! I told my husband John, and he said someone would kill me someday for being so frank." Webster, of course, already knew John and Mary from the Kansas City scene, and he and John had gone to the same high school in the twenties, when John was boarding with his aunt and uncle. Webster was a year older than Mary, already a "Peck's bad boy" well on his way to earning a later nickname, "the Brute," for his transformation from gentle to wild when he drank too much. John Williams called him "a terrible Jekyll and Hyde." Perhaps on account of a relatively careful, even pampered, upbringing by a clutch of female relations, Webster was immediately attracted to the vital street life swirling around him. After studying piano, he switched in 1928 to saxophone. When he declared he was going to be a professional musician, he disappointed his family, as John Williams and Doc Cheatham had done, by failing to follow a respectable career path. But Webster went his way, joined the Young family band (where he became a close friend of young Lester, his brother Lee, and sister Mary), and then played in the band led by Blanche Calloway, before returning to Kansas City and a job with the Clouds in 1932.

"From the moment I met him I was fascinated because he was always up to something," Mary wrote about Webster's restless personality. "Then, too, I liked his tenor. If he felt over-anxious, Ben would play roughly, distorting a style which was already full of vitality. Sometimes John Williams yelled at him on the stand to stop experimenting and play. But after being around with the guys awhile Ben became less boisterous, which made me like him better. We used to walk for miles together and he always took me to jam sessions."

At first, she wrote, she went out with Webster "to counteract my love for the married guy." Her marriage had accustomed her to men running strings of girls—and Webster was no different. "All the time Ben and I were together, he'd see another girl and tell me about a desire to be with her and I'd tell him I'd see him later. I wouldn't say anything. It seemed I was happy if he was. Sometimes while playing on the stand, I'd even point out someone good to him. I never was jealous of him, because of being around guys all my life. I knew they always felt they still loved their wives even if they cheated once in a while."

Webster, however, applied a different standard to her. "Ben and I went everywhere together. One night we were in Kansas City and I was supposed to meet Ben," said Mary. "He saw me walking down the street with Johnny [Harrington] and he really slapped me around and threatened Johnny. I was afraid to go home. I hadn't told my husband that I liked Ben yet. My married lover couldn't understand me and one day *he* said he felt like killing me, that I didn't care for anyone. I couldn't respond, I had nothing to say."

But she was by now madly in love with Ben, and broke off her liaison with Harrington. "He [Webster] stayed with us two or three years—longer than he'd stuck with anyone," she wrote almost wistfully. "Then Ben left the band and Lester Young replaced him. As sensational as Lester was, I could think only of Ben. I lost 25 pounds. I couldn't eat; I didn't realize how much I'd miss him. I got mail from him often and sometimes money. I had told John I loved him."

The love affair was not over: Webster wanted Mary to join him in New York. She wavered. When the Clouds of Joy went to New York in '37, she stayed with him at the Dewey Square Hotel, according to tenor saxophonist Harold Arnold. She also told John she wanted them to live apart for a year, and after that, Webster would take care of the divorce. Still exerting what little control he had over her, John put his foot down: if she left, it had to be permanent. And he talked frankly with her about "the Brute's" unsavory reputation, which did give her pause.

But for her, whatever the failings of the man, there was the music. "Ben Webster was the type of guy that could put so much in one bar— he could do more with one bar than any other man could do," Mary said, paying him her highest artistic compliment. It appears he even collaborated with her to some extent on a composition that would become one of her best known, the ambitious and luminous "Walkin' and Swingin'." John Williams remembered driving Mary to Ben Webster's house to work on "Walkin'" while Webster was with the band. The melody of the piece was inspired by a pop tune called "The Moon Is Low" (which was recorded by the Arnold Ross Quintet, featuring saxophonist Benny Carter). But with or without input from Ben Webster, it is Mary's overarching conception and her writing that made "Walkin' and Swingin'" so popular with musicians. "I needed a fourth saxophone, but during that period you had only three," Mary explained. "As I didn't have a fourth, I used a trumpet with a hat—a wah-wah thing—for the eighth notes. This was an innovation for the time; musicians loved it." And they loved the second chorus, a witty, winding 8-bar road of melody. Mary's arrangement for Kirk brought her five dollars, her then standard fee from the band. She earned considerably more from the more prosperous white bands, providing another arrangement for the Casa Loma Orchestra for fifty dollars, and others recorded by Gene Krupa's band in '38 and Les Brown's band in '40. That second chorus went on to inspire quite a few modern-jazz tunes, including one by Thelonious Monk (discussed in chapter 11).

If during the Depression the work of writing and arranging music for a jazz orchestra was ill paid, Mary didn't care a great deal. Like a playwright with a resident company, she had her own troupe to realize her ideas. And although in 1935 no one in the band could know it, the Clouds of Joy were at last on the brink of success, though the major changes in their fortunes would not all be for the good, as it turned out. Mary in particular was poised to begin a highly creative period and to gain high status and visibility in the next era of dance-crazy popular music.

Chapter Six
Silk Stockings
1936–1941

IN 1971, EXACTLY four decades after Mary joined the Clouds of Joy, she and an entourage that included a teenaged son of her attorney took a cross-country train (Mary was afraid of flying) from New York to California, where she was hailed at the Monterey Jazz Festival as a "rediscovery." But as young Matthew Bliss found out, she had never been forgotten by some. "We were stuck in the train for three days," he recalls. "But Mary *loved* it. She got the star treatment the whole way from the old Pullman guys. They couldn't do enough for her."

Stardom within the black community came to her after the Clouds of Joy began to record again in 1936, especially after their hit "Until the Real Thing Comes Along." As the year opened, the band's recording prospects were still dim. The idea of making records had gone dormant in the Depression; the future, many thought, lay in live radio broadcasts—where the listening was free and advertising paid the expenses. The Clouds had certainly proved how an audience could be enlarged through radio, with their broadcasts from the Blossom Heath Club in Oklahoma. Fans, said Kirk, had written hundreds of enthusiastic letters to the station.

Late in 1935, Kirk pushed to get a recording contract again (probably at the urging of Joe Glaser, the canny agent who was involved peripherally with the band at the time). He persuaded Jack Kapp to hear the band in New York, and pointed to their recent success at the

Oklahoma club. Kapp was in a buying mood. He'd left Brunswick, and with a partner he had bought the American rights to the English-owned Decca label and was aggressively signing up musicians. Besides Kirk and other artists brought over from Brunswick, such as Bing Crosby, Guy Lombardo, Fletcher Henderson, the Casa Lomas, and the Mills Brothers, there were Louis Armstrong and the recently discovered Bill Basie. Kapp had made a very smart move. Since the general public could ill afford the 75-cent recordings of competitors RCA and Columbia, he would sell his for 35 cents. To keep costs down, Kapp used inexpensive materials (including cut-rate songs and recycled tunes) and primitive equipment. The strategy worked, and Decca maneuvered a number of artists into commercial success.

The Clouds recorded thirteen tunes for Kapp in March of 1936. Just as she had a large hand in the first records for Kapp at Brunswick in 1929, Mary contributed a quantity of material—seven new, or newly arranged, tunes for the date (including an extensively redone "Froggy Bottom"); and as usual, she had a hand in arranging the rest of the tunes. Her performances were fine and inventive, especially on "Moten Swing," "Lotta Sax Appeal," and "Bearcat Shuffle." But it was her composing that put her in the front rank of jazz writers of the swing era—and pushed the Clouds of Joy to success. The jazz sides Mary wrote throughout her Decca tenure, until 1942, are savored as collector's items today.

To write for the sessions, Mary holed up at the Dewey Square Hotel in Harlem. "For nights I could not leave my room, having my meals brought in to me. And at 7 A.M., I was up again for another session." She added, "I was supposed to get $75 per arrangement—but I didn't. I think I got instead the money for a dress I liked in a shop window on Broadway—$69.75. I was beginning to think they weren't worth much, for no one ever wanted to pay much for them. But I knew Andy couldn't afford to pay a professional arranger. And I was dumb to the business. I got silk stockings for my payment for all those arrangements I did, and that's about it." Unfortunately, too, virtually none of her compositions were even copyrighted, with the result that she could not claim composer royalties.

She was writing for a very different band from the one recorded in 1921–31: smoother, cleaner, tighter-sounding, with seasoned craftsmen and one new outstanding soloist, saxophonist Dick Wilson. The brass and reed sections were tighter, the rhythm section improved. In fact, only five old-timers remained: Mary, John Williams, "Big Jim" Lawson on lead trumpet, Johnny Harrington on clarinet, and Andy Kirk. Earl Thompson, a.k.a. Merle Boatley, was a good trumpet player who had replaced Mouse Randolph in '33 or '34, and he added several arrangements. Trombonist Henry Wells gave more weight to the brass, and Earl "Buddy" Miller, who came in on alto saxophone, freed up John Williams to concentrate on other reeds, especially baritone sax, adding comparable weight to that section. The gifted, handsome, hard-drinking, Chu Berry–inspired Dick Wilson was the latest in a string of terrific saxophonists: Ben Webster in 1932 and 1933; Lester Young until late 1935 (when he joined the Count Basie Orchestra, a happier fit); Buddy Tate until 1936. Wilson was a wonderful foil for Mary's virtuosity, swinging hard with a gruff undercurrent, yet with a delightful lyric touch. To appreciate how the band had matured, one has only to contrast the group's somewhat jerky rhythm on the first recording of "Messa Stomp" with the 1936 version, which features the crisp drumming of Ben Thigpen, solid string bass underpinning of Booker Collins, and Mary's buoyant piano. "Cloudy" had evolved from a simple layout in which the brass and piano were barely audible in the background, to a much lusher instrumental, with a vocal added—and a more confident-sounding piano. (The final chorus of the first "Cloudy," which opened and closed with a hair-raisingly weird full-band chord, was dropped in the 1936 version.) And "Froggy Bottom," considerably refurbished, had become in Mary's hands a shining example of Kansas City swing, with characteristic short, punchy piano and tuneful section riffs.

But the band had little time to establish their honed jazz-based identity on records. As Gunther Schuller observes about "Until the Real Thing Comes Along," "By 1937 and thereafter, as a result of an immensely popular recording by the band's singer, Pha Terrell, its jazz playing days, while not exactly numbered, were certainly threatened." The pressure was on for more commercial successes, few of which Mary had any involvement with except to play the piano. "She did not set the style for Andy Kirk," emphasizes her later manager, Peter O'Brien. "She set the style only for the majority of the 25 pieces or so that are constantly reissued." Still, even many of those non-jazz, strictly commercial sides had a relaxed yet buoyant, danceable appeal:

as a name for the Andy Kirk band, "Clouds" was exactly right, especially until 1937, when it was still a "small" big band of twelve pieces
with a more intimate feel than later, when it expanded to fifteen and
more.

After their first recording for Decca in March, the band recorded
fourteen more tunes—eleven of them written or cowritten, and in
most cases arranged, by Mary. One can hear how well she had
absorbed the interplay of brass and reeds that Don Redman brought
to the fore for Fletcher Henderson's band. Since then, she had also
fallen under the influence of Eddie Durham (related to the Clouds'
Allen Durham), a trombonist and guitarist and arranger who joined
Count Basie's band in 1937. "Durham helped me quite a bit with
sounds," wrote Mary. "He'd arrange a popular tune giving all the
instruments different notes, extending a seventh chord to an eleventh
or thirteenth. All of the arrangers knew by heart each note an instrument should make and when there was a mistake."

Mary, too, had begun to reach out for broader harmonies. Especially at that early phase of her writing, her experiments were not
always appreciated. "If I passed out an arrangement to the band that
was wrong, the guys would laugh. But they'd give me a chance. Musicians like something different when they're playing the same tunes
every night, and they knew that I was going to feed 'em something different." (Take, as one example, the odd "growls" in the second chorus
of her tune "Little Joe from Chicago.") Whitney Balliett has pointed to
her "odd, beautifully constructed background harmonies," which he
said "had an almost schoolmarm purpose and unfailingly pointed up
both the tunes and the frequent solos." And jazz editor Barry Ulanov,
who knew Mary very well, emphasizes another of her talents: "One of
the difficulties about jazz is that it's very hard to notate it, but Duke
Ellington could and so could Mary. Very few other people have been
able to put on paper the feeling of jazz. There are always technical
problems, and the rhythm is the most serious: you have to have such a
tricky system of dots after notes in order to get the slight changes
between values of ordinary eighth, quarter and sixteenth notes. She
had discovered, because of her particular genius, a way to articulate on
paper a jazz pattern—how to accent a measure. And that's why her
best stuff is among the best in jazz." "It was a terrific feeling to hear
what I had written, to be able to hear what my mind was saying and

transform it into music," Mary said simply. "In experimenting, you don't know what it's going to sound like."

Thrifty in her thinking, if she found a congenial phrase, she handily extended or embellished it. If the second chorus of "Walkin' and Swingin'" was inspired at least partly by something that Ben Webster blew, another of her great swing tunes, called "Steppin' Pretty," used a riff melody by Earl Thompson. "A Mellow Bit of Rhythm" was inspired by saxophonist Herman Walder's playing, and "(Keep It) In the Groove," which gives co-composer credit to Dick Wilson, derived in all probability from a solo he played—as was the case with "Mary's Special," where the melodic lines in the first several choruses originated in a Lester Young solo. The same was true for the dreamy and evocative "Big Jim Blues," deriving its inspiration from a phrase played by trumpeter "Big Jim" Lawson.

In "Steppin' Pretty," choruses of Kansas Citian melodic talk between brass and reeds are followed by a relaxed disquisition by Mary and a clarinet, before the tune ends on a lilting new riff. (Mary's particular way of orchestrating clarinets became popular with other bandleaders, notably Glenn Miller of "Chattanooga Choo-Choo.") "A Mellow Bit of Rhythm" features stride piano left-hand accents seguing into swing-era devices including, analyzed musicologist Erica Kaplan, "frequent unison playing and doubling at the octave, a technique that achieves a powerful sound capable of being thrown great distances, thus accommodating the large dance halls of the swing era." And Mary's *playing* was highly advanced within the swing-era tradition as well. Of "Keep It in the Groove," a critic wrote, "Built on jam session-like riffs, Mary Lou's arrangement swings the door open for soloists to do their thing. Note her leaping, hand-hammering solos. No wonder she was an influence on Monk and on the boppers as well as experimental jazz composers."

But aside from such highly crafted pieces, it is likely that Mary also strove for a hit with the Clouds of Joy (she certainly tried to get one later). But she who had perfect pitch had a tin ear for the marketplace. The market in hits was cornered mainly by Tin Pan Alley, that quasi-incestuous warren of song-pluggers, composers, hucksters, hustlers, and businessmen. It was Tin Pan Alley that took credit for "Until the Real Thing Comes Along." "Real Thing" started as a folk tune called "The Slave Song" (as in "slave" of love) that was strummed around the streets of Kansas City by two young boys with ukuleles whose names have been lost. "I'll work for you, slave for you, lay my body down and die for you," went the lyric. Recalled John Williams, "Everybody in Kansas City that could sing or entertain in a little club, they sang 'The Slave Song.' " "They put everybody's name but those two boys' on it—it made me sick," Delilah Jackson reports of Andy Kirk.

"Jack Kapp didn't want us to record 'The Slave Song,' " recalled John Williams. "He said, 'No ballads, we got Guy Lombardo for that.' " (Kirk recalled that Kapp pushed for more things like "Froggy Bottom.") Continues Williams, "I told him we don't got any more songs. And Kapp finally said okay." He liked the wistful, pretty melody and decided it would do with a new lyric and a good arrangement— Mary's job. (In later years, Mary was loath to admit her part in "Real Thing," disliking its corniness. But, says jazz historian Phil Schaap, "I got Mary to admit she wrote the 22-bar saxophone passage in the middle.") The young team of Sammy Cahn and Saul Chaplin, along with help from others, including the team of Holiner and Nichols, who wrote for Ethel Waters, wrote a new lyric. "Cahn and Chaplin, those songwriters, they were little old boys hanging around us," said John Williams. "Cahn was up there in the studio everyday; he would run errands for us.

" 'The Real Thing' put us on big time," John continued, "and that's when we began to make a steady salary. It was on the Hit Parade for two weeks. That was the big thing in New York. Your band made the Hit Parade, whoever wrote the number had it made. Cahn and Chaplin idolized us after we made that, because we really made *them.* Cahn ended up a millionaire."

But no one else associated with the tune did. John Williams ended as a hotel porter and factory worker. Andy Kirk took a clerk's job for the Musicians Union in New York. The two boys with ukuleles never left Kansas City. Mary received her standard fee of fifteen dollars for arranging the tune.

The die was now cast. "After that, Kapp didn't want us to play no more swing music," said Williams. "We had to play all ballads—'What Would I Tell My Heart,' 'I'm Glad for Your Sake,' things like that." The band was now traveling regularly, in demand because of "Real Thing." But it was the same old low-paying grind, Mary complained. "The sidemen were making $8 a night and paying $2 or $3 for a decent room," wrote Mary. "Some of the guys gave me money—60 cents—to save for them every week, so they'd have money when they got to a major city."

Meanwhile, the communal nature of the Clouds of Joy was being compromised. "Different agents and promoters were flying out to Kansas City to try and book the band," recalled Williams. "On Labor Day of '36, Andy flew to Chicago to meet Joe Glaser, who flew in from New York. They had dinner, and he signed Andy up. Glaser paid off the mortgage on Andy's home and bought him some clothes and he had Andy sign him up as half-owner of our band. Which was the first big mistake Andy made, 'cause all the boys was mad about it." "Andy sold them all out," Claude Williams says bluntly, decades later. "And we didn't need him—he was just the leader." John agreed: "Under the old system, I paid off. First I would take out enough money for gasoline, to try to get to wherever we were going, then whatever was left was split 12 ways. If we made $50, we would split it with 12 people. If we only made $12, we'd split that with 12 people! And I have split up 75 cents. It wasn't written, the commonwealth system, it was just one of those things."

The Clouds had never really had a powerful outside manager before. Kansas City–based Harold Duncan, who had been booking the band around the Southwest, was bush-league. Glaser bought out the band's contract with Duncan and elbowed aside other big-time, would-be bookers, including Willard Alexander and John Hammond, the Columbia A&R man who flew in to Kansas City to try to secure the Clouds—too late. Glaser's influence over the Clouds of Joy was immediate and profound. While he certainly recognized and admired Mary as a musician (as their correspondence over several decades makes clear), Glaser was first and last a businessmen. And by all accounts, a tough, crude one if you got on his bad side.

Riding the crest of the "Real Thing" wave, Glaser got the band heavy exposure. "Glaser put us in the Trianon ballroom in Cleveland, where we broadcast nightly over a national hookup on NBC radio with America's top sports commentator. What power and money can do!" Mary noted drily of this important date in the winter of 1937. As John Williams remembered, Glaser exploited the Trianon broadcast by taping the Clouds off the air. "He stole a record from Andy. That dirty rascal." Those Trianon broadcasts, ironically, are among the few examples to document how effervescent the band was when it played for live audiences—reminding us how much this music was meant for dancing. The broadcasts also offer rare examples of Mary's arrangements not recorded elsewhere: a delicate version of "Spring Holiday," a rousing Kansas City–swing version of "Honeysuckle Rose," and an ambitious arrangement of "Dear Old Southland," amusingly studded with quotes from "St. Louis Blues."

Mary was now getting the highest salary in the band. She and Dick Wilson had been given separate contracts at a special rate by Glaser, though they did not receive their pay if the band did not draw enough in a given week. She was now well dressed, in couture-gown copies (many made by Anna Mae back in Pittsburgh), a fur wrap, and her beloved I. Miller shoes. Yet she distrusted the new management, principally because she saw her friends continuing to be paid dismal wages. "I made a nuisance out of myself asking for a raise for others. I became real unhappy." Mary scornfully dubbed the new setup of stars versus sidemen "The Golden System." The egalitarianism of the past was officially over. For John Williams in particular, the arrival of Glaser meant the end of his privileged position in the band. ("I took care of the band. I *was* the band.") But he and the other musicians were helpless to change the situation.

The band never was as big with the public as Benny Goodman's, Artie Shaw's, Jimmie Lunceford's, or Duke Ellington's; but for a time in the late thirties the Clouds of Joy ranked very high with connoisseurs. Despite pressure from Kapp and Glaser to concentrate on "sweet" ballads, the Clouds resisted abandoning their jazz roots, though treacly commercial tunes did begin to dominate. Kirk, says Peter O'Brien, was proud of the "sweet"—i.e., non-jazz—material. "I used to visit Andy Kirk all the time in the '70s, at the local musicians' union in New York where he worked in the office," says O'Brien. "He told me one day that *The Sweet Side of Andy Kirk*, this double-pocket record on MCA, was coming out, and he was very, very happy about that. Andy's idea was not to do that 'jazz stuff.' He used to say he played for the 'elite.' " Remarked Mary pointedly, "When we first began to hit, everybody thought Andy was white—they had never seen a picture of him—because the band sounded like it on some things that we played." "When we played the Apollo in Harlem for the first time," added John, laughing, "the chorus girls were so surprised we were black."

Even if Kirk had wanted to have a jazz band, he had little chance after throwing in with Glaser, who cast Mary and Dick Wilson, and others later, as niche players. They would be allowed their moment of jazz glory for one or two numbers, but the real draw, the real money, came from attracting the well-heeled, unhip society crowd—Kirk's "elite."

"JOE GLASER WAS the most obscene, the most outrageous, and the toughest agent I've ever bought an act from," wrote Max Gordon, impresario of the Village Vanguard jazz club in New York. "Joe had started out managing heavyweight fighters in Chicago in the Twenties and he never got over the manner and style of his Chicago days, even after he took over the management of Louis Armstrong and moved to New York, where he built up an independent talent agency with branches all over America and in Europe. He was tough, but we always got along. He proved to be right more often than wrong, and in the end I learned to like him. He once lent me 10 grand when I sorely needed it. 'No interest, Max. Pay me back when you have it.' That was Joe." Others, like Mary's boss in the forties, Café Society owner Barney Josephson, found no redeeming qualities in the man. But musicians accepted Glaser as a necessary evil. A black man, Louis Armstrong once said, had to have a white man working for him (and Glaser took on that job with Armstrong for the rest of his life). And if this were so, how much truer for a black woman.

In serving as booking agent and occasional manager for Mary over the years, Glaser wrote numerous letters to her, which she saved. They often reveal him as patient to a fault, occasionally sensitive, more often blunt; the letters of a man who liked the role of Big Daddy. She was proud of the esteem he held her in and liked to relate the high compliment he'd paid her: "You're the only woman that's a real musician." She dedicated her hit boogie-woogie "Little Joe from Chicago" to him. Deep down, however, she was ambivalent about his influence. As the thirties wore on, it was no longer her face or Wilson's featured on the posters and ads for the band but that of crooner Pha Terrell, and, later, vocalist June Richmond.

Whatever his failings, Glaser had real regard for the artists he represented. He used his toughness to bargain with tough Jack Kapp for a better contract for the Clouds of Joy, and separately for Andy Kirk, in 1937, demanding that Kapp throw out the contract Kirk had naïvely signed a year before (Kapp had signed up the Basie band to similarly dismal terms).

Still, Andy Kirk had reason to regret his relationship with Glaser. Late in his life, after Glaser had died, Kirk aired his feelings. Publicly, he remained reserved: "I didn't like Joe Glaser too much. But I couldn't dislike him, because he was bringing in the money. I played Yale, Harvard, all of them, through Joe Glaser's office." But speaking in private, many years later, Kirk was blunter. "You know what?" he told Delilah Jackson. "If I could have knocked him in the mouth, he would love me. If you cursed him out, he liked you. But I wasn't that type. He acted like a crook."

John Williams asserted that Glaser kept double books, a practice by which the agent books the band at a certain fee but pays it a lower rate, the agent pocketing the difference—plus his percentage of the "door." (Louis Armstrong is said to have told Glaser that if he found out Glaser was stiffing him that way, he'd kill him.) "Andy told me that myself," repeated Williams. "Andy didn't have no business being a bandleader in the first place, 'cause he was easygoing and easy to take advantage of. It was easy to take the money. Billy Shaw was Glaser's man, and he would be the one out front collecting the money. He would tell Andy how much we took in—and Andy was all trusting. A lot of those promoters stole from the black acts at that time," continued Williams. "I mean, we were so glad to get a job and make money and travel and live like human beings that we were making enough, more than the average black anyway. They was skimming off of the top, but we knew it. Besides Andy, Glaser stole from Louis and all the black acts he had, like Lionel Hampton."

Relates Peter O'Brien, "Mary said that John Hammond told her that Glaser was skimming off Mary's private contract as well." But were there wheels within wheels? Some in the band felt sure that *Andy Kirk* also kept two sets of books for the band, and that John Williams, as the second in command (and long in charge of the payroll) had helped himself to receipts too. (When Kirk opened a barbecue restaurant in Harlem in 1940, run by his wife Mary during the day and John at night, John's gambling habit—and a need for ready cash—caused the business to fail, in Kirk's opinion.) John, on the other hand, felt that

Kirk would not have been "capable" of skimming money from the band. At any rate, to prove any such allegations would have been both difficult and dangerous. A musician who made such an accusation could easily lose his job, not to mention life or limb. And whatever the arrangements that Glaser made concerning the Clouds of Joy, the documents that the Associated Booking Agency kept have long since been shredded, a perfectly legal procedure.

History would judge Mary to be of central importance to the band, but after 1937 she began to clash more and more with Kirk about her role in the Clouds. Kirk was not disingenuous when he said, "There was nothing you could do to make Mary more impressive. So, we just let her do what she could do best." That was only partly true. His vision was of well-oiled, predictable music, the obverse of what drove an artist like Mary. "When I used to play 'Froggy Bottom,' " she remembered, "I would play a different solo each time and this used to make Andy Kirk angry because people wanted you to play exactly the same as the record, but I wouldn't." Indeed, Mary's harmonics on the keyboard, which may have seemed "wrong" then, are conventional today, such as when she added an extra note, "like the sixth of a chord" instead of relying on the "sweet" major chords that predominated in the stock arrangements of the thirties. "Andy Kirk said to me, 'Mary, you can't use that note, that's against the rules.' 'Rules?' I said. 'That's what I hear.' I'd write anything I heard." (She also could fly into a temper when her music was not taken seriously by the band. "I was very high strung and sensitive. And when the boys fooled around at rehearsal with what I wrote, I got mad and snatched the music off their stands and began to cry and went home to bed.")

Years later, when the verdict about the band was in, Andy Kirk realized that the feather-light yet dissonant chords Mary laid down in the background of her creamy, clean arrangements were the very elements that set the Clouds apart from other bands and appealed to listeners. But Kirk, like John Williams, also seemed nettled by all the critical attention that went to Mary. There were other arrangers in the band, they liked to point out, citing trumpeter Earl Thompson, who was a fine player (taking an excellent solo, for example, on "Zonky") and wrote "All the Jive Is Gone" and "Bear Down" and tailored stock arrangements for the band. "Many of the things Mary Lou got credit for were actually done by him, but he was taken for granted," said John

Williams (and Andy Kirk); both felt that Mary was often given credit for compositions that were produced by the band at rehearsals. "We'd get together and we'd take a song that's real popular and we'd make riffs. Trumpets, you do so and so, you make this riff, the guy next to him will do second harmony, third harmony, and you'd work it out." Such claims have been made about Duke Ellington, too: players complained that "their" riffs were coopted (Johnny Hodges's complaints are well documented). Still, it was undeniably Ellington's overarching creative vision—and Mary's in the Clouds of Joy—that gave each band its "sound." Says Schuller, "Arranger Mary Lou Williams, with her light touch and sense of clarity, was the ideal moulder of the band's identity." Not every critic was as enthusiastic. Big-band writer Albert McCarthy feels that her writing contained "little that is really unexpected—unusual voicings or ingenuity of tempo or melodic line. . . . Craft preponderates over genuine creativity." But Schuller, who took a microscope to swing in his history of the era, builds a convincing case for Mary's often cutting-edge skills as arranger and "melodic editor."

A case in point is Mary's very fine Kansas City–swing composition "Twinklin'." "Some of the things that she gave a name to, they were other songs," said John. "She was using the chords out of those songs and improvising. Like 'Twinklin' ' is actually 'I Never Slept a Wink Last Night.' " While John correctly identifies the source of her inspiration, he begs the question of how good jazz material develops. "Of *course,* she used the chords on other songs," says Peter O'Brien. "But everybody does that. Singling her out for it is subtly trying to take credit away from her."

On the other hand, Mary herself complained that *her* ideas were being stolen. It was always others who were making the money, she felt, no matter how hard and how brilliantly she worked. "I did 20 things in one week for Decca. They were all hits and people stole like mad," she said. "They were just snatching tunes like mad." Little wonder she would implode with rage (much more rarely would she explode). She fought for the publishing royalties due for her original compositions, but she rarely won. The fact was that small labels rarely did pay them, and sometimes the large companies as well. Says Peter O'Brien, "Decca Records—they ripped her off. Moe Asch of Asch/Folkways Records didn't pay royalties at all. He *said* as much to me. Mary would go down there to his office in the '40s, cry, scream, throw things—and finally get a check of some kind from him. Fighting to get your royalties: that's a common thing even now. You've got to get a lawyer and raise hell. It's rough. It's very easy to rip off."

In the late 1930s, when everybody went to the movies, there was always a newsreel, a cartoon, and usually a double feature. Mary's niece Helen remembers Mary was visiting at her home soon after the release of one of her great songs, "What's Your Story, Morning Glory?" (popular with the Clouds, but even more popular in the Billy Moore arrangement for Jimmie Lunceford's band). Helen came home excitedly from the movies, announcing: "Aunt Mary, I heard your song 'Morning Glory' playing on the cartoon!" She never forgot her aunt's response. Mary shrugged, knowing she'd never see a dime of royalties from the use of her song and said, pointing at her head, "I don't care. They can take my music but they can't take this. I can always do some more."

"What's Your Story, Morning Glory?" illustrates the complexities of musical borrowing. "Morning Glory" was recorded by the Clouds of Joy in 1938. It was not a completely original idea, strictly speaking; the first three lines of "Morning Glory" have the same chord changes as an old tune called "Aunt Hagar's Blues." And Mary did not take sole credit for the composition. She and trumpeter Paul Webster, in Jimmie Lunceford's band, often corresponded, writing "letters like lyrical talking notes—it would be music," said Mary. "I'd write the letter to music. So this time he said, 'What's your story, morning glory? I haven't heard from you.' And in about 10 or 15 minutes I wrote this tune. And he gave me a starter of two or four bars, so I put his name on it because otherwise I wouldn't have written it." But Webster, according to Mary, then took the 16-bar blues in "Morning Glory," added a bridge of 8 bars with collaborator Sonny Burke, and dubbed it a new song. The result was the hit song "Black Coffee." (Both songs have been recorded by vocalists such as Sarah Vaughan, Ella Fitzgerald, Peggy Lee, Anita O'Day and others, and in band arrangements. Mary herself recorded "Morning Glory" as a solo at least four times.) Mary fought for compensation from Webster and Burke, but although, as she said, she demonstrated that "Black Coffee" was actually her own, she settled for peanuts—$300.

Blatant appropriations, copyright wrangles, and swindles seem built into the music industry. Says jazz pianist Billy Taylor, who knew Mary well, "People used to just take $40 or $50 for a tune until they wised up." And everyone seems to have his or her own example of a ripoff. Mary's anger over the use of another of her tunes may have had its origin in the racist system that barred the door to all but a very few black musicians. "If you'd like to hear where 'Blues in the Night' began," she suggested in frustration, "listen to the clarinet section part in 'Big Time Crip' "—which supplies the "my mama done tole me" hook of that hit song. The clarinet part to which she referred had been adapted from her "Little Joe from Chicago," written in 1938. "Crip," written in '39, was recorded in '41, the same year Harold Arlen's "Blues in the Night" was released. Arlen and lyricist Johnny Mercer both loved jazz and liked to hang out in Harlem listening to bands like the Clouds of Joy (playing "Big Time Crip"?). Mary's resentment about Arlen's hit wasn't about borrowing *per se*, but rather the fact that *he* had the hit in a Hollywood movie. That was something practically unheard of for blacks: about the only black musician-composer who crossed that barrier in those days was Benny Carter. And he was limited by the industry in what he could compose. As he explained, "The studios have always typed their product, their needs and their supplier. So I was typed early."

Mary, meanwhile, was solidifying her early reputation as a musician's musician, and her work for the band plus some much-admired small-group pieces established her as one of the best swing-style writers. If it was often journeyman work, such as recobbling popular material into a swing style, nevertheless she enjoyed it. "I was beginning to get telegrams from Gus Arnheim, Glen Gray, Tommy and Jimmy Dorsey, Bob Crosby, Cab Calloway, Red Norvo, Les Brown, Earl Hines, and Louis Armstrong. I was writing for some half-dozen bands each week," Mary estimated. "As we were making perhaps 500 miles per night, I used to write in the car by flashlight between engagements. The band parts too," she added. "And when we started to hit, and practically every band in the U.S. asked me for arrangements, I'd work twice as hard. I wrote many arrangements while playing with the band on the stand, playing with my left hand and writing with my right." She had achieved, when not yet out of her twenties, her fantasy of playing and writing at the same time, like Lovie Austin back in Chicago. And, she added proudly, "Whenever musicians listened to the band they would ask who made a certain arrangement. Nearly always it was one of mine."

––––––––

AMONG THE BANDLEADERS who sought Mary out was Benny Good-man, at the behest of the peripatetic John Hammond, then his manager. "I was in Kansas City and John Hammond came and liked what I was doing," wrote Mary. "He suggested that I write a blues or something for Benny Goodman. Although most black musicians," she added meaningfully, "never liked to play the blues or boogie. They said it was kindergarten. I liked to experiment. But the blues were the easiest for people to hear and then the boogie caught on. So we did more than our share of them." Her taste for experimenting led her, as usual, to write a number of original, slyly hip boogie-woogies. In 1936 she recorded several with a trio, including a version of "Froggy Bottom" called "Overhand." For the Goodman band's radio show, she arranged "The Count," "Sweet Georgia Brown," "Messa Stomp," and "Toadie Toddle." In the spring of '37 she wrote the theme for Goodman's radio show (sponsored by Camel cigarettes), "Camel Hop," followed by the wonderful "Roll 'Em." The name of the latter tune harked back to the Sunset Club in Kansas City, where Pete Johnson was the piano player. "Ben Webster would yell, 'Roll for me, roll 'em, Pete, make 'em jump,' " said Mary, "and then Pete would play boogie for us."

Mary wrote "Roll 'Em" for her usual fee—peanuts, no more than twenty-five or thirty-five dollars. But it was a very successful song for Goodman and had the effect of widening the breach between Mary and Andy Kirk: Mary had written a hit for a rival bandleader. If Kirk was hopping mad, Benny Goodman, a difficult taskmaster, loved Mary's work, so much so that he asked her to arrange exclusively for his band. She turned him down. "Usually, we'd play five or six arrangements in a set and each would be three minutes," he said. "But some of those arrangements Mary Lou Williams wrote you would want to play for more than three minutes and the dancers would want you to, too." When Teddy Wilson left his small group, Goodman offered her the piano chair; again she turned him down, as she turned down others.

While Mary was diverting her attention to the writing arrangements for other bands and her output for the Clouds of Joy declined, "Real Thing" crooner Pha Terrell suddenly hit big—the first smooth-singing black balladeer to be widely popular with whites. With a commercial success on their hands, Kapp, Glaser, and Kirk set their sights on a repeat of "Real Thing"'s success. That never happened, but in 1938, twenty-two of the band's twenty-seven recordings were vehicles for Terrell, while Mary produced fewer and fewer numbers for the band—just half a dozen more originals for the Clouds after '39, although several of those are among her best.

————

THOUGH THERE ARE only a few recordings to document the fact, Mary was an excellent accompanist of singers, having cut her teeth in vaudeville behind performers. John Hammond was well aware of this. In '38, as A&R man at Columbia Records for jazz, he arranged for her to record with Billie Holiday. Sadly, this pairing of perhaps the two greatest women jazz artists never took place. Instead, Mary was rushed to the hospital in Chicago in June. She kept quiet about her illness, writing only in one diary entry that she had "passed out," and in another, that she had had "female troubles" and needed an "operation." She was replaced, both on the Clouds' gigs and in the record session with Holiday, by an up-and-coming young pianist, "Countess" Margaret Johnson from Kansas City, a friend of Lester Young's. "Margaret Johnson copied all Mary's intros and everything. She tried to play just like her," recalled John Williams, adding, "Of course she was no Mary, but she was good." (Here was yet another bright young musician to die young, cut down by TB—in Johnson's case, hardly more than twenty.)

Mary's personal unhappiness was building. She was already toying with the idea of leaving the band (possibly in part to extricate herself from a turbulent, at times physically abusive affair she was having with Don Byas) when she went to her sister Mamie's to recuperate after her operation. But there Mary soon found herself in the familiar old sea of domestic problems. Though she was still weak, her mother and other relatives pressed her as usual to contribute to the households. Incredibly, unable to find enough steady work as a pianist in Pittsburgh, she took up her sister Mamie's trade—"pressing dresses," as she put it— to earn something. But the hard tedious work of ironing further exhausted her "until I was unable to do it," she wrote. By September 1938, Mary was back with the band.

Almost immediately, Mary recorded as a leader with Booker Collins on bass and Ben Thigpen on drums. In a quietly masterful mood, she recorded her version of Jelly Roll Morton's "The Pearls," which flowed into "Mr. Freddie Blues," "Sweet (Patootie) Patunia," and "The Rocks." They constitute a kind of essay, or précis, of the music on which she had cut her teeth, yet she was experimenting, too, in a delicate way. Especially in "Mr. Freddie" and "Patunia," there are hints of the modern jazz to come in the next decade, of harmonic inversions and complex chords.

The following year, John Hammond finally got to record Mary with a singer—Mildred Bailey—and it was an excellent session of blues material, released under the odd title of *Mildred Bailey and her Oxford Greys* ("greys" then being a hip term for blacks). Bassist John Williams, with whom Mary had played in Memphis a decade before, drummer Eddie Dougherty, and the Clouds' guitarist Floyd Smith were also on hand. The pairing of Mary and Mildred Bailey was brilliant; they were in synch and supremely relaxed as they spun out "Prisoner of Love," "Barrelhouse Music," "Arkansas Blues," "You Don't Know My Mind Blues," "There'll Be Some Changes Made," and "Gulf Coast Blues." On the last two selections, Mary provided especially sparkling backup for Bailey, and turned in a superb solo on "Gulf Coast Blues."

Despite the success of this date with Bailey, it was one of very few times Mary worked for Hammond. Though she gave him his due for his help to musicians and maintained a cordial relationship with him, she found him patronizing, as did Duke Ellington among others, and she didn't appreciate his interference, well-intentioned though it might be, in the music. "I stay friends with John Hammond by staying away from him," she told her own friends. Yet there seems to be little doubt that Hammond would have done more to "build" her career if she had let him.

He had been "pursuing" her since the success of the 1936 recordings. This letter, dated July 1938, makes it very clear that he was interested in shaping her career:

Dear Mary Lou,
Forgive me if you can. The arrangements arrived, they were swell. Leora Henderson copied them, and Benny received them just before he sailed for Europe. I didn't know just how much you should get for them, but something like $50 a piece,

plus an advance from the publishers for the two originals and something additional for the stocks should be about right. Unfortunately Benny sailed before I could see him about paying you, but I had his sister send you an advance of $75 last week, which you should have received by now. The rest will be sent as soon as Benny returns the first week in August.

Now that that business is out of the way—how are you feeling? I really miss seeing you around, for Andy's band is empty indeed without you. I hope that darned female ailment of yours has improved enough so that you get some pleasure out of life and feel like traveling to New York again.

And now, Mary Lou, I've got an idea. As you probably know Basie opened at the Famous Door two weeks ago, and has suddenly become the greatest attraction in the entire city. The place is jammed to the doors every night with bandleaders, musicians, actors, gamblers, tarts, and plain Basie enthusiasts. The joint, although it holds no more than 150 people, is making more money than any place in the entire city (I know, because I have an interest in the place) and it is absolutely the ideal spot for Basie. Acoustics are perfect, the management is fair enough (Negroes are not only welcome as customers but dance on the small floor) and altogether the place rocks more than any place I can remember in downtown New York. The poor old Onyx Club has practically had to fold up in the interim. Basie is signed there for six months solid, with the likelihood that he'll become a permanent fixture there eight months out of the year.

They hired Rose Murphy from Cleveland for the intermissions. I think Rose is swell: a fine pianist, mediocre singer, and delightful personality; but she hasn't clicked too well with the Broadway crowd, which seems to want either a terrific singer (which she is not) or somebody who just plays piano. Now here's my idea: while you are recuperating would you like to take this job (I think it pays $75) which doesn't begin until 10 at night and is really very simple? Certainly it is much better than traveling around in cars sleepless and knocking yourself out working in a band. You also could arrange for whomever you wished—Andy, Benny, or even the Count, and make yourself additional change. The important thing is that you would be very much in the spotlight, you would get some inspiration every night, and you could be sure of getting your New York card.

I don't want you to think that I want you to do anything that might hurt Andy. He is a swell guy and deserves every possible break. But those terrific jumps every night are hard enough on the guys in a band, to say nothing of a reasonably fragile person like you, and I think that you owe it to yourself and your public (maybe that means me) to take it a little easy and work in a permanent spot. Anyway, I wish you'd let me know pronto so that I can complete arrangements here.

Everybody tells me that Louise Mann is pretty fine, but I would prefer hearing her myself before sending you any advice.

In the meantime take care of yourself—and be good.

> Affectionately,
> John H.

In August, Hammond wrote her again:

Dear Mary Lou,

It sounds like bad news that you are signed up to Andy and Joe Glaser, but if you can get a release the job is open for you at the Door. My suspicion is that they won't let you do it, but anyway there's no harm in asking.

It seems that your arrangement of "After You've Gone" was a little too elaborate for Benny's men, which may mean that he'll want to fix it up a bit before playing it. As soon as he starts using the stuff, we'll get you the whole amount. I hope you are really well by now and I'm sure looking forward to seeing and hearing you again soon.

> Best luck,
> John

Nothing came of these plans, though he did help her a couple of years later in New York. She remained tied to the Clouds, legally, emotionally, and musically—and this fact comes through in a very important recording she made in 1940 with six of her colleagues, including an assertively lyrical Dick Wilson. Dubbed *Six Men and a Girl,* it was one of her favorite records, like a relaxed jam session: "The vibes were right on this date," as she said, "and it was straight ahead."

Containing one of Mary's outstanding compositions from the period, "Scratchin' in the Gravel," a piece she revisited often to reshape as jazz styles progressed, and with majestic solos by both Mary and Wilson, the session also looked ahead in other pieces. In both "Tea for Two" and "Zonky," Mary's fast and forward-reaching harmonies sketched the next movement in jazz now known as bop, which Mary was to become engrossed with—what Schuller describes as her "cubistically modern 'comping.' " "I was one of the first with these frozen sounds, and after a night's jamming would sit and play weird harmonies (just chord progressions) with Dick Wilson," she commented. "Those screwy chords reminded us of music from *Frankenstein* or any horror film," she added with relish (Mary also loved lurid *True Confessions*–type magazines). Later that year, the band's version of "I'll Be Glad When You're Dead, You Rascal, You" is notable for what Schuller calls Mary's "zig-zagging, astoundingly adventurous modulations in and out of the key. Is there an influence on Thelonious Monk in all this?" he wonders. (Within a decade, Mary and Monk would be close friends, co-composing at least one piece).

Mary closed out 1940 with another brilliant recording as a leader. In November, at producer Dave Dexter's behest, she returned to the studio, billed as Mary Lou Williams and Her Kansas City Seven. Dexter parceled out two tunes each to various southwestern leaders for an album of Kansas City swing (though Mary actually is on four: two are arrangements of Bennie Moten riff tunes, two are material by the full Clouds of Joy).

Again, she used musicians she worked with in the Clouds, and again, too, there is a jam-session feel to the date. As it turns out, "Kansas City Seven" is the sole example of a small-group recording of Mary with her soon-to-be second husband, trumpeter Harold "Shorty" Baker, playing lovely obligatos contrasting with Dick Wilson's gruff tenor. Although she stayed in the Clouds of Joy for a year and half longer, Mary was more or less marking time after 1940.

Though Mary was not a prolific melodist, tending instead to weave her work from found objects of riffs, voicings, and rhythmic patterns with the same economy and attention to particularities as, say, a quilter or regional novelist, it is her harmonics and the subtle rhythms of jazz that place her in the inner circle, a musician's musician. Said the late pianist Jimmy Rowles, "I learned how to accompany singers and horn players by listening to the backgrounds that arrangers like Sy Oliver and Duke Ellington and Mary Lou Williams wrote for their soloists. Particularly Mary Lou when she was with Andy Kirk. It's unbelievable how much I owe that woman."

Chapter Seven
Why Go On Pretending?
1941–1942

PUBLICLY, MARY LOU WILLIAMS rarely expressed regret over her failed marriages and love affairs, often making instead the kind of flip, partially true comments that sounded good—and forestalled further scrutiny. "I fell in love with horns, not men," she would say, preferring to keep her disappointments to herself. But later in life, in her sixties, Mary offered a young bassist she thought had promise the bitter fruit of her own experience. He should scrap his plans to get married, she said. A jazz musician shouldn't marry; he can't be a great artist and have a marriage.

From the time Kirk's band hit big, Mary's life became frenetic with travel. Her tendency to exaggerate the time spent on the road getting from gig to gig is understandable: "5,000 or 6,000 miles a week on one-nighters all through the South, repeating most of the dates before coming west again—for nearly three years," she remembered. It must have *seemed* like 5,000 miles. "We arrived in most places in time to play, and left right afterwards. I have gone to sleep with my fur coat on, near to freezing, and woken up in the car hours later wet with perspiration in the sub-tropics of Florida. . . . I remember jumping from St. Louis to Canada: over 750 miles in one day. We played St. Louis until 3 A.M., slept and left for Canada around 11 A.M., and arrived at 10 at night—one hour late for the job."

Under such conditions, a normal life was impossible (part of the reason also cited for the lack of women in the business—though plenty of female singers stood the test). Food was taken on the run, accommodations were uneven, exercise and sleep inadequate, privacy lacking. Like traveling salesmen, musicians existed at the fringes of society, their lives a steady diet of boredom, loneliness, and chance encounters. Cards and crap games, pool rooms and dice, booze, drugs, and sex countered the tedium for many.

It was the world Mary had known since she was fourteen. She had learned to watch out for herself, but by 1941 the camaraderie and mutual support of Kansas City had faded. Mary herself had become, in her quiet way, one of the hip musicians, disdaining alcohol, developing a taste for gambling, marijuana, and men. But her living standard was hardly secure, though certainly more so than during the starved years of the early Depression. Much of her pay was still spent on road life, or sent to support her family. And how she resented never being paid royalties for her compositions for the Clouds of Joy, or compensated adequately for arrangements she had contributed to the band book! "I could not play or write my best for thinking about my share of the loot," she wrote, "and my sacrifices before we made a hit."

She pressed Andy Kirk for her share, as she pressed him for more money for the others in the band. But she accomplished little in this way and was increasingly restless with the routine. Before, she had been willing to put up with a certain amount of unpleasantness, as long as she could "expand with the band." But as the 1940s (Mary's thirties) began, and others were featured far more often, the same old material bored her. Her name now appeared in small print on the marquees announcing the band, while newcomer vocalist June Richmond's name headlined with Andy Kirk's. Mary turned her solos over to another new "star," the guitarist Floyd "Wonderful" Smith (as he was billed). She would often sit doodling at the piano, working crossword puzzles, barely accompanying the band. "Our repertoire consisted of recorded hits, and the solos had to be exactly like those on the records," she told Marsha Vick. "Once the boys said, 'You're snoring, what's the matter with you?' I was still playing—sleeping and playing."

A few times she simply disappeared, contract or no contract. On one tour, "when we reached Kansas City, I ran off. I must have had $200 or more and I went to St. Louis and balled [forties slang for "partied"] and then ran into my old love, Ben Webster, in Chicago at a musician's hangout called the Chicken Shack where I had too much fun. I didn't have carfare home," she added. "But I had a contract with the band—I had to return." She borrowed the money that time from Mamie. Later, the Clouds of Joy went to California for an engagement, where all of her new clothes and shoes were stolen, even the tires on her car, she wrote.

By then Mary and Andy Kirk were not on speaking terms. They "hated each other," confirms O'Brien. "She said he called her crazy, a destroyer of men and many other names." By her own reckoning, Mary had had, among her many romances within the band, an affair with a married man (John Harrington) and an engaged man (saxophonist Earl "Buddy Miller), whose girlfriend tried to commit suicide in front of Mary by drinking a vial of iodine and ending up in Bellevue. Her lover Don Byas, who wrote Mary tenderly lyrical love notes, was fired from the Clouds of Joy by Kirk after slapping her around publicly at a gig: possibly the last straw for Kirk, who warned her to leave the men in the band "alone." But the last straw for Mary was the chance discovery that she was not getting full credit for her compositions. "The valet was cleaning out a trunk and showed me a list of all my tunes and royalties being paid to two other people. I got only one-third."

Though Mary and Andy Kirk strove to be cordial to each other in later decades, a sour-grapes attitude crept into their reminiscences of the swing era. Kirk alternated between praise and slights of her achievements, and was grudging at times in his praise, while Mary was at times frankly bitter, knowing full well her importance to the Clouds of Joy—and that she could hardly be replaced by another woman pianist. She told Peter O'Brien that when she had heard that Dorothy Donegan, a pianist whose show-biz antics she disliked, was claiming that Kirk had offered her a job after Mary left, Mary quipped, "Why would he do that when he's in love with me?" For to complicate matters, the straight-arrow Andy Kirk, according to Mary, was or had been in love with her. When Mary took up with the last of her lovers, during the end of her tenure with the band, Kirk exploded. "Harold Baker and I hit it off quite well, causing the worst jealousy!" she wrote. "But Harold and I were doing very nicely together—he gave me everything I wanted." If Andy Kirk had fallen for her, though, it is highly unlikely that it led to a romance: she liked hip musicians, while Kirk, she hinted, was rather the opposite of hip. Delilah Jackson, who knew both of them in the sixties and seventies concurs: "I don't think they ever had an affair, no. Not Andy Kirk. I did ask Mary [Kirk's wife] if she was jealous of Mary Lou in the band and she said, 'Oh no, we used to do each other's hair, clothes, we were like family.' "

Even if Mary had some sort of convoluted or sublimated lover's quarrel with Kirk, their personal relationship did mellow in time. "When I would visit Kirk in the seventies, Mary Lou would come," recalls Delilah Jackson. "And on the phone, Mary Lou would tell him her troubles and vice versa."

Meanwhile, there remained Mary's husband: Mary seemed to have stayed with John Williams from sheer habit, developing a kind of stubbornly placid indifference even as both pursued other romances outside the marriage. When Mary's half-brother Willis Scruggs saw them together in '37 and '38, he described the marriage as "pleasant. He'd be in the hotel sleeping and she'd be gone with us. He'd always be very friendly. I never saw any problem as husband and wife. She was the HNC—Head Nigger in Charge—as we used to say." But by then, said John, "There was never no kissing or hugging or sex, but we talked, drank, had our laughs, slept together."

———

AT LAST, THOUGH, MARY had enough of her husband's constant womanizing. "I had heard strange tales about John and chorus girls and decided to move," wrote Mary of 1938. "I was kinda sick of being married anyway." A year later they did split up. "Christmastime of 1939," said John. "She asked me for a year's space. She said then after that we could see if we wanted to get back together. But I said, 'If you leave, that's it.' " John quit the Clouds of Joy, to join Coleman Hawkins's big band. "She asked me would I sign that I deserted her so she could get a divorce," said John. "I said yeah, any way you want it. Joe Glaser had told her she might get famous someday and I might sue her. And he wanted her to change her name and a lot of stuff. And she had gone from $50 to $125 a week without even telling me, while we're still married—well, she always wanted her money separate from mine."

"John gave me a lot of trouble," Mary wrote. "After trying to get me to return to him he finally left for Chicago. I felt sorry, yet he had destroyed what little feelings I had left. I never return to somebody after I'm finished with them. I could only be his friend, and I offered to help him get on his feet. He refused. I decided to get a divorce."

Mary filed for divorce from John in January 1941 and the divorce became final in February 1942. After Kirk's restaurant failed, John went out on the road again with Earl Hines's big band (where he played with Charlie Parker and Dizzy Gillespie), but by the mid-forties he quit the music business and got a job, first as a hotel porter and then as a factory worker in Chicago, remarried, and settled after his retirement in Columbus, Ohio, where he died in 1996.

Well before the divorce from John was final, Mary was planning to be married again, to Harold "Shorty" Baker. He joined the Clouds in 1940, and shortly after that, he and Mary began to live together. (Baker neglected to tell her about an unofficial engagement to a girl back in his hometown of St. Louis.) Both were unhappy with the mostly commercial focus of the Clouds by this time. As Mary complained to Baker, "They're burying me in the band." They began to make plans to leave and form a group of their own. Moreover, they had sketched a domestic fantasy for themselves: they would get married, maybe buy a house and start a family, dreams that Mary had put on hold since the breakup with Ben Webster.

It was just a matter of time before Mary quit. At the Apollo Theater in '41, while her highly creative arrangements for Ellington of "Ring Dem Bells," "The Sheik of Araby," and "Handy Eyes" were on the program, they were sideshows to vocalist June Richmond and guitarist Floyd "Wonderful" Smith. Also in 1941, Mary told Glaser she was going to quit unless she was properly paid for the music she'd written all those years. Glaser placated her, but also let her see his teeth: he would, he promised, "look into" the situation; in the meantime, she had a contract with the band. Didn't she realize it would jeopardize her future career if she broke it?

Mary backed down and hung on for one more unhappy year, but finally she walked for good. Andy Kirk said bluntly that "June [Richmond] was . . . the cause of Mary Lou Williams leaving the band in 1942. We were playing a date in Washington, D.C., and at some point during the evening Mary Lou got up from the piano and walked out. . . . Mary Lou, although she was appreciated, would never get that kind of applause because of June's showmanship. . . . I didn't even know she'd left. . . . She'd usually walk off the stand to have a smoke, and with Floyd's amplifier turned way up I didn't notice a thing. She caught the train for Pittsburgh."

"For 12 years with the band I'd known swell times and bad times, but barnstorming and the 'New System' of Management were bringing me down," Mary wrote. "Towards the end, there was no more brotherly love. Nearly everyone, I discovered, either had a knife or a gun. I had lost so much through thefts that for a solid year I had to sleep with everything I owned. When someone broke in my trunk and took earrings, Indian-head pennies and silver dollars which I cherished, I decided to leave. No more respect left—everyone was loud and boisterous. I decided it was too tough in the band. There was no more happiness. Everyone was like a hoodlum. And the piano at the next job we played in Washington, D.C., was the worst. I was fed up. Dragging my trunk off the bus, I drove to Pittsburgh. So ended my long association with the Kirk orchestra."

It was summertime, World War II was raging, and there was a ban on recordings. Mary went to Mamie's, to wait for Baker. She had no work lined up as yet, but lots of plans.

Chapter Eight
Trumpets No End
1942–1943

June 4, 1942
Case #1445
To: the International Executive Board of the Musicians' Union

Dear Sir and Brother:
I beg to file herein complaint against Mary Lou Williams, pianist with my orchestra, who left my band in Washington, D.C., on May 31, 1942, without notice of any kind and has failed to return. She has a contract with me which she utterly disregarded. This has placed me in a very embarrassing position as she was a featured member of the band and was advertised as such.

Fraternally yours,
Andy Kirk

KIRK (AND HIS driving force, Joe Glaser) were determined to punish Mary for breaking her contract and instigated legal action so that she could not get what was called a "transfer card," a crucially important piece of union paper that gave a traveling player the legal right to work around the country. Without it, she was the musician's equivalent of an illegal alien, reduced to working jobs too small for the union to bother policing and fining. Kirk replaced Mary with boogie-woogie stylist

Kenny Kersey in July of '42. Mary appealed to her old friend William Shaw, the well-connected president of Local 627 in Kansas City, for help. Shaw was interested in luring Mary back to K.C., where he assured her she'd find work, but he wrote her rather weakly, "I don't think Kirk has the right to keep your transfer card as it belongs to you and I suggest that you request Andy to send it to you." Mary had other plans. In Pittsburgh, she was soon joined by Harold Baker. "The Clouds came through Pittsburgh and he went to a movie with my brother-in-law while the bus was waiting for him downtown," Mary wrote. After holding the bus for some time, Andy Kirk realized Baker had bailed on him, to join Mary. Both received letters from the musicians' union, advising them they risked breach-of-contract suits. Mary fought back. "I countered this move by stating I would make it very unpleasant for the 'new system' if I answered. Nothing further happened to me. Baker was fined, I think." She was playing a tricky game, however, when she threatened to expose Glaser's "new system," writing that she "knew things." Glaser, furious, acted the part of the betrayed lover: after all, he had given her a personal contract and a raise when he took over the band. And he had plans, he'd told her, to make her a star. In exchange, he demanded loyalty. But now the mask of the doting papa, which he often donned in his letters to Mary, was gone: "I'll bury you because you've fucked the band. I have advised my attorney to take your case before the American Federation of Musicians. I am at a loss to understand your attitude. Your behavior during the past year is a mystery to me and on top of that your letter just received is a mystery."

Mary's departure, while not a death blow to the Clouds, did signal its real decline. It would bob along for some time, recombining periodically into the 1950s, but the glory days for the band (as for nearly all big bands) were over. Modern jazz, eventually known as bop, would replace it, played mostly by smaller, more economical combos—precisely the kind Mary was planning to organize. At the time, however, many of Mary's friends and family thought she had made a great mistake in leaving her secure spot in an established band that had given her national exposure, recordings, and a good salary. What more could she want, they wondered, in such a tough and uncertain business? Yet Mary never regretted leaving the Clouds, even though she did indeed undergo a professional roller-coaster ride afterwards.

She left during a time of terrific upheaval on many fronts. First, the nation and the world were at war. Of secondary importance, except to the musicians and their serious fans, of course, was the close of the era known as swing, at a period when the music business was in upheaval as well. ASCAP (the American Society of Composers, Authors and Publishers) had demanded that radio stations pay their composers a higher fee whenever they played their work. When the radio stations refused, ASCAP forbade the stations to play any of its members' music on radio for a full year. The fight escalated. James Petrillo, the powerful head of the American Federation of Musicians, joined the fight, banning his union's musicians from making records. Unfortunately for Mary, who became a member of ASCAP in the winter of 1943—the first black woman in that organization—the ban coincided with the period when she and Baker played together, which meant that they and their short-lived group would never be recorded together; the recording ban stretched from August of 1942 until November of 1944. (Even without the ban, it would have been a bad time for the record business, as the government commandeered for the war effort most of the copper and shellac needed to make record masters. A limited number of records—the V-discs (V for Victory) *were* allowed to be made, but for the noncommercial use of the troops. Mary did perform on a few of these records.

That June at the Floyds' in East Liberty, Baker and Mary set up camp in the attic. There they, or rather Mary, pulled together new arrangements and hired personnel for the combo. As much as he loved Mary—and he had proposed marriage several times while they were in the Kirk band—Baker was neither a practical man nor a man of much drive. Focused only on music and his horn, he was the quintessential improvising jazz musician and, like a good number of his contemporaries, he liked the bottle too much. It was Mary who made the contacts, who had the vision and energy to put a group together.

She found local men. For a drummer, she picked a very young Art Blakey, who was back in his hometown after a failed stint on the West Coast. "He was born bopping, like J. C. Heard with Teddy Wilson's great band," Mary wrote. "They had to hold them back to get a dance beat going. I had a difficult time with him on ballads and dance tempos. He was a real eager beaver." Other Pittsburghers who came to rehearse at the house were Oliver McLean on reeds (principally clarinet), Edgar Willis on bass, and Orlando Wright, who later changed his name to Musa Kaleem, on tenor saxophone. "We rehearsed the new outfit every day, Harold Baker and myself, and through John Hammond contacted some people who were able to find us work," wrote Mary. "Our first job was in Cleveland, at Mason's Farm, where we followed Coleman Hawkins's group in, and the combo went over well enough for us to be kept on from August to October—way past the summer season."

Mason's Farm catered to a black clientele, including musicians, remembers tenor saxophonist Harold Arnold, an Ohioan then with Lucky Millinder's band. It was "a place with a dancehall, a bar, a restaurant, and horses, at the Cedar Country Club in Solon, Ohio, about 10 or 15 miles from Cleveland. It was run by Bennie Mason, a prosperous numbers racketeer. You could rent cabins. And no, I don't recall any whites out there at all." On the bill with Mary's band was Ted Blackman's Revue, which featured the very young, undiscovered, and, Mary said, great and unique blues singer the late Joe Williams. When he sat in with her combo, Joe Williams was so poor, she said, that he had to camouflage a big gap in his smile with a stick of gum.

One can only speculate about what Mary's group sounded like—Kansas City swing, probably (like the 1940 recording Mary and Baker and company had made as the Kansas City Seven for Decca), but with more of the forward-reaching harmonies she'd been employing. "Tadd Dameron and most of the musicians around came out to hear us," she wrote. Dameron gave her some of his arrangements to try out as well.

It was at Mason's Farm that Mary began her lifelong habit of notating every expense, quite literally down to the penny, that she and her combos incurred. So from the receipts for the band's food and drink we learn that the chubby Harold Baker customarily ate two platefuls of dinner, three or four cups of coffee, and ran up a large bar tab. Her record-keeping was a futile attempt on her part, then and later, to keep expenses under control.

For some reason, Mary noted in her diary, the other players, all Pittsburghers, had taken a dislike to Baker, a St. Louisian. Perhaps because he was already big time, having played with big bands (Duke Ellington's, 1938; Teddy Wilson's, 1939; Kirk's, 1940–42), while they were locals hoping to break into the big time. Perhaps he swaggered.

At any rate, they resented him, and he was made to feel the odd man out.

When members of the Ellington band stopped by Mason's Farm in late September on their way back from a tour of the West Coast, Ellington, short a good lead trumpet, was eager to acquire the commandingly lyrical playing of Baker. He was easily persuaded to join (and appears on the payroll from the fall of that year). He would stay with the Ellington Orchestra, with intervals away, for eight years.

Mary was crushed, but loyal to Harold. "I felt depressed," she confessed. "I made up my mind to join Harold as soon as I could." In the meantime, she had dates to fill for the band. She'd not only lost her lover but her best player and had to find a replacement immediately. She was far from satisfied with the new man, Marion Hazel, whom Mary, typically, did not mention by name when she criticized him. "Art Blakey and the rest had me stop by Pittsburgh to pick up what they said was 'the greatest on trumpet,' " she noted drily. "But we were playing tricky arrangements that called for a bit of reading, and I couldn't find a sound reader on trumpet. No one in the band realized the value of Harold Baker. He could play 10 solos and fall back in a fast-moving ensemble without splitting notes. The new trumpet man would split a D in the staff."

Mary went on to New York, along with Blakey and the others, but promised work fell through. "I was practically stranded in New York but I wouldn't tell anyone. I got myself a room at the Dewey Square and I stayed inside that hotel. I ate and slept for about two weeks and thought over things and meditated as to which way I was going." Just months before, in the summer, she and Baker had taken a lease on a house they planned to use as a base between road trips with their new combo. Now that plan was dashed and all her dreams were again on hold. "Then," Mary went on, "I called John Hammond and he got me in touch with an agent, Louise Crane, who was an heiress."

Crane booked Mary and her combo at Kelly's Stable, a Fifty-second Street club. But her band couldn't cut it; she still couldn't find a trumpet player in the same class as Baker. "The people who were backing me had confidence," she wrote in her diary, "yet I gave it up. I decided I'd join Harold as soon as possible."

It was not quite as simple as that. Walking away from the job had brought her fresh legal difficulty: Louise Crane was demanding

$1,300 in lost income from the gig. Feistily, Mary counterclaimed that Crane had tried to assert improper control over the music and the musicians. "She insisted I bring them in before I thought they were ready. Then, after two and a half weeks she insisted that I break up the combination and fire all the boys. She purchased them railroad tickets back to Pittsburgh and then charged *me* for them." The union, however, found in Crane's favor, although reducing Mary's debt to $300. Meanwhile, Mary was seething at Art Blakey. He had returned to Pittsburgh, taking some of her arrangements with him without her permission—as she angrily informed him. He wrote back, attempting to defend himself. (Typically, Mary never said a word against him publicly, but she never worked with him again, either.)

After the Crane fiasco, Mary knew she needed a manager: she simply couldn't handle the business end of the music. It was more than enough work to put (and keep) together a band of her own. She tried to form a new group—saxophonist Paul King and others telegraphed that they were eager to join—but it didn't jell. "She was just interested in her music. She had nobody in her corner to be a son of a bitch on her behalf," said Peter O'Brien, who would assume a manager's role in the seventies. There was only one person she could think of. Humbling herself, Mary contacted Joe Glaser.

Glaser responded with another of his avuncular, condescending missives, dated November 10, 1942:

Dear Mary,
Your letter of November 8th received and I am really at a loss to understand some of the things you wrote about. First you say you want a combination and then you tell me that you are going to Pittsburgh because someone is sick there and that you are going to get in touch with me and work out a deal whereby I can book the combination in Chicago and now you turn up in Chicago and tell me that you went there because Harold Baker sent for you and now you tell me you have no money and have to live off Harold Baker. Personally I have the highest respect and regard for you and know that you are a great artist, one of the greatest pianists and composers in the country. Well, Mary, for you to write a letter and tell me that you haven't any money and that you are financially obligated to Harold Baker, it

doesn't make sense. You know deep down in your heart that you are not doing the right thing and I assure you that it is time for you to come to your senses—it will only be a question of a few months before you again will be making the money that you used to make, but if you want to stay with Harold Baker and forget all about your music that is entirely up to you.

With every good wish, I am

Sincerely yours,

Joe Glaser

Mary chose not to "forget all about her music" and later that month signed a contract with him as her personal manager (an agreement more symbolic than real, since performers often signed "exclusive" agreements with more than one manager). Over the next decade in New York, Mary went through more than a dozen agents, managers, publicity people, and lawyers. But she always returned to Glaser, and not only because he was the one who got her the best work. There was another dynamic to their relationship, a kind of attraction-repulsion element that kept them crashing together.

Glaser, an astute reader of character despite his crudeness, knew that Mary's backing and filling was not play-acting, but real angst. He could handle her as no one else ever could, mixing a long-suffering tone with hectoring and threats when he felt it was necessary. Eventually he became reconciled to the fact that Mary would move on a project only when she wanted to move. As for Mary, she took it as a great compliment when Glaser threw up his hands, saying, "You're quite a woman. I can't keep you down."

In the late fall of 1942, Mary was clearly in much confusion, as Glaser had spelled out in his letter. Was she planning simply to live with Baker, tagging along with the new band, as she had done in the early years with John and the Clouds of Joy? A girlfriend, living off a musician's irregular earnings, not performing? Impossible—Mary was now an established national presence in jazz in an era when swing was *the* national pop music, a glamorous music queen in sequined gowns who had written hits for the top bands.

Now began a curious interlude in her life, one that led to a great deal of new work, and one that is all but unknown. Mary went back with Shorty Baker to New York, and from there to Baltimore, where the Ellington band was booked for a long engagement at the Royal Theater. And in Baltimore, in a simple ceremony presided over by the Reverend Frederick Douglas, Mary and Harold were married on December 10, 1942. If there was a party or reception or any kind of celebration to mark the wedding, Mary never said. And although she was now officially Mary Lou *Baker* and would remain so for the rest of her life, it was a name she used but rarely. And, although the couple didn't stay together long, they never bothered to get a divorce. When Baker died in 1966, at age fifty-two, at the Veterans Administration Hospital in New York, of throat cancer, Mary was, on paper at least, his widow.

Back in New York, in January 1943, there was a more momentous event than a wedding: Ellington's first Carnegie Hall concert, at which he presented his innovative and controversial composition "Black, Brown and Beige." Mary's ambitions for her own music were fired: *Carnegie Hall?* It was a great, groundbreaking achievement for a jazz composer. And within three years, she was to present a concert there herself.

But Mary, who had seen many incarnations of the Ellington Orchestra, was not at first impressed with the 1943 band. "What a strange group. I guess there were too many stars, because so many of them weren't speaking to each other." The band, she thought, was in a creative slump. "They'd go for months and months and wouldn't play anything much. Harold and I hung out with Lawrence Brown, Juan Tizol, Tricky Sam. For about three months, nothing happened. Really draggy music." Despite her love of Ellington's and Strayhorn's work, Mary decided she'd better go back to New York, find work and an apartment for herself and Baker. "I said to Johnny Hodges, 'I'm gonna have to leave cause the band isn't blowin'.' And he said, 'Oh don't do that, Lou,' because he'd write eight bars and would expect me to put 16 bars to it and finish the tune off. But you know he didn't want to lose me. And there were several others like that."

Then came an extraordinary night. "This particular time we were in Ohio. I said, 'I'm gonna listen one more night, but I want to get out of here and leave.' And I'm telling you, when that band hit, I've never heard anything like that before in my life. And I think everybody else was just in hysterics or something. Duke was vamping. They played 'Caravan.' When the band hit, his vamp—I never heard anything like that before. It sounded like Stravinsky and I said, 'Well, this is the greatest band on earth.' It *was*. Everything had fallen into place. When they finished I screamed and everybody in the place screamed. Everything they played was like that. I said, 'Well, I can't leave this.' Duke's chords and harmonies were way out," she explained, "Different things that nobody'd ever heard before. You've heard all the masters but this was completely different." Mary stuck around.

Back in New York with the Ellington band for a spring engagement at the Hurricane Club, Mary was badly in need of work. But she couldn't perform in the city until accepted into Local 802 of the Musicians Union, a lengthy process. She took a few jobs out of town as a single, but just then a new avenue opened up for her: arranging for the Ellington band. For a week's work in February 1943, for instance, she was paid $100 for arrangements, the same weekly salary that Billy Strayhorn got that year, and more than anyone else in the band at the time for her contributions to the band book.

Mary had hooked up with Harold just as the radio and recording ban rendered the bulk of the Ellington orchestra's band book unavailable for play. "Suddenly Duke was screaming for new material," says Derek Jewell, an Ellington biographer. "Ellington was still leading a band which went from dance halls to theatres, wherever the money and conditions were attractive enough. These venues usually demanded swing and sway rather than suites."

"Duke," Mary reminisced, "asked me to write some arrangements. I told him: 'What in the world am I going to write for you?' "

His way of writing voicings "was quite different than what I was doing. I did learn some of the secrets," she added. "Like one trumpet player played out of tune and Ellington had me write his parts in a different key; that had something to do with it. Instead of everybody playing in C, I wrote *him* in C sharp. And that gave a different sound. He was much better playing in C sharp than in C: it blended much better with what was happening in Duke's band." "Sometimes there was a mistake," she added, "and I'd say, 'Oh my goodness, I got sleepy and I copied the wrong parts.' Once Duke Ellington said, 'Let's try it the way it is.' And it worked out. It didn't matter what I wrote, he said, "Mary, you're a genius,' and he'd hype me to write something else. He knew how to do it, you know. He talked me into it. He'd play anything that I gave him while I was traveling with them. For years and years afterward, he played 'Trumpets No End,' which I wrote for the Ellington Band." Often she had a chance to rehearse the numbers she prepared with the band. Even after Mary stopped traveling with Baker and settled in New York, she continued to prepare arrangements for Ellington. In 1944 or 1945, while Mary was a featured artist at the important club Café Society Downtown, Susan Reed, who played zither there, recalled coming across Mary sitting in a closet with a music pad and pencils. "What are you doing?" Reed asked, and Mary replied, "Writing something for Duke Ellington."

What Duke Ellington's son, Mercer, then a young trumpet player and budding arranger for the band, described in a radio interview with Phil Schaap as "chaos" in the rehearsals of the band in the forties were the conditions Mary had cut her teeth on in the twenties; written arrangements were often only jumping-off points. For Mary, the creative ferment of an Ellington band rehearsal was heaven, although she was less comfortable with the man himself. "I never had too much to say to Duke," she wrote. "I always liked being around sidemen or little people. *This* was my greatest enjoyment." Although she never discussed it publicly, Mary simmered for decades about the way she felt misused by Ellington. In 1967, when she needed an income and was hoping he would pay her for fresh arrangements she'd tailored for his band, she wrote a pointedly worded letter (keeping a carbon copy in her files): "I really do not believe that you did not know that your personal manager did not pay me one cent for the 15 arrangements I did for the band then, including 'Blue Skies.'" For his part, Ellington made certain to credit her musical imagination. "Mary Lou Williams is perpetually contemporary," he wrote. "Her writing and performing are and have always been a little ahead throughout her career . . . her music retains—and maintains—a standard of quality that is timeless. She is like soul on soul."

Mary's best-known arrangement for Ellington was the aforementioned "Trumpets No End," her clever reworking of Irving Berlin's "Blue Skies," in which the melody was coyly hidden, only to show itself in exuberantly cascading trumpet solos. The bravura high notes of "Trumpets"—it was intended as a showcase for Harold Baker—made it a perfect finale, from its debut in 1943 at a Carnegie Hall concert well into the fifties. Mary's arrangement called for solos for clarinet, tenor sax, and trumpet but was edited by Ellington for unison trumpets only, and in the process Baker lost his solo showcase. "Harold called me and he said, 'Guess what? *All* the trumpets are playing in my solo,' " Mary recalled. Mary also wrote a beautiful arrangement, now housed in the Ellington Archive, called "Variations on Stardust," for the band's '43 Carnegie Hall date, as a present for Baker—she gave him two choruses. Besides "Trumpets No End," several other of Mary's arrangements for Ellington were recorded. Her version of "Sweet Georgia Brown" (identified as Mary's by musician Loren Schoenberg), and featuring Ben Webster, then in the Ellington band, was recorded in June 1943. Five years later, Webster and other Ellingtonians (including Billy Strayhorn on piano and Al Hibbler on vocals) recorded Mary's tune "Ghost of Love." Mary's slyly pretty ballad "You Know, Baby" was, Hibbler thinks, also recorded circa 1943, when he joined the band with Ben Webster and others, but the record was not issued. We know that Mary contributed at least forty-seven compositions and arrangements to the Ellington Orchestra between the 1940s and 1960s, and there may well be others. For example, Hibbler thinks that Mary arranged "Stompin' at the Savoy," and Mary's papers indicate that she also arranged Ellington's "Marquetta." But with very few exceptions, her work for the band was soon buried in the mountains of papers that accrued during Ellington's lifetime. It was not until his musical effects were put in order some years after his death that her contribution could begin to be quantified and assessed, an ongoing effort.

And though Mary's contributions were quite secondary to the overall Ellington oeuvre, many of her pieces for him are resplendent, part of a very productive period of work for her that extended through the 1940s and into the 1950s.

———

UNWISELY, BEFORE SHE had her New York union card, Mary took a nonunion job at a Bronx dancehall in the spring of '43 as leader, with Illinois Jacquet on tenor and Oscar Pettiford on bass. The union got wind of it and Mary was called in for a hearing at which she risked a large fine. Luckily, she was let off with only a warning; and through the influence of John Hammond, a backer of Café Society, Mary finally did get her union card—and a job at that club. Hammond had long been after Mary to move to New York; back in 1938 he had tried to get her to help open Café Society Downtown at its highly publicized New

Year's Eve debut, and he kept after her. His persistence paid off. Mary performed for the first time at the Greenwich Village club early in the summer of '43. But Manhattan nightclubs and businesses customarily shut down for August in those pre–air conditioning years, and with no other work, Mary joined Harold on the road again until October. When she was invited to open the new season at Café Society, she agreed immediately. As she wrote, "I moved around with Duke's orchestra until we reached Canada, and I came close to freezing. Then I caught the first train out to New York, leaving Harold with the band."

Though Harold wrote her affectionate letters from the Hotel Piccadilly in Toronto, where the band was playing, money problems predominated. "Go on and take care of things," he urged. "I'm going to try and send at least $150 in the next three or four days. If I send you the money, take some of mine and put it with yours and pay on the coat. You're going to get it, believe me when I tell you." There is something touching about this craving for a mink coat at a time when it was hard for her to pay for her room at the Cecil Hotel on 112th Street. She was glad indeed for the Café Society offer.

In November, the Ellington band returned to New York. Mary and Harold spent the Thanksgiving holiday together, hoping to find an apartment despite wartime shortages in New York, and still talked about starting a family. A few months later, through a tip from Doc Cheatham, who was also working at Café Society in the house band, Mary heard about a vacant two-and-a-half-room apartment—a small kitchen, a bedroom, a sunny livingroom—in the building where he lived, near 144th Street and St. Nicholas Avenue in Harlem. The building also had a doorman and was rent-controlled. Mary grabbed it. For the first time in her life, she had her own place: apartment 21 at 63 Hamilton Terrace, on a quiet, curving tree-lined block convenient to the shops and markets of uptown's commercial thoroughfares.

She kept that apartment for the rest of her life, even after the neighborhood declined and it was broken into numerous times; even after she moved to North Carolina in the late seventies; it was cheaper than a hotel for stays in New York, she reasoned. And—it was home.

In the mid-1940s, Hamilton Terrace was ideal for Mary—a comfortable place to live and entertain. She made sure musicians felt welcome to drop in for music, food, rest. Mary decorated the place simply, painting the kitchen lemon yellow—including the appliances—reapplying the paint as the years went by. It was by the mid-sixties, says Peter O'Brien, who met her then, that the place had declined. The landlord had let the building go and everything was ancient. "A real rattrap of a refrigerator," he recalls of the kitchen, the heart of the apartment, "an old stove, just one window, a sink that was tilting away from the wall, and no cabinets underneath, but rather an old-fashioned, built-in cupboard with glass doors. She had a little tiny round table and two backless stools, where she'd sit and talk. But she did so many things in that little kitchen. She would do her hair at the stove, with a curling iron in the fire. There was no maid, no nothing. She cooked the same thing, over and over: good chicken, fried in lard with garlic. Delicious. With greens, corn and a lettuce and tomato salad. Never anything sweet."

Mary bought a large plush white rug for the living room for friends to loll on. And of course a piano—her favorite, a Baldwin upright, three-quarter size, decorated with photos that couldn't disguise the many cigarette burns. In the bedroom were twin pink satin upholstered Hollywood beds, stacks of cabinets and files. "Mary wrote on her bed and conducted business from her bed," says O'Brien. "Next to the bed when I knew her were her Princess phone and ashtrays, her horror comics—and her missal."

It was meant to be a place for two, of course, but Harold Baker never moved in. Just when she got the apartment, Baker was drafted—either at the end of 1943 or the beginning of 1944. He had ignored his draft notice from the War Department, and, said fellow trumpeter Irving "Mouse" Randolph, "they came and just grabbed him off the bandstand. Taken right out off the Apollo where he was playing with Duke's band."

At first, Baker's letters to Mary were cheerful and warmly affectionate. He was well fed ("getting fat," he boasted), with a cushy job—no responsibilities other than playing in the army band. But by March, his invitations for Mary to come down and visit him for a weekend sounded rather perfunctory: his old sweetheart from St. Louis had resurfaced and she was pressing him to get back together.

The marriage was over in all but name sometime in the spring. In Mary's words, she and Harold were too different in their likes and dislikes; they couldn't compromise. There were also heated quarrels. A couple of years earlier, when they were still in the Clouds of Joy, Andy Kirk recalled to Peter O'Brien, "he saw Mary come running around a corner after a fight with Harold Baker. She'd hit him on the forehead with a Coke bottle and it was bleeding. 'Save me!' she yelled to Kirk, as she dashed by with Baker barreling after her. 'Save yourself,' Kirk reportedly replied." "Yeah, Baker beat her up too when he was drunk," John Williams asserted. "And that lasted about one year. But she never found another John Williams to encourage her in her music." (Not so: the man who followed Baker as Mary's lover, artist David Stone Martin, couldn't have been more supportive of her art and would remain a life-long devoted friend.) Mary and Baker did maintain a civil, if distant, relationship after they split up. When he was ill and nearly destitute in the sixties (having made a terrific record with Doc Cheatham in 1961 for the Swingville label) she sent him money—fifty dollars on one occasion, at a time when she was living on loans herself. She cooked and brought food to him at the hospital as well until he died in '66. He had been a great musician, and Mary revered that above all else.

John Williams failed to see, for all his astuteness about Mary, that while he did play a kind of father-figure role in her life, he had been as much a disappointment to her as Ben Webster, Don Byas, and Harold Baker—but without their greatness as musicians.

Chapter Nine
Café Society Blues
1943–1946

ANY CLUB THAT liked to bill itself as "The Wrong Place for the Right People" had to be at least a little different from the usual nightclub. And Café Society Downtown *was* unusual: not just a business venture, but a social experiment, a somewhat raffish meeting place for the *au courant* of jazz and progressive politics, including many young and wealthy New Yorkers whose taste for the bohemian had been whetted by their parents' experiences in speakeasies and Harlem boîtes in the twenties.

For some, Café Society was chic slumming. For others, it was, as one of its founders, journalist Helen Lawrenson, described it, "our first political nightclub. Jazz and politics were what it was all about. Some people hated it; others were all agog. It was the most exciting night spot in town and the proving ground for more remarkable talent than possibly any similar place before or since. . . . From the beginning, it was completely integrated: black and white performers, black and white patrons. This had never happened before, outside of a few Harlem places where whites got the best tables. Not at Café Society they didn't!" "It *was* the only place for mixed couples to go," confirms Johnnie Garry, the club's bandboy and later Sarah Vaughan's personal manager, who became a friend of Mary's.

Not only was Café Society fully integrated—a radical political stance when de facto segregation was still the norm in the North—it was not a front for vice, as were so many mob-controlled nightclubs. At the Café, there were no hustlers, no cigarette girls or chorus girls. Indeed, Mary recalled that the club had a policy of barring entrance to unescorted female patrons after the first "family" show at eight o'clock (hardly a policy either feminists or the ACLU would applaud today, but effective in keeping out hustlers). Some of its founders—most notably Helen Lawrenson and John Hammond—were openly active in the Communist Party's Popular Front, a radical leftist organization. Hammond booked the talent for the club, Lawrenson initially acted as hostess and publicity person.

It is impossible to say if Mary's employment at Café Society made her vulnerable to suspicions during the McCarthy era when some artists were hounded from their jobs for their political beliefs. Certainly Café Society itself was suspect in the eyes of the many powerful people who saw Communism as a synonym for Evil. Then, too, entertainers who protested against segregation and unequal treatment of the races in America in the postwar years were suspected of "Communist leanings"—FBI director J. Edgar Hoover was not only a fierce anti-Communist but fearful that any attempt to upset the status quo might inspire a Communist takeover. The fact that Café Society was, at bottom, a music venue, and that a lot of people went to the club to enjoy the entertainment, was irrelevant: a performer (and especially a *black* performer) who worked at the Café was tainted, in the FBI's view.

"I got hung up in politics through working at the Café," Mary observed in her diary, "but I think all musicians or people like me would get mixed up in something, looking for some people to help them and help the race. But they can never be anything but a musician." She played fund-raisers for the NAACP—Mary headlined a benefit for the Syracuse University chapter in 1947—and played for the left-leaning Committee for the Negro in the Arts. Probably most disturbing to the FBI, though, was her attempt to perform in an interracial, all-female combo at a revue in her hometown of Atlanta, in 1947. Such a "mixed-race" concert was of course old hat for Mary, who had played with white musicians for decades and performed in such shows as *The People's Bandwagon,* a 1945 revue of white and black entertainers that sought to help reelect President Roosevelt. But her plan to play in an integrated group in the Deep South was a radical idea, as well she knew. Still, she, actor Canada Lee, and others persisted, going so far as to petition Georgia's governor, Ellis Arnall, to override the local laws banning integrated performance. In vain, and to no one's surprise: it would be too dangerous and inflammatory of the "wrong elements," Arnall wrote back, to put on an integrated jazz concert in Atlanta.

Did Mary's career suffer on account of her involvement with the Left, the well-documented fate of many Hollywood writers? Anecdotal evidence suggests that entertainers as well as Hollywood writers and others suffered from a kind of behind-the-scenes blacklisting. Trumpeter Frankie Newton, for instance, was probably cut out of work as a result of his politics. "Frankie was going to Communist Party cell meetings, yes," confirms bassist John Williams (not Mary's John). "But this was part of the scene then. Newton never got the breaks he should have. He was a good arranger, but he ended up as a janitor."

Even Duke Ellington, who once said, "I've never been interested in politics in my whole life," participated in a raft of rallies and benefits, especially in the turbulent late thirties and forties. Benny Goodman appeared at some antifascist and war-aid efforts sponsored by the Popular Front in the forties. And later, Louis Armstrong responded to the ugly 1957 battle to desegregate a public high school in Little Rock, Arkansas, by saying, "The way they are treating my people in the South, the government can go to hell." All three were under surveillance for years by the FBI. As for Mary, who, some friends from the forties have said, hosted Communist cell meetings in her apartment, no evidence of an FBI file has yet surfaced about her.

The Café's owner, Barney Josephson, a shoe salesman from New Jersey who invested money (along with others) in the progressive club, is a controversial figure. At first he was the on-site manager—what Helen Lawrenson describes as the "front man" for the club bankrolled by leftist money—but soon Josephson bought out other interests. It was a business venture that he saw as noble, even self-sacrificing, telling the *New York Post* in 1946, "My friends thought I was balmy. But I was sick of discrimination, had seen too much of it. My first year was tough. I lost $20,000, was flat against the wall, but I wanted to keep going and in my own way. All I want," he added, "is performers, Negro or white, on exactly the same artistic footing."

He did better than that. In 1940, Josephson was able to open a second club, the more upscale Café Society Uptown on Manhattan's East Side. But trouble brewed. Whispers of Communist ties within the Café became full-scale FBI investigations during the McCarthy era. "Not only were Reds assigned as entertainers, waiters and captains," alleged an FBI report in 1947, "but Josephson was advised to use Communist propaganda in shows for the cover-charge customers." The file was massive, some 2,100 pages of documents about alleged Red activities by Café Society employees and the boss. But though Barney's brother Leon, an avowed Communist who had invested start-up money in the club, was sent to prison after refusing to answer questions by the House Un-American Activities Committee (HUAC) in 1948, Barney maintained his innocence.

That Barney Josephson was not indicted was resented, both by forthright leftists like Lawrenson, who dismissed him as "spineless," and by featured entertainers at Café Society such as pianist Hazel Scott. Like Mary and countless others, Scott had performed at benefits and charity causes during World War II, many of them sponsored by the Left. When pressured to testify against Josephson, in Peter O'Brien's words, Hazel Scott "ratted on him." Many years later, with tears in his eyes, Josephson confided to Mary, "I don't know why Hazel would do that to me."

But if Josephson saw himself as a kind of benefactor especially to black show people, they generally viewed him less benignly. Perhaps the entertainers' expectations of him were unrealistic. "When I really got to know him," comments Johnnie Garry, "I realized that he would seem to make you feel that he was in the black people's corner—or in the black *entertainers'* corner—but I never saw him do anything for them." Hazel Scott felt she had been underpaid and manipulated. "Barney was extremely proud of his largesse towards others, but he was *not* a generous man," concurs Peter O'Brien, who had dealings with him as Mary's manager at a later club, the Cookery, in the '70s. "In fact, he was a very good businessman: he had access to a lot of talent nobody else was at all interested in. He made out like a bandit. His idea was to not pay artists very much but help them in other ways." Josephson helped Mary by providing her with gowns, securing her weekly radio show on WNEW, paying for the rental of Town Hall when Mary produced her long work, *The Zodiac Suite*. "But that's how he got to keep the money, by doing other things for her but not paying her much," O'Brien observes. "Joe Glaser was like that, too. He had all kinds of things in his office that he'd give the artist—a mink coat, a prize dog, a jeweled compact."

But Josephson was a survivor in a very tough business. He was savvy enough so that even after Café Society was blackballed by several New York newspapers—right-wing columnist Westbrook Pegler was particularly vehement—he was able to keep it going until finally, in the spring of 1949, he had to close it down. He not only kept his name clear with the government, but was able to salvage enough financially to open several new restaurants, including the Cookery, where Mary would establish a New York presence again in the 1970s.

WHAT WAS CAFÉ SOCIETY like during its glory days in the forties? The war-stimulated economy drew in southern soldiers and socialites, jazz lovers and political radicals—everybody who went out at night came to the Café, which got invaluable publicity by having its talent featured in broadcasts to the armed forces.

Club-goers would descend a flight of rather grubby stairs to a basement room where murals by Village artists adorned the wall. Tables lined the walls, there was a good kitchen and a short bar on the floor, with an elevated bandstand but no stage. Shows started at 8 P.M., when the house band began playing the first of three sets of entertainment; the 8 P.M. show was, in Mary's words, geared for "dad, mother and the smaller kids." Performers sought to be booked into the club: although Josephson did not pay big salaries, the exposure made it worthwhile. On a given night, a patron would catch great pianists—Mary, Teddy Wilson, Art Tatum, Earl Hines, Bud Powell, Hazel Scott—and singers like Billie Holiday, Lena Horne, and Georgia Gibbs; the zither player Susan Reed; songwriter Cy Coleman; comedians Zero Mostel, Jack Gilford, and Imogene Coca; and dancers like Pearl Primus, many of them at the start of their careers. "Then Sunday night," recalled Doc Cheatham, who was in the house band led by pianist Eddie Heywood for about six years, "everybody in show business would come in—Billy Strayhorn, Paul Robeson, Lena Horne, Joe Louis, Canada Lee, Josh White."

"The musicians would go out between shows, wouldn't mingle with customers," recalls Gray Weingarten (née Marjorie Merwin), who as a close friend of Mary's did have the honor of mingling. "On pay night, after the performances were all over, about 2 A.M., they'd all take their paychecks and go throw dice against the back stairs. All the performers would play."

DESPITE BEING A veteran performer, Mary suffered acute stage fright at Café Society when she began working there. "After being with a big band, I felt so alone," she explained about playing with only a bass and drums behind her. "I missed many shows that first month—I wasn't drinking at the time, but I must have consumed a pint that first night without effect." But when she surrounded herself with excellent musicians, many of them old friends, Mary quickly adjusted. She put together arrangements for her rhythm section. "On my way to the club, I'd write an arrangement in my head, and I'd tell drummer J. C. Heard, for example, 'I'd like to do "Limehouse Blues." Follow me.' And he did." "There was the difference," said Doc Cheatham, "from being an accompanist and a soloist, and every night she was better and better and she was very happy then." "Being in one place was quite to my liking," she wrote, "since I had traveled for at least 12 to 15 years."

"You could always tell when Mary Lou was getting ready, when she really felt like playing," recalls Johnnie Garry. "She'd take that right heel and she'd cock it and start stompin' on that floor. We'd say she's in the groove tonight." Slim, attractive, and stylish, her captivating piano style combining sensitivity with relentless swing, Mary became one of the toasts of New York's hip society. A nationwide Mary Lou Williams fan club was established; presided over by her half-cousin, the comedian Nipsy Russell, it distributed a newsletter, pins, and posters. Glaser, cut out by her direct dealing with Hammond, was enraged again. Having signed an exclusive contract with her, he demanded she pay him his 10-percent commission from the Café Society job. But either the suit was dropped or a deal worked out. Mary's career future had never looked so good.

AT THE CAFÉ, Mary sometimes alternated with Hazel Scott as the featured pianist. Like Mary, Scott had shown precocious musical talent as a little girl; she had begun by studying classical piano at Juilliard. But Scott also loved jazz. Ten years younger than Mary, she idolized her as the star of the Clouds of Joy and cut out Mary's picture from the "window cards"—posters put up in store windows around Harlem that advertised coming appearances of the band. At eighteen Hazel Scott dropped out of Juilliard to front a band in Harlem and began to make a name for herself.

If the similarities between the two gifted women pianists are obvious, the differences are crucial. Scott was an extrovert who lit up the stage with her personality, a fabulous-looking player who developed a technique of "jazzin' the classics" that was wildly popular with audiences. Mary, on the other hand, was a subdued beauty, shy and introverted, although once ignited, her inner fire could sear the listener.

Leonard Feather, who lived above Café Society, was crazy about Hazel Scott and steered her career before Barney Josephson became her personal manager; both coached her in ways Mary would never have stood for. And it would be pale-brown Hazel Scott, not chocolate Mary Lou Williams, who was called to Hollywood, where she played cameo roles emphasizing her sex appeal (most memorable: a scene in *Rhapsody in Blue* in which she played the piano in a fairy-princess gown while the camera lingered on her creamy decolletage). Avoided in most discussions of Hazel Scott's quick rise to popularity was the taboo subject of color, or rather caste. "The racism that existed in that world! I don't just mean the white world, either," says Peter O'Brien. "That light, half-caste, almost white look was the acceptable, pleasing thing. Hazel was light-skinned. Mary was dark." Mary was still the undisputed "queen" of the ivories, accepted into the highest ranks of musicianship. But by 1945, it was Hazel Scott who was enjoying its trappings: she carried a trademark red rose wherever she went, had her hands insured by Lloyd's of London, bought her jewelry from Harry Winston, and that same year, at age twenty-five, married *the* power broker of black America, the Reverend Adam Clayton Powell, Jr., minister of the powerful Abyssinian Baptist Church in Harlem. (At the wedding, Mary was a bridesmaid and Hazel was given away by Barney Josephson, standing in for her long-deceased father.) Mary and Hazel remained friends, each helping the other later on at difficult junctures in their lives. "Although Mary had been very jealous and hurt by how far Hazel could go," thinks Peter O'Brien, "I think she didn't mind it *that* much because Hazel was a talented musician."

Mary hoped to get movie deals, throughout the forties, and later a television show, but her plans seldom materialized. Decades later Barney Josephson acknowledged the futility of trying to mold Mary as he'd molded Hazel. "Mary Lou was very self-effacing. . . . If she'd had

the bounce of Hazel Scott, she'd have been *bigger* than Hazel and gotten all the publicity, because she was a better pianist. *Nobody* could
touch her, man or woman. . . . That she didn't emphasize showmanship was the only thing that held Mary back. I know, one afternoon, I
tried to show Mary what I wanted her to do. It was a matter of repeating things over and over again to excite people. Mary got mad. I tried
to get her to sell what she had by playing to the audience, but Mary
wouldn't sell herself that way." O'Brien agrees: "She didn't *want* the
limelight. Mary Lou was *not* a performer. She would barely speak or
take a bow, and she didn't and couldn't sing. She just didn't have the
kind of personality that grabs the mike and holds the attention."

Occasionally, she would break out of her shell. "One night at the
Café I made up my mind to try a song," Mary remembered. "I went out
on the floor and began singing 'You Know, Baby.' Even the guy in the
men's room came to see what was happening. Word got to Barney at
Café Uptown and he came down hoping to dig the next performance.
But I had sobered up quite a bit by then and refused to sing again."
Indeed, there are only rare examples of Mary's mild, pleasant voice on
record.

"She was more than just a damn piano player," O'Brien emphasizes. "She was black, a woman, and an artist. And people often didn't
understand her because of this. Mary knew just how musical *she* was
and how she couldn't become a star. I don't know if she *understood* it,
but she *knew* it. And it hurt."

———

ALTHOUGH JOHN HAMMOND had been key in getting Mary into Café
Society, and was highly influential as a record producer, Mary was as
wary of his interference in her artistic life as she was of Barney Josephson's. For all her ambition to get a recording contract with a major
label—something she wrote about repeatedly in her diary—she
chafed in his company, wary of his very fixed opinions about musicians and his insistence that others fall in line. (Nor was she alone in
this. "Hammond himself said that it 'nearly broke Basie's heart' when
he had to fire a man to take on one of Hammond's discoveries," writes
James Lincoln Collier. Teddy Wilson, when he was leading his excellent orchestra, reportedly turned down a steady job at the Café before
Mary, because, he said, "I would have to take his men, his personnel.

He wouldn't take the men out of my big band." (Mary knew all of the musicians well.) Like Teddy Wilson, Duke Ellington, Louis Armstrong, and Benny Goodman later in his career (though Goodman was Hammond's brother-in-law), Mary withdrew from Hammond's orbit. All during the forties, when Mary was writing stunning music and Hammond was in charge of jazz production at Columbia, Mary seems to have made no more recordings for him: her last one was a 1939 entry, the swing-era pieces "Little Joe from Chicago" and "Margie," only recently released for the first time. Though she admired Hammond's political commitment, including a trip he made down south to support the Scottsboro boys during that famous trial, she later maintained that the best way to be friends with him was not to be around him. However, by the 1970s, John Hammond was once more a keen supporter of Mary's music and facilitated record dates for her.

"I don't think she could have conformed to his idea of what the music was supposed to be like," thinks Peter O'Brien. "He would have wanted to continue to record her only if she kept playing like the Mary Lou of '36 and '38. Here was a really intelligent person, a creative artist who did not produce on demand, but from inside herself. But this was not allowed black women in that period." However, it is possible that Hammond was the executive producer for a date Mary did for Mercury in 1948—two recently discovered, very good bop arrangements she made of "Just You, Just Me" and "Just an Idea," her own composition. Mary recalled later that there had been some "unpleasantness" on that date, cutting short the project, and the two tunes languished in the record company vaults for fifty years. (Happily, they have finally been issued.)

For a good deal of her career, though certainly in the 1940s, music critics seemed uneasy about how to categorize a black female jazz composer. A review in *Time* magazine when Mary first played Café Society in June 1943 is larded with a patronizing attitude (not the less objectionable because it is unconscious), headlining Mary as a "Kitten on the Keys," and describing her as a "sinewy young Negro woman playing the solid, unpretentious, flesh & bone kind of jazz piano that is expected from such vigorous Negro masters." This about a woman who was producing highly sophisticated versions of Ellington, Gershwin, and her own richly harmonic pieces! Another review of Mary at

Café Society merely called her the "plain unassuming girl who plays a solid boogie-woogie."

Although Mary waited in vain for a major label to sign her on, in 1944 she began a unique and very productive association with the record producer Moses (Moe) Asch, who presided over his own small, idiosyncratic record company. Over the years, he went on to produce a huge and far-flung group of recordings for his labels, Asch, Disc, then Folkways (today Smithsonian Folkways). After beginning a career recording Jewish folk material, Asch became a jazz and then a folk enthusiast and recorded, besides Mary, Art Tatum, Erroll Garner, Lead Belly, Burl Ives, Woody Guthrie, Pete Seeger, and many others. Moe Asch gave Mary carte blanche for the next several years. "Anytime she wanted to record all she had to do was call him," recalls Johnnie Garry. Asch would see that everything was set up, turn on the recording equipment—and leave the room. "He never told a musician how to record or what to do," Mary said admiringly. "If you burped, he'd record that." For this she loved Moe Asch. It was almost like having her own record company without the financial and administrative headaches. Also important, Asch was well ahead of his time in terms of his overall presentation of the material. "He provided his albums with background notes, cover notes, lyrics to the music; records that were superbly packaged," noted a connoisseur of early record cover art.

The downside of Asch's laissez-faire approach was that everything was done on the cheap. Distribution of the records was limited, nothing was spent on advertising, and the inferior materials he used to make his records doomed them to wear out quickly. Certainly his musicians didn't get rich working for Asch; Mary had to ask repeatedly for her money. But Asch, for all his economies, often simply didn't have it to give. "The poor guy," Mary wrote, "never quite made it financially because he was too nice to musicians, paying their price even if he had to sleep out in the rain. He'd always treat musicians to big steak dinners and drinks. Some deserved this but many did not." And, she admitted, "We ruined a couple of sessions being too high."

By 1948, in fact, Moe Asch was bankrupt, and Mary was out of a record company. Regrouping, Asch decided to avoid competition with the major labels producing jazz and turned to folk music exclusively. Nevertheless, the volume of her recording for Asch from 1944 to 1946 meant that she received more royalties over the years from Asch than from any other record company during her lifetime. "Moe Asch was the only one who would record me in the forties," she told Peter O'Brien. She was hardly exaggerating.

In 1944 alone, she produced a total of twenty-five sides for Asch on his Disc label. On the first session that winter, she recorded solos of three favorites she had recently arranged for Ellington, and again for Harold Baker with her short-lived combo—"Blue Skies," "Caravan," and "Yesterdays," charming examples of Mary at the peak of her swing playing (though unreleased until half a century later). In March, she recorded with Café Society's house band, including the fine trumpeter Frankie Newton, arrangements with creamy voicings and mellow harmonies, including an original, "Satchel Mouth Baby" (later called "Pretty Eyed Baby"), and "Yesterday's Kisses" with clarinetist Edmond Hall. In April, she recorded more solos, including of her own "Mary's Boogie" and "Drag 'Em" (a.k.a. "New Drag 'Em Blues"), and her fine arrangement of "St. Louis Blues" called "Handy Eyes."

Back in the studio that summer, with a septet that included Don Byas on tenor, Dick Vance on trumpet, Vic Dickenson on trombone, Claude Greene on clarinet, and her preferred rhythm players from Café Society, Al Lucas on bass and Jack Parker on drums, Mary recorded her swing-style bouquet to the photographer Gjon Mili ("Gjon Mili Jam Session") and a co-composition with Don Byas ("Man O'Mine," which quite possibly was also titled "My Last Affair"). And again she reworked a favorite in "Stardust," taking two quite different approaches, one a languid piano feature, the other by ensemble.

In July, Mary rested, but in August she was back in the studio as a trio with bassist Al Hall and trumpeter Bill Coleman—with novel arrangements of six standards. The interplay between the musicians was hand-in-glove; after he heard that August date and the one that followed in December, Dizzy Gillespie wanted her to do a similar record with him (it didn't happen). Mary's muse was in an impish mood that summer. The music was full of high spirits, even near-slapstick at times: for example, in "Russian Lullaby," Bill Coleman shouts "Oh heave ho!" before Mary launches into a brilliant spring cleaning of the tune. On "Persian Rug" (where, for some reason, Al Hall is made to play at the top of his bass in what is apparently a cuckoo-clock imitation), the melody is cleverly interwoven with "It Ain't Necessarily So" and ends with a laughing trumpet. Mary's composition "You Know, Baby" is a droll send-up of sexiness and the popular boogie-woogie style that bored her, a tune complete with air kisses and grunts. But it is "Night and Day" that best displays her wit. A piano introduction that sets the melody straight on its head is followed by a mellow trumpet reading of the melody, a quick bass solo, and a trio reading, before again turning the melody upside down. "Night and Day" ends with a rumba rhythm and a last "ha ha, ha ha" from Coleman's merry trumpet. Many years later, a reviewer judged these records, and Mary's solos in particular, to be "full of joys—brilliant flourishes and treble calligraphies in 'Blue Skies' and 'Persian Rug,' sardonic boogie in 'You Know, Baby' . . . [and a] readiness to vary the mood by changes of tempo that bespeaks an artistic approach to arrangement and a bold challenge to the functional image of jazz to which few could rise in those days."

But it was a very different musical kettle of fish in December. Or rather, *kettles*. The first was "The Minute Man," a weak excuse for a patriotic song on which Josh White sang flat and Mary dutifully laid down chords, with yet another version of "Froggy Bottom" thrown in on the B side. (She had produced another overtly political tune the previous August, "The Ballot Box Boogie in the Time of Franklin D," in support of FDR's reelection.) The important musical business came a few days later, when Mary made her only recording with Coleman Hawkins on tenor saxophone (Bill Coleman was on trumpet again, along with Eddie Robinson on bass and Denzil Best on drums, Joe Evans on alto sax, and Claude Greene on clarinet on "Song in My Soul" and "This and That," Greene's tune). Mary, Bill Coleman, and Coleman Hawkins were three of a minority of prominent swing-era musicians who had begun to explore the then revolutionary musical challenges to the status quo, the new music that came to be called bop. Mary's "Song in My Soul" was a new and sophisticated blues lament, beautifully played by Mary (though it could be heard in a better arrangement the following year on her radio program, with a vocal added, sung by the young, Billie Holiday–ish Sylvia Sims). Despite its unfortunate title, "Carcinoma" (formerly called "Cancer," for the sign in the zodiac) was lovely, "a slow, insinuating riff opus with a delightful atmosphere," as reviewer Barry Ulanov described it in *Metronome*.

But the *pièce de résistance* of that session was Mary's arrangement of "Lady Be Good," in which the melody is disguised. Here is the first concrete evidence of Mary's shift from swing to the new style of jazz—the rather boppish figures with their "modern" oddness of turns and shifts in phrasing and even in her voicings. "Lady Be Good" signaled her deepening involvement in a more demanding, more sophisticated brand of jazz.

————

IT WAS PROBABLY no coincidence that the music sparkled so much on the Asch recordings in '44, for Mary was involved in a new love affair. Until she settled in New York and began to perform at Café Society, Mary had lived and loved in a largely self-contained black world in which whites existed, for the most part, only as exotics, criminals, or authority figures—cops, theater owners, managers, agents, record producers: white males who controlled a musician's destiny. Some white musicians, natural bohemians like Mary and her friends, had slipped through the fence of race and racism to become her friends, colleagues, or admirers, but they were exceptions.

Then came Café Society, the epicenter of a new exchange between blacks and whites. Mary made friends with men and women from all kinds of backgrounds she had never really known before. And there was David Stone Martin—DSM, as he signed his paintings. Very tall, very thin, with blond hair and a big fluffy mustache, he was a night owl, a drinker, an iconoclast, a gifted artist with a social conscience who instinctively related deeply to jazz and musicians. With a studio a few blocks from Café Society, he soon became a habitué of the club—and fell in love with Mary. He was probably her first white lover, at a time when interracial love affairs were unusual, even in places like Greenwich Village. Just as unusual, he was probably her first *non-musician* lover.

But they had a great deal in common. Both were child prodigies— he had shown unmistakable talent at the drawing board as a little boy. And for both, art was a passport—he from Chicago, the son of a Presbyterian minister. They were about the same age (he was three years younger), and both were committed to the reality of equality for all Americans. Both had also gone hungry for their art. The older artist Ben Shahn had fanned Martin's passion for social realism; later, he was lucky to get work painting murals on power houses for the TVA, and on public buildings for the WPA, in Chicago, during the Great Depression.

It was not long after that Martin took his first wife, Thelma (he would have three), and two young sons and moved to the East Coast to work as an artist, drawing distinctive, heavy black-ink portraits for *Life* and later for the covers of *Time* before photographs became standard. While Martin's family was ensconced in Roosevelt, New Jersey, he also kept for himself his Village studio. There, he and Mary kept their rendezvous after her Café Society work ended in the wee small hours.

Mary's love life was no less entangled than his. Even as her husband, Harold Baker, entertained his former fiancée down south on weekend passes from the army base where he was stationed, Mary had taken up with tenor saxophonist Herschel Evans, according to bassist John Williams, who knew her well. But David Stone Martin was attractive on several counts. He courted her attentively at the Café, he had a quick, mordant sense of humor. Crucially, too, he listened to music almost the way a musician would and he knew what it meant to her. And he also intrigued her as an artist in a completely different medium. They became good friends right away. "He had an apartment close by in the Village and he rented a piano for me to play or write music while he painted," Mary wrote primly. During the day, they would sometimes meet in Central Park for lunch, Mary wearing the dress and heels that were at that time de rigueur.

A public liaison between a white man and a black woman was still taboo. And for all its social and political progressiveness, even Greenwich Village could be quite an unwelcome place for blacks. A young Sarah Vaughan, just starting her career, was roughed up by street thugs after a performance at the Café one night. Nor was the club itself always safe. "We had plenty of southern soldiers come in there, and plenty good fist fights in that place," reminisces Johnnie Garry. "A guy once dropped a champagne bucket of water on Mary—he was nuts, drunk. We took care of *him*."

Mary and Martin were set upon, too. As Mary wrote, "One night we left the club to go to the next block to get some spaghetti, and three soldiers—Southerners—got mad when they saw him with me and started jumping on him. Poor David—he couldn't defend himself too well, but afterwards he laughed."

Chafing against the constraints of marriage and family, mesmerized by Mary's beauty and brilliance, Martin plied her with love letters, often written after she had left his Village studio to go uptown to her apartment. "I will love you always *in spite of* my fashion," he wrote in

one. He was the pursuer, she the pursued, throughout the spring, summer, and fall of 1944.

[Undated]
Tuesday at 5:30 p.m.
Mary darling, I wanted to kiss you and I had a sinking feeling in
my stomach when you left in the cab. I'm going to miss you darling, more than you know. *I want you forever.* We can make each
other great people.

No rats can keep you down dearest, too many fine people
love you. The fight underneath is bigger than us but we're part
of the side that's winning. I'm sure you can trick your enemies
and your friends are solid.

You are the kind of person who has a great purpose. Most
jazz musicians are sitting on a dung heap and never will get off.
You have the ability for creative invention and the feeling for
modern music to make a big contribution to its realization.

I love you (David)

He was right: she was then in one of her most creative periods, as
he was, and they did achieve great things together. Without realizing it,
Mary launched Martin on a fabulous new career when she asked him
to do a cover for an album of 78s for Asch, something to fill the square
blank covers of the record box. The result was a moody portrait of her,
the beginning of a new art form: record cover art. Martin "was the first
visual artist to provide deeply felt imaging about jazz and jazz people."
Typically, Moe Asch not only recognized DSM's gift but gave him a free
hand. Martin went on to illustrate more than 200 record covers for
Moe Asch, and hundreds more for Norman Granz's record labels,
including Verve, Clef, and Norgram, among others. And he continued
to make record covers for Mary and draw her portrait. As she wrote,
"David never forgot me and always credited me with his success." He
also remained fascinated by her high cheekbones, lustrous skin tone,
her soft, inward-gazing eyes.

But though they remained close friends, their love affair did not
last long. Martin's sad and impassioned farewell gives a rare glimpse at
the emotional turmoil that for Mary was only to build in the coming
years.

[undated]
3:00 a.m. Thursday

Mary darling—
It would be too easy to say it's finished—it's not. Even if I never
see you again you are with me like a burn in my heart. At odd
times for the rest of my life you will be my eyes suddenly moist-
ening, a sharp pain in my stomach remembering the times we
hollered together. When a big lump rises in my throat I will
remember the times you cried in my arms. Possessive—of
course! The things we possess of each other will never be damaged—nor can they ever be shared.

*The hard times you couldn't endure, that annoyed you, that made
you evil with distrust and suspicion and hard talk—these things I cannot love about you. But those things are understandable. There are too
many wonderful things to remember.*

My life will never follow the accepted patterns even without
you. It seems so foolish and unnecessary being without you.
The thought is very hard to digest. There was a big gaping hole
in my life that you filled that will never be empty again, but it
will grow to a bigger emptiness which is the loss of you—shut-
ting off the growth of love. That will be a big painful emptiness
which no one else will ever close up.

As usual, Mary kept her private life very much to herself. Friends
and colleagues could only speculate about Mary and Martin. "Sometimes you see women with a boyfriend—but not Mary Lou," emphasizes Johnnie Garry. "And I really liked David Stone Martin. But I don't
know what happened: he just wasn't around any more." "I can't keep
husbands or sweethearts. I forget about them," Mary told an interviewer soon after, with candor and a peculiar kind of resignation. "I
forget about friends, too. I guess the only thing I really love is music."
If Martin wrote with regret about his lost intimacy with Mary—"shut-
ting off the growth of love"—she, on the other hand, seemed relieved
when an affair was over, preferring to maintain friendships, as she did
with most of her ex-lovers. Even after he had married again, Mary visited Martin and his later, and third, wife. Yet at that time, in the mid-
forties, Mary must have felt deep regret over her inability to maintain

an intimate relationship with a man who so clearly adored her: about the time that she split with Martin, she revised and retitled a tune she'd co-written called "Man O' Mine." The new title: "My Last Affair."

But she had little time to brood about an affair, as by 1945 she was as busy as she would ever be. For a planned musical of *The Glass Menagerie* (it never materialized), to be called *Amanda's House*, she wrote at least one song, called "The Adding Machine." The previous year, radio producer Norman Corwin commissioned her to write music for Josh White for a radio drama called "Dorie," but the show was never aired. (Later, Mary wrote incidental music for a popular variety show, also produced by Corwin, called "We the People.") She had lengthy engagements, six nights a week, at Café Society; benefit performances all over town for the Red Cross, war orphans, soldiers, and so on; radio appearances for Mildred Bailey and Paul Whiteman's shows; plus her own radio show and even a part in a Broadway revue. As if that weren't enough, it was also the year that she wrote and arranged her set of twelve pieces called *The Zodiac Suite* for a chamber-jazz ensemble at Town Hall (discussed in the next chapter).

So it was a time of constant work for Mary, and 1945 was a year of changes. She began to appear at Café Society's sister club, Café Society Uptown. Where Downtown was relaxed and casual, Uptown, located on East Fifty-eighth Street, was chic, attracting a far different clientele that wouldn't ordinarily go down to the Village. That club, too, was a success, until it was sold in 1947 and became a bistro, Le Directoire, which featured French music. (The buyer was Josephson's downtown rival, Max Gordon, of the Village Vanguard. Le Directoire quickly failed.)

The entertainers and political leftists who'd made Café Society Downtown a success tended to look down their noses at the East Side venue as pretentious, more suited for squares. "Downtown was the more soulful, more of a jazz club, more intimate and less stiff. You would never have Meade Lux Lewis or Pete Johnson uptown. It was the tuxedo crowd," says Johnnie Garry. "So who does he take with him as piano player? He takes Hazel Scott. If you were Mary Lou, you would have to resent that." Then in late 1945, when Hazel Scott left to marry Adam Clayton Powell, Jr., Josephson installed her as Scott's reluctant replacement. "After the waiters and so on heard I was on my way uptown after Hazel Scott left, they tried to discourage me. They said the club was a jinx. I tried to get Barney to hire Erroll Garner uptown and leave me downtown," she added.

However, Mary was a success on East Fifty-eighth Street, both with the audience and musically. She was surrounded by old friends in the house band—clarinetist and leader Edmond Hall (whom Benny Goodman used to drop in to hear), the exquisite Ellis Larkins on piano, "Mouse" Randolph on trumpet, John Williams on bass. Already moving away mentally from the swing-era music that made her a draw, she experimented with new arrangements for the house band to ease her swing colleagues into the modern sounds that were fascinating her after hours. Among her arrangements was a version of "Tempus Fugit," Bud Powell's composition that Mary claimed he dedicated to her (these arrangements have not been located). In the spring of the year, Mary got tremendous publicity from her weekly radio show on WNEW, which Teddy Wilson had turned over to her before leaving New York to tour. She and Wilson were among several black pianists—Billy Taylor was another—who gained invaluable exposure over the airwaves. Television was not yet popular, and film work was scarce. If Hazel Scott's cameos in movies from that era had to be excised when they were shown in the Deep South, radio was like the "blind screen" auditions that orchestras later adopted (with the result that far more female, black, and uncomely musicians were hired). "You couldn't see the performers," Taylor remarks pointedly of radio.

Mary's half-hour show on Sunday afternoons consisted of several piano pieces, solo or with a rhythm section, and guest appearances by various Café Society performers, accompanied by Mary and her combo. On many weeks, Mary introduced a short new solo dedicated to a sign of the zodiac. After an initial run of twelve weeks, response by listeners was so good that her contract was extended. She was at the peak of her New York fame.

Fortunately, a good number of those radio shows were taped. And while many of the indifferently talented guests, and certainly the announcers' plummy, pseudo-English accents, date those 1945 radio shows, Mary's playing remains fresh and uncontrived. There was often a kind of amateur-night quality to the proceedings—the star Josh White sang duets with his frantically off-key little daughter, Bunny, and so on. Even Mary sang from time to time, in her soft, shy voice—her own compositions, like "It's Amazing," a pre-bop goof, and "You Know,

Baby." The shows contain some simply outstanding examples of her ability as a musician, as when she played an incredibly swift and witty Gershwin medley, and her continued honing of arrangements of favorites like "Honeysuckle Rose" and "Limehouse Blues." And although she didn't record bop till two years later, she provided modern accompaniment on April 11th for "Put Another Nickel In," sung by Joe Carroll, and on "It's Amazing."

While her radio show and performances at both Cafés were going full-tilt, and while she was running to do benefits between sets, Mary was offered that featured role in a Broadway revue—her first.

For all her success—and in part because of it—a shadow had begun to appear behind Mary's shy smile, and she often had a tired, sad expression that became more noticeable as the forties wore on. There was her hectic schedule, of course. But the failure of her love affairs pointed also to an exhaustion that was fed by long-standing emotional and psychic conflicts. Then, not long before *Blue Holiday* was to open, Mary suddenly stopped performing at Café Society. The rumor swirled that she had been hospitalized for drug use. Hospitalized, yes; but not for drugs. Rather, she had abruptly decided to have a nose job, as a few close friends later learned. As Johnnie Garry recounts: "She calls, she's in the Lincoln Hospital, you gotta come get me. I get her and she was all bandaged up like a mummy. I brought her to her apartment, I said, 'Who mugged you?' " Mary replied: " 'You better never tell this 'til the day I die. I had a nose job. But you tell Barney I was in a car accident.' Then I had to take her back to the hospital and they had to re-break it because it didn't come out right." Concerned and mystified, Josephson showed up at her apartment, offering her the name of lawyers who could help her sue after the "accident," but Mary sent him away, arousing his suspicions that there had been no car accident but a deliberate and misguided attempt to make herself more glamorous. "It looked grotesque," he complained. "She was much more attractive with her own nose."

If Josephson was right to mistrust Mary's story, the truth was darker than he supposed: her nose had been broken when she was punched in the face during an argument. It was only many years later that the truth came out. Jazz musicians are as protective and clubby as any other fraternity, with a great many closet doors slammed shut to this day. "One time when she was working at Café Society, Barney Josephson told me she came in with these big shiners," recalls Peter O'Brien. "But not a word was said by either party. She just went on and played." But bassist John Williams, who was in the house band at Café Society Uptown, eventually divulged the identity, if not the name, of the culprit: "That bass player with Eddie Heywood; he broke her nose. He was from Florida, came to New York with the Sunset Royal entertainers." This was Al Lucas, one of Mary's closest playing partners at the time. Why did he hit her? Nobody from that time knows for sure; but Lucas was at times a brawler, and Mary could be a demanding leader whose criticism could cut deep. Her half-brother, Jerry Burley, with whom she was close after he settled in Manhattan in the forties, once mentioned to O'Brien that he was surprised that somebody hadn't killed her: he had often seen her deliver a stinging tongue-lashing to musicians who weren't cutting it. She was even known for throwing a punch or two herself, for when pushed too far Mary could be a formidable opponent. "I come on like a bear," she said proudly. The pianist and bandleader Phil Moore, who developed many careers, learned this at Café Society, where at one point he led the band. "He had a big diamond ring," says Johnnie Garry. "My job every night was to wash and wipe off the piano keys, get the dust off them and stuff. And there would be these big nicks on the keys from his ring. Mary asked him, 'Would you take that ring off? I'm cutting my hand.' But he didn't. He was arrogant that way. And then one night she did cut her hand, and she got up off the piano and walked over and punched him in the mouth. She was for *real*. I tell you, Mary Lou was the only thing that kept me in this business. And, after that nose operation she was OK—we laughed about the whole thing."

———

THE BROADWAY VENTURE, mounted at the Belasco Theater in May of 1945—first called *The Wishing Tree* (after the great tree in Harlem that was a talisman for black performers), and then *Blue Holiday*—was meant to be a vehicle for Ethel Waters's comeback. She had not had a good part in several years and was anxious to reestablish herself as the star she'd been in *Cabin in the Sky*. Unwisely, perhaps, she insisted on opening her new all-black show at the same time as her rival, Bill "Bojangles" Robinson, was opening his—*Memphis Bound*. After years of few opportunities on the Great White Way, the theater was opening up again for African-American actors: Paul Robeson had scored as Othello on Broadway, Canada Lee had played Caliban in *The Tempest* and a role in Alfred Hitchcock's film *Lifeboat* with Tallulah Bankhead.

Not only did the name of the show change; so did its cast, and it was finally decided to simply use Café Society talent. Besides Mary (who played two numbers), there was Josh White, dancer Josephine Premice, the Hall Johnson singers, comic Willie Bryant, and Katherine Dunham's dance troupe. The pit band, with the awful name of "The Chocolateers," featured Benny Morton, Wilbur De Paris, and a young Billy Taylor on piano. Though a press release promised music by Duke Ellington and Yip Harburg, it was apparently written by Al Moritz, who had conceived the revue and found the backers. (There was, however, at least one Yip Harburg–Earl Robinson tune, "Free and Equal Blues," sung by Josh White.)

Ethel Waters worked frantically to pull the revue together, redoing the choreography—"which improved it, though not much," wrote Mary. "The whole thing was kind of thrown together." And the cast, Mary recalled later, treated Ethel Waters as an "old has-been" (though she was not yet fifty!), laughing at her star airs. (Five years later, Waters had her revenge with a glorious comeback in the Carson McCullers play *The Member of the Wedding*.) *Blue Holiday* folded after five nights. But if the reviewers complained that the show lacked continuity and conviction, they also singled out outstanding performances. "We could listen forever to the piano-playing of Mary Lou Williams, but in *Blue Holiday* she does exactly two numbers," mourned critic Irene Kittle. Billy Taylor, down in the pit, recalls that she was "on stage with her trio for about six or eight minutes. And she was so great that she held her spot *simply by her music*—which was a very impressive thing to do for a theatrical, *visually* attuned audience." "As usual," Mary wrote resignedly, "I went back to work at the Café."

All summer she continued working constantly—at the Café, with Josh White doing USO service shows for black soldiers and sailors, plus the radio show. Little wonder that in August, Mary collapsed. "When I went into the Café I was weighing 163 pounds. Someone told me to go on a Benzedrine diet. Not knowing the effects, I felt that it was harmless. And also I needed something since I never got any sleep at all—I worked all night and jammed all morning. Well at first the tablets gave me a lot of vitality and took away my appetite. But in about 10 days I couldn't eat at all and was having chills. I lost a lot of weight and looked skinny and sickly. This one night before we went on, I took two tablets of Benzedrine plus black coffee. On stage, I blacked out and fainted. Back at the club Barney sent for the doctor. He gave me something to counteract the drug and sent me home for a week." Although she stopped taking pills, Mary, driven by a deeply felt need to be taken seriously as a musician, was unable to stop pushing herself hard.

Chapter Ten
The Zodiac Suite
1945–1946

IN 1942, WHILE still with the Clouds of Joy, Mary borrowed an astrology book from a bandmate and became intrigued with the possibilities of writing psychological portraits of musicians she knew based on their sun signs. "I wrote 'Scorpio,' 'Taurus,' and 'Gemini,' not finishing the rest until years later," she recalled. Given her predeliction for the supernatural, the zodiac seemed an ideal vehicle for Mary as a composer.

Since her *Zodiac Suite*, first recorded in the summer of 1945, several jazz musicians have titled tunes after sun signs. (The English classical composer Robert Forsythe, Mary later learned, also wrote a suite about the zodiac.) But at the time she produced her suite, it was a unique idea in jazz that generated much interest, especially when she attempted to cross over into classical ground in the compositions. On December 30, 1945, the afternoon before New Year's Eve, she presented *Zodiac* for chamber-jazz ensemble at Town Hall. This was followed six months later at Carnegie Hall by a full-scale arrangement of three of the pieces for piano and symphony orchestra. As Dan Morgenstern observes of the latter event, "The concert marked the first time, to the best of my knowledge, that a *symphony orchestra* performed music by a genuine jazz composer." (Emphasis added.) Not the first time jazz apeared at Carnegie Hall, however: in January of 1943, two and a half years before Mary's symphonic debut there, Ellington and his orchestra performed his groundbreaking *Black, Brown and Beige,* his first concert on America's premier concert stage. Classical critics tended to pan *Black, Brown and Beige,* saying that Ellington, along with other jazz composers, lacked sufficient formal training to deal with the structural cohesion required in longer works. Mary and her *Zodiac Suite* were criticized along the same lines by some.

There can be little doubt that Mary's ambition to mount a symphonic work orchestrated for instruments not usually associated with jazz was fired by Ellington's potent example. Like Ellington, Mary refused to take a backseat as a composer because she wrote from the jazz tradition—in other words, black music. *The Zodiac Suite,* she wrote, was "the beginning of a real fulfillment of one of my ambitions. As a composer and musician, I have worked all my life to write and develop serious music that is both original and creative." Acutely aware of much of the musical establishment's general disdain for jazz, she wrote with satisfaction about the reception by jazz musicians of her Town Hall concert of the suite in a letter to Joe Glaser: "From *Zodiac,* I received the name of musicians' musician instead of the Boogie Woogie Queen."

––––––––

IN EXPANDING THE twelve pieces of *Zodiac* from solo and trio works to instrumentations for chamber-jazz, Mary indulged a passion for the darker, rich colors of the orchestral palate, what Gunther Schuller described as "a grand love affair with the bass clarinet." It was a love affair that endured; she afterwards wrote many arrangements for woodwinds. And although Mary employed modern jazz techniques, as Billy Taylor has observed of her then-innovative use of the rhythm section, she had also recently immersed herself in the work of twentieth-century symphonic composers—Bartok, the French impressionists, the German modernists. *Zodiac* represents a synthesis of everything she had absorbed to that point, while it is at the same time forward-looking—for instance, as a critic notes, her use of the "many pedal-point ostinatos developing into a blue-boogie played in thirds reminiscent of Miles Davis' 1959 'Kind of Blue.' "

Having written three signs by 1945, Mary simply improvised many of the other nine during her WNEW live radio show. "I thought perhaps I'd have all of them finished by the time they were aired but unfortunately I had ceased to think. On WNEW, I'd just compose them while I was playing during the broadcasts and Al [Lucas, bass] and Jack [Parker, drums] followed without missing. I'd nod my head when I wished for them to stop." The radio audience responded enthusiastically, and in June of 1945, Mary recorded the signs for Moe Asch, as solos or with Lucas and Parker.

"Aries" was intended to reflect the qualities of Ben Webster and Billie Holiday. They were "moody pioneers; people who create sounds and things you've never heard before." Taurus was Mary's and Duke Ellington's sign, also Ellis Larkins's. Taurans, Mary wrote, are "creative, lovers of the arts. They procrastinate, but they also know in what direction they're going. That's real jazz. I have tried to portray the stubborn quality. My music for the Sign of the Bull begins and ends with the same theme to indicate the personality that only changes when it is forced to do so." The music is soft, understated, with an underlying deep wistfulness, and the gorgeous chords of the 6-bar theme framing "Taurus" pay obvious homage to Ellington (though for some reason she also included a quote from "Penthouse Serenade," not an Ellington composition). "Gemini" was meant to be a sketch of Harold Baker. "He is described 'playfully' with a bit too much to drink," Mary wrote. "He'd get real barrelhouse and then gentle and playful again. These people are at home doing 'two things at one time' and so in my music I have used two themes, in discord—the bass moving in one direction and the piano in the other—but equally balanced to set the pattern of those born under the Sign of the Twin."

"Cancer," dedicated to alto saxophonist Lem Davis, then working with pianist Eddie Heywood at Café Society, was supposed to reflect "the order, peace and tranquility in the Sign of the Crab." The chamber version at Town Hall featured a beautiful solo by Ben Webster. "Leo," a bit of pomp and fanfare, was written for one of her favorite trombonists, Vic Dickenson. Leos are "proud and very strong," Mary wrote, "born to rule. Leos really know what they're doing." The opening chords of the piano solo version were given "a trumpet-like effect to set the stage" and expanded to a fanfare for the chamber group. "Virgo" was the "jazziest" of the signs; its "flowing rhythms and running chords suggest those people who seem to have more intellectual than emotional personalities." "Libra" represented no less than six heavy-weights: Art Tatum, Dizzy Gillespie, Bud Powell, Thelonious Monk,

Charlie Parker, and, later, John Coltrane. "Framed by a 1 2-bar prelude and ending that structurally display the balance for which that constellation is known," Mary said in the liner notes, it was "written in a harmonious and melodic mood." "Libra," "the sign for those who love beauty and art," was beautifully orchestrated for reeds (flute, oboe, clarinet, and bassoon), and brass (French horn, trumpet, and trombone), as well as strings (cello and double bass), piano, and drums. "Scorpio," one of the first pieces Mary wrote, was "the sign of those who are creative, intense and passionate," such as Ethel Waters, Katherine Dunham, Al Lucas. She set the music to this sign "in a strong and forceful pattern to indicate some of the moods which they follow," stressing "tonal intensity." This was one of Mary's most successful "signs"; she wrote and recorded several arrangements: for trio; a fifteen-piece ensemble version; and a seventy-piece orchestral version—all three in '45 and '46—as well as a score intended for Ellington's orchestra. An octet version recorded by bassist Oscar Pettiford for the Bethlehem label in the fifties is outstanding.

Mary sketched "Sagittarius" for pianist Eddie Heywood, and while it is among the most interesting musical experiments of the twelve, it is at the same time one of the least satisfactorily developed. "I set this piece in a triumphant and varied mood for those headed for 'success and glory.' And I made the bars of the music as full and resounding as possible to achieve the kind of effect I wanted," wrote Mary. But the piece, never achieving resolution, falls flat. "Capricorn," for dancer Pearl Primus and trumpeter Frankie Newton, was one of Mary's favorites, "the most ominous of all the movements because Capricorns are very good people, very deep people, very sad people. When they become discouraged, they go down, down, down. This has a mood to it and I knew the people." Built on "Yesterdays," a favorite tune of hers, "Capricorn," as Mary described it, "is written with a dirge-like, half hammer beat, and it builds slowly to suggest a deliberate and headstrong personality." But like "Sagittarius," its ending is inconclusive.

"Aquarius," dedicated to Josh White and Eartha Kitt, was written as "a light, happy and jovial composition written for outgoing people," the opposite of the brooding and heavy "Capricorn" (but both reminiscent of Gershwin's piano "Preludes"). "Aquarius," too, lacks a developed structure. "Pisces," on the other hand, written for bassist Al Hall (and for Barney Josephson), was deliberately free-form, an airy waltz reminiscent of Brazilian composer Heitor Villa-Lobos's "Bachianas," the sole "sign" to include a vocal, sung by operatic soprano Hope Foye. "It's a tricky sign," Mary wrote. "I composed this while broadcasting one Sunday afternoon on the radio show. There is no set theme pattern written for this composition, because I think of Pisces people as freedom-loving and imaginative. Of course, those influenced by this sign are thought to be arrogant too—and as the music unfolds I have injected those notes which I thought best captured the spirit of these people."

––––––––

IF THE CHIEF drawback of some of the pieces was their fragmentary nature, the piano solo and trio version of *Zodiac* that Mary recorded builds a whole demonstrably greater than its parts, a lovely, lingering meditation. Jazz reviewers generally responded favorably: the attractively packaged album of 78s, with a portrait by David Stone Martin, was chosen as the "Record of the Month Club Selection" by *The Record Review*, which described *Zodiac Suite* as a "series of vividly evocative tone-poems in the jazz idiom," adding that "fortunately she has not confined herself to jazz but uses modern symphonic composition."

By the time Mary began work on her new arrangements of *Zodiac*, with her vision of a concert-hall setting, she and DSM were no longer lovers, though he remained a close friend. The new man in her life was Milton Orent, a bass player with formal training in the classics who assisted her in scoring *Zodiac* both for chamber ensemble and then for symphony orchestra.

Mary had met Orent right before she quit the Clouds of Joy, when he prepared a couple of arrangements for the band, and she ran into him again after she and Martin had parted. Orent had become a staff arranger for NBC radio, a job he hated. "If he had to do a score for Kate Smith or someone like that, he'd have the wildest things imaginable on it," Mary recalled. "I'd say, 'Milt, you can't do that, she can't sing on top of that!' And he'd shout, 'I'm sick of this!' and start throwing paper. Milt was so far out they finally fired him."

Orent served as a kind of inspiration for Mary. While other friends, like Gray Weingarten, recall listening to symphonic music (as well as jazz) with Mary, with Orent she could talk about the music technically. "I studied with Milt," Mary wrote. "In the latter part of 1945 we used to visit the library on East 58th Street and listen to music with earphones, reading scores—Hindemith, Schoenberg, Berg and all of the German composers. Milt made a present of a few scores and records. The reason I was so ahead in modern harmony was that I absorbed from Milt. He knew so much about chords and things. He knew a great deal about Schoenberg, Hindemith, and others before it became the thing. After being around him awhile I decided to dig intellectual music." Orent had another useful talent: he was a lyricist. "It was always difficult to get him to finish anything he'd started," Mary complained, "but he was the only lyricist who actually wrote the kind of story I wanted for my music."

It was at this point too that Mary decided to take some lessons from a Russian emigré called Ray Lev who, Mary hoped, could advise her on tone production and legato technique. The experience was disastrous: like all largely self-taught musicians, Mary had acquired "wrong" approaches. She had never, for example, learned "proper" pedal technique; instead, she had absorbed the jazz equivalent—controlling the keyboard with the hands—from masters like Art Tatum. Lev, she wrote, "sneered" at her playing technique. Mary swept out in a rage. A less secure artist might have crumpled under such withering criticism, but Mary eventually became clearer about where her artistic temperament and taste lay and felt that twentieth-century Western classical music did not voice the feeling that was all-important to jazz. Except for learning strengthening exercises of the hands and fingers in the seventies, when her hands were giving her trouble because of age and illness, Mary never again sought the approval of Western classicists. With the clarity of hindsight, she added, "The more I studied, the sillier and colder I got. When I played the classical composers for musicians at my apartment, they'd say the music made them feel as if they were crazy." As for Milt Orent, attracted to jazz but trained outside it, "He was a great musician technically speaking, yet he was not too original. I lost my beat for a while after playing with him."

Their affair, though, seemed almost purely musical, and their surviving letters seem businesslike, without a whiff of the romance or passion that had suffused other relationships. Mary's friends didn't care much for Orent. "Milt was what we used to call a drag, like depressed and always trying to be hip or something," remarks Gray Weingarten. "He just, you know, smoked a lot of pot. I didn't like to be around him too much and he didn't have much to say to me." Adds Johnnie Garry, "Milt Orent was just a bass player. Mary Lou did all of the *Zodiac*—but he was her boyfriend and she gave him credit. Mary would say, 'Milt's a great arranger.' And why? Because she's got to give him *something* to do. But *I'm* saying Milt was just a bass player, and anyway, there were only two bass players she liked to play with her—Al Lucas and Al Hall." Still, Mary had always preferred to mix music and romance, and Milt Orent was useful to her and loyal—very important qualities to Mary. "Mary was very controlling," observes Gray Weingarten. "Her friends were all her friends. *She* could have her boyfriends in and out of the house, but when I got engaged, that was different: she acted as if she were losing a friend. She was very insecure." Which may be why she liked Milt Orent; he remained steadfast. Long after their affair had blown over and he had gotten married and moved away, they still worked together periodically.

Milt Orent's actual contribution to *Zodiac*'s chamber-jazz version (presented at Town Hall) may never be completely clarified. The ideas were Mary's; Orent helped with elaboration and development. Certainly, what Barry Ulanov terms the "strikingly unorthodox instrumentation of woodwinds, French horns, trumpet, trombone, strings and rhythm" was Mary's plan, exactly the kind of blend she sought in the next few years, in compositions such as "Waltz Boogie," "Elijah and the Juniper Tree," "Tisherome," "Knowledge," and "In the Land of Oo-bla-dee." And it was Mary's idea as well to write jazz-inspired lines for instruments seldom associated with jazz. Indeed, she poured a wealth of ideas into the mix with Orent's help. "Stylistically the suite is wide-ranging," wrote scholar Richard Thompson, "including 20th century European piano preludes, blues boogie-woogie, vamps, ABA sectional forms, which often contrast jazz and classical writing, free piano cadenzas, standard song progressions and forms. Throughout the suite her invention is high; each piece has an individual spirit and feeling."

To present *Zodiac*, Mary persuaded Barney Josephson to rent Town Hall at the end of 1945. Other expenses—for orchestrating and copying the music and for rehearsing the musicians—she had to beg, borrow, or pay for out of pocket (she complained she had to pay $500 alone for copyists). She had a startling amount of work to accomplish and took a leave from the Café to do so nonstop. Friends who dropped by her apartment that autumn were accustomed to finding *Zodiac* music manuscript everywhere. "She'd leave that music around on her bed," remembers Johnnie Garry, "and piled up on the floor." For the Christmas holidays, Mary's niece Helen came up from Pittsburgh. "She'd sit in a chair with her legs crossed, or else she'd stay in bed, writing music, just oblivious to everything," Helen says. "Then sometimes she'd go to a park and just sit there for hours. *Hours.* Just looking around."

If Mary put her best face on in public, recalling it as a "wonderful concert," privately she endured the anguish known to every artist who confronts the abyss between the vision and the finished work. "Everything went wrong," she wrote in a diary passage filled with anguish. When Mary was not required on stage during the performance, Helen Floyd, who was backstage, says, "I remember she ran down in the basement and hid when they were doing it." Nor was the concert hall filled. Mary blamed "the publicity man who was working on a concert the day before for drummer Specs Powell, which split the audience"; then, too, 5:30 P.M. the day before New Year's Eve was not the best time for a concert. As Mary put it, the audience consisted of "a pack of musicians, newspapermen, disc jockeys and theatre people."

Mary's favorite drummer, Jack Parker, couldn't make the date, so she substituted J. C. Heard, then also working at the Café. While Ben Webster was a brilliant choice on tenor, her friend and Hamilton Terrace neighbor "Mouse" Randolph fluffed a lot of notes. The remaining musicians were mostly symphony players—flute, clarinet, bassoon, trombone, French horn, strings. And the meeting of jazz and the classics on Mary's "Gjon Mili Jam Session" was the weakest: Mary's idea to have a jam session needed more than one rehearsal to prepare both camps for the treacherous waters of improvisation. The result was chamber players who sounded stiff with fear. Nor were they helped by the fact that Milt Orent, who conducted the concert, lost a page of music. Mary reminisced, "The long, drawn-out strings threw some of the other musicians. So the musicians began to play on the wrong page and got lost. Everyone seemed to be playing a different page and I'll never forget Ben Webster's big eyes fixed on me. I remember yelling, 'Count eight and play letter *J*.' I thought I would blow a blood vessel any second. Somehow we got out of it." Mary's characteristic wit and vitality at the keyboard were overtaken, perhaps, by her anxiety and her playing was somewhat static. After the event, she wrote, "I was sick for about a week and could not work."

Critical reaction broke fairly predictably along the classical-jazz fault line, with jazz reviewers responding more sympathetically than the sterner classical critics. Barry Ulanov was one of her most eloquent supporters, seeing *Zodiac* as further proof of the coming-of-age of the jazz composer. Though he conceded weaknesses—the concert had been underrehearsed, with sloppy ensemble work, and some weak spots in the construction—overall he regarded the concert a success. "This is the way music must go from here. Jazz cannot exist on jive and kicks and nostalgia alone; classical music will stop short unless it is infused with the warmth and drive and spontaneity of jazz. Mary Lou Williams, even if she was not altogether successful, made the case for this position almost unassailable." "Fortunately," agreed another writer, "she has not confined herself solely to the harmonic and rhythmic sequences of jazz alone, but has drawn freely from the scales and chords used so effectively in modern symphonic composition."

Classical critics tended to review Mary much less favorably. It was acceptable to use black "folk" themes in symphonic works, as composers like Gershwin and Copland did. But it was another thing entirely for a jazz composer to propose meeting the canon of Western classical music on equal ground.

Paul Bowles, the avant-garde writer who later moved to Morocco, where he wrote the *The Sheltering Sky* and other books, was also a conservatory-trained composer, and in the 1940s he wrote reviews of adventurous music. In reviewing *Zodiac Suite* for the now-defunct *Herald Tribune,* he resharpened the red pencil he had used on Ellington after *Black, Brown and Beige,* ticking off the ailments he found in *Zodiac* with a world-weary efficiency. Mary's "ambitious and sometimes amusing project was neither fish nor fowl," Bowles complained, "often purely improvisational in character, although it had all been painstakingly orchestrated." Indeed the only parts Bowles liked about *Zodiac* were the spots where Mary simply played jazz in her usual way. It was, he wrote with hardly veiled exasperation, "another attempt to bring about a wedding between French Impressionism and American jazz, a perfectly valid concept but it necessitates much more knowledge of the achievements of latter-day serious composers than is generally evident." Other reviewers concurred. For Colin McPhee, writing in *Modern Music,* "when she turns to composing in a 'modern, experimental' way, the results are naive and unfortunate."

Recent critical attention generally follows Bowles's line, while ascribing more credit to Mary's musicianship. "As pure instrumental music, it does not hold together," thinks one reviewer. "Positively speaking, however, Williams is a master of harmony and this piece demonstrates a rich chromatic language." Another writer agrees: With the exception of "Capricorn" and "Cancer"—the best examples of "a real jazz/classical integration"—Mary is "a very talented composer using disparate elements, unable to achieve formal clarity, development or a dialectic between different musical worlds, which emphasize respectively improvisation and premeditated, notated composition. This," he adds, "has always been one of the severest challenges for the jazz musician, to extend composition beyond the realm of cyclic forms without losing that essential spirit which makes jazz what it is."

Apart from the testimony of those fans and critics who were actually in the audience on December 30, 1945, there was no way of assessing *Zodiac Suite* until half a century after the concert, when Mary was no longer alive, because no recording was released until the 1990s, even though the concert was taped for a planned record issue. The reason for this has all the elements of a tragicomedy. Most likely Moe Asch had agreed to issue a record of the Town Hall *Zodiac,* and was responsible for providing a recording machine at the hall—a portable but cumbersome machine that cut acetates of live music from which record masters were then made. Immediately after the concert, Mary had fled the hall, distraught and exhausted. When she returned the next day to retrieve the acetates of *Zodiac,* they had vanished. "For the first time in the history of the hall, the records [sic] had been stolen," she wrote. "So I never heard how my music sounded." Years later, she learned what had happened, writing in a letter to a lawyer she had hired to help her retrieve copyrights, "My Town Hall recording was stolen by Timme Rosenkrantz and released on a record in Denmark on the Baronet label."

Baron Timme Rosenkrantz was one of those fabulous characters who inhabit the fringes of jazz. Affectionately called the Jazz Baron by some, not so affectionately known as the Robber Baron by others, he was very much the genuine aristocrat; indeed, it was his family name that Shakespeare gave to one of the minor characters in *Hamlet.* By the time he was born, in the early 1900s, the Rosenkrantzes retained only a remnant (but a comfortable one) of their once-great fortune. Jazz critic Dan Morgenstern, a fellow Dane, recalls as a young man seeing

Rosenkrantz's father, a venerable writer of Danish historical fiction, strolling the Tivoli gardens in a long white beard.

Timme, the classic black sheep, was a great disappointment to his family. (His waywardness was matched, if not topped, by a younger, wealthier aristocrat called the Baroness Nica de Koenigswarter, who was born a Rothschild. Both the Jazz Baron and the baroness were friends of Mary's.) Jazz and cocktails played the largest part in the baron's life; by the 1930s, he had moved to New York to be at the center of things. There he fell in love with, or under the spell of, another larger-than-life character: the clever, sexually ambiguous Inez Cavanaugh, an elegant, attractive black woman who tried her hand at several occupations and maintained an open relationship with Timme. As a journalist she wrote good descriptive pieces for *Metronome,* worked as a publicist for Duke Ellington, and wrote the liner notes to *Black, Brown and Beige,* as well as admiring notes about Mary's playing. Sometimes Cavanaugh worked as a singer. She had presence, not much voice, but was intelligent about lyrics. And she and Baron Timme started a number of business ventures: a record shop in Harlem, a radio program, a music magazine (which lasted for only one issue), a club.

Their forte, however, was entertaining. They kept a constant party going in their New York apartment. The baron's many friends found him lovable, generous, and easy to forgive—his chief fault, apparently, was the fecklessness that stemmed from his drinking. It was an era of much greater tolerance for excessive drinking, however, and the baron's charm, his genuine enthusiasm and love for jazz and jazz people balanced the sloppiness, broken promises, and so on. "Timme was never sober when I knew him, but he was a *congenial* drunk," recalls Gray Weingarten.

It was through Rosenkrantz and Cavanaugh that Gray Weingarten met great artists like Billie Holiday and subsequently befriended Mary. Chafing under the rules of her strict, well-to-do Christian Scientist family, she rebelled, falling in love with a young man named Hugh Shannon, a cabaret pianist, during the war. When Shannon was drafted into the army, Gray sent him jazz records at his request and developed her own interest in the music. "When Hugh was on leave, he took me to Café Uptown to see a very glamorous, marvelous pianist called Mary Lou Williams—Hugh was a pianist so he was a connoisseur. And Mary was part of the older scene, the Café Society set, along with players like Teddy Wilson, Eddie Heywood, Billie Holiday. She had a white, sparkling dress and she looked very beautiful. She didn't say anything, she just came out, sort of bowed and just played up a storm. It was wonderful! That was my first introduction to her. And Hugh was very friendly with Billie Holiday, so I got to know her and then the Rosenkrantzes. They had an apartment, a really far-out apartment around 32nd Street not far from Fifth Avenue. There were two lions in front of it and it was owned by an eccentric guy who collected bathtubs. A lot of very famous people came there: Langston Hughes and Duke Ellington at one point. I guess anybody who was anybody came up there, it was like a perpetual open house, just a one-room apartment with a kitchen and a bathroom. And a big piano. Quite an atmosphere. When I'd come home from college on weekends, I'd hang out there.

"I learned a lot about life at Timme's. Billie Holiday was there one night, and to my horror I walked in the kitchen just as she had a tourniquet on her arm and she was shooting up. That was my first introduction to drugs."

Rosenkrantz's unflattering nickname, the Robber Baron, resulted from his production of pirate records on labels like Baronet and New York Jazz, for sale abroad during the recording ban in the forties. "Danish guy? The thief, yeah," says Johnnie Garry. "He would hide microphones and record people at his apartment. During the war, he was doing the black market records." "I don't know what the quality of the tape was, but good for the times, probably," adds Gray Weingarten. "The equipment was right out there, on a table behind the piano. And Timme used to tape musicians at these parties at his place. He had this recorder which cut wax with a needle. I remember him taping Willie 'the Lion' Smith, for example. I'm not sure the artists were really aware that he was going to sell the stuff, or whether he told them that he would use it to get them jobs in Europe. There could have been all kinds of angles. I know *he* made money on the tapes, the musicians didn't."

But others who knew Rosenkrantz had a more charitable view of the man. Dan Morgenstern remembers the baron's love of jazz, his larger-than-life personality. Says jazz writer Chris Albertson, "In the early 60's, we were roommates in New York for a bit, but he was always disorganized and poor. He was a baron, but *he* never had any money and people ripped *him* off. I remember after the war, in Copenhagen, he had this Model T Ford without a heater. His brother would drive it and Timme would emerge from this pile of blankets in the back of the car, with piles of records to sell at the stores."

Besides acting as a record "producer," Rosenkrantz also played the impresario. "I helped him put together guys for this orchestra he wanted to take over to Europe after the war," recalls Weingarten. "All the musicians on the Street used to go to this bar on the corner of Sixth Avenue and 52nd Street for their break between sets. And there Timme would try to sign them up for his European excursion. He was drunk almost all the time I knew him. But that's where he got his orchestra together. He was promising them they'd have a great time in Europe, see all the sights and so on. Billy Taylor was the pianist hired, along with Peanuts Holland, Tyree Glenn, and Don Redman as conductor. But when they got over, their luggage was in hock because he hadn't paid certain fees. I was stuck with this band equipment he'd left me with—and the bill for sending it was about $850, a lot of money then. My mother paid for it. Also, my boyfriend Hugh had left me for a male lover around then. I was just crushed. But then I really hooked up with Inez Cavanaugh and that whole crowd in New York. It was fascinating. And one day, Inez, who knew everybody, was going up to see Mary Lou and I went along because I had a car. Inez said I needed a friend. Well, Mary Lou turned out to be a great friend to me, a confidante. After I'd gotten stuck with Timme's huge bill, I went up to see Mary Lou and told her what I had done. She told me not to expect any money back from Rosenkrantz and Inez. That was their style and they were pretty slick. She said Inez was a very clever and conniving kind of woman.

"Most everybody thinks that after *The Zodiac Suite* was played at Town Hall, that Timme definitely was the one that went backstage and simply asked for the tapes. As if he was an official and entitled to them and supposed to have them," Weingarten continues. "But nobody *saw* him do it." Confirms Chris Albertson, "Timme *did* put out something of Mary Lou's, one of her *Zodiac* pieces [retitled as the "Stars," "Moon," "Sunset" and "Sunrise," on Selmer Records] and he never paid her."

Yet the Timme Rosenkrantz–*Zodiac* connection gets curiouser and curiouser. In a plot line that no self-respecting writer would attempt, he *repeated* his theft six months later.

In the winter of 1946, Norman Granz was then at the beginning of a highly successful career as impresario of large-scale concerts called Jazz at the Philharmonic, popularly known as JATP. He approached Mary about performing in an upcoming concert. She was not interested in being one of many in a concert lineup, but she made a counteroffer. "I said, 'I'll do a concert if you get me a job playing with the New York Philharmonic symphony orchestra.' I didn't realize he was going to do it. I was just talking, you know, because we used to argue a lot when we met." Granz waffled at first: jazz with the New York Philharmonic, or any symphony orchestra? It had never been done; and it would be expensive to produce, obviously. Finally, he agreed, and worked out a deal with the Carnegie Pops Orchestra, many of whose members also played for the New York Philharmonic. However, Granz told Mary, the concert was hers on condition that she work for minimum scale *and* pay for copying arrangements for the seventy-piece orchestra herself; also, he insisted, she must include some Café Society material along with the *Zodiac*. Mary accepted. "Being determined," as she wrote, "I tried it once again." There was barely enough time to pull it together. "You talk about being scared!" she wrote. "I was shaking in my boots. I had only eight or nine days to work, and 70 pieces to score for, so I got my old friend, Milton Orent, to help out."

Orent collaborated on the orchestrations to two of the three pieces selected, "Sagittarius" and "Aquarius," but then had to leave town on a job, so Mary was left to complete the scoring for "Scorpio." "I said, 'Oh my goodness, I'll finish them myself.' He was so surprised. I had never written for a symphony in my life." For "Scorpio," she adapted the score she'd arranged for Ellington's orchestra. Then, only a day or two before the sole rehearsal in June, Mary had "this brilliant idea, this piece of craziness. This was an idea that came on at the last minute. I called Milt. 'What do you think about having the "paper men" '—her term for symphonic players—'do a jazz thing?' 'Don't do it, Pussycat,' Milt Orent warned me." Later that day, when David Stone Martin stopped by to visit, he found Mary seated on the floor with music manuscript spread out all around her, writing furiously. "I'm going to have the New York Philharmonic play a jazz boogie-woogie," she told him proudly. Martin burst out laughing. "No one knows what you'll do next."

Her decision to program a "boogie woogie" for symphony orchestra was especially dicey; she was intent on getting the classical musical world to take her seriously—as more than a "boogie woogie" pianist. "A lot of blacks felt that it was a derogatory kind of music to them," comments Gray Weingarten. "Once in 1947, Mary and I went to hear Art Tatum play up in Buffalo at a very fancy club and somebody requested a boogie-woogie. Instead, Art Tatum played a marvelous classical thing, maybe Bach, with an occasional boogie-woogie bass, just a hint of it." Mary intended to do the same. Anticipating the mixing of strings with jazz by other bop musicians, especially Charlie Parker (who in fact took great interest in what Mary was doing at Carnegie Hall), she scored for unison strings a long bebop line inspired by a Parker solo she'd heard on a record, and instructed them to play it *swingingly*.

"It was 6:30 P.M. when I began this piece of craziness," she wrote in her diary. "I had to write and copy for 100 pieces! I worked all night and went in at one the next afternoon." David Stone Martin stayed up with her all night, a kind of one-man cheerleading section. Copying music by the hour is grueling work and one can only imagine the shape her hands and finger muscles were in afterwards.

At the rehearsal the next day, June 21, Mary learned to her dismay that she had been assigned a green young conductor, Ann Kullmer, who "knew nothing about jazz and was frightened by 100 men sitting in front of her. At first, I was afraid to pass out the parts I had written for the Boogie Woogie. But then the manager, Mr. Ripp, was called away to the phone and I said to the musicians, 'Do this for me.' " The result was chaotic. She and Kullmer looked at each other, near panic. "We both at one point were shaking like a dog," wrote Mary. Mary decided that she would conduct the boogie-woogie herself after simplifying the arrangement: "I quickly changed the intro to a chord, asking Kullmer to start them and count eight beats, then cut out." Mary led the orchestra from the piano. "After the intro, I played four choruses of a fast boogie and had the four bass men moving on chords and a fifth one doubling on the tonic. After the piano chorus, I had the oboe take a solo I had written. Then, 30-some violins stood and played two choruses, the piano came in once again, then the ensemble, the works, and a piano ending." With Mary at the helm, laying down those strong, rock-steady rhythms, the musicians relaxed.

The next day, June 22, she whirled into Carnegie Hall for her performance at the "Spring Finale" of the Carnegie Pops concerts series—sandwiched between soprano Gertrude Ribla and an offering of orchestral excerpts by Gounod, Brahms, and Mendelssohn, under the baton of Herman Neuman. She opened with "Sagittarius," taking it at a considerably faster pace than at Town Hall and featuring piano rather than flutes and woodwinds. It was a curious choice: at ninety seconds, it was not much more than a fragment, and one of the least developed of the signs. Moreover, the string section sounded confused: clearly, there had not been adequate rehearsal time. But Mary's next selection (misspelled "Boogie Voogie" in the program) went over better. The strings played the looping bebop line in unison—even with a hint of swing. Mary's adrenaline was sky high. She'd played a flying piano solo introduction on the boogie-woogie; on "Scorpio," her next and best selection (save for the horror-movie background effects scored for orchestra), she began her piano introduction with a key-splintering chord, followed by more jazz-paced unison lines for the orchestra. But then "Aquarius" was taken at a near-funereal tempo that only underscored both the static quality of the piece and a hopelessly lost string section. Again Mary rallied, closing her program with a sparkling solo encore of "The Man I Love," folding bebop phrasing into advanced swing-era technique.

Mary was sailing high after the concert, writing in her diary that the musicians especially had loved playing the boogie-woogie. "And later I was asked to do more things like this. I collected my music and went home much elated." But her strong playing could not counterbalance the poor showing of the string section in particular. Like the overly ambitious fisherman's wife of the Grimms' fairy tale, who moves from hut to ever-grander abodes until she reaches too far, *Zodiac Suite* had gone from the simple to the grandiose, only to collapse under the weight of a full orchestra. With enough money, and especially with more rehearsal time, the challenges she'd set herself with *Zodiac* might well have been met. But it was a case of too little too late. The ad hoc approach she had mastered with swing bands wasn't appropriate for a symphony orchestra.

Mary had again arranged to have the Carnegie concert taped for an intended recording. Not yet aware that Rosenkrantz had purloined her Town Hall material, she wrote in her journal with unintended irony, "This time I did not forget the sides. I asked Inez Cavanaugh and her husband, the Danish Baron Timme Rosenkrantz, to guard them for me." And lo! again the acetates mysteriously disappeared. They resurfaced later, if briefly. "Timme Rosenkrantz owed me a lot of money," says Weingarten, "and gave me a whole bunch of records, his way of paying me back. Mary Lou's *Zodiac* at Carnegie Hall, a twelve-inch vinyl record with a radio station's name printed on it, was among them. And I think I may have the only copy of that record." Mary discovered that theft at the same time she learned of the previous year's. "My Carnegie Hall recording was also stolen by Timme Rosenkrantz," she wrote more than a decade later.

Mary seldom if ever spoke of that concert again. Uncharacteristically, there were no reviews of the Carnegie effort in her voluminous scrapbooks, only a program. Decades later, Mary's *Zodiac* concert at Carnegie had acquired something of a mythic quality, and some even wondered if it had really taken place! But the program and a tape recording made by Weingarten of the twelve-inch vinyl exist to attest to Mary's daring, if not completely successful, experiment with a symphony orchestra.

————

DANCERS ESPECIALLY WERE intrigued by the *Zodiac Suite* in the forties: Katherine Dunham, along with the brilliant choreographer and dancer Talley Beatty, adapted "Scorpio" for a ballet for her company. And Pearl Primus, then a young dancer at Café Society who became a friend of Mary's, adapted some of the signs for a dance series.

Nor did Mary forget her suite. "Mary expressed a desire to have the *Zodiac* played in symphonic form again," remembers Weingarten, then a student at Syracuse University. "She had all the music and I thought that it would be great to do at Syracuse. So I played my tape for a violinist who put on experimental concerts. He thought it was wonderful. I called Mary Lou and told her he'd love to do it. But she wanted too much money—$2,000, way out of the ballpark for Syracuse at the time."

Instead, Mary played portions of the suite at Syracuse with her trio as a benefit for the NAACP. "We had only a few days to put out some pamphlets and publicize it, but it went very well. She played pieces from *Zodiac*, standards, and her own boogies." Then, in 1957, after several years of near-complete absence from public performance, Mary played with Dizzy Gillespie's big band at the Newport Jazz Festival, presenting "Aries," "Libra," and "Virgo" in arrangements by trombonist Melba Liston. Later, in 1969, while she was in Rome, Mary played new arrangements of *Zodiac* pieces over Vatican Radio. And when she returned to the States a few months later, she had still another idea: to rearrange the suite for Thelonious Monk. Nothing, though, came of this intriguing plan.

———

THE ZODIAC SUITE had brought her a flurry of critical attention, and within the black community there was intense pride in her accomplishment. Mary's Carnegie performance, wrote journalist Lorna McDaniel, "completely eroded the whites-only barrier to the Carnegie Hall stage." But the commissions she'd thought would come her way did not materialize. "One of my greatest ambitions will be realized," she told an interviewer the next year, "when I am called to present some of my work at a concert with the New York Philharmonic or the Boston Symphony Orchestra." She soon learned differently. "Even if you had studied for symphonic music, there was no opening for blacks at the time in that field," she told student musicians later. Although Mary's life would be crowned by many achievements and honors, she was never invited to appear with the New York Philharmonic or the Boston Symphony.

After the Carnegie Hall venture, Mary told Barney Josephson she needed some time off from Café Society. She had been working hard for more than twenty years; she now retreated from performing. "After I left the Café, I turned down work that would have paid $400 a week, and was told I should be in a straitjacket," she noted drily. "Now," she added privately in her diary, "for a while, I'd take it easy and ball."

issues in society. All of the ongoing conflicts in America—racial, class, sexual—impacted on post–World War II America. Bop strongly signified a passionate and relentless velocity, complexity, even superiority—a breathtaking command of the idiom in the hands of the best players, who were African-Americans. The musicians themselves who were experimenting with bop intrigued Mary as well, and she made a point of getting to know them. Though she had an established reputation, especially among musicians, while they were unknowns, Mary was only seven years older than Thelonious Monk, and fourteen years older than Bud Powell.

———

ALTHOUGH MARY DIDN'T record full-fledged bop until 1947, there was plenty of evidence earlier of her interest in expanding her musical boundaries. Besides certain forward-looking harmonies she wrote while with the Clouds of Joy, she was using modern harmonies in recordings as early in 1944, and specifically in certain chord changes in *The Zodiac Suite,* in her arrangements of "Caravan" and "Stardust," and in her composition "Bobo and Doodles," which had elements of blues, boogie, and bop, including thirteenths, which were quite modern voicings for that era.

By 1946, she was clearly immersed in the possibilities of modern jazz harmonies, as shown in her recording of "These Foolish Things," and the bop-oriented charts she arranged for the house band at Café Society Uptown. "Lonely Moments," a riff-built swing tune Mary wrote in '43, was one of her favorites, and she arranged it with modern harmonies for various combinations and a piano solo. By '47, she'd written a flat-out bop version for big band (not performed in full until 1994, about fifty years later, at Carnegie Hall, although a "small" big-band version was recorded in '47) that anticipated in its judicious use of flatted fifths her best-known bop tune, "In the Land of Oo-bla-dee," written a year later. And there was her excellent "Kool," based, like so many other bop tunes of the era, on the changes of "I Got Rhythm." "Kool," writes scholar Erica Kaplan, contains "an enormous variety of rhythmic figures. . . . The florid and angular melody line is highly ornamental, utilizing frequent embellishing notes and figures as well as diatonic and whole-tone scale passages. Sharp 11ths, augmented 5ths, 13ths, and raised and lowered 9ths are prominently featured."

But for all the influence of Thelonious Monk, Bud Powell, and Dizzy Gillespie, Duke Ellington's "ultra modern phrasing" remained Mary's most important influence. "Even though the Ellington band hasn't the bop phrasing," she wrote, "what composer in the jazz field can get a jazz sound out of an oboe or flute? None but Duke." That she had a strong sense of the historical importance of the forms of black music preceding modern jazz is clear. In November of 1946, she performed with Ethel Waters in an innovative "Concert in Blue" at Cornell University, the music linked to a text prepared by a young Marshall Stearns, who would become the eminent jazz historian. Later, when Mary performed her important "history of jazz" concerts, she drew on Stearns's writing that traced jazz from slave-era spirituals.

Mary's need to communicate her rich musical heritage led her, in the mid-1940s, in another direction: teaching. She attracted many pupils, among them young Eddie Bonnemere, who had won a radio contest with his version of Mary's "Lonely Moments." She also turned many away. A flock of Juilliard students approached her in 1946, but of them she wrote, "I kept two out of this group. I felt the others should continue with the classics as they did not have much imagination."

——————

MARY HAD recorded certain important new compositions like "Kool" for Moe Asch, who continued to give her complete artistic freedom in her recordings. But she was eager both to record with a major label and to be paid reasonably well for her work, while Moe Asch continued to operate on a shoestring. Yet a lucrative record contract was still only a dim prospect, which may be why she accepted an offer from producer Leonard Feather to record some of her new originals, despite her reluctance. Feather's plan called for an "all-girl" band, which Mary viewed as a gimmick.

It was not that she didn't esteem women musicians. She had many friends and role models among women in jazz—from Lovie Austin to Lil Hardin Armstrong in the twenties; singers like Ethel Waters, Billie Holiday, and the new singer on the block, Sarah Vaughan; piano players such as Bobbie Jones, Julia Lee, Margaret Johnson, Barbara Carroll, and Beryl Booker; trumpet player Dolly Jones; and guitarist Mary Osborne, whom Feather had booked for her date as a leader. But long accustomed as she was to picking top sidemen, Mary chafed under

Feather's insistence that she use June Rotenberg and Bridget O'Flynn on bass and drums, respectively. (She would also play with bassist Bonnie Wetzel and drummer Elaine Leighton.) She did not disparage their musicianship publicly; Mary fought all her musical battles privately, almost never knocking another player to the press. But she was frankly wary about the wisdom of choosing sidemen on the basis of gender. Ironically, when June Rotenberg could not make the first recording session (for Continental Records), Feather didn't hesitate to substitute a male bassist (Billy Taylor, masquerading as "Bea" Taylor).

Later in 1946, after the Continental date, Mary made more records with Feather as producer for RCA Victor; though she was booked to play Carnegie Hall also as leader of an all-woman group, opposite Mildred Bailey and her orchestra, there is no record of such a concert.

Feather thought the combo successful enough to plan further dates (including the Atlanta concert nixed by the Georgia governor because it was a mixed-race group). But Mary bowed out of further commitments with Feather, distressed by what she termed "nasty vibrations" from certain of the musicians. The first recording session had lived up to her fears. "It was the cattiest session I'd ever encountered; the girls talked more music than they played."

When Feather managed to persuade her to record with the women again for RCA, "I said to myself, 'This time I'm going to see if they can think like a male.'" But there were "words" between the musicians, scenes in the studio. "This kind of thing upset my entire system and I kept putting future dates off." Another problem was Mary's artistic relationship with the producer, who several times imposed "his" tunes on the dates, which incensed Mary. Indeed, many years later she wrote Feather a letter in which she lambasted him for what she called his manipulativeness, coldness, and meanness.

Two of the most brilliant tunes that Mary recorded with women, either in late '47 or early '48, never made it out of the studio until discovered in Mercury's vaults nearly fifty years later. One was "Just You, Just Me," in which she reveals a firm command of Monk's techniques; the other was a modern version of "Mary's Idea." They may have been the result of a budding record deal with Mercury, an important label. As Mary later recalled, producer Mitch Miller also wanted to record her around that time, as did John Hammond.

But no deal materialized with either producer, and Mary continued to be spottily recorded, mostly by minor labels. Still, musicians and critics prized her few offerings during the rest of the decade. To pianist Billy Taylor, who met her in 1945, "Mary Lou Williams was, as usual, far-thinking." For Gary Giddins, writing in the seventies, "her bop recordings are notable for the absolute avoidance of clichés."

FROM THE TIME Mary settled in New York, in the early forties, she liked to drop by Minton's Playhouse on 118th Street. Minton's, a new club on the renovated ground floor of Cecil's Hotel, played a big part in the beginnings of bop, as did Clark Monroe's Uptown House, where younger musicians who had not yet made their mark formed the core of regulars. Thelonious Monk was the house pianist at Minton's, and Dizzy Gillespie, Charlie Parker, and Kenny Clarke were constantly in attendance, working out complex harmonies. "We all used to hang out at Minton's," Mary told Phil Schaap. "I'd go there practically every night and hang out. I only sat in once, very short, I was there listening to sounds, it was something new to me, I was absorbing it. It was the new way of playing—never heard before."

Minton's Playhouse was not too large a place—"intimate," she described it. "The bar was at the front and the cabaret in the back, and the bandstand was in the rear of the back room, with a strange painting that covered the entire wall at the back, with weird characters sitting on a brass bed, some jamming, some talking to chicks and one chick lying across the bed. I always thought the painting was out of place. During the day characters played the jukebox and danced. I used to visit frequently during the day and got a lot of laughs. One big family on 118th Street, that's how we were. The club was run by Teddy Hill, who was the manager, a bandleader at one time.

"All the bop musicians were jamming or playing there because there was no work for them on 52nd Street," continued Mary. "Nobody understood what they were playing. I lost the friendship of a lot of older musicians by hanging out with the young musicians. When bop came along they felt that it was so strange that it wasn't right, it wasn't good. You know, you always have that dissension. They didn't understand: it was so far out."

But soon the creative explosion drew other musicians, some of them inspired innovators, others talented consolidators, white as well

Mary listening to a playback at a recording session in 1948. *(W. Eugene Smith Archive, Center for Creative Photography, The University of Arizona. Copyright © The Heirs of W. Eugene Smith, Courtesy Black Star, Inc., New York)*

Mary at home, 1944.

Mary in performance at Café Society Downtown, one of the first fully integrated nightspots in New York, circa 1945.

Mary and members of her fan club at WNEW, where she had a weekly radio
show, "The Mary Lou Williams Piano Workshop," for much of 1945.

Mary at Child's Paramount Theatre, with Oscar Pettiford, bass, and unidentified drummer, in 1948.

Mary's jazz "salon" at 63 Hamilton Terrace, in 1945 or 1946. Left to right: Dizzy Gillespie, Mary, Tadd Dameron, Hank Jones, Milt Orent, Jack Teagarden's girlfriend Dixie, Jack Teagarden. *(Photograph by William P. Gottlieb. Copyright © William P. Gottlieb. From the Collection of The Library of Congress)*

Mary with *Melody Maker*
editor Max Jones in London, 1953.

At Chez Mary Lou, the old Perdido
Club, in Paris, November 1954.

Paris, spring of 1953. The Baroness Nica de Koenigswarter is between a
look-alike daughter and pianist Garland Wilson. Mary introduced
Nica to Thelonious Monk during this time.

Saxophonist Don Byas, about 1938, as a member of the Clouds of Joy. Although in love with Mary, Byas would be fired from the band, partly for his alcohol-related physical abuse of her.

Trumpeter Harold "Shorty" Baker, Mary's second husband, in the 1940s. Though they soon parted, they never divorced.

Mary with trombonist Jack Teagarden, her close friend, in 1946. Teagarden proposed marriage at least once, possibly twice. *(Photograph by William P. Gottlieb. Copyright © William P. Gottlieb. From the Collection of The Library of Congress)*

Lindsay Steele, a non-musician who was Mary's lover from 1948 until she left for Europe in late 1952.

Drummer Gérard "Dave" Pochonet, Mary's lover in France in 1954, and friend later.

Artist David Stone Martin, Mary's lover in the mid-1940s, and a lifelong friend.

Photograph taken in 1958 during the legendary "Great Day in Harlem" communal jazz photo shoot. Left to right: drummer Ronnie Free, singer Mose Allison, saxophonist Lester Young, Mary, saxophonist Charlie Rouse, bassist Oscar Pettiford. *(Photograph by Art Kane. Copyright © The Estate of Art Kane)*

as black. As in every art, there were also poseurs of hip, imitators who were happy to coopt the ideas of others and make money off them. " 'Leeches' would scribble music on their cuffs at Minton's, stealing it, and even our own guys, I'm afraid, did not give Monk the credit he had coming," Mary wrote.

The "big family" at Minton's, however, did not provide the same camaraderie for Mary as the Kansas City scene had. Her success, her age, and, to a certain extent, her gender—all were barriers, despite her assertions to the contrary. Her male colleagues respected her as an equal professionally, but trumpeter Howard McGhee, then just coming along, may have been speaking for many when he said: "When a woman is on the scene, it's different. Even with the grandmother of all the lady musicians, jazz pianist Mary Lou Williams, you really have to be extra respectful. She expects it. So if you hire women, it's just going to mean hassles."

The most profound division, however, between Mary and many of the bop musicians was not age or gender or style of playing, but their use of heroin. "It must have really hurt her, when heroin came in and she saw so many people destroyed," remarks Peter O'Brien. "She never said anything but it must have taken a toll." Marijuana was different; she, like Louis Armstrong (who smoked it every day, which Mary did not), found it calming, useful for reflecting and relaxing at times. Ironically, given the epidemic of hard drugs at the time, Barney Josephson actually fired her for smoking pot one night at Café Uptown. (He had forbidden the use of drugs of any kind in the clubs). "I was set up," she wrote, "by a jealous 'big name' musician. I protested to Barney and he relented." But little did Josephson know, as he shuttled between his Downtown and Uptown clubs, that in Doc Cheatham's words, "Everybody in that group smoked pot. They had a little room off the bandstand and some, including Mary Lou and Billie, would smoke pot in there. They would put me outside the door in a chair smoking a pipe that would cover the fumes of the pot." Mary and Doc Cheatham often shared a cab home after the gig to the apartment building they both lived in. Cheatham said, "We would come home together. She would light up. One time she said, 'Take one.' I said, 'Man, I don't want to smoke.' She said, 'Take one.' So I took a little and blew all the smoke out. She said, 'Don't you waste that!'" He added elsewhere, ruefully, "She never did invite me to those after-hours they had, like with Billie Holiday."

But heroin was out for her—the scourge of her community, as Mary saw so soon and so painfully, although alcohol remained a big problem as well, particularly for some older musicians. It was then that Mary—aided by her friend Gray Weingarten—began a lifelong crusade to help musicians troubled by addiction. One of those they tried to help was Billie Holiday, who had been arrested in 1947 for possession of heroin. "I heard that Billie Holiday was on drugs and was not well and had been busted," recalls Gray Weingarten. "I talked to Mary Lou about it. She said, 'Oh yeah, it's terrible, but I don't know what we could do about it. She belongs to Joe Glaser, you know.' But I convinced Mary to talk to him. She made an appointment, and we went into Joe's office. There he sat behind his great big desk. And Mary Lou said, 'This is my friend, she's got something she wants to say to you.' And I told him, since he made money off of her, why wouldn't he help her? And he said he would put her in the hospital and try to help her kick the habit. He didn't think it would do any good, though. And of course he was right.

"Another time she called and said, 'Gray, you got to get right up here, we got a lot of work to do, don't ask any questions. Come on up. Wear your work clothes.' It was Jack 'the Bear' Parker, the drummer from Café Society. His wife had been sick and he had some kids, two or three boys, and he just couldn't cope. He gave Mary Lou the keys to the apartment. There were dirty clothes from one end of this place to the other and toys all over. So we went out and bought soap and Mary Lou and I washed the dishes and did all this laundry. Then we strung a big long rope we'd bought from one end of the place to the other and back again, three times, and hung up all this laundry. Straightened up the place and left. It took us all day. That was a typical good-will trip with Mary Lou.

"At another point, Willie 'the Lion' Smith was sick and really down on his luck. Mary and I went over and we cleaned house and brought him some groceries—he wanted some ice cream. He was very grateful."

But Mary was powerless to clean up the mess in many of her friends' lives, a fact that caused her endless pain. "More than once I have gone up to 52nd Street to catch a favorite," she wrote sadly, "and have found one of my best friends asleep at the piano, not even aware that there was an audience. Fifty-second Street by this time was loaded with dope peddlers . . . but my friends did not know that they were being destroyed and I dared not tell them for I loved them too much. . . ."

Mary herself never tried heroin, and in fact, she later forced an out-of-court settlement from then-media giant RKO (which owned WOR radio) for headlining an ad about an upcoming radio interview with her: "From Heroin to Heroine in the '60s." It was not that she didn't have an interest in stronger drugs. "I consulted a doctor and asked him which of the dope I could try without becoming an addict the first time," she recalled. "He asked me if I was crazy and said he'd not permit me to do it. He asked why I wanted to try dope. I answered that I'd like to know the kicks that my friends were getting. On my own I decided to try cocaine when the opportunity presented itself, for I'd gotten up enough nerve to do so." If she did try cocaine, though, neither she nor anyone else who knew her ever made any mention of it. Perhaps the memory of her nightmarish experience with Benzedrine in '45 was enough to check that impulse.

EVEN AS HEROIN was digging its claws into modern jazz musicians, Mary's attractive three-room apartment on Hamilton Terrace was a kind of haven, a salon for the music. "After finishing work at Café each morning," Mary wrote, "I'd either pick up several musicians and take them along with me or else we would meet at my apartment when I got home around 4 o'clock. The guys used to come to my house then— Bud Powell, Tadd Dameron, Monk, Miles, Mel Torme, Sarah Vaughan, Dizzy—all the boppers. Even Benny Goodman. See, they weren't working and would write music and play all morning, almost 'til it was time to go to work. Sometimes Tadd Dameron would get stuck with his arrangements and he'd say, 'Come on and play something, Lou.' And while I was creating, it would push him off again. And Aaron Bridgers and Billy Strayhorn, plus various disc jockeys and newspapermen, would be in and out of my place at all hours, and we'd really ball."

Mary had a thick white carpet in the living room on which the group would all gather, snacking, drinking coffee or mixed drinks, talking. Mary enjoyed playing hostess. "The first thing I'd do was prepare breakfast or serve drinks." And there was the scent and haze of marijuana in the air—Mary liked to relax with a joint after a gig—but no hard drugs: the musicians had too much respect for Mary. And above all, there was the music. Piano players especially liked to congregate around Mary's Baldwin upright, which was rapidly gathering battle scars from cigarette burns and water spots. "We'd sit and talk until somebody felt like playing. Often a pianist would try out a composition he'd just written," Mary reminisced. Adds Weingarten, who was raised in downtown white privilege, "I was never afraid to go there in the '40s. Somehow, it was safe—except, Mary Lou said, for the park. You could drive up there alone, park in front of the building and go up. Or other times I'd walk the lonely streets down from Hamilton Terrace to the subway at three o'clock in the morning, not a care in the world."

———

STARS LIKE ART TATUM would drop by Hamilton Terrace, but most of the musicians were unknowns trying to prove themselves—like Sarah Vaughan, an awkward, high-spirited young nightingale from Newark. "I met her," said Mary, "while she was touring with Earl Hines. John Williams, who was with Earl's band then, told me how great Sarah was. Tadd Dameron later brought Sarah to the house and we became great friends. She'd either sing or play piano with me." Dizzy Gillespie, one of Mary's closest musical friends for life, was another visitor.

Another unknown at the time was Earl "Bud" Powell. In '46 he was just out of his teens when Mary, who'd heard him at Minton's, persuaded Barney Josephson to give him a job at Café Society Downtown, as the house pianist with John Kirby's group. Though his job at Café Society did not last long, a close friendship formed between Powell and Mary.

Powell was already showing signs of the mental turmoil that was to torment him. The year before, a breakdown (allegedly triggered by a blow to the head) had taken him from the ranks of Cootie Williams's band to Pilgrim State Mental Hospital on Long Island. It was the first of many hospitalizations.

Mary became Powell's guide and mentor. At Café Society, the show included comedienne Imogene Coca. Mary wrote, "I had quite a bit of trouble trying to get Bud to play the show music which was not too modern. He kept saying that this type of music was too corny and it was an insult to his musical ability. I told him that a musician was only considered great who played everything. It finally soaked in and he promised to let me show him how to play Imogene's music, eliminating the modern harmonies. I insisted he play it as written.

"Everything went along smoothly, until one night he came in polluted and the talk was they'd have to let him go. I got to Bud and told him he shouldn't drink too much while working and if he'd listen to me I'd tell him when and how much to drink. I was so surprised that he listened to me and did just what I told him. After playing a set he'd go to the dressing room and sit in the corner waiting for me if I was out, frightening the girls in the show as he'd have the meanest expression on his face until I came in. I began feeling like Mother Mary. I'd sometimes give him one drink and later he'd ask if he could have another and I'd tell him to wait until later.

"One night his little combo really blew and Bud was in the best of form. He had people standing around the piano, amazed at his technique and ideas. Out of 10 choruses he'd not repeat; he told the greatest story and I had to hug him when he came off. We were inseparable after this and he always came to the house and played new things he had written or tunes he was going to record on session, waiting for me to say whether or not they were good."

Mary's mentoring included coaching Powell on the piano. She who had developed a great left hand from the stride-era giants told her friend Billy Taylor that she pinpointed a weakness in bop players, telling Bud Powell, "Everybody's playin' without a left hand, so let's fill up the chords." Johnnie Garry remembers after-hours sessions at the apartment where "she had a little ruler in her hand and she used to hit Bud on his hand and say, 'Left hand, Bud, left hand.' " "She made them [Powell *and* Monk] both more aware of touch," insists Billy Taylor. "You could hear the difference in touch between the early and later Powell records. You can hear the same with Monk: when he was recording for Blue Note, it was one touch. And then later he began to record for other labels . . . it wasn't just the change in sound, *he* changed. And you could hear a more pianistic approach. This was, in my opinion, a result of his close association with Mary Lou."

But Mary was quick to acknowledge that she was also learning a great deal from Powell's daring flights and brilliant turn-on-a-dime improvisations. She wrote that "the things Bud wrote for me improved what little originality I had and inspired me to experiment with my own things."

Although there was never any possibility of a love affair with Bud Powell in *her* mind, he pursued her for some time. He called her "Baby Doll." Everything about her enchanted him: her musical brilliance,

her looks; even her age gave her a sexy-maternal aura. Mary's past difficulties in relationships paled before the chaos that emanated from
Bud Powell. By the later 1940s he was becoming as much renowned
for his unstable personality, exacerbated by drinking and drug-taking,
as for his brilliance at the keyboard. Mary continued to try to exert a
helpful influence on him. When Powell was at Birdland, Garry, working as an assistant manager at the club, recalls that "they called Mary
because they were afraid he was going to tear the whole place up. And
she could calm him down," he adds. "He used to dip into the cash register. He got very angry, furious, that they weren't paying him more."

"I was the only one who could do things for Bud," she wrote in her
diary. "Bud had a tendency to go overboard; I'd make him take a bath
or go to sleep. At one time, Birdland wanted to pay me $75 to take care
of him. But I said, 'I have to look after myself, too. I can't sit in the
house for that. But I'll help when he needs help.' " Yet there was not
much she could do as Powell deteriorated. He was put into mental hospitals in 1947 and 1948, later taken to Bellevue, and again admitted to
a state hospital in 1953. He became dangerous even to Mary. "Once or
twice when he almost lost his mind I had to hide away because I think
he felt he was in love with me—he wouldn't allow me even to sit with
one of my little nephews, and he kicked him—well, not hard. But the
kid was only about three or four years old. He wanted nobody around
me. If I walked down the street with anybody he'd push them away
from me. He began to depend on me emotionally."

Then one night, drunk and in a rage of jealousy, Powell stormed
into Mary's apartment, threatening to kill her. Somehow she managed
to reach a musician friend by phone, who came immediately and got
Powell to go home. After that, said Mary, "I wouldn't let Bud Powell in
my house when he'd come in high."

Despite all this, there was a bond between the two, and years later
Mary tried to help Powell again. She was touched by the dedication of
his composition "Tempus Fugit," written partly at 63 Hamilton Terrace, and she carefully preserved a poem that he had written at her
apartment in block letters with a pencil:

THE GREAT AWAKENING

I was sitting in the garden one late afternoon
And out of the sky a feather fell

And not a moment too soon.
I didn't stop to regard from what source it came
I only know it lifted me out of the depths of shame . . .

After several more verses of increasingly maudlin confession, Powell, vowing to "live the way God intended," ends the poem declaring that "God had sent the feather to me." "I pray that some day Bud will know how straight he was when he wrote that," Mary wrote in her diary. To her, every bop pianist after Bud Powell played Bud Powell.

There were other extraordinary pianistic talents emerging then whom Mary nurtured. Like Bud Powell, the singleminded Erroll Garner was a brilliant original. Eleven years younger than Mary, Garner was a Pittsburgh-born pianist who went to school at Westinghouse School, Mary's alma mater. When Mary first heard him, he was still a teenager. "He was about as fast as Art Tatum; fabulous. But sometimes he'd get overanxious and all I did was just keep him straight—I didn't teach him. Like one time he was playing like Art Tatum and I said, 'No, you'll never make a success like that.' "

When Garner moved to New York in 1945, a shy and inarticulate unknown, Mary took him under her wing. "We used to go out to concerts and listen to various musicians. We went to New York University to hear a big orchestra—I forget the name of it—and he came back to my house playing everything practically he had heard. He was going out to Inez Cavanaugh's apartment, which was very inspiring to most of the musicians, composing and playing practically all day for Inez, who used to record some of the things he'd composed on the spot."

Garner couldn't read music, but drew the line at her tentative offer to teach him. Mary understood: "If you touch someone like Erroll Garner or myself you can destroy everything," she told an interviewer."

When Mary was making the switch from Café Society Downtown to the Uptown club in 1946, "I tried to get the manager to put Erroll in the Downtown club. I wasn't successful until I got him up to the house to hear him play. He played my favorite, 'The Man I Love,' in his sensuous way. Oh what a morning! We enjoyed Erroll for at least three hours."

Garner went on to become famous, with an immediately identifiable style, an independent, rock-steady left hand and a far-reaching, melodic right. Mary recalled often, as here in her diary: "The four-four beat that he had going? That happened in my apartment. I was in the back room, I had gotten a little tired and so I had left him at the piano. Then he ran to the back room, he said, 'I got it, I got it! I don't have to be bothered with a rhythm section.' You know how they sometimes don't play with you?" Garner had worked out a way to be a one-man band.

Mary always retained a special fondness for the elfin Garner. "He and Thelonious Monk never got up off the piano. And Erroll Garner tied 'em *all* up one night. There were about five of them there one night, including Bud Powell, and when Erroll played, they couldn't play! Bud said, 'Baby Doll, I can't play!' and I said go back and try. I never bothered them when they were there because they were composing things, finding things."

Yet a third pianistic genius became an intimate friend: Thelonious Monk. "When Bud came to me for help and if he got a little bit out of line, I'd say: 'I'll tell Monk.' He'd say: 'Don't do that, Baby Doll.' He respected Monk, he was crazy about Monk. We were going to do three-piano things. The three of us rehearsed on one piano and that was so funny. Yes, it was a very happy time. It seemed to me that no one could think as Monk did except Charlie Christian, Kenny Clarke and a couple others."

Monk's music, while consistent with bop, was that of an iconoclast. Mary recalled that during the thirties Monk had come through Kansas City, playing with an evangelist. "In Kansas City Monk was employing a lot more technique than he does today. He plays the way he does today because he got fed up," she explained in later years. "Whatever people may tell you, I know how Monk can play. He felt that musicians should play something new and started doing it. He was one of the original modernists all right, playing pretty much the same harmonies then that he's playing now.

"There's no precedent for his conceptions," she noted. "When he wrote a tune he'd bring it to me and I'd try to play it and he'd say, 'No, you phrased it like this'—maybe a couple of 16th notes or something and that would be a part of the melody—but I couldn't phrase the way that he wanted me to, so I just played it my way."

Mary found Monk's elusive personality hard to describe. "Thelonious is a nice guy," she said, but added, "He's odd. He's odd. He doesn't talk much at all. You can't get words out of him at all. A very grand guy. And he was kind of a funny guy if you asked him to do something. Like he was working at Minton's and the owner of the club told him to put the cover on the piano to preserve it. And he said, 'No, I'm not a busboy.' And he walked out."

Monk at times could provide comic relief: "One morning I felt extra tired and I left the guys in the living room to enjoy themselves and went to bed," Mary wrote. "Eventually everybody went and the last one out left the front door open, since it could only be locked from inside or with a key. I had twin beds in my room. When I awoke around noon, I was surprised to see a figure stretched out on the other one with a beret on. I yelled and the figure jumped up and ran into my closet, where all the clothes fell down. It was Monk. He explained he'd come to see me. Finding the door open, he came in but since I was asleep he decided not to play piano but wait for me, which he did. And he fell asleep. We always laughed about that."

Yet, not only was Monk not well-known as a jazz pianist in the mid-forties, he was disparaged as a player by many. This did not bother him, Mary said, for Monk had artistic hauteur: he "always had that thing." Like most musicians, too, he was poor, sometimes almost penniless, and Mary bought groceries more than once so that he could feed his children.

"Usually," Mary wrote, "when Monk composed a song he'd play it both night and day if you didn't stop him. He always said that was the only way to find out if it was going to be good. It either grew on you or it didn't. His music is . . . a conversation. It could be angry or love. Monk has an awful lot of that in his music."

Of course, Monk and Powell had a direct influence on Mary's approach to music. But Mary was an influence on Monk as well as on Powell, too. "In the forties," notes Whitney Balliett of Mary's evolving style, "she advanced certain dissonant chords that became part of Thelonious Monk's permanent furniture." *Direct* evidence of her influence on Monk is apparent in several compositions: in his "52nd Street Theme," particularly the bass line, which is straight out of Mary's "Scorpio"; in Monk's "Hackensack," which refers to Mary's 1944 arrangement of "Lady Be Good"; and in his "Rhythm-a-ning," based on the second chorus of her "Walkin' and Swingin'."

In the case of Bud Powell, Mary noted that he "took some licks of mine" for his "Un Poco Loco." She was not apparently bothered by such borrowing because the musicians were her close friends; indeed,

she saw it as a compliment, as when she herself retailored Monk's
" 'Round Midnight," a composition she loved. Her version of Monk's
tune, recorded in 1955, was called "I Love Him," a title intended to
make clear that she was throwing a musical bouquet to Monk by
reworking an admired tune.

Many musical "borrowings" belong to the "imitation as flattery"
school, or they are the innocent, unconscious applications of others'
ideas. Others are not imitations at all, but deliberate "lifts"—a polite
word for theft. Such thievery occurred many times over with Mary's
compositions, and as Peter O'Brien notes, "She was angry—angry at
not being given credit for what she actually did." In the forties, as Mary
often told friends like Marsha Vick, "Musicians used to come and sit
beside me because they'd hear during a set maybe a couple of new
things that they could use." Explains Billy Taylor, "She was in a very
fertile period then, writing a lot for all of them and people just took
the music and somebody else's name got on it." Examples? Coleman
Hawkins recorded Mary's hip arrangement on the changes of "Lady
Be Good," a session she recorded for Asch with Hawkins, calling it
"Rifftide"—which Monk later did as "Hackensack." The same disguised "Lady Be Good" was recorded by trumpeter Fats Navarro as
"Fats Blows." Also, as noted above, the second chorus from Mary's
"Walkin' and Swingin' " was adapted by Monk in his tune "Rhythm-a-
ning." *Then* pianist Al Haig used Monk's version in his own "Opus
Caprice"; and two years later it reappeared in Sonny Stitt's nearly iden-
tical "Symphony Hall Swing." There are undoubtedly other borrowings. The important thing, as the writer Ira Gitler emphasizes, is this:
"Nowhere does Mary Lou receive credit of any kind." Of course, many
creative jazz musicians have been dealt similar bad hands. But it was
the repetition of uncredited borrowings over the years, the piling up
of incident upon incident in Mary's case, that was a big factor in her
eventual loss of heart over the whole business of jazz for a long time.

———

ONCE, AND PERHAPS only once, Mary played with both Bud Powell
and Thelonious Monk at a concert—but the occasion of three of the
greatest jazz pianists playing together was just another shabby gig.
"Someone booked the three of us at a concert in Philadelphia. Real
pitiful—we played in the Elks clubhouse. Stan Getz and Red Rodney

and group were booked in the adjoining room. It cost me money, for Monk as usual was without even train fare and I had to sponsor the trip. At the concert someone slipped Bud a few drinks and he really clowned after this. Poor Bud's mother was with him, trying to keep him from going overboard. I felt sorry for her, she was a kind mother. But I never laughed so much. Even the audience laughed: Bud would sit and stare at everyone, then play 24 bars of the Minute Waltz, stop and sit."

It was Monk, Mary wrote, who asked her in 1944 to participate in a project for all three pianists. "I had Monk write one that he later recorded as 'Criss-cross' with a small combo," Mary said. Powell's contribution was probably what Mary later termed "a solo on 'Cherokee' " and Mary's contribution was a new arrangement of "Scorpio" for three pianos. "I arranged Monk's part so that it would be more or less in his style. And Bud Powell's was quite different and my part was my style. It was really quite wonderful—the three of us were working on one piano, six hands. But our rehearsal turned out to be funny. Monk was reaching over Bud's shoulder to play his chords and Bud turning around, giving Monk a mean look. This rehearsing every day on one piano in my apartment went on for some time until I got sick of it. And before I could get the idea done, I had to go away. Anyway, it was just an experiment."

Monk's musical ideas and approach exerted a powerful influence on Mary, and they remained friendly until the last phase of his life, when, his personality damaged by his addictions and mental instability, he withdrew from society almost totally. Peter O'Brien recalls that in the early 1970s, as a new young priest (and Mary's manager), he visited Monk's dressing room with Mary. "Monk was in the dressing room and he went into the bathroom. He was nodding when he came out and Mary just sat there. She didn't bat an eye. All I saw was a little flicker of sadness in her face, but she knew how to deal with that, she just stayed right there. That was early on in my exposure to these things."

Chapter Twelve
Benny's Bop
1948

IN THE SUMMER of 1948, Mary took a step that surprised many in the jazz world, joining Benny Goodman's recently formed combo. She knew firsthand of Goodman's reputation for being hard on musicians, and had turned down an offer, nine years earlier, to replace Teddy Wilson when Wilson left Goodman's combo. But since then, Goodman had broken up his big band, forming a new group to feature modern jazz; and this development much intrigued Mary, who was eager to write more bop charts (and be paid the kind of fees she had received occasionally in the thirties for her work for the established big bands).

The crusty Goodman had something of a soft spot for Mary—no surprise, since in the thirties she had given him a hit with "Roll 'Em." Also, years before she had recommended a fantastic but unknown guitarist named Charlie Christian to Goodman's then manager, John Hammond, who was stunned by Christian's virtuosity and immediately wanted him for the Goodman ensemble. Then Mary, who was a friend, talked Christian into leaving his safe surroundings for the wide white world of fame in music. But Goodman was reluctant to hire a black guitarist. "John Hammond said, 'Benny didn't want to start no revolution,'" related Delilah Jackson, a historian of black entertainment who knew Hammond. "Benny told him, 'It's not me; it's the guys. All this business of black and white guys upsets the band. And Roseland [the Manhattan ballroom] don't want you to bring black guys in.' Eventually, Mary told me, Hammond just sprung Christian on the band."

Once Goodman heard Christian play, it was a done deal. For the brief period of 1939 to 1941, when Christian was with Goodman's sextet, the group was wildly popular, Christian's creativity and lyrical playing adding invaluable luster. Christian spun out beautifully improvised patterns that grew titles like "Gone with What Wind," "Air Mail Special," "Flying Home," "Seven Come Eleven." "But after he had been with Benny Goodman a while," Delilah Jackson relates, "he says to Mary, 'You got to stop him! Benny Goodman's stealing everything I do. One night I play a riff, and it's my riff, and the next night he's got it in his licks. This has been going on ever since I been there.' Well, Mary said she spoke to Benny Goodman and told him that Charlie had been doing these musical things since he's a kid in Oklahoma."

When Mary and Christian were not on the road with their respective bands in 1939–41, they would get together to jam in the basement of the Dewey Square Hotel, which had a piano. "Charlie and I used to play and write all night long. I still have the music—16 bars—of a song he started but never completed," Mary said. Benny Goodman once stopped by and was charmed by a musical side of Christian he hadn't known existed. "Charlie played the classics, lovely things such as 'Rhapsody in Blue,' " wrote Mary.

But the young guitarist was ill. Mary had already lost several friends to tuberculosis, mostly recently the brilliant saxophonist Dick Wilson. Charlie Christian was to follow, collapsing during a tour at the end of 1941. Back in New York, he ended up in Seaview Hospital, a city-run sanatorium notorious among the poor for its indifferent care. There, Christian lingered until March of 1942, with Count Basie paying his doctor to visit him weekly, while Goodman, as John Hammond pointedly mentions in his autobiography, did not even find the time to visit Christian at his sickbed. Charlie Christian was just twenty-five when he died.

———

IN 1946, BENNY GOODMAN recorded as air checks both "Lonely Moments" and Mary's jaunty, riff-tiered "Whistle Blues" (also called "Whistling Blues"). Goodman had recently settled in Los Angeles, broken up his big band, and switched from Columbia to the more pop-oriented Capitol Records. "Lonely Moments" is the superior tune, building to a bravura finale, and Goodman's recording of it, according to a Goodman discographer, was a signal "that Benny is building a new book for the band, that it will be oriented toward 'bop.' "

However, Benny Goodman had serious reservations about bop. He complained to George Simon that it "jarred his ear. Everybody is trying to see just how much he can put in it. It's nervous more than exciting music. If some of them would just try to simplify their arrangements and solos, they'd come off much better. . . . And as for some of those chords they're using, they're just pretentious tripe." Mary was among the few with whom Goodman felt secure venturing into the new musical territory. But it was not a smooth transition, even with her. On "Lonely Moments," says biographer Ross Firestone, "Benny had scoffed 'Oh, bebop!' when Mary Lou first showed him the chart and insisted she simplify some of the more harmonically complex passages." Adds another Goodman expert, James L. Collier, "Eventually Williams persuaded Goodman to use it by telling him to play the blues on his solo. Goodman, however, as he frequently did, tinkered with the arrangement, in particular removing the flatted fifths." Still, the performance was deemed a critical success, fresher and more adventurous than anything Benny had tried in some time.

———

AS GOODMAN WAS casting around for more modern-sounding material he liked, he happened to hear a superb young tenor saxophonist. Wardell Gray's smooth blending of the styles of Lester Young and Charlie Parker appealed to Goodman, and he offered him a job. Then Goodman heard the young Swedish clarinetist Ake "Stan" Hasselgard, who also straddled swing and bop. Hasselgard had an easy charm and the ability to laugh off Goodman's often grating eccentricities; more important, he served as a kind of bridge between earlier and current clarinet styles. Goodman took the unusual step of hiring Hasselgard as second clarinet in his new group, and brought Gray and Hasselgard back east in the spring of 1948. There, he assembled a rhythm section sympathetic to bop: Billy Bauer on guitar (later replaced by Mundell Lowe), Arnold Fishkind on bass (replaced by Clyde Lombardi), and Mel Zelnick on drums, as well as a very young Patti Page, the first of several vocalists to pass through that band. Other brief sojourners were the trumpeters Red Rodney, Fats Navarro, and Doug Mettome. A reluctant Teddy Wilson had been persuaded to rejoin Goodman on piano.

Although lack of ticket sales forced a Carnegie Hall concert for the band to be canceled, Goodman remained optimistic about his bop group's future. In May 1948, they were booked for much of the month at the big, popular Click Club Restaurant in Philadelphia. For the new band book, Goodman commissioned Mary to be one of his principal arrangers, also using material by Mel Powell, Eddie Sauter, Shorty Rogers, and others.

Radio broadcasts, recorded off the air and later released as bootleg records, give invaluable evidence of the fresh new sound of a band that was almost entirely unrecorded. Although Mary was not yet in the band in May, many of her arrangements were played. Among them was a favorite of Goodman's, "Mary's Idea," (a.k.a. "Just an Idea"), one of Mary's first compositions, and one which she had continued to refashion to fit the ways jazz had evolved since 1930. By 1948, "Mary's Idea" was clothed in long, sinuous lines, more complex riffs, and tightly voiced ensemble passages. She also contributed, among others, hip new versions of "Bye Bye Blues," "Blue Views," and an excellent "There's a Small Hotel." But despite their quality and Mary's established standing as an arranger, Goodman paid her, she said, only $10 an arrangement, promising her more as the band became successful. Mary fumed in private. (Like most musicians, she had her stories about the bandleader's tightfistedness. After calling rehearsals that would last into the wee hours of the morning, she said, Goodman expected his band members to pay for their own taxis home.)

From the start, there were problems attracting an audience with the Goodman bop band. Younger people especially liked what they heard, but the legions of die-hard swing-era Benny Goodman fans—his bread and butter—wanted no part of bop, not even a bop as polished as it was in his repertoire. The Click Club tried to renegotiate its fee with Goodman in mid-May, but Goodman resisted. He was determined to hold on until he got back to New York, where he had big plans: he wanted to book the group for a whole summer of dance concerts, as soon as the ban was lifted, and make some records. Teddy Wilson, tired of road life and Benny Goodman, gave notice when the Click Club date ended, and Goodman immediately got in touch with

Mary, offering her the job. After some hesitation, Mary consented, swayed when she heard Goodman's plans to record her arrangements for Capitol in the fall. She still had no major recording contract and knew she'd get valuable exposure through Goodman.

"The first two nights Benny used bass, drums, piano and clarinet," Mary wrote about the new band's initial performances in early June. "We had quite a ball and sounded very good. After this we played weekends with the Sextet." For his part, Benny Goodman was, as he told George Simon, "of course, very enthusiastic about Mary Lou, about her writing and about her playing."

The weekend job was an innovative experiment for the times—not just musically but socially. Promoted and financially backed in part by Goodman himself, the combo played its first weekend concert on June 26th at the huge Westchester County Center in White Plains, and was broadcast over radio station WNEW as "The Benny Goodman Show." The County Center could accommodate thousands and as BG himself said on the air, it was "just a block from the train station at White Plains—the cost only $1.25, and soft drinks only." Goodman apparently envisioned the teenagers of New York and its suburbs flocking to the County Center all summer to hear a different band on Friday nights, and his own group on Saturday nights.

The gamble didn't pay off. Nor, it seems, was it the music alone that kept the fans away. The County Center backed a mixed race policy, which Goodman, to his credit, supported fully as the leader of his combo, but it was a highly controversial policy, as George Simon pointed out in *Metronome* later that summer. It was one thing for an integrated Café Society to cater to a sophisticated New York crowd of blacks and whites; but the White Plains venture catered to the white masses. It would, after all, be some twenty years before Martin Luther King, Jr., was to galvanize the civil rights movement in America, so after just three weekends, Goodman canceled the rest of the summer engagement at the Center.

———

THOUGH BENNY GOODMAN continued to waffle about the merits of bop, the little he and his combo managed to record is extremely well rehearsed, well thought out, and listenable: two WNEW air checks from the Westchester County Center, two V-discs, and some material recorded during rehearsals in September 1948 for a Capitol album that was not released. That there is *any* music on record is serendipity: there was another recording ban at the time, extending from January 1948 until early in 1949. There were still, however, those government-issued V-discs, and radio broadcast transcriptions for the AFRS (Armed Forces Radio Service), which had begun during the war. Bootleg records also cropped up later.

The County Center broadcasts featured Goodman, Mary, Stan Hasselgard, Wardell Gray, Red Rodney on trumpet, and the rhythm section of Billy Bauer on guitar, Clyde Lombardi on bass, and Mel Zelnick on drums, as well as several young male and female vocalists who mostly faded from sight afterwards. (Bop singer Babs Gonzales, a friend of Mary's, turned up for one set but wasn't recorded.) In an attempt to please both his swing fans and the younger crowd he wanted to attract, Goodman's repertoire ranged from swing-style arrangements like "Back Home in Indiana" to bop favorites like "Swedish Pastry." The air checks of the band make clear that he was most at ease with the swing material, but to his (and Mary's) credit, her arrangements of tunes like "Mary's Idea" made Goodman sound as comfortable as one could imagine him sounding playing flatted fifths and ninths.

He had little reason to feel optimistic about his bop plans after the failure of the County Center dates, but Goodman pressed on. While unsure about the music itself—as George Simon put it, Goodman "blows hot and cold"—he did want to make lots of records with the group, and he planned to expand it into a new big band that he would take out on a concert tour. For this, as he told jazz writers, he would need more arrangers to "supplement manuscripts by Mary Lou and Mel Powell." (He did go on to build a basic bop band book, with new charts by Chico O'Farrill and others, and more by Mary as well.)

In the summer of '48, the bop combo found itself without a gig. However, they kept busy rehearsing and made two V-discs in New York in July, including an old Goodman standby, "Stealin' Apples," wittily updated by Mary. (This material is now available on compact discs.)

The group (Benny Goodman, Wardell Gray, Clyde Lombardi, Mel Zelnick, and an unidentified pianist who was actually Mary) recorded Mary's reworking of "Limehouse Blues," calling it "Benny's Bop." With its complex and tricky unison lines, the writing reminded bop critics of

Lennie Tristano, a pianist whom Mary much admired at the time (it was a short-lived musical infatuation). "Benny's Bop" was exactly that: a challenging bop tune written for Goodman to take flight.

Negotiations to end the recording ban were proceeding (it would end in January 1949), and Goodman—and probably Capitol—were anxious to have material ready to record. Mary went to work, polishing the material she had been providing Goodman since the spring and adding new compositions. On September 8, 1948, she showed up for an all-day rehearsal and recording date at Capitol's studios in New York. The band had changed personnel somewhat—Fats Navarro was now on trumpet, and Mundell Lowe had replaced Billy Bauer on guitar—but otherwise it was the same as on the V-disc sessions. Yet it was an unknown pianist, the Brooklyn-based Gene Di Novi, who ended up recording with the group and not Mary.

Tension had been building between Mary and Benny all summer. Venting her frustrations with rare candor in her diary, she wrote of the County Center dates, "That was one of the most awful engagements of my career. We never made it except when Benny had to go home early one night and left us to finish off. The guys really blew like mad this particular night. Babs Gonzales sat in one night and shook it up—and Benny was unpleasant. When Benny *was* on the stand he made everyone uneasy by the discouraging look he gave them. It seemed he wasn't happy, which made everybody uncomfortable. Once in awhile he'd walk over to the piano and remark that he didn't like the way someone played."

Although Mary had liked Benny Goodman well enough in the thirties and early forties, "now I had found either a real neurotic or a monster—he was either too rich to blow or too sick. And the job paid me practically nothing. I struggled along." Mary chafed under the restrictions Goodman imposed on her as a writer. (She was not alone. The arranger Eddie Sauter also had to submit to numerous cuts by the leader.) "Of course she wasn't going to allow herself to be under anybody after her early years, with Kirk and her husband," says Gray Weingarten. "I've always been a leader of men," was the way Mary herself put it. To be fair, Goodman was by no means the only bandleader to change his writers' work: Count Basie, to mention one of many, is said to have red-penciled material blithely if he thought it unduly complicated. According to some of Goodman's former sidemen, however, he was capable of a terrific insensitivity that led many to shake their heads in wonder—and others to quit. Mary, however, *forced* Goodman to do things her way, or at least tried. "When I was doing arrangements for Benny Goodman, he never liked for anyone to lead the band but him," Mary told Marsha Vick. "So I'd step up and say, 'You're not messin' up *my* arrangements,' and he'd sit down and let me show them how to do them." But Goodman was then likely to go ahead and change them anyway.

By the day of the recording session, Mary had become so frustrated that, after something was said that upset her, she did the unheard-of: she left the studio and didn't come back. Shades of 1943, walking off the bandstand of Clouds of Joy.

The very next day, Joe Glaser, who was again representing her, dashed off one of his vintage epistles:

Walter Rivers, the Capitol producer, was completely mystified as to your behavior on the Goodman recording date. He says one moment you were there and the next moment you weren't and after a long wait, they finally made up their minds that you were nowhere around. They sat down to try to figure what had happened. Benny swore that he had done nothing and said nothing. But Rivers didn't quite believe him, knowing Benny. Benny said that a call had come into him from a pianist that you might have overheard and that you took a burn believing that he had been dickering with someone else for the date. Anyhow, they got another pianist in your place and the date proceeded.

That young pianist, Gene Di Novi, recalled "receiving a last-minute phone call from Hasselgard offering me the job. He told me that Mary Lou and Benny had just had a big fight, so I ran in from Brooklyn to make the date."

Mary privately expressed misgivings. "I was quite fed up anyway, so I walked out on the date, something I've never done in my life and regretted later on. This set me back financially for about a month. I did not see Benny until later when he was rehearsing for a new band."

It may have been coincidence, but without Mary the combo collapsed, and Goodman disbanded it within weeks, although in Novem-

ber he did record several tunes with Barbara Carroll on piano. Goodman was more interested anyway in assembling a new big band to take
on the road, keeping Wardell Gray and Fats Navarro (who was soon
replaced by Doug Mettome), and the then Bud Powell–inspired
pianist Buddy Greco, who also sang with the band. But this plan didn't
work out either; it was very rough going financially by then for all the
big bands that remained. By the end of 1949, Benny Goodman dis-
solved both his bop big band and his new combo and, one imagines,
sighed with relief.

––––––––––

IN THE FALL of 1948, Mary chose to hole up again. She wanted, she
said, "to take the next six months off to write a symphony and several
other compositions." Since she had no income, she appealed to Joe
Glaser for $5,000, which she calculated she needed to live on while
writing. Glaser responded with a scolding:

> It is unbelievable that you should conduct your business affairs
> the way you do and my only hope is that you realize that is the
> only reason you are in the predicament you are in.

But Mary soon patched things up enough with Benny Goodman to
supply him with several new numbers, which he recorded with the big
band or the new combo. He recorded "Oo-bla-dee" in April 1949 with
Buddy Greco as vocalist and pianist, Wardell Gray and Doug Mettome
on tenor sax and trumpet respectively; and he continued to play her
arrangements (such as "Just an Idea"), while "Blue Lou" and "There's
a Small Hotel" were issued on a Capitol LP, now available on CD. Then
in November of 1950, he recorded Mary's new composition "Walkin'
Out the Door," with Terry Gibbs on vibes and Teddy Wilson back again
on piano, with Nancy Reed and the Pastels handling the vocals. It was a
tune Mary was sure could be a hit, but it never caught on.

Goodman fans, and Mary's own considerable swing-era following,
seemed to show no more enthusiasm for the new bop charts than for
the earlier ones. D. Russell Connor spoke for the Goodman masses in
dismissing the bop groups the leader put together as "a controversial
chapter in his long career. . . . Few Goodman enthusiasts champion
this band." Yet decades later, the music, now mostly available on

compact discs, sounds seamlessly smooth and airy, if Mary's cooler approach to her piano is tinged with a note of world-weariness. As musician Loren Schoenberg has observed in writing about the 1948 Goodman group, "to present-day ears it is hard to understand what all the fuss was about between the musical generations when this recording was made."

Chapter Thirteen
Walkin' Out the Door
1948–1952

BY AUTUMN 1948 Mary was in an ambiguous position. "No other pianist, male or female, has so steadily met the demands of the increasingly demanding art of jazz keyboard performance," asserted Barry Ulanov. "A brilliant musician. . . . It is entirely possible that future generations will consider her as one of the few geniuses of this era," concurred pianist and critic Sharon Pease. But not yet. Another critic and admirer, *Ebony* writer Allan Morison, noted sadly that "commercial success has eluded her thus far." Just as her New York audience still associated her with Café Society and not Minton's, so was she regarded by the recording industry in general as neither fish nor fowl, and a record deal continued to elude her. Even Moe Asch was recording only folk music on his new label, Folkways. Asch had paid her little, but he had been an anchor in Mary's professional life.

Not that offers for work didn't come along. She was still, after all, a name. Glaser periodically called with offers of work. But Mary was essentially on her own. "How many Negro performers can afford a press agent of the caliber that put Sinatra across?" she asked rhetorically. "No, it seems to me that we must make it the hard way."

Even harder was making it as a serious composer. Mary had withdrawn for several months to write one of her most original and ambitious works for piano and mixed adult chorus. Called *Elijah and the Juniper Tree*, it presaged her involvement with choral jazz in coming decades, especially her masses. Set to the poetry of Monty Carr, the biblically based *Elijah* concerned social activism. The work had been commissioned by the director of a sixty-voice choir in Pittsburgh who, as Mary recalled, urged her to "do something like that 'Blue Skies' you arranged for Duke." But *Elijah*'s jazz-oriented rhythmic inflections and difficult harmonies presented major challenges for classically tutored voices. The piece had only one performance in 1948; it was simply too demanding a work. "It seems no one can sing it," Mary wrote forlornly and put it in the drawer. Then, nine years later, she was reported to be scoring it for a hundred voices and orchestra for a Town Hall concert that did not come to pass, and *Elijah and the Juniper Tree* languished until 1996, when it was performed again at the LYNX jazz festival in Florida.

Disheartened by the uphill battles she faced as a composer and pianist, Mary wrote in her diary in the winter of 1949, "I continued to stay up working nights and gambling, never getting any rest until I had a breakdown," adding elliptically, "I went to a doctor and he gave me a transfusion immediately." In all likelihood, however, the "breakdown" and "transfusion" actually referred to an unwanted pregnancy and a traumatic abortion, an event she referred to cryptically. She wrote in one diary entry that she had a "miscarriage" in 1946; another entry said 1948, and a third referred to a "procedure" in '49. She made sure to keep the matter a secret. Even close friends were unaware of it at the time. Garry, who was a frequent friend and attendant, jokes, "I didn't think she had time to lay down and have a baby."

It was not until decades later that she confided in a few friends about the procedure. Peter O'Brien says, "She said that Dr. Logan, the physician who treated Duke Ellington, came and gave her an injection of some kind, a muscle relaxant probably. This all happened in her bedroom. Then, she said, 'Something fell out like a turkey heart. And I know how bad all that is because I saw the devil out of the corner of my eyes—it was like a great big ostrich with long legs.' "

The abortion was certainly a great trauma for Mary. Years later, she sometimes suffered from apparitions of small children who had died, and there seems a special urgency in the efforts she made in helping to raise a nephew, whom she loved as her own child. Then too, Mary's later conversion to Roman Catholicism must have underscored her guilt, even if she was taught that her sins were forgiven. In any case, she became overwrought and overextended in the months after her operation.

———

MARY HAD SUPPLIED her mother with money as often as she could from the time she was a preteen wunderkind. But now, as she approached forty, with nearly a quarter-century of road life already behind her, her exhaustion, combined with long-simmering resentment, exploded into rage; for the first time she turned her back on the Pittsburgh Burleys. "I'd always sent money home, which wasn't appreciated," she wrote flatly. "Later when I was ill and went home to convalesce, my people wondered when I'd be working again. I sent money to my mother and sister. And I had a charge at Gimbel's they'd use. And if I bought things too small or large for them, they wouldn't return them. They gave them to the neighbors, saying, 'Don't worry, my daughter is rich.' I was hurt and I didn't send them anything, fully convinced they didn't need it." But guilt is rarely rational. As long as Mary had a decent roof over her head and three meals a day, she was ahead of the Burleys. Recalls Gray Weingarten: "She told me she felt so bad because her sisters back in Pittsburgh would have to go gather the coal that fell by the railroad tracks so they'd have fuel for the winter, while she was 'living it up' in New York." By the Burleys' standards, Mary, of course, *was* rich.

Around that time, Mary's younger half-brothers, Jerry and Howard, who were war veterans, stayed with her temporarily; Jerry, her favorite relation next to Mamie, was stable, finding lifelong work as a bellhop, but Howard was another story. He had clear talent and dreamed of becoming a visual artist. But he hung out in the bars, got involved with heroin, and soon left Hamilton Terrace.

———

NOW CAME a disastrous time for her. Like many musicians, Mary had developed a taste for card games to while away the long hours on the road. Everyone always played for money, including Mary, but now she took it more seriously—so much so that she became addicted. "I had always loved to gamble with musicians who played mild games of tonk or poker to pass the time away between shows, but I had never gone into it in a big way. I got mixed up with the wrong characters. When someone gave me a line I swallowed it hook, line and sinker. Someone I considered a friend had got me in a swindle and I lost so much money, over $12,000. I was so regularly drawing it from my postal savings that the authorities thought some goon was blackmailing me."

Her escort during that time was a seasoned player whom she referred to simply and dismissively as "the old man." But he was no benevolent Roland Mayfield, bailing her out, no strings attached, and supplying her with Cadillacs. The "old man" in Harlem wanted a return on his investment. "I finally let him kiss me. Then I decided to stay home. But not too long, for the urge to play [gamble] got the best of me." Her would-be lover staked her to $100, then finally ran out of patience the next time they met. "I was greeted at the door," Mary wrote, "by a very angry old monster who picked up a knife as if to stab me. I told him off, telling him I never loved him, had no intention of being his girlfriend and that he forced the loot and trinkets on me. I went home. By this time he must have given me over $1,000 to lose in the games. I decided to change and stop."

The compulsion chipped away at her resolve. "I determined I'd only take a small amount with me. If I lost this, I'd stop. But I continued to lose—although they were smaller amounts." The web Mary was weaving grew more tangled. She who had never been a drinker, wrote that she was suddenly drinking too much, a measure of what she called her "nervousness." There was a raid at the house where she went to gamble; she just managed to escape. "But I still hadn't had enough," she added drily. She began running a game out of her own home. "My apartment was so packed that I thought we'd be raided any minute. There were four tables going. All the hustlers in town came up to see what the apartment looked like and the game lasted almost two days."

She had stopped working, lost her savings and much of her self-respect. Her old friends, and her ex-husband John Williams, blamed most of her troubles on her new friends. "She didn't have nobody to treat her like a lady," he protested. "That place that she had, her apartment, and fooling around with those dope fiends and all! You know, dope fiends will rob you, don't care who you are if they can get more stuff. She should have gotten out of that neighborhood." Nevertheless, she had her standards: "She didn't use profanity. She always used a soft tone of voice and there were some rough characters. She was that kind of woman," said Buttercup Powell (Bud Powell's common-law wife, who had a son, John, by the pianist) in admiration. And yet, Mary couldn't stop gambling. "I have been hungry and broke but never this," she lamented.

———

AND THEN MARY, who described herself during this period as a "bachelor girl," was rescued, in a manner of speaking, when she met the man who was to be her lover for the next several years and who showed her, as she put it, how to "protect myself from cheaters." She met him at Minton's, no longer the cool bop club but still an important neighborhood bar. Lindsay Steele was "sharp looking and rather a fast talker," Mary said, "and he and I became friendly."

"Lindsay was also a numbers runner, like a bookie for the numbers; that's really how she met him," adds Gray Weingarten; she and her then-fiancé Keeva Weingarten used to double-date with Mary and Steele. "Mary'd have a dream and translate the dream into numbers, then go down and play it at Minton's, and Lindsay took the bets. That's all I knew about what he did." Apparently he had other talents, too—at least Mary thought so, describing him as a cook and a good mixer at the restaurant who often sang during intermissions. Others demurred. "Lindsay *sang*?" sniffs Johnnie Garry. "He was a numbers runner, understand? And he had no talent for music." Significantly, the good-looking and suave Steele was the first of Mary's lovers who was not an artist. That may have been part of the appeal. She'd had several unsuccessful affairs after Orent—with Orlando Wright, the tenor saxophonist, for one. Steele at least represented a different kind of life, at a time when she was particularly world-weary. "The trouble with me is that everything happened when I was young," she told an interviewer, "and now nothing fazes me." In Lindsay Steele, she may have felt she had also found a strong shoulder to lean on—at least in the Harlem sense. He seemed intelligent, street-smart, was well presented, and, in the beginning at least, was protective and watchful of her welfare. There was a disastrous encounter with Bud Powell and his girlfriend that Christmas at which Steele intervened to remove the troubled Powell. And he could certainly be charming when he wanted to be. "He didn't live with her—she wouldn't let anyone live with her—but they were lovers," says Weingarten. "We'd go out partying. He had a sense of humor and was really handsome. I liked him better than any boyfriend Mary Lou had."

———

MARY COULDN'T AFFORD to rest long. There was the rent to pay. "I realized I must work again," she wrote. "But as a result of disappearing for six months, it was like starting from the bottom all over again." When a well-paying offer came her way from Critelli's Nightclub in Des Moines, with a stopover in Chicago, Mary grabbed it. But she returned to New York to a ransacked apartment. Many of her prized records were gone, along with her fur coat, jewelry, and gowns. Papers were also missing, which made documenting the losses for tax purposes a problem. "I had lost most of my receipts when my apartment was broken into. One [IRS] investigator remarked to me that a Negro would never pay as high as $500 for a gown," she added matter-of-factly. "So they wouldn't let me deduct for my gowns. There was income tax, leeches, there was paying the funeral expenses of a couple of people." And, she might have added, there were the losses sustained at poker.

Financially, she was in as bad a way as she had ever been and she didn't hesitate to accept the first recording offer to come along, a deal orchestrated by Joe Glaser. It would be hard to think of a label less suitable for Mary than King Records, which had started as a purveyor of hillbilly music, and went on to build a reputation as a rhythm-and-blues label. But it had been three years since she'd made a record as a leader, and her work for Benny Goodman had evaporated.

———

THOUGH SHE WAS eager to record right away, "it took them over two months to record me," she wrote of King Records, "and because I recorded modern music they were disappointed. They'd expected me to do the older things." In fact, Mary recorded four of her most original bop-oriented pieces, arranged for octet: "Tisherome," "Knowledge," "Shorty Boo," and "In the Land of Oo-bla-dee" (with Gillespie's vocalist Kenny "Pancho" Hagood on the vocals written by Milt Orent).

If King hated the sides, jazz critics immediately hailed them. "Knowledge," a variation on "What Is This Thing Called Love?," showcased Mary's trademark use of deft and witty interpolations. "Tisherome" (a partial anagram for "more shit") is a variant of "Knowledge," sharing its melodic line but exemplifying Mary's interest in harmonies and rhythm more vividly, with Monk-like stylings. "Shorty Boo," a languid, bluesy ballad, had been rearranged to good effect, but was saddled with mediocre lyrics. "In the Land of Oo-bla-dee" fared better, with its slightly loopy, mildly marijuana-scented words, and it became an underground hit. *Downbeat,* which awarded it four stars, declared "Oo-bla-dee" a "neat little tale of a bop princess wooed by a young man, the attempt to shuffle off a substitute bride, and the happy outcome. . . . With the use of flute [it] has managed to make the usual bop unisons sound almost colorful." But this and other rave reviews fell on deaf ears at King, which dismissed the four compositions as "bop platters" that had virtually no market. Desperate to get her records out to the stores, Mary called and telegraphed the irascible president, Sydney Nathan, repeatedly, complaining that she got no promotion. In response, Nathan shot back a snarly letter, so mean-spirited it seemed a parody. But it was for real:

> A lot of you boys seem to think that the sound of your melodious voices will influence me to do things you think you could not accomplish by means of wire or letter, but *you are wrong.* Forget about a response, 'cause you aren't getting one.

Stunned and furious, Mary began to promote "Oo-bla-dee" herself, the first of several intense efforts at self-promotion she would make in the coming decades. She roped in Lindsay and Milt Orent and anybody else she could find to help. "Milt and I sent letters and records out to hundreds of d.j.'s around the country, even to friends in radio in Canada and Paris, Italy, Johannesburg, Germany."

And she got results. "In five months, I secured three major recordings—Dizzy Gillespie on Victor; Benny Goodman on Capitol; and Les Brown, with a 60-voiced choral group for Decca. Sarah Vaughan wanted to do it, but her company, Columbia, wouldn't." Her efforts, however, were largely wasted. Gillespie's and Brown's recordings were not released, and the Goodman version, which the leader had cleansed of the more interesting bop harmonies, was not particularly successful, coming as it did just before he was about to break up his bop band. At least part of the problem was a backlash against bop, which many in that era of growing conservatism and fear of Communist subversion associated with unsavory, subversive elements; even a bop fairy tale was suspect.

Mary calculated that she spent about $1,000 to promote her records—serious money for her a half-century ago—and borrowed more. Not only would King not advance her more money toward promotion, but at the end of the year he informed her that her royalties for the entire year of 1949 amounted to only $49.25. Bound to King like a sharecropper, Mary stood by in frustration as the company insisted on extending her contract for one more year to try to recoup the "debt" of her $1,000 advance.

Glaser took Syd Nathan's side against Mary in her fight with King, writing to him:

> I realize she has been sort of a problem child to you and regret the fact you have been caused any trouble; however I am sure you realize I greatly appreciate your having recorded her at my request and if ever an opportunity presents itself where I can reciprocate you by working out deals with you for any of our attractions, it will be a pleasure.

While continuing to promote her two King 78s, Mary had a date at Café Society, with Buck Clayton on trumpet, before the club closed for good in the spring of '49. She finally had a lucky break when the Village Vanguard decided to feature jazz and offered her the debut position, opposite drummer J. C. Heard and group, in late August.

The Vanguard engagement, with Bill Clarke on drums, and Billy Moore, Jr., on bass, reestablished Mary's importance as an accomplished presence on the New York jazz scene. She was reviewed in all the important papers, and her initial two-week date was extended through the fall and into the winter. One critic noted of Mary's performance of her bop arrangement of Grieg's "Anitra's Dance": "When she comes on a particularly novel progression she nods swiftly and minutely (her neck nudges forward like a Hindoo dancer's) as if approving the hands that thought that one up. . . . Never once does the music become noisy. Just very very steady with an insistence that prickles one's spine and sends one just where it wants one to go. . . . Miss Williams . . . seems always ahead of her playing, thinking into the next phrase. . . . Bach would like what she is doing—all this building and scattering, clustering and dispersing, by-path pointing while keeping to the direction . . . creation going on under the audience's very noses."

"I always had bop ideas," she told another reviewer. "So I was glad when it got popular and I could use them more often. Right now I've got chords way ahead of bop."

Not all the reviewers were as enraptured. Many disliked bop; several felt it robbed her playing of vitality. And Mary had personnel problems. Heard, she wrote in her diary, was jealous and treated her insolently, surrounding himself with friends who were "ignorant types: loud-talking and loud-dressed." Bill Clarke also, she added somewhat cryptically, "became jealous and the friendship ended."

She had plenty of offers for work now, but distrusted agents and turned everything over to Glaser, her next best thing to a personal manager (a dream that perpetually eluded her). "Since leaving Kirk," she lamented in her writing, "I haven't ever been lucky enough to get an agent to do anything. After signing, they sit and *you* bring your own work to them. After working hard to keep going, they'll offer you a job you have to take at half the price you could have gotten yourself."

The Vanguard was a springboard, however, to other important jobs. She appeared in Boston at John Hancock Hall for a week in October of '49, opposite pianist Lennie Tristano and his group, performing bop arrangements of her material, including pieces from *Zodiac*. Her admiration for Tristano cooled a little after the date; she felt on further listening that there was too little contrast in his music.

That she felt desperate for someone to straighten out her career (or life) is something she revealed only to her diaries. "Harlem," she wrote, "had taken me to the cleaners." In the early winter of 1950, while appearing in Chicago's Music Bar, she reached out to John Williams, who had moved to Chicago after leaving the music business in the early forties. She still admired his intelligence and his ability "to maneuver" and "exploit"—two of her most positive verbs.

But Williams turned her down. "Mary was in town with a group," recalled Williams. "She asked me to come by, so I visited her at her hotel. She said, 'Come back and handle this band for me.' Mary was having problems with the group, controlling them, and she was really asking for help, you see. I was like a big brother to her. She said, why didn't we get back together. I said no, 'It is over.' I was in love. I had a girlfriend, Kathleen Duncan, who would become my wife in 1951."

Mary said nothing about this meeting to anyone, as was her custom. But she returned to a life lived constantly on the edge. To pay bills, she turned out arrangements: Benny Goodman, Earl Hines, Woody Herman, and Nat Cole all gave her work. As for recording, it had been ten months since she made a record for King. King wanted her to record some organ music, presumably more in the R&B vein, while Mary wanted to make a solo piano jazz record. Insisting on control of the next recording session, they sent a black producer to take her in hand, and in January of 1950 she went into the studio again. Mary detested this producer (in her fashion, she does not identify him in her diary, though in all probability it was Henry Glover, an important presence at King). The only input allowed her was the choice of a rhythm section: she went with the excellent players George Duvivier on bass, Denzil Best on drums, and Mundell Lowe on guitar. Of this session she notes merely: "I sat down and played a distorted organ and piano and then I got out of the place."

The results were predictable. "Willow Weep for Me" was "pleasant, with Garnerish overtones," as one reviewer said, but it was paired with an unremarkable "I'm in the Mood for Love." Worse was the odd, rather disjointed sound of organ with piano overdubbed on "Bye Bye Blues" and its flip side, "Moonglow." The January sides sank with barely a ripple of interest. Now Mary was on the warpath. She had performed as King wanted. Now she pressed the company hard to let her record a solo recording, as specified in her contract, before she began a club date in March 1950. But King kept stalling her. Doubtless there had been words at the disastrous organ-piano session. "She was not pliable and couldn't be used by other people. No matter what anybody did, she could not be deterred. And that could be enraging," notes Peter O'Brien, who managed her career later.

It was guerrilla warfare. The producer claimed he arrived at her apartment to pick her up for the recording date but that she was "passed out, drunk." As the consummate professional, Mary was incensed by such an assertion. She tried to break her contract, pleaded with them to let her go. The company stood firm. Ironically, now, after years of neglect, her Village Vanguard date had brought expressions of interest in recordings from important labels. One record producer suggested she do an album of her modern work; another wanted an album of piano rags. Mary went so far as to prepare material and a budget for a recording session of all new originals—but with another artist, Bobby Tucker, on piano. (Fragments of pieces probably intended for that session, including lyrics without music to "Bebop Blues" and "Lessons in Bopology," survive, in Mary's hand, among her papers.)

King still would not let her go, but neither would they record her. Finally, in September 1950, Mary took the drastic step of filing a claim with the American Federation of Musicians for breach of contract. James Petrillo, head of the AFM, seethed when he learned the facts from her. "The idea of tying up this artist for two or three years without doing anything with her!" he fumed at King, and he got her a release at the end of the year. It was something of a Pyrrhic victory. It was "detrimental to an artist to secure a release this way," Mary wrote, fearing that she would be viewed as a troublemaker by other record companies, and ostracized. She was right. On top of that, she was suspended from Union Local 802 in New York for nonpayment of dues, which meant she could not work where she lived until she paid up. It had not been a good year.

Mary tried once more, now desperate—there is no other word to describe the fever pitch of urgency in her correspondence—to get a record contract. She borrowed money again and made test pressings of new ideas—a bop piano trio version of "The Sheik of Araby," and vocal experiments on "Cloudy" and "Yes, We Have No Bananas," hiring professional singers to tackle the difficult harmonies. "For years I had been experimenting with voices the way I heard them. I wanted to have them sing like instruments. I had used several groups for tests." She took her test pressings all around New York, but over and over, "I was turned down." Nor did other plans pan out, including an offer by David Stone Martin's brother to record her for a label he hoped to start. He didn't have enough money to get it off the ground.

Mary's urgency may have been driven by a sense of being preempted. She explained, "I had to get my experiments recorded along with a piano thing with bongo, because already a few people were trying to pick up on this sound. I had decided to start a bop era," she added, referring to the general dearth of recording of the new crop of beboppers—a claim teetering between hubris, on the one hand, and artistic self-confidence on the other, with a rich lode of fantasy in the middle. "By 1951 no one cared to record me until a friend of mine, Nicole Barclay, came in from Europe. Nicole took me to Jimmy Ryan's Dixieland Club to meet kind Rudi Blesh, whom I shall always be very grateful to. I asked him for a record date and he immediately said yes."

Rudi Blesh owned and operated Circle Records. He was a great fan of ragtime and "trad" jazz, caring nothing for bop, but to his credit, he indulged Mary out of his high regard for her—that and the fact that she probably managed to convince him that there was a significant market niche to be tapped for her kind of jazz. She brought him her test records. In Mary's honor, Blesh inaugurated a line of modern trends in jazz on Circle, but as it turned out, hers was to be the first and last in this category.

Nicole Barclay, who had brought Mary and Blesh together and would reappear a few years later in Mary's story, was a chic, wealthy Frenchwoman, a jazz lover married to Eddie Barclay, with whom she started the record companies Blue Star and Barclay. The labels produced mostly expatriate American musicians and also reissued American-made jazz. Nicole Barclay had come to New York to promote a proposed jazz festival in Paris. She hoped to get Art Tatum to headline the event, but Tatum pulled out, so she tried to persuade Mary to take his place. But Mary balked, claiming the salary was too low—and fearful of being stranded in Europe, as had happened to a number of her friends. (But Barclay's offer had planted the seed, and in two years Mary did leave for Europe, where she recorded for Barclay in Paris, including the lovely modern blues ballad "Nicole.")

Blesh gave Mary studio time in June 1951. But before Mary's Circle date, in March 1951, she recorded an LP for Atlantic Records. Here she showed herself to be under the sway of Erroll Garner, especially with respect to his use of time lags and voicings, but there was rather a tentative feeling to her playing, perhaps reflecting the strain she was under. The record got a good critical reception, but Mary was far more interested in her projects for Circle and hardly mentioned the Atlantic date, though it does contain several new originals and works by Herbie Nichols. By June of 1951, Mary had her arrangements ready and went into the studio on June 10th. That first session was one of her most creative and productive. With Billy Taylor on bass, Al Walker on drums and bongos, she recorded three of her modern originals—"Bobo," "Kool," and "Tisherome"—plus modern arrangements of "The Sheik of Araby" and "St. Louis Blues/Handy Eyes."

"Kool" had a lighter feel than in the Asch version, and "Tisherome" in particular was beautifully played and more effective than in its earlier King version. Opening to a rumba beat, it moved into straight 4/4 jazz time with strong, atmospheric chords. "Handy Eyes" (Mary's reworking of "St. Louis Blues") had of course been evolving for years, "typical of her application of modern harmonies to the folk blues," as Allan Morison wrote in the liner notes. Similarly, her highly rhythmic "Sheik of Araby" showed how far she had come.

"Bobo," adapted from "Bobo and Doodles," is the most musically advanced of the eight tunes on the album *Piano Contempo: Modern Piano Jazz*. It is one of her strangest pieces, mixing Afro-Cuban rhythms and chants (invocations by Willie Bobo that Mary may or may not have known were chants to santería deities), with Schoenbergian dissonances and bop harmonies, ending with a quote from Bud Powell's "Tempus Fugit." Sadly, though much of the material on the Circle record was brilliant, it went out of print almost immediately.

On June 15, five days later, Mary was back in the studio. "I thought up an idea of voices singing like instruments, also piano solos with bongo, bass and drums," she wrote, describing an idea she had already tried out in works like *Elijah* and her test record the year before. Now she used a singer friend, then-struggling Dave Lambert (later well known as part of Lambert, Hendricks, and Ross), who brought with him a group of eight musician-singers to work on four arrangements.

The results were dismal. As the rehearsal tapes Mary kept document, the group was simply not up to the job of Mary's close harmonies and difficult rhythms. Mary's piano weaves precisely through take after mushy take. At times she lets loose a slammed chord that cracks like a slap, signaling her loss of patience.

It must have been instantly apparent to her on that June day that her ideas, so carefully burnished, were not to be implemented. There were other, curious lapses. "Da Function" is a repetitive West Indian ditty, sung by a mediocre calypso singer, that simply had no place with Mary's compositions. Perhaps she chose it because calypso was then enjoying a vogue; perhaps, too, to help out the composer, pianist Herbie Nichols, a new friend introduced by Monk. (Besides the wretched "Da Function," she recorded his lackluster ballad "I Won't Let It Bother Me," as well as several of his tunes on her Atlantic record.) A sensitive, literate man, Nichols wrote Mary a letter that hinted at romantic feelings on his part: "I suppose the reason I left so many tunes with you were selfish ones—I derived pleasure from watching you smile at the different morsels."

Neither did Mary's ambitious vocal arrangements work. On two old warhorses, "Cloudy" and "Froggy Bottom," the group never comes close to the kind of ethereal, sighing vocal effects she aimed for. After what Mary called a "discussion," she then reluctantly agreed to the singers' demands that she speed up the tempos (they were funereal) and change the key signature: that, she complained, "immediately gave it a different sound and we struggled through rehearsal." To loosen things up, she added, she "let the musicians use stimulants but still nothing. I gave up. I never saw such a crazy session in all my life."

The tune that Mary pinned her hopes on was "Walking Out the Door," a.k.a. "Walkin'," her jaunty modern blues with bop piano accents and vocals, which Benny Goodman had recorded in 1949. A creditable take of "Walkin'" was finally made and released with "Sheik of Araby" on a 78, but it was not a hit, although musicians and hip listeners liked it. (The best version of "Walkin'" was made by Nat Cole for Capitol Records in an arrangement by Billy May.) Several other tunes from the June sessions were released on Circle 78s, notably "Caravan" and Mary's amusing bop version of "Yes, We Have No Bananas," the latter with a short intro by Dave Lambert. Rehearsal tapes Mary kept of "Caravan" are highly indicative of her wide-ranging musicality. In one take, she interpolates "her" Bud Powell tune "Tempus Fugit" along with bass and/or conga, while another builds a brooding, subtle bop version on piano alone.

Then Mary cut what should have been one of her most important record albums of the post-Kirk period: for about twenty minutes, she simply improvised on favorite tunes alone at the piano, achieving the intimate feeling that her nightclub and living room listeners always said showed Mary to best advantage. Here were her advanced harmonies, her trademark ethereal-sounding chords ("Yesterdays" and "People Will Say We're in Love"), her architectonic knowledge of jazz music (turning "Stompin' at the Savoy" into a modern blues). On "For the Man I Love," a.k.a. "For You," dedicated to Thelonious Monk, she constructed a wistful spiral of emotion that climaxed with a perfectly placed quote from *Rhapsody in Blue*. But once again, a major effort went nowhere: provisionally titled *Mary Lou at Midnight*, the recording was never released.

The disappointments surrounding Circle—her unsatisfactory ensemble sessions, the withdrawal of the promised release of much material, the poor sales of the few tunes that were halfheartedly marketed—all compounded Mary's growing depression, and her sense of personal crisis deepened. "I really saw the toughest time of my entire life," she wrote. Steele, no longer the romantic cavalier, grew jealous and controlling. "He was very narrow-minded and after a while, no one would come around. When I went out he'd almost get in fights if anyone looked at me. I was a nervous wreck. I'd say to myself, 'Well you've gotten yourself in a real mess now, experimenting.' "

Steele, who had notions of starting a singing career, used Mary as a springboard on the Circle dates; his voice is impressively present on several of the unreleased cuts, especially "Cloudy." Steele also demanded that Mary give him co-composer credit for "Walkin' Out the Door" (which they both hoped would become a hit song), claiming she'd taken his idea, a line from a letter of apology he wrote after an argument: "I'm walking out the door (had you on my mind)." Mary refused: she had written the music and, with help from Orent, most of the lyric. Nevertheless, Steele threatened a lawsuit unless he got half the composer's royalties. A fine romance. Reluctantly, Mary gave in. "I must have lost two years off my life, trying to analyze him and the situation," Mary wrote, adding that he was loyal to his friends but had "no confidence in women."

Mary's sense of frustration is palpable in a letter she wrote to ASCAP in 1951 canceling her membership. If she had been justly proud in '43 to be the first black woman accepted into the organization that represented composers of the stature of Ellington and Gershwin and Kern, in 1951—less than a decade later—she could no longer afford to belong. "I have not made enough royalties from my compositions to be paying an additional amount of money for dues," she wrote plainly. "I have received less money in the last five years than for my entire years of writing. Have visited your office trying to obtain help. I'm sorry but publishers do not pay me. I have spent a fortune with lawyers in New York."

The sad fact was, she had not registered many of her earlier compositions with the U.S. Copyright Office, with the result that she could not claim ownership. She tried to redress the situation, as thick files of letters and lists she typed of her songs attest. And though a stream of lawyers, short-lived personal managers, and publicity agents came in and out of her life, none of them was ever able to straighten out the tangled mess of copyright issues. "I really don't think I'll be writing music for publication again," she said, adding with self-mocking half-humor, "I told a friend if he ever caught me writing again, to kick me."

At least there were a few bright spots in '51. In the fall, she had engagements at the Savoy in Boston, at the Hi Note in Chicago, and at the Blue Note in Philadelphia. Then, bad news when she lost a royalty fight on "Pretty-Eyed Baby," her tune that had begun life as "Satchel Mouth Baby." An R&B singer changed a piece of the lyric and trombonist Snub Moseley, who had added a tag at the end of the song, sued for co-composer credit. Mary fought them both. "But I finally had to compromise," she wrote glumly. "There were a lot of meetings with lawyers, and Johnson and Snub Moseley got ⅓ of the song."

Badly in need of "loot," as she always called money, Mary went once again to Joe Glaser, but he had nothing for her. In November, her pent-up frustration and rage poured out in a letter to Glaser, in which she accused him of exploiting Negro entertainers, especially women, and blamed him for her money problems. Everything was going wrong for her, it seemed. There was Steele, her ball-and-chain, and a fresh disappointment with a well-known publicity agent who had begun plotting a career for Mary in the new medium of television. At first, things looked promising. The agent booked her on a good number of shows, and she also received a tentative offer for a fifteen-minute weekly show of her own. But that fell through, too, when the agent fell in love with her. "I began having trouble with him. He did great publicity but was revengeful. He'd call me all morning, came to the house, tried to kick the door in." Her only real friends, she wrote sadly, were "David Stone Martin and musicians like Milt Orent, Bernie Levin, Billy Jacobs and Allan Felman." Gone from the list were family and the bop musicians who been such close friends only a few years before. Still, there were a few bright moments. Joe Glaser, who knew Mary's moods very well, forged a reconciliation with her and by Christmas they were back on their old footing, with Glaser taking over where the possessive publicity man had left off.

The year 1952 was an improvement over 1951. She was booked with her old friend Mildred Bailey in the summer at a club on Fifty-second Street, "a terrific engagement except that Mildred used to become disturbed." In October Mary was fêted at Town Hall by a group called the Committee for the Negro in the Arts. Sidney Poitier was the host, and many of her friends performed, including Monk, Billy Taylor, Eartha Kitt, and others. That same year, the creamy-voiced Billy Eckstine, a fellow Pittsburgher, asked Mary to join his group at

Bop City, which led to jobs at Kelly's Stables, Storyville, and the Rhythm Room in New York, and clubs in Philadelphia.

By far her most important engagement in 1952 was at the Downbeat Club, where she was booked with a trio on and off, starting in September. There Mary put together what she called a dream band with Kenny "Klook" Clarke on drums and Oscar Pettiford on bass. Clarke knew Mary from Pittsburgh and Pettiford was one of Mary's favorites, though she noted he could be difficult when he drank his favorite cocktail, called a Moscow Mule. "There wasn't a set we didn't compose on the spot when I played with the trio. Pettiford would start something and I'd add to it with Klook carrying on in the background," she wrote. Among those ideas was a tune called "Swingin' Til the Guys Come Home," that Pettiford cited as "Swingin' Til the *Girls* Come Home." (When Mary recorded it in France in 1954, she gave co-composer credit to Pettiford.)

Playing opposite Mary and her dream team was the young and fiery Billy Taylor with his trio. He inspired her further, helped "keep her up," said Mary. Taylor adds affectionately, "She'd try to swing me out of the club. She was *very* competitive musically but she was never mean, and off the bandstand, she was quite shy." They often exchanged lead sheets for favorite tunes, including their own. Fine players passed through the band: trumpeter Kenny Dorham, trombonists Bill Harris and Kai Winding, saxophonists Zoot Sims and Charlie Parker. It was around that time that Charlie Parker, she recalled, asked her to come down to Birdland (where he was regularly hired and fired, depending on his drug use); he wanted her to hear his experiments playing with strings there. Mary was all for it. A little later, kicked out of Birdland again, Parker was hanging around the clubs and stopped in the Downbeat. Mary wrote in her diary, "Charlie Parker came in one night and he said to me, 'Lou, let's get a band or something together. You know all the cats always want me to get a band with you.' I said, 'No, man, not the condition you're in.' He said, 'Mary, anything you tell me I'll do.' He said, 'You know I'm not allowed to play in Birdland or any of the clubs.' So I told him, 'Get up on the stand and let the people see how great you are.' The place was really packed because a lot of the people had followed me from the East Side. Charlie Parker got up on the stand and he said, 'Play the Kansas City blues.' Listen, I've never heard Coltrane play what that boy did! No! During the time that he played I don't know what carried us along with him because there were sounds that we'd never played before. . . . Charlie Parker kept going to keys and he kept going through changes. Oscar said, 'Mary, where is he now?' I said, 'Man, don't talk to me now.' . . . When he finished everybody just screamed. He said, 'How was that?' I said, 'Man, that was too great for me.' "

That Charlie Parker should not be allowed to work at Birdland, the club named after him, registered deeply with Mary. "I was in New York when musicians were barred from several clubs, even those that weren't using heroin," she wrote. But she knew she had been stigmatized as well, by her close association with musicians known to be addicts, so that some people just assumed she was a junkie. She was also distressed by what she saw as the opportunism of some white musicians, who seemed bent on eliminating competition from black musicians. "All during the war when they were trying to learn bop and didn't have time to listen to prejudiced talk, they were lovey-dovey," Mary wrote. In her diary, she detailed a rare specific complaint against a fellow musician: "Oscar [Pettiford] had employed Lee Konitz and Kai Winding the first time he took his small combo into Snookie's. Lee Konitz at the time hadn't worked in quite awhile and was working part-time in a record shop. First he was happy to work with Oscar until an offer came for him to either join Stan Kenton or some other outfit, and then he made deprecating remarks."

———

AS SUCH THINGS tend to do, Mary's dream band drifted apart. She went on tour and came back to find that Pettiford had joined another band. In her absence, Mary had been booked to play with a band made up of former Woody Herman sidemen. "Out of six musicians I was the only Negro. I played along with them until I felt it was the worst. So I left without giving notice." There was an angry phone confrontation with the club's management about the dearth of black musicians on the bandstand. Mary got her way. "I returned—after the manager consented to equalize—that is, use a mixed outfit." Furthermore, she added with satisfaction, she was given a raise.

But by then, Mary had received an intriguing offer to go abroad, by liner, from booking agent Joe Marsolais, who worked for Moe Gale's agency, a rival of Joe Glaser's Associated Booking. It was billed as a nine-day tour of England, with Mary as the featured star of an enter-tainment package—an excellent opportunity, Marsolais pointed out, to internationalize her audience. Mary hesitated. Europe was an unknown quantity. Also, England presented a special problem: its musicians' union had, in effect, banned American jazz groups by demanding that for every American jazz musician who performed in England, an English jazz musician be booked in the United States. Worse, the only American musicians allowed to work in British night-clubs were singers.

Mary turned the offer down, but Marsolais persisted: how much of a risk could it be? She would be the star of the show, with guaranteed salary and expenses. She could sail back after the Christmas holidays, and the Downbeat Club promised to keep her job open.

A great sticking point in their negotiations was Mary's insistence that she have a return ticket in hand before she sailed. In the end, Mar-solais managed to convince her it would be waiting for her on the other side, so she consented, well aware that her career needed a boost. In fact, the only record she had made that year was a swing-style jam session in July; Mary led a septet that included Harold Baker on trumpet.

Before sailing on the 28th of November, Mary went to Pittsburgh for an early Thanksgiving with the Burleys. While there, her aunt Anna Mae made her several stunning couture-copied gowns for the trip. Returning to New York, she was booked on the airwaves on Thanksgiv-ing, playing "Lullaby of Birdland" with Roy Haynes and Oscar Petti-ford on a CBS radio show, then down the hall to perform "Lullaby" again and "Tea for Two," for Steve Allen's show.

All was not roses that night. Hovering in the background through-out was Lindsay Steele; he made certain he accompanied Mary every-where, both to boost his fledgling singing career and to keep an eye on her. At the radio station, recalls Peter O'Brien, "She told me that he tried to intervene with an engineer at the studio and she told him to stay out of it, that he didn't know anything about it. Then he knocked her down." Mary, O'Brien added, sounded simply matter-of-fact years later when she related this latest incidence of physical violence.

Afterwards, she partied until early in the morning with friends Oscar Pettiford and Erroll Garner, arriving home at dawn to grab some sleep before finishing her packing. In the afternoon she went down to the pier to board ship, still accompanied by Steele, to whom she had entrusted the keys of her apartment and who was supposed to look after things in her absence.

Aboard the *Queen Elizabeth,* on which Marsolais had booked passage in a handsome stateroom in exchange for her playing nightly for the passengers, she must have felt a great sense of relief as the liner pulled away from shore. How bracing the sea air must have been— breathed alone, in the blessed quiet that feeds an introvert's soul. Free of Steele at last. Later she would tell close friends like Barry Ulanov and Peter O'Brien about her apprehensions, but not then; as usual, she kept her troubles to herself. But Mary was afraid of Steele.

As she faced the gray, cold expanse of the Atlantic, did Mary, as sensitive as she was, have a premonition that her voyage would turn out to be a sea change indeed? First, she would not be away only two weeks, as planned, but two *years.* And during that time, her life would take a painful, profound turn: she was about to enter her "dark night of the soul."

As the *Queen Elizabeth* headed out of New York harbor that November evening in 1952, away from the city that for a decade had schooled her in so many hard lessons, one can imagine Mary alone on the deck in the night, the collar of her mink coat turned up, until the cold air at last drove her inside, where the passengers waited to be entertained below by boogie-woogie in the lounge.

Chapter Fourteen
Chez Mary Lou
1952–1954

DESPITE HER RELIEF at escaping her problems at home, Mary's mood did not improve. As she wrote of the passengers who gathered in the lounge of the ship to listen to what they thought of as "jazz," "I said to myself, here is that commercial shit again. Well, I know what I'll have to do, return to the ol' training, and play what they like. And I broke it up until we had to be run off to bed at about three in the morning."

She was run-down, and soon a combination of seasickness and flu made her consider canceling the English tour and simply heading for home again once they docked in England. Her mood worsened once the ship came in at Southampton and she'd cleared Customs. She was made to wait in the unheated station for several hours until a "weasel-looking chap came to pick me up. Now I was cold as a Norwegian turd and evil. Here I was alone in a strange country . . . blanketed in fog. . . . Being alone threw me off balance at first. Forget it and work if you can, I told myself."

In London, however, she was mollified when greeted with due ceremony by a small but extremely devoted jazz coterie: English jazz fans waving flags, presenting her with bouquets, sending mounds of telegrams and invitations to parties. They were starved for the real thing. She was booked for a radio broadcast on the BBC's "In Town Tonight" before her debut concert at the Royal Albert Hall on December 7, and made an invaluable friend in a tireless young editor named

Max Jones, who worked for the English paper *Melody Maker*. Mary's fears were soothed, and her health somewhat strengthened, at her enthusiastic reception. "Firsts" were important to Mary, and for her the tour of England had missionary overtones. "I was sent to England to break the ban that prevented American musicians from playing in England," she was wont to recall, adding with a touch of her typical bravado that she was allowed to play with all the bands and musicians there. Another first: this, she said, had never happened in thirty years.

This was only partly true, as she soon learned. As far as the union was concerned, jazz pianists were not "concert musicians" but "variety" artists—the English equivalent of vaudeville performers. When she became aware of this distinction, so reminiscent of the patronizing of jazz she had detested at home, Mary's mood fell. She felt "sick and blue," she confided. "Being in Europe made me realize how great being black is. But, I haven't the least idea what I'm doing in Europe. I'm here, so what." Worse was to come. The big show, of which she was billed as the star—"The Big Rhythm Show of 1952"—was a package that consisted mostly of variety acts, and she shared headliner status with Cab Calloway and Marie Bryant, two unmodern entertainers. All of this had been put together by agent Harry Dawson, the same "weasel-looking chap" she'd met at Southampton, who promoted Mary in ads as "America's Queen of the Ivories." Hardly the serious artistic consideration she had been led to expect.

But reviews of her Albert Hall concert were ecstatic; as Max Jones wrote, even those who were familiar with her work after the Clouds of Joy were unprepared for her high level of artistry. It was, he wrote, "nothing less than a revelation. It is the overall impact of her greatness that is quite overwhelming." Mary was also overwhelmed, but negatively again, by the playing and living conditions. "The fog in Albert Hall was so bad I couldn't even see my rhythm," she wrote, and complained about the local sidemen (as she would do often back in New York). "I expected too much. The bassist should be so relaxed that if the pianist decides to make different changes, or to modulate, he can automatically follow."

Mary was unhappy, too, with her accommodations at the Airways Mansions (which did not live up to its name), the poor quality of the food, and the lack of heat that postwar England still endured. In a funk she wrote: "Terrible fog . . . What a dreary lonesome kinda world to be in, I'm sad, I wanta go home." She went so far as to inquire about her return ticket at Fosters, the English booking agent handling the tour. But they were firm: she had to complete her contract first. There were eight more concerts to go—in Manchester, Southampton, Leicester, and elsewhere—culminating in one on the 28th of December, at which time she would be at liberty to sail to New York.

It had been one thing to be young and foolish in the 1930s, living on poor-boy sandwiches and corn taken from the field, with her buddies in the Clouds of Joy. It was quite another to be a woman in her forties, enduring unheated bus trips through icy fog, and always, she wrote with astonishment, offered the same thing for dinner: fish and chips. And, ominously, in several theaters the house was only half-full and Dawson was having trouble making the payroll. Lil Hardin Armstrong arrived to take Cab Calloway's place, played one show, then refused to go on again until she had cash in hand. Mary got in a fight with Dawson. "At one point, I went for my shoe to crown the Weasel—Higgins intervened."

"Higgins"—Jack Higgins, a young English agent—was one of the bright spots. Having instantly fallen in love with Mary, he was trying to help her sort out her problems. "Back then, in terms of the business, it was dog eat dog in Europe," says British-born singer Annie Ross, who was to meet Mary there as a neophyte jazz singer who liked to hang out with expatriate American performers. "Agents would book you at one rate, but have a higher rate actually with the club. They would take in the difference *plus* their commission." Not so different from what went on in America, but with maneuvers and hustles unfamiliar to a Yank. Still, Mary had learned to fight for her rights as a performer. "Women had to have a sense of aggressiveness to survive, it was absolutely necessary, and Mary had that," Annie Ross recalls.

Despite her unhappiness, Mary looked decidedly glamorous—and younger than forty-two—in chic gowns that emphasized her smooth satin skin and ripe figure. She wore her lustrous black hair short, or swept up so as to emphasize her beautiful cheekbones. And she had a demure self-possession tinged with hauteur that appealed to the English. It was only her eyes, often tired and wary, that gave evidence of her inner turbulence.

Jack Higgins saw to it that Mary got her money, paid her little attentions, such as putting fresh flowers in her dressing rooms, and located more interesting food for her. They began an affair, according to singers Thelma Carpenter and Annie Ross, who were on the scene; she was, he wrote, his "dearest Mary Lou," "my love," and "Pussycat." When they were apart, he counted the days until he'd see her again. But Mary tired quickly of the affair. He was, she wrote in her diary, her "kind associate," nothing more. Then followed an argument: she had learned that he owed money to everybody in London. He became the "jinx," an agent, someone to keep at arm's length. Eventually, a rapprochement, but for Mary, the affair was over. Years later, Higgins and Mary did business again when he booked her at Ronnie Scott's club in London.

Toward the end of the run Dawson was not able to meet his "Big Rhythm Show" payroll at all and at least one or two concerts had to be delayed; in limbo, Mary could not return to the States as planned. The money was very important to her, but she was so angry that when the last concert was rescheduled for the first week in January of 1953, she had to be threatened with a lawsuit before she'd show up and play.

After completing the tour, Mary told the British press she "was bitterly disappointed." By then, though, she had second thoughts about going home, saying she "wanted to play and record with British musicians, compose and arrange for British bands." Yet with no more work lined up, she would be compelled by British law to leave the country. Nor could she afford to wait for work. She was, by now, reduced to sharing a flat with two tap dancers whose tall figures it amused her to watch as they bent over a tiny alcohol stove, cooking a supper of franks and beans. Sometimes they got lucky: stewards she'd befriended on the voyage over snuck in steaks from America for favorites like Mary. As for restaurants, her friend Gray Weingarten, who was in London on her honeymoon in early January, recalls that "Mary advised us to eat just at this one little Jewish deli she knew, because at least it was clean."

Max Jones and other friends managed to get around the strict British music union laws and lined up some concert appearances for her, the first with jazz bandleader Ted Heath at the Palladium on January 25th. Three days before, Mary cut an impressive recording for the Vogue label with a British rhythm section, playing mostly bop compositions unfamiliar to many of her European listeners. Reviewers praised her phrasing and ideas. There was humor on "Koolbongo," fire on "Titoros," lyricism on "Lady Bird" and "Perdido," and a pensive quality to "'Round Midnight"—"so uncompromisingly grave," wrote one reviewer, "that it will have limited appeal; yet its unsmiling beauty covers an inner warmth."

There were also negative reviews for the record. The "trads" stopped at the swing era, and one self-styled "critic" of their breed wrote, "Her ideas are so banal and cliche-ridden that any discerning listener must soon suffer an onslaught of ennui."

Probably around the same time (though discographies date it a year later) she recorded again for Vogue, with a different combo, several more of her original compositions and an outstanding bop-tinged treatment of "The Man I Love" that swings relentlessly but unobtrusively.

After playing Royal Festival Hall on February 15 and Royal Albert Hall for a second time on February 22 with Sarah Vaughan, Mary was signed in March by the London label for a series of records. Disappointingly, only two of the four tunes she recorded were issued, and both in a style she did not often visit: ragtime. "Laughing Rag," by Derek New, and "Rag of Rags," by David Bee, were produced, as one review explained, "with an eye to sales to the general public." But the idea may well have been Mary's, for she had almost produced a ragtime album in the forties and would certainly play ragtime again. Although her foray into ragtime was received well by the "trad" critics, who noted that her playing was "gay and full of the tunefulness typical of years ago . . . [with] great elegance and precision," the record passed quickly into obscurity.

By March, Mary decided to prolong her stay. She had various plans in mind—and she had begun to work on her autobiography, a project especially dear to her heart.

———

HER STORY, SHE felt, was unique; and Max Jones had offered to help. They planned for Mary to write up notes on her life for a series of articles that Jones would edit and publish in *Melody Maker*. After that, it seemed certain that a book publisher would express interest. But she soon discovered how treacherous the path to writing about one's own past can be. Faced with the blank page, and the dilemma of what to reveal and what to suppress, she froze. Musicians were family, and Mary wrote to Jones that she didn't want to reveal things that might damage their reputation. The letters that flew back and forth between them in 1953—while Mary was touring on the Continent a good deal—reveal Jones to be a patient man but harassed by missed editorial deadlines (his own editor's motto was, he said, "I don't want it good, I want it Friday"). Still, together they managed to produce a well-told, entertaining version of her life in eleven articles, totaling around 20,000 words. Entitled *Mary Lou Williams: My Life with the Kings of Jazz,* the series veiled Mary's serious purpose in writing about her life. Headings like "Gambler's Mascot," "Then Came Zombie Music," and "The Mad Monk" were calculated to appeal to the foreign fantasy of an America that had produced Al Capone, cowboys, flappers—and jazz. The BBC aired readings of some of the episodes, and Max Jones took steps to help her organize a book, providing suggestions, even a possible title, *Piano for Sale.* But for whatever reason, he bowed out as collaborator on a book, and after the series had run in the magazine, the project lay dormant for several years.

Mary continued to concertize in the spring. Then, in June of '53, she was offered a job touring on the continent with Louis Armstrong and the All-Stars, a well-paying, steady job for the rest of the summer. But, warned Joe Glaser, "I am sure you know the group plays a certain type of music and it would be necessary for you to conform, and if you are willing to do this let me hear from you immediately." Not surprisingly, Mary turned down the offer, telling friends she wanted to form her own group and be happy in her work. In fact, she had plans to put together a big band in Europe for one-nighters on the continent, though she soon scaled things back to a more manageable combo size. But even that proved impossible. She did not have her membership card yet in the British Musicians' Union, a necessity; and she could not get it for six more months, after she had been in Britain a year. Her friends and fans were furious. Wrote Max Jones: "As Mary Lou has been so ill-served in this country, it seems as though there is no real demand for good jazz pianists." But she did at least make more records in May, including her originals "Music Maker" and the interesting, boppish "Musical Express."

After touring Paris and Holland in June, and playing several engagements in London, Mary decided to move to Paris in November. She was booked at a club renamed the Chez Mary Lou (the old Perdido Club at 49 rue de Ponthieu, which had gone bust) while doubling at the elegant Ringside (27 rue d'Artois), where she was touted as "*la célèbre pianiste noire américaine.*" A nice touch were the embossed cards distributed by nightclubs to publicize performers. "You are cordially invited to hear Mary Lou Williams," cooed the Ringside—in French, naturally. Best of all for Mary, there were no hassles over union membership.

In Paris, Mary met up with old friends like Don Byas and dozens of expatriate Americans who preferred France. She became friendly with the venerable clarinetist Sidney Bechet, who had settled there, and was much beloved. Mary took a reluctant young Annie Ross to hear Bechet, advising her not to close her mind to *any* music. "I was knocked out, Bechet swung beautifully, I *loved* it," Ross says. "Bechet's hobby was collecting loose emeralds, and he gave Mary a handful that evening."

From the isolation of England, Mary was plunged into the gaiety of Parisian society. "She knew everybody!" writes another expatriate pianist, her friend Aaron Bridgers. Mary moved into the modest Hotel Cristal on the Left Bank, home to such struggling writers as James Baldwin and Chester Himes, actor Canada Lee, and Eartha Kitt, and Baron Timme Rosenkrantz, who with Inez Cavanaugh ran a little soul-food bar. Hazel Scott, who was then at the height of her career and had a glamorous flat in another arrondissement, often dropped by to visit. Accommodations were rudimentary, recalls Annie Ross. "No one at the Cristal had a private bath. I remember Inez sang a song about 'Pissin' in the warm bidet because the loo in the hall's too cold,' something like that."

For a while Mary shared digs at the Cristal with Annie Ross (the dancer Taps Miller, who became Ross's lover, was down the hall). Often Mary took Ross to jam with her in a basement room of a restaurant on the Champs Élysées; just like the Dewey Square Hotel, it boasted a piano, and whoever was in town would drop in to jam, Ross recalls: Jack Teagarden, Don Byas. And Jack Higgins hung around, still in love with Mary.

Paris was then also full of American artists, veterans of the war who came to Paris supported by the GI Bill. Romare Bearden was there, though he had stopped painting at the time. James Baldwin had been there since '49, and had just published his first novel, *Go Tell It on the Mountain*. "Baldwin was 'Jimmy' to us then," says Annie Ross. "I remember we used to collect milk bottles for the deposit money. It was expensive in Paris. Nobody had any money, we lived day to day, including Mary Lou."

"I must say, Paris was the happiest place for me," Mary wrote. Mainly she meant the music. There were plenty of places to listen, from the elegant Ringside to the musicians' and writers' hangout, the Mars Club, and the established but still bohemian Le Boeuf sur le Toit. In December, she recorded again for Vogue, arguably the best recording of her stay in Europe, with Don Byas providing sweet-and-sour poetry with his tenor saxophone on her bop blues "O.W." and on a softly shimmering duet in the yearningly lovely ballad "Why?" With this recording, no longer did bop predominate in her playing but was, rather, incorporated seamlessly into the mix. Above all, there was a sheen of sadness that overlaid the recording, an accurate reading of Mary's state of mind.

She was still restless, unhappy, and decided to return to Britain after Christmas. Finally, she wrote excitedly in her diary, she had an offer to tour England with her own band, playing her new material instead of the swing-era pieces still associated with her from the Clouds of Joy days. Also on the bill would be the neophyte Ross, with Taps Miller dancing. On Christmas night, she played in a glittering concert billed as the "Concert de l'École Française Moderne de Jazz" at the commodious Palais de Chaillot in Paris and then took the boat-train with Ross and Miller to Dover. The plan was to fill an engagement at the Bandbox Club in London and then put together her band.

It was a debacle. Max Jones was there to greet them—with a brass band, at that—but both Mary and Taps Miller were refused entry when their papers were found to be technically not in order (Mary lacked a work permit from the Ministry of Labor). "They just decided not to let them in," remembers Annie Ross. "We had to go all the way back to Cherbourg, and then sleep in the waiting room there while we waited to get back to Paris. And everybody was broke."

"The Jazz Wagon," announced an English paper in February, "starring the British band led by Jack Parnell, will not include Mary Lou Williams as originally planned."

———

MARY MOVED BACK to the Cristal, where her luck improved only a little. On the one hand, work was far more abundant than in England. "I had many job offers from Delaunay [the modern jazz enthusiast and impresario]," she wrote, "but I refused them due to the low salaries paid in Paris. Instead I played many radio and TV programs in Paris, Holland, Switzerland, Belgium, Sweden, Italy." Occasionally she also played in Paris clubs, like the Metro. But the work was more sporadic than it sounds, and Mary had resumed her old "nite life" gambling binges. The result was that she was scuffling, and decided she should go home, where surely things would get better. She turned to friends in the States trying to raise enough money for her passage (her original return ticket had long since been cashed in, or reneged upon). But she was unable to raise much cash, and when she gritted her teeth and asked Joe Glaser for a loan of $5,000, he responded with one of his vintage lectures—no doubt remembering how she had turned down the tour with Louis Armstrong the previous summer.

Yet there was feasting in the midst of famine for Mary, who was fêted by wealthy continentals in Paris, even royals. "I was surrounded with the rich, it seems they go there to stay rich," she wrote. She played for the Hon. Gerald Lascelles, for Lord and Lady Donegal, the Hennessys of the cognac fortune, and the Duke and Duchess of Windsor, who, said a press release, "invited her to play 'Alexander's Ragtime Band' and the 'Birth of the Blues' for them at a private party." She also met and befriended the Baroness Nica de Koenigswarter, introducing her shortly thereafter in Paris to Thelonious Monk, who became her great protégé. And she met many others, particularly at the elegant Mars Club. "She attracted both the jazz audience and the general public," recalls drummer Gérard "Dave" Pochonet, who grew very close to Mary during her Paris stay. "There were stars, too—I remember Errol Flynn, for example. And of course she was friendly with Nicole Barclay, who was wealthy and of the jet set." Indeed, Mary became even fonder of Nicole Barclay, writing, "She was such a fabulous friend to musicians, she always helped musicians when they were stranded or in distress. She'd see they got money or a ticket back to America. So I recorded a song and dedicated this to her." "Nicole" is notable both for its spare, hornlike phrasing and its deceptively cool-seeming surface, a classic modern blues. The tune appears on an LP she cut that spring (1954), on which Mary plays several originals and standards in fresh, subtly modern treatments. "Not only in solos but also in her orchestrations [there is] a subtle sense of delicacy, an extremely sensitive temperament. These feelings give her music a special originality and a unique place in the world of jazz," the uncredited writer of the liner notes (Nicole Barclay?) commented. Yet later, despite Mary's fondness for her benefactress, she complained that she got no money by making the disc nor received any royalties. It was a lament reflective of Mary's entire recording history, and common to many other American artists who cut records overseas.

Professionally, it continued to be a slow time for her. "Although most of my jobs were successful," she wrote to a friend, "one has to wait a month or more for other work." A well-received tour of Holland and Scandinavia in the spring, for example, was followed by unemployment. Feast or famine. When Mary was flush, she bought gowns, furs, the best perfume, and so on, often on credit, and suffered the consequences during hard times. Once she was unable to pay a dressmaker who specialized in couture copies a fee of 60,000 francs. The dressmaker sent a detective *and* a lawyer to the Cristal, who somehow insinuated themselves into Mary's room, where they demanded the money, threatening to take Mary's new mink coat in forfeit. There followed a humiliating scene in the hall, a shouting match for all the hotel to hear—Mary refusing to be bullied, the lawyer threatening to have her thrown in jail if she dared wear her fur coat until her bill was settled. In the end, a distraught Mary called one of her benefactors for help. Colonel Edward L. Brennan, one of the wealthy American expatriates who frequented clubs like the Mars and the Ringside, settled that bill. To show her gratitude, Mary wrote a song for him, "The Colonel's in Love with Nancy." It was Mary's lifelong habit to reward friends, especially wealthy friends, with songs. She wrote "Joycie" for Joyce Breach, and "Miss D.D." for Doris Duke.

But Colonel Brennan had far greater significance in Mary's life than being her "bread and butter," to use a phrase she liked. He was a devout Roman Catholic, and one afternoon he showed Mary a small church with a walled garden and statuary. Mary, in ever greater turmoil, soon returned to this peaceful setting alone. There, she experienced a religious epiphany, writing that "I found God in a little garden in Paris." To friends and family she added that she had the most powerful vision of her life there, of the Virgin Mary, and marked it as the beginning of an intensely mystical journey, filled with supernatural symbolism. It was only after she became a Roman Catholic, several years later, and her spiritual life became regularized under the guidance of a wise confessor, that the visions subsided.

––––––––

AMONG MARY'S CLOSEST friends in Paris was an expatriate American pianist regarded as a fine accompanist for singers. Garland Wilson, who had lived earlier in Europe, had returned to Paris permanently in 1953. Wilson held court at Le Boeuf sur le Toit, a club long famous among hip Parisians, but by 1954 he was very ill. Through the spring of '54, Mary and Wilson clung together in an intense, though not sexual, relationship (Wilson was homosexual). "I'd either go by the Mars Club for Garland or wait up for him," she wrote. "I often left my door open, and would wake up finding Garland snoring, lying on top of my legs, and I'd make him get in bed on the other side of me." When Mary's bags were seized until a friend's bill was paid up, Mary packed up and moved to the Hotel La Boëtie. "Garland Wilson thought I was running out on him and he packed up and came with me. Then, one night I went by to pick him up from his job and he was crying and could barely walk. I took him home and put him in bed. The next day he was back on his feet and happy."

After her vision in the church garden, as Mary began to retreat from her friends and associations, she avoided Garland Wilson as well. "I unpacked, getting in bed and relaxing and going over my life to dig what I had done wrong. I seldom left my room except to eat or play gigs. Everyone began to enquire about my sudden disappearance. Garland ran into me on the Champs Élysées, and said, 'I've been trying to reach you.' Well, I was really depressed."

Yet she continued to pick up a good deal of work, including radio appearances and occasional television spots. On one radio program, poet François Valorbe, a disciple of André Breton, read a poem dedicated to Mary from his recent collection called *Carte Noire* (Black Card) inspired by American jazz musicians and decorated with an Art Deco cover. It begins:

> *It rains bells over the nighttime laugh of the piano . . .*
> *A summer of tar hopes,*
> *another summer jingling the keys of this night*
> *in our fingers . . .*

As summer approached, Mary's despondency had become debili-
tating. But she had to work. In June, she accepted a gig at a New
Orleans–style jazz festival in June at the Salle Pleyel. At least she could
take comfort in her unusual versatility: in France as in England, the
"trads" and the "moderns" went to each other's concerts to boo rival
stylists, but both camps admired Mary. "Actually I'm the only pianist
who can play with anybody," she remarked in her direct manner. Yet
after appearing in Germany—and a tape of that concert, in Baden-
Baden, shows her to be in fine form, both soloing and accompanying a
band led by Kurt Edelhagen—she wrote in her diary that she lost all
appetite for her music. She kept going because she had to support
herself.

And despite her despair, Mary produced a fresh body of work,
much of it excellent, although little known today—"Nicole," "I Love
Him," "Twilight," "Amy," "Nirees," "Musical Express"/"NME," "Melody
Maker," "Blues Pour le Club Français," "The Colonel Is in Love with
Nancy," to name several. As ever, turning to her music soothed and
inspired her.

But not for much longer.

She kept trying to borrow enough money to get back to the States,
but her cash shortages continued. Efforts to reclaim royalties were
fruitless; her business letters are full of confused and frantic language
and repetitions. And another record she made around that time, produced by the Club Français du Disque, marked the nadir of her
recording career abroad, a squandering of her talent on mediocre
sidemen and poorly rehearsed, ragged sessions. Mary, who provided
businesslike but colorless comping, came to life briefly on the several
tunes where the rhythm section was inoffensive, and especially where
she was left alone to solo, out-Shearing Shearing on "Memories of You"
and giving an Erroll Garner treatment to "(I Made You) Love Paris."

Soon after, on the 31st of May, Mary was sitting at the bar of her
hotel with her old friend Mae Mezzrow when another friend rushed in
to announce that Garland Wilson had collapsed and been taken to the
American Hospital. Hysterical, Mary rushed there with her friend,
only to be turned away. They were told to come back in the morning.

As it turned out, Wilson had already died (pianist Aaron Bridgers
says the cause was an "exploded liver") soon after arriving at the hospital. "Garland Wilson was well loved by many," writes Bridgers, "and the

next night people came to the Boeuf in sympathy. That night no one played; they simply placed an orchid on the piano." Added Mary in her diary, "There was a big expensive funeral for Garland Wilson. . . . I did a benefit for Garland and the Baroness [Nica] contributed quite a lot."

Wilson's death was the catalyst for the next downturn in Mary's spiraling depression. Feeling incapable of doing or caring much about anything, she simply retreated to her cheap hotel room. When M. Henrion, the manager of the Boeuf, called and asked her to take Wilson's job at the club, she wrote, "I asked him, 'Why me?' And he said, 'Because I looked in his billfold and he was carrying your photo next to his heart.' " "But," adds Aaron Bridgers, "she was too upset over his passing to commence immediately, so *I* played a few nights until she felt capable."

———

LE BOEUF SUR LE TOIT, at 34 rue du Colisée, is a play on words: though the name translates literally as "beef over the roof," but *boeuf* was also slang for "jam session." Taking its name from a surrealist ballet by Jean Cocteau, with music by Darius Milhaud, the club, which opened in 1922, was a home to jazz enthusiasts and artists, including writers like Cocteau, Max Jacob, André Breton; painters such as Picasso, Picabia, Derain, and Marcel Duchamp; the composers Ravel, Honegger, Poulenc, and Auric. "Le Boeuf sur le Toit seemed to characterize French intellectual life in the twenties," notes writer Chris Goddard. "The prevailing philosophy was not so much non-conformist as anti-conformist"; it was an era where European and especially French-centered art was informed by a new sensibility, fascinated by African and by American music and art, as he adds elsewhere.

But by the 1950s, the Boeuf, seedy old bohemian that it was, was showing its age. Mary was unfazed. "It was a gay bar, but it wasn't obvious," explains Gérard Pochonet. "Many of the women were really dressed—and many of them were men. But it was also for the general public." Mary put it with more characteristically prim indirection: "It's a place where the customers that really frequent this place didn't like women, but I got in because I was a friend of Garland Wilson's." Mary began working at the Boeuf in the middle of June, and between shows at the club, she also appeared at the Olympia Theatre on a bill with the very popular singer Jean Sablon. She received rave reviews: "a remarkable pianist, the best part of the program, the highest quality jazz."

These new engagements seemed to bring her out of her depression, and she went on a shopping spree, buying, as she put it, "all kinds of crazy gowns." She was beautiful in a white lace dress with cut-out sleeves and heart-shaped décolletage at the gala party—a traditional French "presse cocktail" to officially welcome the "World's Greatest Female Jazz Pianist" at the newest "Chez Mary Lou." Everyone Mary knew in Paris came, people like drummer Kansas Fields, James Baldwin, the Brennans, the Baroness; also such visitors as Sugar Ray Robinson, Billy Eckstine, and Bill Coleman. But Mary cast an ironic eye on the hoopla. "The producer wanted to make money. There are certain seasons that the Americans are in Paris or Europe and when they go home there's nobody left. Well, they had only one musician left—and that was me."

At the Boeuf, Mary used Wilson's bass player, the Austrian Heinz Grah, or the Belgian bassist Benoit Quersin, but she wanted more rhythm, so she brought in "the best brush man in Paris," her friend Gérard Pochonet. "She was very inventive, always," he remembers. "Nothing far ahead, modern but also back to boogie-woogie, which was her claim to fame, but normally no more bop. She always wanted to play it her way, always." To Mary, her way meant keeping continuity with the blues: "That offbeat can easily throw you," she said. "Those changes sound new but it's the blues right on; the blues is a matter of feeling and the blues is basic and all the other styles telescope out of it."

Basie's band had come to Paris the month before, and it was manna to her. "After fooling around with the frozen sounds since 1945, and hearing potentially good musicians playing this frozen sound in Europe, I was most distressed. But when Count Basie came to Paris in May of 1954, they floored everyone, including myself. I couldn't sit down during the concert, I couldn't stop dancing. Now I cannot readjust myself to listen to those frozen sounds anymore. They belong in the classics and not warm God-loving music like the spirituals and bop." She still felt the blues when she played, but, she complained, she was increasingly distracted and jittery. Significantly, too, she was less and less interested in playing. "In Europe, I became a frustrated musical wreck," she wrote later, "with a nervous heart and a kidney ailment." But it was not her own musicianship that caused her anxiety: "I did feel discouraged, fed up," but not, she emphasized, with her own playing. "I didn't feel that way at all because I never become discouraged—maybe for a fraction of a second." Yet in the intensifying isolation of her malaise, the music she made was becoming a mockery of her own agonized sense of inner emptiness.

Clearly, her problems went deeper than music alone could cure.

———

HER PAIN WAS almost palpable. Around Bastille Day, Mary wrote, "I stood the Boeuf as long as I could. Billy Eckstine, my good friend, came back to Paris and I threw a birthday party for him." She invited her own crowd—Hazel Scott, Sugar Ray Robinson, the Mezzrows, harmonica player Larry Adler—and Pochonet, who by now was madly in love with her. Not that Mary noticed him. Gérard Pochonet, thirty years old, good-looking, and the best available drummer in town, was simply "the poor lil drummer" in her diary. "I met her at the end of November 1953," he recalls, "and I became very interested in the way she played, so I played with her in a couple of places including the Boeuf sur Le Toit for free." When, in late June, Mary's mood blackened and she walked away from the club after a party one night, needing solitude, he was concerned. "The poor lil drummer followed me to my hotel saying 'Lou, what is wrong?' I screamed and told him to get out. He wouldn't, he just sat there and looked pitiful. This got to me. He said, 'Come and move out to the house with Grandmaman and me.' I said, 'What? Me? I'm used to being around young brilliant musicians and you want me to live with *you* in the country?' (Oh, how I've regretted all these remarks.) Well, it was too late for his train so I yelled, 'Here take this money and get a room here, why do you keep trailing after me, blow!' He hung his head. The next morning he knocked on the door fresh and with a beautiful smile. 'Lou, you need a rest. I don't make much but you won't starve. Come out with us. Grandma is an excellent cook. I said, 'I'm sick of French food. Please go home,' and slammed the door.

"I felt I had absolutely no one to turn to, no one to talk my troubles over with. I grew bitter at life, at people, and for several days I walked around as though I were in a fog. I met people who spoke but I didn't see them. My mind wasn't on them. I was searching for something I did not see and I did not know what it was. But I know I was searching for something."

In the midst of her anguish and mental instability, Pochonet returned, a veritable white knight. "I was glad to see him. I was scared to no end, I had terrible nightmares all night. I said how's about sleeping at the foot of the bed tonight? This the poor fellow did. The next couple of nights I let him sleep on top of the second sheet. I'd wake up and he'd have his arms around me. I'd go into the craziest fits. He'd look at me and smile or look sad." They became lovers.

And it was there, in a third-rate hotel far from home, that the end of one kind of life for Mary began—an exquisitely painful explosion of the validity of many of the assumptions she had developed since childhood. Instead: the anguish of awareness that her life held no redeeming purpose that she could see, no meaning. And as the old life was falling apart around her, there was raw pain and tremendous fear. As she came to view it later, she was being given a gift of great value: the old self dying in order to be reborn, a concept particularly resonant within the context of Christianity, which Mary soon embraced. But as yet, she felt very little hope.

————

NO ONE WHO knew Mary well has suggested that she had any kind of chronic problem with drink or drugs. If anything, she much more closely fit the classic pattern of the para-alcoholic in her attempts (mostly futile) to manage, help and/or control the alcoholics around her. Yet quite clearly also, her spiraling despair and self-destructive behavior paralleled the downward progression of the alcoholic. While she was in Paris, Mary herself noted that she was self-medicating, noting: "I was never a heavy drinker for my system has never been able to take it. Yet I was quite high practically every night on champagne, my favorite drink." "Quite amazing," she added in a letter, "for before 1946, beverages made me sick, my system never could take strong drinks, but I began to cultivate a taste for it, etc." Then there was the "partying," as Annie Ross called it, with Mary's old standby, marijuana. Did she try other drugs long familiar to the nightlife crowd—"poppers" (amyl nitrate), speed, cocaine, sleeping pills? If so, she was discreet; though years later, back in New York, Peter O'Brien recalls finding an old bottle of amyl nitrate with a French label in her medicine chest, and when he asked her about it Mary, he said, became "flustered."

In Paris, then, she hit bottom. "I was in my hotel room alone and all of a sudden it seemed as though everything I had done up to then meant absolutely nothing. I was despondent because everything seemed so meaningless and useless. Even my beloved music, the piano I played, all seemed to have lost their appeal. So had my former associates in show business, the musicians, the night club owners and the wealthy men and women who were my patrons and who had been dining and wining me—none of them seemed important any more. There was no feeling for me to end it all. It was just despondency based on the fact that I felt everything I had been doing was no good."

———

MARY MOVED OUT of Paris to live with Pochonet at his grandmother's, commuting to work in Paris almost every night by train or cab in July. But in August, she severed her ties to the Boeuf sur le Toit. "Now, Mary Lou didn't just up and walk out of the place she was playing," emphasizes Aaron Bridgers. "She was going through a sort of spiritual calling. And she felt that she couldn't continue the way her career was going on. She sat down with her employer and explained her feelings, after which he released her from her contract."

Mary herself saw her crisis in a spiritual context and used spiritual metaphors to understand her experience. She looked back over her European stay to find what she called "signs" and "messengers" that led her, eventually, to God. Her first messenger had been a soldier—a white soldier she'd met the previous November at a party thrown for Mary by the jazz-loving Hon. Gerald Lascelles, a member of the British royal family. Mary had too much to drink and was nervous and silly—her words—but the soldier, sensing her distress, began talking with her about religion, suggesting she read the Ninety-sixth Psalm. Misunderstanding him, she went home and dug out her little white Bible and read *all* of the psalms, continuing to do so for years afterwards in an unconscious imitation of the regime of the Benedictine monks. "The psalms cooled me and made me feel protected, but I still didn't feel right." Colonel Brennan was her second messenger, introducing her to the Roman Catholic church where she had her ecstatic vision. Her third messenger was Pochonet, a completely nonreligious person who showered her with love and provided her a retreat from the world.

Now came the fourth and most powerful message, sent by an unlikely candidate on the face of it—Hazel Scott, whom Mary once described in a letter as "a wild chick, had tried suicide, was quite sinful." But, Mary continues, "after absorbing what I had to tell her, she looked at me and said, 'Lou, have you a Bible? Get one immediately, read it and pray, pray, pray. What you need is peace of mind.' Hazel Scott, bless her soul. She made me see my oversight of God. I returned to my hotel room, closed and locked the door and fell down on my knees and I prayed for hours. I had never felt a conscious desire to get close to God. But it seemed that night that it all came to a head."

———

ON HER MOVE to Pochonet's grandmother's place, Mary commented, "I'm sure that I was on my way to a real crack-up. I had to walk at least two miles to the train station (this kept me home)." She added elsewhere, "I did not trust myself around the old gang and the places they frequented." Grand'maman Pochonet's was literally a refuge, an asylum. In her diary Mary wrote, "We call Grandma's place 'Paradise Lane,' a garden of flowers, away from everybody, in the country." (Mary exaggerates a bit: according to Pochonet, his grandmother's house was in the small town of Vaucresson, twenty minutes by train from Paris.) "And Grandma," Mary went on, "was a beautiful spry white-haired lady. She cooked for us." There was no instant cure, however. "Life looked mean and ugly to me. Music bored and irritated me. I just ate and stayed in bed. I'm sure that I left the print of my body in Grandma's bed. Late at night I'd go downstairs in the kitchen and pray and cry. Slowly, however, the deep spell of despondency began to lift and I saw things I had never seen before in my mind's eye: bright things, clean and pure. I received a message: 'Be calm.' "

It appears that she never shared her feelings about this transformation with her French lover. "Mary Lou and I would go in by train to work in the club, or in a taxi," says Pochonet, "but she never talked about religion, the psalms, prayer, *to me*—absolutely not; we talked about music mostly." They were bound by music, sexual passion, and his love for her, but they were as unlike as chalk and cheese.

Thus alone did Mary go through her breakdown and breakthrough, confronting her guilt over the past: "I'd pray and thank God and cry for all the bad things I've done. I've never been selfish, mean or very bad. I had helped and listened to so many poor people and unfortunate musicians. But I had never reached God before and I was 44 years old." It was prayer, she felt strongly, that helped her recover.

The chaotic state of her emotions was mirrored by the disorder of her finances and business affairs. "She had a whole suitcase of con-tracts and music and letters all mixed up together. A complete mess," recalls Pochonet. "I really tried to help her with that, but it was very dif-ficult because she didn't have much common sense. Much talent, but not much common sense. She would do things which I told her in advance wouldn't work but she kept doing them."

She made attempts to straighten things out, contacting the Gale agency in New York to ask for a return ticket. On August 6 they replied with a Glaser-like lecture: "The only reason you are in this difficulty at the moment is due to the fact that you yourself decided to stay in England and on the Continent. We do not feel that we are in any way responsible for returning a performer to this country close to two years after an engagement has been played." But friends in the States did raise some money for the ticket.

By September, Mary had "gained some spiritual strength," as she wrote in a frank and mystic-leaning article for *Sepia* Magazine several years later. That fall she agreed to go on a tour of concert halls and army camps in Europe on a bill with Sarah Vaughan, Coleman Hawkins, Illinois Jacquet, and sidemen. The money, recalls Johnnie Garry, who had become Sarah Vaughan's valet, was very good.

Mary was eager now to go back to the States, though Pochonet tried to persuade her to stay in France. He was thirty and thought Mary was thirty-eight, though she was actually forty-four. "But she didn't look her age at the time. I proposed to marry her but she said no. Well, she was still married to Baker and she never got divorced—it's too costly, she told me. And then, I was not in a position to get her the kind of work she could get in New York, and I was not ready to leave France and go to the States and emigrate."

Mary finally booked passage on a liner leaving the 15th of Decem-ber, two years after she'd arrived for what she thought was a two-week tour. Pochonet accompanied her on the boat train to the port of Le Havre, still trying to persuade her to stay. Neither was happy when she sailed for New York. Mary stayed in her cabin, praying, asking God to help her live a different life, and "wondering what will I find there in America." Her old partying friend Inez Cavanaugh was on board also, but Mary avoided her, staying in her cabin except at mealtime.

Mary had begun to withdraw from the world in earnest. "It's possi-ble I was her last lover; to my knowledge I was," muses Pochonet.

"Before she got religion, she was not a nun at all, I can tell you. But after that, the pleasures of the flesh fell away.

"She'd been offered some big engagements back in America by Joe Glaser, but she canceled everything before returning to America," he adds. In her diary Mary wrote, "I was still looking for peace of mind, and I was determined to give up music, night life and all else that was sinful in the eyes of God. After that, I wouldn't play anymore."

Chapter Fifteen
Praying Through My Fingertips
1955–1962

AS MUCH AS Mary longed to turn her back on "music, night life," and other "sins," when she arrived back in New York during the Christmas season of 1954 she was not able to do so right away. With no savings, she had to work at something. (When the IRS contacted her about unpaid back taxes, Mary responded flatly, "I arrived back from Europe on December 21, 1954, completely broke," and invited the tax collectors to come see her spare living conditions for themselves.) Soon after she went to Europe, she had stopped corresponding with Lindsay Steele (and stopped sending him money), and he was gone, but her apartment had been ransacked. Mary all but accused Steele of having ripped her off, joked mordantly that at least he had left her Royal typewriter, so she could work on her autobiography.

Needing money urgently, she turned to Joe Glaser and publicist Bert Block, both of whom held out possibilities of performance work for her, but at a lower salary than Mary expected. In vain they explained to her that her time in Europe had not added to her drawing power in the States. And conditions had worsened; there were fewer venues for jazz musicians. "The Street is gone," Mary complained, a reference to the lively jazz-club scene along Fifty-second Street. She was offered a job in April at the Composer, a congenial club for pianists in midtown Manhattan, but she turned it down, ostensibly because of the money. And again, when she was lined up to play the

Hickory House, another good spot for piano players, Mary canceled the date.

In truth, Mary was simply loath to perform in nightclubs, and would avoid them as much as possible for many years. She readily agreed to appear on radio and TV that spring, including May appearances on the Steve Allen and Gary Moore shows. And she was still active in the jazz community. After Charlie Parker died in March, she agreed to serve as a co-chairperson of the Charlie Parker Foundation, along with Hazel Scott and Dizzy Gillespie. The foundation had a purpose dear to her heart—to raise money to help educate Parker's children. But although a sum was raised for the Charlie Parker Memorial Fund, Mary became disillusioned and tendered her resignation in July. However, her experience with the Parker Foundation had planted an important seed: from it Mary got the idea to set up her own nonprofit foundation to help poor musicians and children.

Buoyed by the interest and favorable press she'd received in Europe with her *Melody Maker* reminiscences, Mary set about getting a contract for a book. John Hammond was enthusiastic and showed the *Melody Maker* articles to *Life* and book ediors, and her friend the writer Allan Morison did the same at *Ebony*, where he was the New York editor. No one was buying. Though disappointed, Mary continued to write pieces of her story on an informal basis.

Most important, she cut a record called *A Keyboard History*, the first example of the synoptic "history of jazz" approach she'd developed since the forties. The album, produced by the Jazztone Society (an offshoot of the Concert Hall Society, an established classical music mail-order club), was an excellent example of Mary's lucid musicality and mastery of the various styles of jazz. "She used to say," recalls Peter O'Brien, "that one of the things about good jazz is when it's like a good conversation. No babbling, no wasted notes." Her swinging, up-tempo arrangement of the spiritual "(Joshua Fit the Battle of) Jericho"; her renditions of the ragtime piece "Fandango"; the old-time blues "My Mama Pinned a Rose on Me"; and her swing hit "Roll 'Em" demonstrate her great ease with the styles of jazz preceding bop, while her composition "I Love Him," a study of "'Round Midnight," and her "Amy" are fine examples of modern jazz. In the liner notes, Mary wrote that she had been "part of each jazz era and didn't realize it. It was my pleasure to bring you through the history of jazz." Then with wry humor she added, "You may not realize this, but you're lucky. On the other hand, to bring this history to you, I had to go through muck and mud."

The reviews were enthusiastic, almost pleading for the record industry to keep recording her. "She's back in America now," *Downbeat* reminded its readers, "and I hope a bright recording company will ask her to do a series of autobiographical LP's because Mary's history is that of an influential artist-composer with three decades of deep involvement with the growth of jazz." Three years later, when *A Keyboard History* was reissued, came fresh praise. "This collection makes up one of the most satisfying piano albums to be recorded in recent years," wrote one critic.

There was no hint of a troubled mind or anguished spirit on the recording; on the contrary, her clarity and precision of thought and execution were at a high level. Yet, although she recorded quite a few 45s over the next decade (some never issued), Mary did not make another LP as a leader for eight more years. Meanwhile, she watched as Marian McPartland clinched a five-record deal with Capitol, Thelonious Monk recorded for Riverside, and pianists like Horace Silver, Erroll Garner, George Shearing, and Ahmad Jamal cut albums.

Even as Mary had picked up the reins again in New York, facing the old familiar problems of money and music, her personal life foundered in a disastrous second crisis of the spirit, as she was drawn back into old habits now hateful to her. As usual, she only hints at these habits—gambling, nightlife—in letters and her diary, writing to a friend called Dan (no last name was given), "After six months of devout praying, I was taken for a ride by two sinful people. It took me at least three months to get out of these people's clutches and I have really prayed sincerely since first feeling God in Paris." If she was, as usual, evasive about the details, Mary was eloquent about the effects of "sin." Satan, she wrote, was "the man" who set cunning traps for the unwary. "An evil person will cause a good person to stumble, will throw you in a trance and take your natural soul if you are not really down with it, for the man is hustling madly for souls."

Mary's decision to turn from the "sinful" world of entertainment to a self-cloistered religiosity, said some who knew her, was understandable—a matter of a tender nature crushed by abuse. Said John Williams, "She trusted everybody and was treated so bad."

Seeking solace, she joined the Abyssinian Baptist Church, which was led by the Reverend Adam Clayton Powell, Jr. (by then Hazel Scott's ex-husband). It was a logical choice. Mary had been baptized by Great-Aunt Hattie in that denomination, her grandfather was a Baptist deacon, and, most significantly, the Abyssinian Church was the most powerful black religious institution in Harlem.

But by June, disillusioned with that church, she handed in a crisp letter of resignation. At the same time she more or less stopped looking for work as a musician. It was, perhaps, an even more painful withdrawal than in France. The music that had always been at once Mary's bulwark, her frame, her canvas, her delight—indeed, her reality—ceased to matter. "Music had left my head," Mary said, "and I hardly remembered playing." "About six months or so after she went back to New York her letters changed," remembers Pochonet, a steadfast correspondent. It was as if the musical "faucet" had been turned off, yet Mary's need for self-expression had to find an outlet. She developed a new passion in a gush of energy, an obsession to rescue the world. Mary set upon her new full-time work of rehabilitating troubled people—starting with her own family in Pittsburgh, some of whom were in a pitiful state. At Mamie's house, when she announced she was giving up show business and everything that went with it, she stunned and angered her better-off family members. "The whole family thought I was crazy. I gave away my Dior gowns and sold a $6,500 mink for $50." They simply could not understand her: Was this the same woman who was a famous piano star, the woman who had just come back from a triumphant European tour, as they thought? The same Mary who had regularly sent expensive presents to them in the past? "When I graduated from high school [in the thirties]," said Helen Floyd, "she gave me fox furs. She said, 'If you'd have been on the honor roll, I'd have bought you a car.' "

Mary explained that her life was different now that she had found God. She was quitting the world of nightclubs and simply could not stand by while, for example, her half-sister Grace Mickles lived in squalor, an alcoholic single mother on welfare with four children (and one grandchild). Although Mamie, who herself had tried to help Grace, warned her against it, Mary decided to take Grace back to New York and straighten her out.

Into her car, an old but sturdy Cadillac, piled Grace, Victoria, Carl,

Don, Cab, and teenaged Victoria's son, Clifford. On the way back to New York, Mary got into an accident. Narrowly avoiding being thrown through the windshield, she had her face cut by glass and her knee damaged, and one of the children was hurt. Mary had always been a safe, steady driver; now she was shaken by guilt.

With six people dependent on her (soon to be seven, for shortly after they arrived in New York, Grace was pregnant again), Mary became desperate for money. She wrote to her attorney, who was holding on to her ASCAP check, a quarterly payment of her royalties, until she paid him for legal services. She had to have that money, she wrote furiously: she had five kids to feed! And why were his fees so high in the first place? And where was all this money he had promised to recoup for her? Old familiar questions, old familiar battles. Meanwhile, Grace's life was in predictable chaos. Heavyset, with beautiful brown eyes, she was usually meek and soft-spoken, but when she drank, Mary said, she was a "typical Jekyll and Hyde" alcoholic. In her drunken haze, Grace, a frustrated singer who sounded something like Billie Holiday, lashed out in jealous rages at Mary, the successful one.

Grace had no marketable skills, but after she had her baby, Robert, in 1956, Mary lined her up a job with a well-to-do friend, Elaine Lorillard, called Robbie (she had cofounded the Newport Jazz Festival). "I hired Mary Lou's sister as a maid," Mrs. Lorillard recalls. "But she was a big fat woman, totally ignorant and not at all nice. And she couldn't do anything—nothing. Not even clean silver."

Mary found herself completely responsible for Grace and her brood, recalling that "I cooked for them, washed for them and slept on the floor so they could live in my apartment in Harlem." At times she even rented a small room down the hall from her apartment for other troubled souls she was trying to help. The strain was tremendous, the following diary entry from the winter of '56 makes clear (Mary refers to herself sometimes as "Mary," sometimes as "she," and sometimes as "I"; Grace is "she" and the children "they"):

> They have just about demolished everything she has, yet she keeps them looking good. She gave her a cute dress from Saks Fifth Avenue for Christmas. She must have iron nerves for there are six of us in two rooms and Carl is awful! I imagine she has always been kindhearted but to go through what she goes

through every day she must have a good story to tell us about praying to God.

I know the only way one can make it through the world is through reading psalms everyday and doing the rosary. Mary even forgot about her artistic work and pitches in laundering, even big sheets etc., our clothes, like a regular wash-woman and thinks nothing about it, often saying I love God and it's a pleasure to do all this. I bring my entire salary home, about $35 a week. None of us have anything but every little bit helps.

After a year of caring for Grace and her family, Mary had had it: she drove them all back to Pittsburgh, where she left them with Mamie, the only other stable person in the family. Mamie was furious, but as Mary explained in a letter, "I had to get my strength back up." "Carry your cross and cease grumbling," she added, advice scarcely bound to mollify. Please, she begged Mamie, "keep the kids a little more. Very strange kids, grit your teeth and carry on." She added that she had just taken in Bud Powell and helped him straighten out temporarily so that he could make a date at Birdland.

By September, Mamie was at the end of her tether. She was charging Grace room and board—which angered Mary, who shot off a letter:

We have always loved each other very much but my being away from Pittsburgh so much kinda separated that fine love of ours. You weren't supposed to charge poor Grace. You asked in your letter why I didn't buy them clothes etc. Well, I dressed those kids like rich kids. What happened to all the things I sent over there? Anybody would call me crazy the kind things I did for them. But don't you remember I was born like that? Now I could care less for money and material things—the flesh is evil. I have given away practically everything I get.

You must relax and read your Bible and wait on God—Believe it. I didn't have furniture, street clothes and underwear and owe close to $900 or more on my charges because of the things I've bought for the unfortunates. And I was down to about my last $20 in the post office savings account. Yes, I got some money to rehearse and go to work, but God wasn't ready for me to work yet. But I was completely relaxed. And a check came in for $608.03. Mamie, you were not doing God right, that's why you had no work except for Fridays. I have prayed madly for you.

She added about Grace,

I have been going to church at 6 A.M. or 7 A.M. reading and praying madly and God is working fast miracles. Watch and see if you won't be healing soon, just keep praying the way we used to. Let me know if I am reaching you spiritually. This is what I'm praying to be able to do.

It would be many years of sorrow and destruction, however, before Grace is said to have stopped drinking. "Grace often acts like Lucifer," Mary wrote a friend sadly. "I gave her everything I had, went without. She ruined five beautiful talented kids. Nobody worries but me about the relatives."

AMID THE CONSTANT pressure of her daily domestic drudgery and frequent crises, Mary set herself an absolutely incredible discipline of prayer and meditation, in the grip of the passionate urgency she had first felt in France the year before. Guilt seemed to press in upon her like a vise; clearly she was in the grip of a chronic mental disturbance. In a struggle both heroic and appalling, she beat back "the old self" and the old friends and lifestyle, all of which she now found noxious. She set herself goals to protect and purify herself from the wrongful ways and the vengeful impulses she called her "blocks." Quite possibly she was suffering from paranoia; undoubtedly she needed good counsel and guidance. But it was not to come yet. For the time being, she withdrew into herself, sustained by an improvised philosophy that comprised Christian tenets, spiritualist practices, and African-American folk beliefs. The old spirits and hallucinations that had haunted her in childhood, and had returned in France, now flourished an array of good and evil emanations, on one side a firmament of angels, intercessors, and saints, and on the other, dark side, a host of demons, "ghouls," and such-like. "The spirits are asleep during the day in the corners. One has to read the psalms, use holy water, etc. to get rid of them," she wrote in a typical passage. She had psychic flashes, many of them concerned with troubled jazz musicians and with jazz as an art form in peril of commercialism: "When I stopped playing in 1954 (I had never been away from my music over two months straight), while talking to individuals the future would flash before my eyes as to what was going to happen to them. For awhile I was miserable, but I learned to live with it. And the future of jazz flashed before me. I saw the enemy (Satan, evil, negativity) trying to destroy the spirituality and healing of this great art."

In 1956, Mary composed long lists of people she prayed for every day. One list contains an astounding 900 names, a fascinating group that includes Babe Ruth, Valaida Snow, Bojangles, Charlie Parker, and Rudolph Valentino. That year also, she discovered a local Roman Catholic church that propitiously kept its doors unlocked all day. Soon, in addition to her regular (voluminous) prayers, she was making entreaties to saints for the removal of physical and emotional afflictions, and to guardian angels for the lost souls of the living. Nor did she fail to list admonitions for herself: "Watch out for nervousness, gossip, worry, anger, fear and anxiety. Don't swear. Be calm, sweet, pious, helpful to all. Learn to be patient and God will help you, this is difficult but is for your future happiness. Pray madly for all our relatives. Please help my relatives with their jealousies." She read aloud, morning and night, the Tenth, Fifteenth, Twenty-third, and Twenty-fourth psalms. And she sent up one simple prayer every day: "Stop Grace from drinking . . . care for myself . . . for all musicians." Forgiving her mother was hardest of all. Says Peter O'Brien, "When she became a Catholic, the first thing she prayed for was not to hate her mother." Mary held her mother responsible for the failure in life of many of her brothers and sisters—her mother, who drank as Grace did. "No one ever knew it but my people had always been a terrible cross to bear, worrying about how they were making out, especially my brothers and sisters," she wrote in a draft of her autobiography. "I had always wanted to send them to a private school but my mother would not hear of this. I thought that doing this might give them a chance in the world."

But in the personal mythology that Mary evolved after her conversion experience, a myth of tragic female heroism, her mother—

whom other family members never remembered as a musician—became a tragic heroine, a thwarted artist whom the white world insisted stop "improvising" and learn the "rules," thereby rendering her incapable of playing music. Then along came Mary, the daughter who broke the spell, who restored musical power and speech—and thus the black cultural heritage—as a fiercely gifted and self-reliant improviser. In Mary's myth, the black woman triumphs and does not allow her "soul" to be repressed or "taken." Reinventing her mother (and herself) in such a way gave Mary the opportunity both to exonerate her mother and to cast herself as her mother's rescuer. Mary could not wish away the envy and rage between herself and her vanquished mother, nor the guilt she must have felt at her own triumph while her mother's life was such a failure; but her new spirituality healed much of the hurt within her. "I used to get mad every time I had to bring my money home to contribute to the support of Mom and the kids—now since I've reached God, I'm happy to do it. Gee! This is a wonderful feeling. I seldom get angry." Still, as Peter O'Brien is quick to point out, "she would *not* stay at her mother's house when she was in Pittsburgh."

————

BY THE FALL of 1956, Grace and her children returned to Hamilton Terrace from Mamie's. In January 1957, Mary wrote to a sympathetic lawyer, Maxwell Cohen, who was trying to help Bud Powell: "Please help me! I had to take my sister to Belleview [sic] hospital Monday, what with three babies crying all day. I'd appreciate your calling the Doctor on Ward N7 and ask if they'll keep her until we can get her a place in the country. I'm afraid that they will release her before the Catholic charity can do so."

Interestingly, Mary was now coming back to life musically and longed for privacy and peace in her own home. She had, she continued to Cohen, some "big, big projects" in mind, but "I'm so very very tired." She even took a rare engagement later in the year at the Blue Note in Chicago, taking along her one-year-old nephew, Robbie, whom Mary was to part-raise and all but consider the son she never had. The family situation continued to be desperate, requiring her constant attention. Years later, Mary wrote of this period in a *cri de coeur* to Robbie, who had failed to turn out as she'd hoped:

When you were between one and five years of age Grace would get her Welfare check, drink, fight and sing. And once she cut your brother Cab when they were in the Bronx. I had to tie her in bed to stop her. She couldn't sleep for weeks when she drank. I took her twice to Dr. Miller [a psychiatrist] and now she can sleep when she drinks. What happens with most in the family is a nervous condition which does not allow one to sleep except when doped or full of wine and whiskey. Robert, when you were a baby I'd run to the Bronx and bring you home with me to keep you safe. Ask your sister Vic. It has hurt to hear you say at times that you hated me, but I push it aside because Grace was crazy and jealous and you heard her say this when you were small.

"He was beaten with pipes, left hungry, stomped etc. when nothing but a baby, you see," Mary added in a letter to a friend defending her continued support years later of a boy others called a "bad egg" and crazy. "He's frightened half the time. He'd like to hurt his mother now." Mary spoke prophetically. But it was she whom Robbie wished to hurt, and did.

———————

THE IRS CONTINUED to dun Mary for taxes, and again in 1956 she wrote the agency a letter notable for its degree of naked despair:

> My future in show business is very vague due to heavy competition and my ill health. I have been broke since 1947 and the few jobs I was able to obtain at indefinite intervals went toward my many mounting bills and expenses.
>
> Steady employment is just about impossible for me. I am completely bankrupt and my future in show business is closed until I can have a plastic surgeon fix my face which of course is impossible as I have no income and am unemployed.
>
> If it were through some miraculous way that I was able to work again it would take me at least a year or two to pay back the personal loans and get my few last possessions out of pawn, plus get the adequate medical treatment that I need. Kindly favor me with a humane reply.

(There is no record of a response from the IRS.)

In fact, Mary, whose frame of mind seemed as extreme as her financial straits, could barely bring herself to work as a musician anymore. She continued to turn aside jobs offers, as she had done since 1954. "I got the feeling that I would never play jazz again nor would I return to my old life, although people were offering me all kinds of good-paying jobs, all of which I turned down." Instead, for the next several years, she lived on very little, her "quarterly ASCAP check [about $300], occasional royalties from old records, and credit," as she said late in '57 to a *Time* reporter. She could not have survived without the credit, which came in the form of loans and hand-outs from old friends—the Baroness Nica, Nicole Barclay, and a few musicians, notably Dizzy Gillespie. Mary had tried to help the baroness, who was bereft after Charlie Parker died, with her own drug problem. As for the Gillespies, they "used to call and ask if I had enough to eat. Then a few minutes later the doorbell would ring and Lorraine would bring me a big basket of food," Mary reminisced. The Gillespies were well aware of the help Mary was giving to other musicians.

Indeed, Mary had taken on several new "cases," including dancer Baby Lawrence, seldom mentioned today. Lawrence was known as a wonderful drummer with his feet, and Mary prized playing with him, so much so that in the spring of 1955 she briefly put together a trio with Lawrence and bassist Oscar Pettiford—an interesting concept, but one that could find no bookings. Baby Lawrence and Mary (she on a portable keyboard) began performing together on street corners, sharing a religious fervor. Lawrence would exhort passersby to come and be baptized. Lawrence wrote literate letters of penetrating insight, but he was also a troubled alcoholic, in and out of institutions.

WITH WRITER ALLAN MORISON, Mary visited Bud Powell at Birdland. "Birdland's vibrations are bad for him," she wrote. "When Bud played, I was surprised to hear him playing like Shearing, Marian McPartland, and others. Later we went to his dressing room, and he was too knocked out to even talk. Heroin. The next day I prayed at the altar. Trying to shake off the vibrations of Birdland, I stayed in church five hours." Mary managed to persuade some musicians—Kenny Clarke, Harold Baker, Dizzy Gillespie, even Thelonious Monk—to attend church with her, although one wonders whether it was worth the effort. "She offered to take Monk in her car to Our Lady of Lourdes to meditate for the first time in his life," recalls Mary's friend Joyce Breach. "He was reluctant to go and stalled her, then he tried to get his wife to come along too, but Nellie told him to go on by himself. Then, Mary said, he had her stop the car on the way up. Unbeknownst to her, he bought himself a pint of wine and drank it all up. And when they got to the church, he fell down inside and Mary kept pulling on him, trying to get him up, calling him a big ape. Fortunately, no one else was there in the church. Monk wouldn't tell her what was going on but finally he got up and sat in a pew and prayed. Then a few days later he confessed he'd drunk the wine because he'd never been in a church and was afraid he'd die or something."

Some musicians refused to humor Mary. Miles Davis respected Mary's musicianship (several years later he admitted to her, "I should have asked you to be in my band"); but he also mockingly called her "Reverend Williams." Others, says Lorraine Gillespie, "started running when they saw her coming—she was always trying to get them to go in the church and pray. They'd tell her, everybody's got his own way. And they said to me, she used to be *wild*. And I said to them, 'If a person changes, isn't that something?' They should be praising her, not putting her down. But musicians, you know, ummmmhum."

"She was like a bag lady—not crazy, but odd, running here and there with bags of groceries, trying to help these strung-out musicians," recalls Helen Floyd. "People laughed at her, you know." Her apartment was like a homeless shelter, with musicians convalescing in her living room (Grace having been moved out to an apartment in the Bronx).

Many of Mary's white friends were as uncomfortable about the change in her as her family and the community of black musicians, but they remained loyal. Joyce Breach, a wealthy young jazz lover from Greenwich, Connecticut, simply accepted her. "She was very unrealistic about some things, like Alice in Wonderland, and street-smart at the same time. But that was Mary, and I never tried to change her." Explains Gray Weingarten, "In the '50s, I started having children and didn't get into New York very much. Next time I saw Mary Lou, she was in a stage of intense religious conversion." Weingarten herself had converted to Judaism, but remained intellectually skeptical of all religion. "I couldn't deal with Mary Lou, almost a maternal figure in my life, becoming a religious convert—a fanatic. That was a big difficulty for me. Later on, Mary Lou got better about the religious thing. She 'sobered up.' But still, when she came to visit me at my home, she'd put her Jesuses and her Marys all over before she even unpacked." Adds Elaine Lorillard pointedly, "She was very determined to do what she wanted to do—which was bad for her career."

Revealing that she was well aware of the criticism about her, Mary wrote to her friend Barry Ulanov, "Whenever God heals or performs a miracle they say I'm crazy, fanatic, a witch, anything evil." She was exhausted and often discouraged by her efforts, and felt keenly the conflict between helping others full-time while her own material and artistic needs were neglected. "All my life I've thought that my greatest block to big success was my weakness in stopping along the way to help an unfortunate," she wrote. "This set up many obstacles." Yet she had so projected the urgency of her own situation onto the world at large that she felt compelled to keep trying to rescue burnt-out cases.

Mary's life narrowed to a monastic leanness. Mornings were spent at Our Lady of Lourdes, the church around the corner; then home to fix lunch for whoever was staying with her; then back to church to meditate. At times her meals consisted of apples and water. She often gave up her bed to some addicted patient, sleeping on a pad on the floor. If she had to go somewhere, she walked; the little money she had went to feed and care for her patients.

Already comfortable praying at a Roman Catholic church, Mary began following Catholic disciplines well before she converted. Out walking one day, she "heard a sound"—her term for intuition—and bought a rosary she saw on display in a religious shop. She called her lapsed Catholic friend, Hazel Scott, for the words of the prayer. Then Mary began taking the classes in religious instruction required of all converts, at Our Lady of Lourdes. She loved her local church: its convenience and quiet, its cool meditative atmosphere, even the meeting room next to the downstairs chapel where parishioners socialized, playing penny-ante card games. In time, remarked Bernice Daniels, "I remember she was always playing cards in the church, even though she didn't win very often." And significantly, Mary was gradually drawn back to playing her music. Sitting in the quiet chapel for hours at a time, all sorts of "important sounds" came to her. "I'd go down and meditate in that church and hear some crazy arrangements. They come so fast I can't write them," she said. But she did begin to write them: her music notebooks from then on were full of fragments, riffs, sketches for pieces like "Gabriel's Horn," and "The 23rd Psalm," which would in time become one of her important new compositions, blending jazz with a spiritual intent. And if she still had no desire to play publicly, even during her most reclusive period—1956 into late 1957—there was a piano in her apartment and a piano in the church basement next to the card tables; and friends from the period, like Joyce Breach and Conchita "Niki" Nakatani, a journalist from Philadelphia who stayed at Hamilton Terrace for several weeks in 1958, recall that Mary would, in fact, occasionally play. She even offered to perform for Our Lady of Lourdes Church to help raise money for the grammar school the church was struggling to keep open, and which one of her nephews was attending. (But there is no record that the parish priest, a Father Dolan, took her up on the offer.) "She remained very concentrated in her music, and I suspect she never stopped playing," emphasizes Barry Ulanov. "Something musical happened all the time I knew her—from the early 1940s until her death. She was a true artist and music was everything for her. Too much weight is given to heavily publicized public appearances by musicians, while other venues—schools, churches, homes—are every bit as valid. If it's an artist of quality, both arenas are important. And Mary is a superb example of this."

However, Mary soon became disenchanted with the instruction she was receiving at Our Lady of Lourdes, complaining in a letter to Father Dolan of "strange vibrations." Temporarily adrift again, she turned back to her marathon prayer sessions, obsessed, like a prophet of old, that doom was near for the whole world, and that striving for salvation was paramount. It was a home-grown personal faith that depended on continuously surrendering her own needs. "Sacrifice was it for her. If you were destitute, she would go in your house and give you food and clothing and clean your floor and all that," recalls Helen Floyd. Mary herself had only one pair of shoes and a single dress, which she washed out in the bathroom basin and hung up to dry as needed.

———

GIVEN MARY'S STATE of mind at the time, it can fairly be called providential that she met two priests who possessed the rare blend of sensibilities she needed. The first, Father John Crowley, was a Redemptorist missionary in Paraguay who loved jazz (he was a former saxophone player). While on a goodwill tour of South America leading a band in '56, the Gillespies struck up a friendship with the priest, who encouraged Lorraine Gillespie in her desire to become a Roman Catholic. Later that year, Crowley was reassigned to a mission in Boston; on his way, he stopped in New York and looked up Lorraine, who introduced him to Mary. Their meeting was highly significant. At last Mary had met someone she would listen to: a priest who loved jazz. Crowley was able to temper her extremism. Concerned for her safety, he warned her not to take in any more people addled by narcotics or alcohol. In response, Mary quoted scripture to Father Crowley. "What a beat up guinea-pig I was," Mary wrote later. "And Father Crowley told me that with all that praying, I was doing what *he* was supposed to do."

Crucially, Crowley succeeded in nudging Mary back to performing her music—in effect, integrating the roles of healer and musician. "Father Crowley told me to get back to my work and offer this up as a prayer for others. That I should be playing the piano again," Mary remembered. The seed was planted.

Soon after, Mary met another critical religious influence, the erudite and brilliant priest Father Anthony Woods, a Jesuit, who was to have the greatest influence in shaping and balancing her religious energy with her musical persona. It was Barry Ulanov who introduced Mary to Woods. Ulanov, a Jew, had converted to Roman Catholicism and was a brilliant and articulate bridge between jazz and liberal Catholic theology and practice (later, after a divorce, he became an Anglo-Catholic Episcopalian). Ulanov, who had by then left jazz journalism to become a theology professor, wrote for the magazine *Jesuit Missions,* which Woods edited. His urging and that of Lorraine Gillespie, who had begun taking catechism classes with Woods, decided Mary. She joined his classes of instruction once a week throughout the winter and spring of 1957, at the well-to-do (and lily-white) St. Ignatius Loyola Church, on Park Avenue.

––––––

WOODS WAS TALL and large, kindly, but, says Ulanov, "tough minded at the same time." Father Peter O'Brien knew him when he attended high school at St. Francis Xavier in Greenwich Village, an intellectually and artistically vibrant church where Woods became parish priest late in 1957. "He wore a Homburg, a Chesterfield coat and all that kind of thing."

Mary and Lorraine were both baptized on May 9, 1957, one day after Mary's forty-seventh birthday. (Barry Ulanov was Mary's godfather; Bricktop, the Paris-based jazz hostess, was Lorraine's.) One month later, the women were confirmed together.

From then on, "Woods was her spiritual adviser and they were very close," says Peter O'Brien. Woods gave Mary the same advice that Crowley had: "Father Woods was telling me I was doing it the wrong way," she told her niece Helen. But Mary enchanted Woods with her passionate, childlike ardor and her musical intelligence. He confided, "She has the beauty of being simple without any affectation—and simplicity with her is a very deep thing. And I have heard her discuss the aesthetics of music with great penetration. She seems to have an understanding of what is good, of what is beautiful. And in her uncomplicated way, she can't understand how anybody can't be sincere. To me, she is one of the greatest persons I have ever met—really a very great soul. She has exquisite taste, and where there is goodness, she gravitates to it naturally.

"But," he went on, "she is an emotional thinker, a disorganized thinker and sometimes she has to sort out her ideas. And that's where I come in. She's simple and direct, primitive in a very good sense, and not spoiled by the sophistication around her. I don't believe that Mary is capable of producing anything except what is good."

Woods was an adept diplomat. By the time she began meeting with him for instruction into the church, Mary's prayer list topped 1,000 names—each of which she prayed for daily! Mary calculated that between prayers and one or two attendances at mass, she spent nine hours a day in church. Woods curbed her excesses in a kind but firm way. "One of the first things I taught Mary Lou," Woods said, "was how to pray for the thousand friends on her prayer list without naming each one."

Then there was the business of the visions. Her clairvoyance was, of course, long-standing—and not only visual; as a musician, she picked up information about feelings from sounds. But a good part of her spiritual rebirth was inspired by apocalyptic visions about individuals and society in general, causing her acute distress. "When I stopped playing, the sounds I picked up concerned the world," she wrote. "God gifted me with reading minds and I was most disturbed, thinking *I* had evil thoughts. The worst. Some people," she added, "lose their minds."

"I was a born medium," Mary added in a letter to her friend "Dan" of her breakdown and breakthrough in Paris, "but I saw awful things because I was not praying. I asked God in Paris to not let me see anything more except good." During the intensity of her early spiritual rebirth, she resorted to what many might see as superstitious practices, but the rituals gave her a measure of security. She sprinkled holy water on sites that seemed disturbed; she signed the cross over the area; she burned colored candles to shine on the dead and the psychically troubled that she saw in visions and dreams (in one, she wrote, trumpeter Buck Clayton was staring out of the darkness of a balcony). And, being Mary, she loved burning candles—candles to try to get a "lucky number" when she played the numbers, candles to "purify" a room of evil spirits, and so on. "I've tried the black cat, ladder, whistling, fortunetellers," she wrote later of her various efforts to control fate by manipulating the supernatural, "as well as peanuts backstage, and the round truck," practices passed along from black vaudeville.

And there were more visions, at times ravishing, as of the Virgin Mary in Paris, but more often frightening. Recalls Father John Dear (now a Jesuit priest, but in 1979 a Duke University student when Mary was there as artist-in-residence): "She told me about this great priest, Woods, coming and telling her very gently that you should ask God not to have visions anymore, so that you can get back to having an ordinary spiritual life, loving people and serving them through music. A profound thing, I thought. She's having these visions of the saints—and this Jesuit says there's a deeper thing. I was very taken by it and she was too."

Under Father Woods's guidance, Mary's obsessiveness subsided. Her fears of being "tricked" by sad spirits and the souls of the unsaved lessened. Gradually, she no longer worried that a person might be hypnotized by bad spirits while awake, or one's soul "taken" while asleep; at a deep level she let go of her magical thinking.

"Woods was made to order for Mary—quick, accommodating, unjudgmental; so strong and strong-willed yet with delicate apprehensions," reflects Barry Ulanov. "He was interested in music, yes, but the *last* thing Mary needed was somebody to deal with her jazz feelings.

She needed somebody to deal with her feelings and her understanding of herself. He was her spiritual advisor, her counselor—and the man who accompanied her through the gates." The happiest moments of her life, Mary wrote, were when she was going for instruction from Father Woods.

————

FATHER WOODS, FRESH to tenure in 1957 as parish priest at St. Francis Xavier, at 30 West Sixteenth Street, provided Mary, as did Father Crowley, with the inspiration to create music again—jazz with a spiritual content. Xavier supported a thriving arts community. Besides a boys' high school, there was a small, beautifully proportioned theater with a curving balcony and boxes, where the Village Light Opera Company, the Village Players, and the Xavier Symphony Orchestra performed. Xavier also hosted the St. Thomas More Society, a sodality, or Roman Catholic fellowship, that had quickly evolved into an intellectually vibrant forum for professionals to meet and discuss contemporary theology and its applications. Woods was the moderator, and Ulanov was a key member. Mary soon joined, and found there a bridge to Catholic activism, for the More Society definitely appealed to liberal and radical Catholics at a time when civil rights issues were heating up. But it was still the McCarthy era, a time of growing rifts within the Church, as within society at large. A Village friend of Mary's and fellow parishioner, Gemma Biggi, recalls a homily given by Father Woods in the late 1950s admonishing his congregation "not to find a Communist under every pew"; afterwards, contributions plummeted, and he was admonished by higher Church authorities. Woods marched for civil rights and pressed for inclusion of jazz music in the liturgy. "Woods had guts," Biggi says simply.

Sometimes, Mary walked all the way from her Harlem apartment to the church, more than a hundred city blocks, to be with Father Woods. "She said she had to walk," says Peter O'Brien. "She still didn't have any money for transportation." Yet she could only rarely be persuaded to play, even at private parties. A new friend she made in the fifties was the heiress Joyce Ekblom Breach. "At that time I still had money and gave a lot of big private parties, and my thing was the music," recalls Breach. "Marian McPartland played at a number of my parties and I wanted her for my parents' 35th wedding anniversary, but Marian was

booked and she recommended Mary. We talked on the phone and hit
it off, but Mary said she wasn't into playing. No. 'Too much evil in the
world.' Jimmy McPartland ended up playing the party."

Deeply in debt, Mary was on the verge of turning her back on the
world completely and becoming a nun, "so that I would be able to help
unfortunates," she wrote. It was Father Woods who helped her to realize how she could live, in the words of Romans 12:2, "not conformed
to the world but transformed from the world." He had a hard time,
however, convincing Mary to return to performing. "I'm a loner," she
would protest; but he knew that she needed to balance her intense
introversion with the gift that linked her to the world. "He told her,
says Helen Floyd, to "use her music! It wasn't the music doing her
harm. And that's how she got started into the liturgical music."

———————

EVEN BEFORE SHE had met Woods, however, Mary had begun sketch-
ing plans for a comeback to involve music and religion, writing to
lawyer Max Cohen in January of 1957, "I'll have to talk with you about
my plans concerning my return to the music field. I have great ideas
for creative music that are at a standstill now." She envisioned playing
music as a means of helping down-and-out musicians, but pinned
her hopes—at once grandiose and pathetic—on her autobiography
becoming a bestseller. She wrote:

> I'm sure that when you read my letter and notes on my story
> [her autobiography], you will probably think that I'm either
> nuts, eccentric, a genius or a queer—there's no end to the
> names one might be called. And I've gotta think how to write the
> good part of my experiences so I don't hurt anyone . . . many
> big names.
>
> I'd like $700 advance on my story. You may think that is a
> big amount. . . . Then too a movie can be done with some of my
> compositions as the background. Anyone connected with this
> story will become famous overnight and it also means the
> return of creative music—every time I recorded modern music
> it brought back people like Monk, Bud—it may not have
> helped me but it certainly did help others. I need a great deal
> of money for other things I have in mind, too. But I'm very very
> very tired, it seems I haven't slept for years. At the present, I

need donations for rosaries and masses while I'm resting and practicing. . . . I had contemplated not working until after Lent—I'd rather write new material and prepare my story. My story will start me back in big money.

There was no "big money" in the offing. However, when Mary made a rare excursion out in the spring with the Gillespies, sitting in on a date Dizzy had in Atlantic City (at Dizzy's repeated urging), Mary played as well as ever. "And Dizzy was lecturing Mary, telling her she's not helping things by not playing. She should get out there and play and hire musicians, keep them from trouble," Lorraine Gillespie recalls. "He said, 'God gave you all that talent—get back and work; maybe you'll get some musicians so occupied they'll stay off the streets.' He wanted her to be arranging, writing, rehearsing."

Gillespie also convinced Mary that an appearance at the Newport Jazz Festival would reignite her career. True, she would be paid only $300, but, he convinced her, her performance there could open up her mission to bring the spirituality of jazz to the world. "Mary hopes that her music will once more bring happiness to the world of music," she wrote of herself with regard to that event. With Gillespie's big band in 1957, she played three pieces from *Zodiac:* "Virgo," "Libra," and "Aries"—newly arranged by the talented young Melba Liston, then a trombonist with Gillespie—and a version of "Carioca" featuring Mary on piano. Father Crowley, living in Boston, called to make sure that she was practicing an hour every day, she wrote, to make up for the time she had been away from the piano, and the Gillespies bought Mary a gown, a mink stole, and a watch for the date. Mary tried to give the furs back. As for the watch, "I just lost it again."

Though Mary made a strong showing at Newport—Gary Giddins raved about Mary's use of "dissonances, dynamics, wit, subtle quotations, liveliness of ideas and clarity of articulation"—the band was underrehearsed. With her characteristic keyboard mastery, Mary laid to rest any rumors about her mental state, although in photographs from the period she seems almost to sag with sadness.

There is other evidence from 1957 of undiminished pianistic brilliance—evidence that has never been made available to the public. Later in the summer, Mary did a three-hour recording session for Roulette Records (now unavailable except on a tape Mary kept), working again with Melba Liston on updated arrangements of her own compositions, including a lilting "Waltz Boogie," one of her finest tunes, scored for reeds, rhythm, and piano. And Mary began, reluctantly, to work in nightclubs again—in Canada, at the Town Tavern in Toronto with bassist Tommy Potter and drummer Denzil Best, and later in Manhattan, at the Composer, which she felt to be sympathetic to modern musicians, with her old rhythm section of Bill Clarke and Bruce Lawrence. Mary told *Time* about the gig that she was "petrified yet unafraid. I'll play good. My fingers are faster than ever. Once I just played. Now I'm sensitive: if anybody don't like me, I'll know it. But I'll pray, and offer up my music."

Although the reviews were excellent (one raved over an "amazing 20-minute specialty of *The Zodiac Suite*"), Mary was, she told friends, "mixed-up and disturbed," her nerves paper-thin. Between sets she'd go directly from the piano to the cloakroom. "I have to watch that I do not allow others to goof me, making me crazy, eccentric etc. and is this ever difficult," she wrote in a letter in October to her new attorney, Herbert Bliss. Ever the perfectionist, she found her friend Bruce Lawrence's bass playing inadequate, writing in her diary, "Before I began praying, I would have broken up Bruce's bass and not because I think I know it all. I just cannot stand hearing someone not trying, even if he cannot play as much as the next guy." When the Composer date was extended to February of 1958, she calmed down and began to enjoy playing in public again. Opposite her was pianist Billy Taylor, her old Downbeat Club partner, who remembers her playing as strong as ever, but "quieter." Together the two agreed to co-write the music for a show called *After Hours,* to be produced by the Composer's owner Cy Baron. Although the show never got off the ground, it marked a sea change for Mary. She took on other jobs at important clubs such as the Blue Note and Bar O'Music in Chicago, and the Village Vanguard and the Cherry Lane in New York; there was even, as she wrote in February, "the possibility of a night club opened in my name." She had moved out the ailing musicians, but Grace had had a relapse and was now back in the apartment with her kids.

———

OF ALL THE ideas Mary came up with to fund her mission, none appealed to her more than an idea she would try to implement for many years after: a charitable foundation. As she wrote to Father Crow-

ley early in 1957, she wanted above all else "to help bring back creativeness and healing of mental patients, cancer and many other dis-
eases. I'd like to stay in the background except for my music."

The manifesto Mary prepared for her nonprofit organization,
which she had named the Bel Canto Foundation, is a paragraph that
speaks as much about Mary's own thwarted dreams for herself as it
does about her hopes for sick musicians:

> Bel Canto has been set up especially for musical performers out
> of a need to help them, which of course helps music. . . . It will
> be a home in the country where musicians, regardless of race,
> color or creed may go for a time to find peace and whatever
> "HELP" they may require to bring us the music we require. . . .
> Bel Canto has grown out of the need to help individual per-
> formers during periods of personal crisis. It hopes in the near
> future to purchase or build a home in the country staffed with
> medical personnel away from the pressures and stifling influ-
> ences of the city.

Through Father Woods, Mary had met a lawyer, Herbert Bliss, a
partner in the firm of Egan and Bliss, who at the request of the priest
agreed to take on Mary's charitable legal work *pro bono*. He helped her
draw up the papers to incorporate the nonprofit organization in 1958,
and a revised version in 1960. The stated aim of the foundation was:
"To voluntarily assist in relief of every kind and nature to those persons
suffering from or exposed to alcohol or drugs to any degree, but primarily to musicians."

Almost immediately, Mary began doling out money to sick musicians, money from the loans and gifts that she gathered from everyone
she could think of. All an applicant had to do was give his name and
address to receive a small check from Mary. This of course could not,
and did not, last long.

As another source of revenue, she tried again to retrieve lost copyrights, mostly on her own, as she could not afford even the reduced
rates Bliss charged for helping with such services. She envisioned a raft
of music-related jobs for her underemployed friends (and herself), if
she could fulfill her plans to establish a recording company, a publishing company, a booking agency, and a magazine. She wrote to an orga-

nization called Catholic Educational Institutions, offering to give a two-hour concert at Catholic colleges and universities, for a fee of $1,250, with a portion to go to Bel Canto. There were no takers; it was a considerable amount of money, after all.

Mary kicked off her fund-raising plans with a concert at Carnegie Hall on September 20, 1958, producing the concert with loans from friends, including two of the world's wealthiest women, Barbara Hutton and Doris Duke (to whom Mary even gave piano lessons for a time). Mary's relationships with her heiresses went sour, though, and Barbara Hutton was going to sue Mary to get her "loan" back, until Herbert Bliss persuaded her to drop the suit. As for the volatile Miss Duke, rumors circulated, said Elaine Lorillard, that she also filed a suit against Mary for unpaid loans. At any rate, the friendship ended abruptly. Lorillard herself lent money for the concert.

The Bel Canto concert featured, besides a group of Mary's old standbys and a new arrangement of "Roll 'Em" by Melba Liston, a jam session with everyone Mary could round up, an impressive lineup including Ben Webster, Thelonious Monk, Eddie "Lockjaw" Davis, Anita O'Day, Shirley Scott, and Baby Lawrence; Sugar Ray Robinson put in a nonmusical appearance. Despite the lineup of talent, though, attendance was weak. "In fact, that concert lost every penny," remembers Lorillard.

———

YET FAR FROM discouraging her, the failure of the Carnegie Hall concert only seemed to energize Mary. Her list of projects lengthened: she wanted to make regular visits to the sick at hospitals; hand-sew and donate scapulars (the badges worn by Catholic religious orders); and solicit donations of musical instruments from music stores for the young people she was beginning to teach at storefront community centers. But above all, there was the thrift shop. She scouted Manhattan for a storefront, finding one she liked around the corner from Bellevue Hospital, at 308 East Twenty-ninth Street. Signing a year's lease in 1959, she set to soliciting "subscribers" and contributions of clothes and other items to sell.

The shop, friends remember, was never well-organized. There were racks of clothes, jumbled-up boxes of things, many of them from Mary's famous friends—Lucille Armstrong, Louis's wife, donated dozens of pairs of size 4½ shoes, Duke Ellington gave a mink bow tie, Elaine Lorillard gave brooches and beaded bags, Esmé Hammond gave couture dresses, and so on. Mary was proud, in a childlike way, of these trophies.

Having at last settled Grace in her own place, Mary's time was now mostly her own; a woman helped out part-time in the shop. She let everyone know she was looking for merchandise, and leaned on buyer friends from Saks and Gimbel's for donations. Mary's favorite way of selling the clothes was to throw a party in the shop as a fund-raiser for a musician in trouble and invite people to make their purchases while she played. Delilah Jackson, today a historian of black entertainment, wandered into the shop one day in 1960, a young single black woman pushing a baby carriage. "Seemed like she knew that I needed things," she recalled. "She introduced herself, but didn't say she was a musician, an entertainer, and she asked if I needed anything. I said I didn't have any money and she said, 'I didn't say anything about money, it's for the kid.' She gave me a big bag of clothes for the baby. She was still beautiful then and she was so excited about this shop, it seemed like she had found a new love. She'd put like $5 or $10 in my hand; she felt sorry for me. She was trying to do everything she could for me, this went on for six or seven months."

Curious as to why Mary had picked a white working-class neighborhood for her shop, Delilah remembers asking, " 'Those Irish people, they like you? They're crackers.' But she said, 'They love me, they can't do enough for me. God's been good to me.' "

If Mary had become "like a nun," as several friends put it, she was still attractive to men. "There was a man who came by her shop who liked her," says Jackson. "I think he drove a taxi, and she'd run out and talk to him, like she was in love. She had these long, slit skirts, with voluptuous legs—sexy." "But," emphasizes Lorraine Gillespie, "I didn't know her to have any boyfriends in the time I knew her. Just the church," she says, adding after a pause, "and *all these priests*."

And friars, she might have added. In the spring of '58, during a chance stop at Graymoor, a monastery and retreat center run by the Franciscan Brothers and Sisters of the Atonement in the Hudson Valley, Mary met and immediately befriended a young black Franciscan, Brother Mario (born Grady Hancock). Attracted by the beauty and aura of the place, Mary—who was traveling back from an engagement in upstate New York with, of all people, Joe Glaser—spent a good deal of the morning there. "She probably had never seen a black Franciscan, and so she was very determined to meet me," recalls Brother Mario. "I was in the gift shop when they walked in. She was thin then and very pretty, in a dark coat with her hair flowing as usual, and I knew immediately she was an exceptional person, not an ordinary person that makes a pilgrimage. She carried herself like a lady. And I thought that Glaser was her husband, but she introduced him as her manager. Joe Glaser seemed in a rush but she was saying, 'Wait, wait.' She was just bubbling over, overjoyed to see a black religious and she gave me her address and sent Glaser back to the car to get some of her records—some 45s. Then Glaser tried to get across to me how important she was. 'She's a very famous jazz pianist.'

"Glaser was a very respectful man; he seemed dedicated to her. He would never interrupt her, although he did want to get on his way. But they must have stayed about another hour. I took them to the guest cafeteria for a cup of coffee. She was in complete control, oblivious. She talked in a sweet, soft voice at a solemn tempo. By then, Glaser was really nervous, looking at his watch and shifting around.

"I didn't know who she was. We didn't know those things, they were considered worldly. We never even read newspapers, and I'd been away from the world about three years. I had gone to Graymoor in 1955 and I was very young, about 21.

"About five months later in the autumn of 1958, she made a retreat, staying at our Sisters' for three days. She was my guest, so we'd have a meal together, talk, and we'd walk around the grounds. And that's when we really got to know one another. We weren't allowed to get too involved with lay people, but she wrote letters that I have. In later years, from '58 to '64, when I was there, working at the gift shop, she'd jump in the car and just show up at any moment. When the Brothers went to New York twice a year, I'd visit her there. And she brought Lorraine Gillespie and Lucille Armstrong, all three together, up to Graymoor in about 1959 or 1960. Lorraine and Lucille, I remember, bought expensive rosaries."

Mary, however, had no money for expensive rosaries. Her shop limped along for several years until, by the end of 1963, it was operating at such a loss that Mary had to close it. Undeterred, she sought fresh financial support to open another storefront, but this time on home ground, between 142nd and 143rd streets in Harlem, just minutes from her apartment. Ever hopeful, she took out an ad in the *Amsterdam News,* announcing:

> New and Old Clothing for the Entire Family donated by such well known artists as Duke Ellington, Dizzy Gillespie, Louis Armstrong, Clark Terry, Hazel Scott, Janet Burwash, Carmen McRae, Randy Weston, and others . . .

Chapter Sixteen
Black Christ of the Andes
1962–1968

THROUGHOUT THE 1960S Mary remained a "jack-in-the-box," in
Peter O'Brien's phrase, in terms of performing. She continued to
loathe nightclubs: not only were they full of bad vibes and selfishness,
but worse, the noise and distraction "broke the telepathy between
players." When out of necessity she did take club dates, though, Mary
felt that her playing had improved. "Before, I was almost wasted," she
wrote in her diary. "Now I can express myself better without 'hoggin'
up'—making mistakes. My thinking is much better. I can really play
from my mind through my heart to my fingertips, and that's what jazz
really is." The best evidence of the strength and clarity of her playing
from this period comes from self-produced recording sessions (for
Mary Records) in '62 and '63. The version of "It Ain't Necessarily So"
released as a record is a buoyant, spare etching of the blues. (An abundance of other material from the same recording sessions, never previously released, may be planned for a CD release.)

Mary's motto now became "Jazz is healing to the soul," a belief she
elaborated upon in her diary, in essays, and even in broadsheets that
decried the polluting effects of commercialism on jazz music and
called for a return to the strongly spiritual roots of the music. But her
convictions, genuine and deeply felt though they were, had the ring of
fanaticism for many people, serving only to isolate her from the very
community she had long taken as her "family."

She was particularly upset by the movement called avant-garde, or "free." "It mirrors destructiveness," she wrote in one of her most controversial essays. "I am very sad for what I hear, it seems that a heritage is being thrown away." The kids—the next generation for jazz—couldn't relate to it, she added, because the avant-gardists got "so far out they forgot about the basic thing—rhythm. So the kids made up their own kind of music with their own kind of rhythm for their own particular kind of dances, while these musicians got so anxious to impress each other with their dazzling techniques and complicated chords they failed to notice that they were losing them."

She distrusted the 1960s craze she called "Afro." "Afro has nothing to do with jazz," she continued. "Jazz grew up on its own here in America. It grew out of the work songs and the psalms of the black people here. Black Americans don't have to go back to Africa to get their dignity. They've got it here. The innovators have introduced sounds that are not compatible to love and jazz is disturbed. These sounds are . . . turned in from love and away from God." She added bluntly, "But these musicians using their talent to become a big star knew *I* was completely different. This talent I have is to help people, period. Yet I have faith that jazz is strong, the roots are deep. We must rid ourselves of evil by becoming charitable. SING OUR SOULS.

"It's the suffering that gives jazz its spiritual dimension," she added later, repeating her fervently felt view of jazz as a healing force. "That's what our jazzmen today have forgotten. Only out of suffering is a true thing born."

Regardless of the lastest fashions in music and painting, Mary now accepted that if she was to have an income it meant performing. After months of back-and-forthing, Joe Glaser finally convinced her that exposure in California could be invaluable to her career. He signed her to an important engagement in San Francisco at the Tudor Room of the Sheraton Palace Hotel in January 1962. Knowing her well, however, he took no chances once she'd accepted and asked Louis Armstrong, then based in California, to stop by to offer moral support. Armstrong did, and squired her to a Chinese restaurant—they both loved Chinese food—where they ate a six-course meal.

Mary got glowing notices at the Tudor Room and settled in for an extended engagement, striking up a friendship with actor Lloyd

Bridges, who was then starring in *Guys and Dolls* at the hotel's adjacent dinner theater.

To all outward appearances in California, Mary was successful and moderately prosperous; few could imagine the true state of her finances. Glaser had had to buy her gowns and help defray expenses because she was broke and up to her ears in debt. She still hoped— or fantasized—that she could recoup decades of lost royalties for old tunes, and to this end, she occupied her free time in California with typing letters to music publishing companies, adding to the thick pile of correspondence she'd carried on with them since the forties.

Wanting badly again to get a record out, Mary also wrote to Frank Sinatra at his new label, Reprise. "She told him she'd like to make a record for him, but she never heard back," recalls Joyce Breach. Then from New York, Glaser wrote that he was trying to put together a record deal to rebuild her presence—first through reissues of old material and then new material. But this plan fell through, too, partly because he learned that Mary was trying on her own to set up a deal (in vain) with a public relations woman she'd become friendly with at the hotel. Glaser shot her one of his furious letters: he and Mary had an exclusive contract, how could she think of trying this?

In the spring Mary returned to New York, where she found new energy and began an impressive series of initiatives. She founded her own music publishing company, Cecilia Music, and a record company, Mary Records, and began actively educating children at storefronts. And finally, too, she began to write the music that most deeply engaged her: spiritual jazz.

————

IN THE YEARS 1962 to 1965, as part of a movement to update and lib- eralize the Roman Catholic Church, Pope John XXIII convened the Second Vatican Council. Religious institutions in America in general were struggling for relevance: for many African-Americans, the lack of inclusion of non-white aesthetics and customs in the Catholic Church was a deep concern. Among Catholics, a debate raged over whether or not jazz was appropriate for a church service. Father Norman O'Con- nor, known then as the "jazz priest," lobbied for including jazz in new liturgical music written for the Church, suggesting that jazz as music was neither sacred nor profane—rather, it was the purpose and the place it was played that made it one or the other. Mary had been thinking of writing spiritual jazz for some time. (Perhaps longer than anyone realized; after her death there was found among her papers a copyrighted "Lord Have Mercy"—from 1945.)

Conchita Nakatani, a friend and houseguest in 1958 and '59, recalled that Mary began writing sacred music then, possibly an extended work based on parts of the Book of Psalms. And with the encouragement of Fathers Crowley and Woods, Mary planned to write a mass. "If anyone is capable of composing a great work in this field it will be she," said Father Woods. "I see her as an apostle in the musical world. Jazz and Catholicism are in harmony with her. Jazz is an expression of the American Negro culture, and it has something beautiful to offer the Church in the way of music."

Her first published work of lasting importance as spiritual jazz was the six-and-a-half-minute modern hymn composed for mixed-voice choir in dense harmony called, alternatively, *St. Martin de Porres*, or *Black Christ of the Andes*. This was music expressing Mary's mystical nature in a formal exploration of jazz elements.

On May 6, 1962, Martin de Porres became the first black (actually a mulatto, or person of color) to be canonized in the Catholic Church. Conferring sainthood on de Porres, a Dominican lay brother born in Peru in the seventeenth century who became revered for his miraculous cures of the poor, was if nothing else politically overdue: many black Catholics were becoming increasingly alienated.

De Porres became the patron saint of justice and harmony among the races. Called "black Christ" by liberal Catholics, he appealed deeply to Mary, at least in part for the same reason Brother Mario had immediately attracted her. Both were rare symbols—and validation—of African-American heritage in a mostly white Church. "She said," relates Brother Mario, "that I walked in her Harlem apartment and I said, 'This is going to make you play,' pointing at a statue of Saint Martin de Porres on top of her piano. And she said that's when she started writing her hymn to Saint Martin." (The friar himself does not recall this incident.) Mary also confided in Father John Dear, who was a student at Duke University when she knew him, that after Saint Martin's canonization, she woke up one night to see a man standing at the foot of her bed. "I remember she told me she said to him, 'You're Martin de

Porres,' and he said 'yes.' And they started talking about life and Jesus and her believing in God."

"Whenever she talked about how the visions or saints spoke to her—especially in her dreams," Brother Mario adds, "I tried to change the subject because I always felt a little uncomfortable that she would speak about visions. She always said she could see things. Later, I accepted it as Mary's way of trying to express herself. That was her way of expressing spirituality."

————

BY THE EARLY 1960s, as the issues of racism and segregation were front and center in the news, and the pain and frustration of the ongoing, often brutal struggle for civil rights for blacks built, Mary's conflicted emotions displayed themselves in seeming contradictions. On the one hand, she was an integrationist, choosing friends and lovers by character, not color. Yet she could also write in her diary: "Ofays [whites] made me nervous, I could not stay around them nor work with them."

But if it was hard for her to deal with the covert and mostly insidious racism of the North, as well as the shocking reports of southern brutality toward blacks, Mary's greatest difficulties with "race" concerned her own people. She noted sorrowfully, "There is no race on earth that is gifted with genius from the go like the Negro, yet he does the worst things in the way of sin." Among the worst of these things, in Mary's eyes, was self-destruction through heroin use. Appalled to see the growing violence and addiction in her neighborhood, she could not reconcile herself to the physical and spiritual degradation she witnessed.

Mary's hymn to Saint Martin de Porres was her pioneering attempt, at once audacious and courageous, to marry jazz with spiritual content, as a means of healing troubled souls, especially the souls of her people. (The original title for the LP that would include *St. Martin,* later dropped, was *Music for Disturbed Souls.*) She premiered the piece on the saint's first feast day, on November 3, 1962, at a concert after a noon mass at St. Francis Xavier Church. It was a carefully arranged work for trio and choir and, as had been the case since *Elijah,* the harmonies for voice were dense, with beautifully unexpected resolutions.

A recording of *St. Martin,* made a month earlier for Mary Records, gave the piece a certain fame. Despite the expense involved, she had insisted on using professionals for the vocals, booking the Ray Charles Singers (no relation to the famous singer), which backed many top acts. "They were the only ones who could do it," Mary explained. Nevertheless, "The chords were so complicated that I had to simplify them and turn to one of the most brilliant voice coaches, conductor and musician Howard Roberts." Milt Hinton was discreetly in the background on mostly bowed bass.

For *St. Martin* Mary drew on a a range of musical influences, from traditional church hymns to spirituals, Latin-American rhythm, and jazz, leaving very little room for improvisation. Conceived as a ballad with a simple melody line, *St. Martin* is in three parts, and is set in a minor key so as to impart a blues flavor. The work is divided into pairs of male and female voices, observes musicologist Gayle Murcheson. "The tenors and basses open the piece with the first minor text singing the phrase 'St. Martin de Porres' as a refrain. However, instead of completing the phrase, they're answered by the female voices and first tenors." As Mary envisioned it, the composition was to swing by virtue of its approach to time in its phrasing, a goal not completely achieved by the somewhat stiff-sounding choir, despite Howard Roberts's direction. "The Devil," an example of African-American humor, was another new choral work with a typically Mary-esque sinuous melody line. Mary described it as being "about the material world and its many snares, with the Devil like an adversary, seeking whom he may devour."

Singer Ada Moore, a sometime collaborator, contributed a witty but rather unwieldy lyric for "The Devil"; Mary fared much better on *St. Martin's* lyric, pressing a reluctant Father Woods into service with his pen. Mary tapped and hummed the melody and Woods came up with this:

St. Martin de Porres,
His shepherd staff a dusty broom.
St. Martin de Porres,
The poor man made a shrine of his tomb.
St. Martin de Porres,
He gentled creatures tame and wild.
St. Martin de Porres,
He sheltered each unwanted child.

O Black Christ of the Andes
Come feed and cure us
While we pray.

———

A WEEK AFTER the church concert debut on November 11, 1962, Mary presented *St. Martin*, "The Devil," and several other new compositions at New York's Philharmonic Hall at Lincoln Center as part of a program she called "New Concepts in Jazz." On the bill with Mary was Dizzy Gillespie and his twenty-five-piece orchestra, also the Argentine jazz-influenced composer and pianist Lalo Schifrin.

———

Reaction to *St. Martin* in performance was mixed, and although Mary had appealed to her lists of friends and patrons to attend the concert, with proceeds to be shared between the Bel Canto Foundation and St. Francis Xavier's arts programs, the concert failed to turn a profit. Although a few critics praised *St. Martin*, and Mary herself as a perennial pioneer in her writing, others were not so kind. One declared that "*St. Martin* was neither fish nor fowl," not "good liturgical music nor good jazz and certainly not a possible fusion of the two," just a "hokey prayer." A French critic, Jean Delmond, very much the French philosopher, agreed, saying that *St. Martin*, although "imbued with the spirit of the blues" was a *denatured* composition, a "blues stripped of its accent." Even the *New York Times* critic, John S. Wilson, soon to become a great and stalwart admirer of Mary's music, was lukewarm about *St. Martin* and "The Devil" in concert. Mary's pieces, he thought, were "neatly turned little cameos, each pleasant in itself but even in sum they did not achieve compelling interest."

Mary responded defensively, remarking that "one must listen attentively." She had big plans for both the music and the saint, telling the press that singing star Johnny Mathis was planning to make a movie about Saint Martin de Porres, with her music supplying the soundtrack, another project that did not get off the ground. But after 1964, she dropped the piece from her repertoire. Peter O'Brien, who met her in that year and heard her play countless times, cannot remember a single performance of *St. Martin*, recalling that she told him in the late sixties that "Martin de Porres likes to stay hidden; he don't like too much publicity." Mary would have been well pleased, though, about the little side chapel dedicated to Saint Martin at St. Francis Xavier after her death. The chapel contains a dark-hued wood statue of the black saint.

————

THROUGH WOODS AND other friends at the St. Thomas More Society, Mary met some of the most interesting radical Catholics of her day. One, well-to-do, somewhat reclusive Janet Burwash, helped to finance Mary's next important concert, in 1967, and helped support her as she concentrated on both writing and performing a jazz mass. Burwash belonged to the influential peace movement, first known in America as Pax Christi, which worked for civil rights of African-Americans and an end to the war in Vietnam. Through Pax, organized in part by the radical Catholic Eileen Egan, Mary met Dorothy Day, the cofounder and voice of the Catholic Worker movement—and at this writing reportedly under consideration for canonization as a saint. Like Woods, Crowley, and other priests and Catholic activists Mary befriended, Day supported Mary in her desire to compose a jazz mass, and Mary performed several times at Tivoli, the farm worked by the Catholic Worker cooperative in the Hudson Valley, near Bard College.

————

AROUND 1961, AFTER Mary had finished composing *St. Martin de Porres,* she began what was to become a long on-again, off-again engagement at Wells Supper Club in Harlem. The club was named for its owner, entrepreneur Joe Wells, a great admirer of Mary's talent. But he was struggling financially in the early sixties. He had just opened his restaurant, and business was so poor in '61 that he thought he might have to close it. Mary, needing money to fund Bel Canto's latest endeavors, offered Wells a deal: she and a rhythm section would play for expenses only. The clear benefit to Wells was that her presence would lend class to the room and bring in the spenders. In turn, he would bankroll her recordings.

Gérard Pochonet, by then married and living in New York, played drums for several stints at Wells's club. "The music was excellent, great—half her tunes, half standards. Her style was still her style to me," Pochonet recalls. "But Wells was a cheap guy." According to Mary's agreement with Wells, in addition to performing for expenses only she promised to give him 15 percent of the sales generated from her new records; later amendments of the agreement gave Wells 50 percent of the royalties.

What did Mary actually get from this deal? Between '62 and '63, she put together enough material in the studio for both an EP (extended play) of eight tunes and a complete LP, *Mary Lou Williams Presents St. Martin de Porres,* a venture probably funded in total by Wells. Cover art for the LP was donated by David Stone Martin, who produced a supremely apt illustration of hands at once praying and flexed, as if for playing the piano—the whole in pink, Mary's favorite color. For the EP, Mary turned to Alisa Mandel, a Greenwich Village artist and fellow St. Thomas More Society member. Born in Czechoslovakia, a Jewish convert to Catholicism, Mandel provided a line portrait drawing of Mary. For inexpensive manufacturing of the vinyl itself, she turned to Moe Asch. "He was pressing the records so badly that they wore out after three or four plays," says Pochonet. "But she didn't pay any attention to it. I told her, but that was the way she was."

The LP featured Mary playing in three different combinations: with bassist Percy Heath; with saxophonist Budd Johnson; and with gospel singer Jimmy Mitchell. Besides *St. Martin,* there was Mary's modern gospel piece "Anima Christi" and "Praise the Lord," set to Psalm 150 (both arranged and conducted by Melba Liston), as well as Mary's tribute to recently assassinated President John F. Kennedy, the beautiful "Dirge Blues"; and "A Fungus Amungus," a critique of the jazz avant-garde whose tartly humorous title derived from a story Lorraine Gillespie told about a frustrated preacher who was heckled until he shouted, 'Everybody stand up! There's a fungus among us!"

Despite the mixed reception of the original concert version of *St. Martin de Porres,* reviews of the album (*Mary Lou Williams Presents . . .*) were good. One critic said the record marked "the triumphant return of a major talent to jazz," and when it was later distributed in Europe, Mary was awarded both the Prix Mondial du Disque de Jazz from the Hot Club of France and the Grand Prix Académie du Disque Français in 1968.

Despite her avowal in the liner notes that "10 percent of the proceeds from this album will be used for the rehabilitation of sick musicians," sales were disappointing and there were no profits. Indeed, this first of her several self-produced albums turned out to be another of what Peter O'Brien calls her "more grandiose dreams," and Mary was once again in financial straits. At Father Woods's urging, Mary finally agreed to an engagement at the Hickory House beginning in January 1964. It was a well-paying job with plenty of exposure. Booked to play a month, with indefinite two-week extensions, Mary ended up playing at the club for well over a year.

Again, the club date was billed as Mary's latest "comeback," leading to TV spots on both the "Today" and "Tonight" shows and a planned weekly half-hour radio show on WABC. *Time* magazine, which in 1957 had run a story about Mary's "comeback," ran another in 1964 in which Mary said prophetically, "I haven't had that feeling of wanting to give up—I think this time that I'm out here to stay." Whitney Balliett's in-depth interview for *The New Yorker* that year also helped reestablish her presence.

Back in 1957, Mary would stew in silence or vent her frustration in her diary when a sideman displeased her. At the Hickory House in 1964, she was far less reserved and showed a sterner side, establishing a reputation among bass players as a strict leader. "It was terrible being on a job with her if the bass player wasn't right—nothing would satisfy her," says Peter O'Brien, who counted eighteen bass players come and go during the lengthy Hickory House engagement. Explains bassist-vocalist Carline Ray, "She would get angry at the kind of bass players who liked to play up near the top of the fingerboard, who wouldn't let her have her space. She liked a bass player who would play down in the lower reaches of the instrument and lay down a nice musical swinging cushion and let her do her thing—in other words, stay out of her way." Famously, Mary not only fired bassist Richard Davis at the Hickory House, but told Balliett, "I'd like to nail his foot to the floor; play them changes, man." Says Marian McPartland, who knew her well, "On the bandstand Mary was demanding and intolerant, but also like a mother, praising the good." If the rhythm section was not "together," Mary told Marian, she would stop playing and let them play by themselves, rejoining them when they were "tight" again. And if they couldn't get it together, she said she'd "play chimes," because, she explained, "you've got to bring a section together to let them hear themselves. But if after this they still don't make it, then I'll start cussing!" As pianist Billy Taylor sums up Mary's professionalism, "She was looking for perfection in playing mates." From the sixties on, she worked mostly with bassists Larry Gales, Bob Cranshaw, Milton Suggs, Brian Torff, and Ronnie Boykins. Probably her most satisfying collaboration was with Buster Williams.

"Bass is important to me," she explained to Billy Taylor. "I don't play any of the bass notes at all when I'm playing. . . . Today, if I don't get a giant, well, he doesn't hear it, 'cause the kids can't hear the bottom of the chord. Often with the bassist I get hung up and have to get out of it."

"We've got to think together," she insisted elsewhere. "You can't think separately when you're in jazz, even when one goes out free. There's got to be a hitch-up of the minds, like mental telepathy. They say I'm difficult to play with. I don't know."

Although at the Hickory House Mary had found a steady income at last, she was more interested in raising money for Bel Canto Foundation projects. After the first thrift shop failed, she considered running a tea shop in a bookshop that Joyce Breach had opened in 1965 in prosperous Bronxville. She would play piano for the "old Mary Lou fan club," she mused, who would presumably make the trek from Manhattan to hear her during tea, and buy books. Nothing came of that, nor did halfhearted plans to earn money from trimming hats with fur or making beaded bags.

However much in debt she remained (and she was also still half-supporting relatives), Mary's image in the black community remained lustrous. When she proposed taking Breach nightclubbing around Harlem, her Greenwich-born friend objected: "But I'm so *white* white." To which Mary replied, "Yeah, but you're with *Mary Lou Williams.*" On one such evening, Breach recalls, Mary took her to hear Sarah Vaughan. "A long line waited to enter the nightclub but Mary just swept in, saying, 'Mary Lou Williams waits for no one.' And once we were inside, they found a table and very happily squeezed us in."

The honorable and reasonable way to raise money, Mary decided, was to seek work through the Catholic Church. Although her letters suggesting concert dates at Catholic college campuses had not yet borne fruit, Mary prevailed on Father Woods to introduce her to Bishop (later Cardinal) John J. Wright of Pittsburgh, an influential clergyman. She hoped he would fund jazz education in the schools.

Their meeting was productive. Bishop Wright steered her toward the Catholic Youth Organization (CYO), which sponsored programs in music and art for young people in poor neighborhoods, but he hesitated at Mary's request to fund her mission to write jazz music for the Church. Jazz, he responded, had an unsavory reputation: it was associated with drugs and dropouts. Her reply was vintage Mary. "I said, 'No, that's not so. It is this commercial rock that has caused havoc in that area.' I ran it down for him!"

She was persuasive enough to win Wright's backing to organize a jazz festival in Pittsburgh for 1964. Mary loved "firsts," and this was a triple play: the first time that an African-American woman produced a jazz festival, the first time that sacred music was commissioned for a jazz festival, and the first time that the Catholic Church was involved in running a jazz festival. The Pittsburgh Jazz Festival was to be a charitable event, with any profits (over and above the initial outlay of "$25,000 or $50,000," as Mary vaguely remembered) going to fund CYO projects.

Putting together a program proved more difficult than expected. Soon veteran George Wein, who had been producing the Newport Jazz Festival since the later 1950s, was brought in. (Mary never said anything negative about Wein for publication, but privately she told a story that revealed her resentment. "She said Ben Webster went after George Wein with a saxophone at a rehearsal at the Pittsburgh Festival," remembers Peter O'Brien, "when Wein said Dave Brubeck had done more for jazz than anybody. Ben Webster had to be restrained. Wein, he liked to keep them humble.")

————

FOR THE FIRST Pittsburgh Jazz Festival, held June 19–20, 1964, at the Civic Arena, Mary and Wein gathered top jazz talent. For m.c.'s there were Willis Conover, the famous disc jockey for Radio Free Europe; Duke Ellington's son, Mercer; and Father Norman J. O'Connor. Among the musicians she hired were Harold Baker, Art Blakey and his Jazz Messengers, Bud Freeman, Thelonious Monk, Jimmy Smith, Ben Webster, Melba Liston, Sarah Vaughan, Dave Brubeck, and Joe Williams.

Much of Mary's work was featured during the two-day event, in a trio setting and by a twenty-five-piece band playing Liston's arrangements of Mary's recent compositions, including *St. Martin de Porres* and "Praise the Lord." Mary had approached choreographer Alvin Ailey about setting *St. Martin* to dance, but when Ailey was not available, the Bernice Johnson Dancers—the choreographer was saxophonist Budd Johnson's wife—performed it along with "Praise the Lord." (A decade later, however, Mary did work with Ailey.)

With good reviews and an enthusiastic crowd, the concert appeared in every sense to have been a success. Mary happily told a

local newspaperman, "It's like Father Woods said. I do seem to be helping people. They kind of hear what I'm telling them through my
music. The sounds reach out and touch you." But when the dust settled, there was only a paltry $1,000 profit.

Mary was undeterred, ignoring certain rumblings about overreach-
ing herself, and produced a festival the following year with an even
more ambitious lineup—Thelonious Monk, Dave Brubeck, the Modern Jazz Quartet, Count Basie, Duke Ellington, Carmen McRae, Earl
Hines, John Coltrane, Billy Taylor, and Woody Herman. Reviewers
were even more enthusiastic about Mary's solos and trio work in the
1965 festival. "Miss Williams has a pair of brilliant solos that ride along
exultantly on her strong, driving attack," one noted. With Larry Gales
on bass and Ben Riley on drums that year, she played one of her
favorites, the Denzil Best composition "45 Degree Angle," as well as
her own "Joycie" (for Breach).

But the 1965 Pittsburgh Jazz Festival was also a financial disappointment. The CYO director, a Father Michael Williams, whom Mary
referred to in one letter as "that priest that was mean to me," eased her
out entirely, made George Wein sole producer, and decided to include
popular and folk music—heresy!—in subsequent festivals. (The festival limped along for a few more years before expiring, to be resur-
rected some years later as a popular summer feature in Pittsburgh.)

———

THREADING THROUGH MARY'S life in the sixties was her continued
relationship with her troubled family, a constant shadow and worry.
"She had these nephews she part-raised," says her old friend Bernice
Daniels. "One was her sister's boy, Robbie, another was her niece's,
Clifford, up in the Bronx." Grace was attempting to stay sober, after
bouncing in and out of dry-out centers. So also was Virginia Burley,
who had cancer. Wrote a penniless Grace in her application for aid to
dependent children in July of 1963, "Mom gave up wine and hooch
since they found these things in her." Getting on welfare regularized
Grace's life to some extent, but her privations were great. Mary gave
what she could, but after 1963 she felt she also had to give to others in
need, particularly musicians (such as her ailing husband, Harold
Baker, and a now-flat Hazel Scott in Paris, to whom she wired money),
as well as giving a huge amount (when measured against her income)

to various Catholic charities. At times, Mary simply had nothing left to give. Where Grace and her family were concerned, she tried to shift the responsibility—if not to Grace herself, then to the New York City Department of Welfare. After school started that fall, for example, Mary went to battle with the Welfare Department on behalf of little Robbie, and won. Her eight-year-old nephew, she wrote, had no coat, no boots, not even a proper pair of shoes; they must buy him some. She also persuaded Ellington's personal physician, Dr. Arthur Logan, to write the Welfare Department, citing the medical necessity of having a telephone at Grace's apartment. When Robbie had his "sick attacks," Mary explained unmedically, he had to be rushed to the emergency room.

Although Robbie Mickles was the closest thing to a son she'd ever known, she could not care for him full-time; that should have been Grace's job. "Anyway, [Mary] would have been incapable of raising him or adopting him in a conventional way, say in Westchester or Long Island," explains O'Brien. "She was not capable of giving up who she was, of giving up the piano, to take care of him. So she raised him about a third of the time." But Grace was not to be depended upon. She continued to relapse. To a friend Mary wrote:

> Got her out of Bellevue today and she's still drinking (sh . . .) Everything is a mess—thanks to God—Just hope I don't lose my mind (smile). Am receiving my salary in dribbles. They had to pay the Ray Charles singers $11,000—whew! Give me a ring—I may split the scene. smile. May God bless you.
>
> > Love, your pal

At the end of May, Mary noted in a postscript in another letter that she was "a nervous wreck," with Grace trying to borrow money again and refusing to empty out her whiskey bottles as part of the deal. "Poor sister Grace," Mary concluded. As for surrogate son Robbie, worse was to come.

––––––––

IT WAS NOT quite true, as Mary half-joked to Joyce Breach, that "Mary Lou Williams waits for no one." She had in fact long been waiting for someone to help run the business side of her life. She had approached a host of agents and public relations people, friends such as Weingarten and Breach; wealthy patrons; even her ex-husband. But nothing had worked out for long.

For moral support Mary had Brother Mario and Father Woods. Then, in the winter of '64, Brother Mario learned that he was being sent to the Vatican by his order. Mary was thrilled for him (and hoped as well that he could facilitate her wish to get a papal commission to write a jazz mass). But it meant the loss of her closest spiritual friend. Typically, she put her own loss to one side and threw a grand party for him at the Hickory House to which she invited luminaries like the Armstrongs, the Gillespies, the Ellingtons, and others. She had hoped the guests would provide the needy friar with farewell cash gifts, but, said Hancock, sounding bemused, he received "only a fancy bookmark. I don't think they understood the purpose of the party."

But as one door closed, another opened: no sooner had Hancock departed for Italy than a new religious man entered Mary's life—literally walked in the door of the Hickory House one night. This was Peter O'Brien, who was a young seminarian breaking his curfew, as he regularly did. He was to become arguably the most important person in Mary's life. Of their first meeting Mary recalled: "My piano faced the door. I could see anybody that was coming. All of a sudden this little boy came in and he looked so funny I had to laugh. He had on a winter coat down to his ankles and it was too big for him. And he came and sat down at the bar and he was lookin' while I was playin'. I said, 'I wonder who that is?' "

"He kept looking up at me," she added elsewhere, "smiling and carrying on. . . . He came regularly the whole time I was there and he's been with me from that day to this." The "little boy," altar-boy handsome, was actually twenty-four, not eighteen as Mary liked to tell it. He was smart and ambitious, with an appetite for the unconventional that belied his innocent appearance.

Peter Francis O'Brien, from Fairview, New Jersey, was born into a working-class family, the first of eleven children and the golden boy intended for the prize of the priesthood. There was a streak of theatricality in the family that Peter O'Brien seems to have inherited. "Some of my father's relatives in the twenties had a radio show called the 'Hawaiian O'Briens,' three Irishmen with Hawaiian guitar. And as early as three or four years old—some fifty years ago—I went to a dancing school called the Swift Sisters. Mae Swift had been in George M. Cohan's touring company of "Mary." A dozen of us at the dancing school did routines—tap, soft-shoe, ballet—at shows for the Elks, the Rainbow Women and so on. There are photos of me standing on a table, wearing a straw hat, ready to perform. I got my lessons free. We couldn't afford them. This was a world I loved. And also the Church. This arena like a stage set, that whole pursuit of something beautiful."

Apart from that, he cares to remember little of the childhood he described as "that awful, dysfunctional world. With the onset of puberty, off I went to New York. My father made certain good moves for me, got me into Xavier, a military high school, attached to the church where Father Woods was the parish priest. Xavier High School was a really wonderful place, with a really almost professional theater." Young O'Brien was soon sneaking off to the forbidden world of Broadway—"I saw the second half of all the shows; that way I didn't have to pay"—and even landed a job as an usher at Radio City Music Hall, which his father made him turn down. "Show business was the only place I felt safe," he explains. "I had this deep fantasy all the way up to 1970 about my own career as an actor. But then I found my arena as a performer as a priest."

In 1962 O'Brien made a move in that direction, entering the Jesuit-run Loyola Seminary in Shrub Oak, New York. In high school, he had already begun escaping into the specialized reality of *black* American show business. The catalyst was discovering Ethel Waters's autobiography, *His Eye Is on the Sparrow.* "I was determined to meet Ethel Waters—I just loved that book of hers. And the seminary was only a train ride from Manhattan. To get to Ethel, I sought out Carson McCullers. Ethel had starred in her play, *The Member of the Wedding.* So I used to go read to McCullers—F. Scott Fitzgerald. And I pursued other artists. I wrote them letters, I found out who knew them." Among these were singer Thelma Carpenter, and the photographer and writer Carl Van Vechten, famous for his portraits of black entertainers—he would photograph the young, winsome O'Brien). And then—Mary. *Time*'s comeback article about her, titled "The Prayerful One," with its twin photo images of Mary kneeling in prayer at church complete with lace mantilla, and in a tight, low-cut gown at a gig, made a powerful impact on the seminarian. O'Brien immediately wrote to her, then followed up with a visit to the Hickory House. "I'd never heard anything like that in my life. I'd heard a little jazz—Duke, Benny Goodman, Dizzy at sixteen at Birdland, Erroll Garner, but that was it. So this music just washed over me and overwhelmed me and that was it—*wham*. Two things were operative in my life, the performing arts and the Church. And then here comes this woman that embodies them both.

"Early on, she would never speak, she was very reserved. I told her I was in seminary to be a priest, and that's all we talked about. Very quiet. She used to go sit in the coatroom to get out of the way."

But their relationship blossomed quickly. "Part of *my* relationship with her, I needed a mother. I'm very jealous and looking for attention and Mary gave me that. I enjoyed an absolute preeminence with her. We would sit in that little yellow kitchen in Hamilton Terrace and talk for hours and hours on end. She would ask me questions about church or about God that I could not answer. I was so young, her searching perplexed me. Nor did I think there were outright answers to her questions. I ranted and raved about the Church, but I think she understood that I wasn't really serious." Indeed, Mary wrote to O'Brien at that time: "Father Woods told me to see that you make it as a good Jesuit Priest. To give you hell when you're wrong, ha!" It was, however, hardly a joke to her: his vocation as a priest was a profound thing for her, as was their relationship. So profound that others who had known her longer came to feel that O'Brien manipulated Mary's credulity and peripheralized her other relationships.

Immediately, O'Brien became part of the warp and woof of her career plans; he had an appetite for the arts, huge energy, and an optimism that proved irresistible to her, as when he wrote soon after: "The Carnegie Concert should be a great thing next October; that should shoot you straight up where you belong." (That particular concert, however, did not take place for three years.)

Mary's letters to O'Brien from the period are warmly confiding, revealing something of the innocent, little-girl quality that other friends remarked on as part of her charm. Apprehensive about an upcoming trip to Pittsburgh, and conflicted about playing publicly, she wrote him:

Also pray that I'm humble and silent the way I use to be. Seems that people upset me and I speak my mind—and there's that question of jealousy in our business. Really a nasty business and half of the musicians are either jealous or nuts! smile.

I'm out here to try and make a big name so this way I'll be able to help the foundation and other unfortunate musicians. I am so very sensitive (after being away from the public so long) to all the sounds on the outside . . . Before I leave this world I'd like to do many great things for our Lord. May God bless you,

Love, Mary

Her motherliness also surfaced immediately with the impetuous priest-in-training. Setting what was to be become a pattern for the relationship, she began sending him money and dispensing advice: "Peter, when something goes wrong with our nerves, it's sin—ask God to show you yourself. This is what I'm doing. I'm jealous, talk too much about others when angered."

Mary's relationship with Anthony Woods was the most mature and intense and the healthiest that she enjoyed with a father figure. But Woods was no attendant; rather he was her confessor, provider of good counsel, restorer of good humor and balance, and a firm, if compassionate, disciplinarian who pressed Mary to focus on priorities. Brother Mario had been more of a companion, a kindly, patient, respectful, fun-loving but *safe* companion. Meeting Peter O'Brien so soon after the friar was gone from her life must have seemed highly auspicious to her—literally a godsend. He too was fun-loving, devoted—and also seemed safe, if somewhat wilder, edgier, and more rebellious than Brother Mario.

But not long after Mary became close to O'Brien, Father Anthony Woods, ill with heart disease for some time, died suddenly in October 1965 (only a year younger than Mary). Mary was in Pittsburgh and received word from Gemma Biggi, her Village friend. "I remember she got a ride back to New York in a truck. Father was laid out full-length at Xavier in a small chapel. Mary and Lorraine were so upset. Outside the chapel, Mary said, 'Why did they have to bury him with shoes with holes in them?' Mary was usually stoic. But she was crying. From there, we went to the burial in silence. We were all sad, but Mary was heartbroken. He meant so much to her, it was such a loss."

"She told me later," adds O'Brien, " 'I thought I was going to die myself, that I couldn't make it anymore.' " Bereft, Mary needed a companion of the spirit more than ever.

———

THE MID-SIXTIES held more difficult losses for Mary (Bud Powell died a year after Father Woods), yet she remained excited about various new projects she planned in order to reach the next generation. She had, of course, long been interested in jazz education; as early as 1946 she wrote an article proposing that jazz be taught in the public schools. Now, in the sixties, it seemed very likely to many people that jazz was in danger of dying out. "Black people don't know anything about the history of their music," Mary said bluntly, noting that they recognized pop star Diana Ross but not Billie Holiday.

When the Jazzmobile began touring the neighborhoods of New York with the music, director Billy Taylor recalls that Mary plied him with questions. And in her diary she noted, "I decided to work with teens to try to save the one American-born art." She set up informal jazz "workshops" on Harlem streetcorners. She'd play a tape and ask the children she had coached (in storefronts like "Our Place") to demonstrate dance techniques for the kids on the street. After playing selections from familiar pop tunes with simple melodies, simple beats, "I'd switch it on them but not too much; the kids are smart. You can't put too much over on them." At the storefronts, she'd work on scat singing and dance patterns, to get kids into the jazz groove. Nor was that all. "She'd blend her music with other things such as etiquette, how to present yourself," says O'Brien.

She also produced records aimed at winning over teenagers to jazz. With Milt Orent she wrote several tunes (released as 45s on the Mary label), among them "Chief Natoma from Tacoma" and a rock-and-roll version of her forties ballad "You Know, Baby." Later, she produced others, but the "hits" she hoped for eluded her. Instead, stacks of undistributed 45s piled up in her apartment. She looked to O'Brien, still in seminary, to publicize her records to disc jockeys. Dutifully, O'Brien tried to help, but he was bewildered. Why didn't she put her energy into mounting another concert at Carnegie Hall (preferably a night of standards and originals with a trio, he thought, not the religious music she wanted to produce)? Why wouldn't she agree, instead, to do a concept album—songs by Gershwin, say? That would interest record companies. "But I couldn't get her to do things like that. And now I see that while it might have been nice to have the Gershwin album, it wouldn't have been important," O'Brien acknowledges.

In late 1966 O'Brien made his maiden voyage as Mary's manager. But Mary prevailed: instead of just a jazz concert, it was to be a sacred concert, an event billed as "Praise the Lord in Many Voices." O'Brien negotiated her contract for this Carnegie Hall event of February 1967. Mary was in her element among the hand-picked group of contemporary composers of "new" and experimental sacred music, with narration by the eminent Jesuit musicologist, Father Clemens J. McNaspy.

The concert took place in a period of intense controversy for the Catholic Church. By 1967, Vatican II was replacing centuries of tradition: not only was the mass now to be celebrated in the vernacular, but church music was to be modernized as well. Throughout the twentieth century, with occasional exceptions, drums, cymbals, and bells were banned from the liturgy, but Pope John XXIII had reversed the ruling—and jazz, too, was (tentatively) deemed worthy of inclusion. But by 1963, Pope John was dead, and his successor, Pope Paul VI, was more conservative. Said a Vatican liturgical expert, the Reverend Annibale Bugnini, pointedly, "Jazz masses violated the norms for sacred music laid down by Pope Saint Pius X, more than 50 years ago."

The timing of the Carnegie Hall concert was no coincidence and expressed the views of a large number of progressive Catholics, both religious and lay. Father Norman O'Connor, in the liner notes to *Jazz Mass,* a Columbia recording, stated bluntly that the Vatican didn't know what was jazz and what wasn't. Father McNaspy, in the Jesuit magazine *America,* joined in, writing that he was in favor of jazz in the Church.

"It was a very exciting time. Such a thing as this concert would not have been possible before," says O'Brien. In fact, a Vatican decree *reversed* the ban on jazz later that year. Mary's involvement in the concert was considered a coup for progressive Catholicism, although her actual liturgical writing was to come a bit later. "Thank You, Jesus" was a modern spiritual with gently satirical overtones arranged by Mary and Bob Banks for solo voice, sung by a young Leon Thomas. "Our Father" was arranged for piano trio and a chorus of thirty-five voices, featuring the creamy-toned Honi Gordon. Mary had also freshly arranged "Praise the Lord" for an ensemble that included French horn, piano, bass, drums, conga, and male vocal soloist.

O'Brien and Mary had the first of many disagreements when she threw her energies into trying to market the recording made of the concert by Avant Garde Records. "Mary took these LPs all over to d.j.s," says O'Brien. "That seemed sort of pitiful to me. What's that record going to do for her?" Not much, as it turned out, for Mary later wrote that although she sought royalties, she never received "a dime."

Frustrated yet again by lack of response, Mary turned to Moe Asch with another project: an interpretation of the history of jazz. She was interviewing and taping her mother, she wrote, about ragtime and the aftershocks of slavery, but it was like pulling teeth. She wanted to tape others—Dizzy, Andy Kirk, John Williams. And she would include her own thoughts (narrated, she hoped, by Father McNaspy):

> From Suffering came the Negro spirituals, the songs of joy, and the songs of sorrow. Because of the deeply religious background of the Negro he was able to translate this into rhythms that reached deep enough into the inner self to give expression to outcries of honest and sincere joy. The origin of Jazz is the Spirituals and out of this comes the growth of four eras of music, Ragtime, Jazz, Swing, and Bop, or modern. Unfortunately however, before Bop was fully developed, some of the younger American musicians lost the heritage by playing modern foreign composers, destroying the basic creativeness, honesty, and truth of the great American art called JAZZ.

Eventually Mary had to self-produce her history-of-jazz record, taping it in her apartment, at her old Baldwin, and O'Brien edited down the tapes to LP length. Asch, however, did agree to distribute the record on Folkways, and soon Mary was writing Asch about producing another project: her first mass. "There's been nothing like it," she exulted, "but all I have is a little tape recorder not worthy of recording it. The Catholic priests and nuns are making a lot of money on records now," she added hopefully. But Moe Asch did not take her up on this suggestion.

"EVERY CENTURY HAS had its best contemporary music written for the church, from Schütz to Bach to Mozart," as Richard Westenburg, music historian and director of Musica Sacra, has pointed out. But it was only toward the final quarter of the twentieth century that jazz came to be included in the liturgy. Mary began formally writing her first mass—that is, composing music to fit the Catholic (and Episco-

pal) liturgy, or church service—in 1967. Hers was not the first, however. Jazz had been included in the worship service before. Perhaps the
earliest example was a 1946 service at the Park Avenue Synagogue in
New York, for which Leonard Bernstein, Morton Gould, and David
Amram were commissioned to write pieces; and in the fifties and early
sixties there were jazz bands and jazz-influenced masses presented in
several Episcopal churches, though "jazz" was often a catch-all term,
covering everything from Dixieland to folk guitar. Nor was Mary the
first to write a specifically Catholic jazz mass. The Reverend Clarence
Joseph Rivers of St. Louis wrote one in 1964; it was even performed at
the Newport Jazz Festival that year, and again in 1967. Eddie Bonnemere, Mary's one-time student, wrote a *Missa Hodierna* for jazz group
and choir performed during a mass at Manhattan's St. Charles Borre-
meo Church in 1966. But most jazz composers with a serious interest
in spiritual music preferred to concertize on sacred themes rather
than write music specifically for the liturgy.

If Mary was not the very first to write a jazz mass, then, hers was successful as few others have managed to be, a happy marriage of the
sacred and the profane, of the formal Western and the African-
American approaches to rhythm and phrasing. As in *Elijah,* and the
more recent *St. Martin de Porres,* she avoided improvisation, offering
instead composed vocal and instrumental parts with the *freshness* of
improvisation and the flavor of African-American swing, without
falling back on well-known formulas of gospel music. In the evolution
of Mary's masses—three in all, in a number of versions—Mary reached
her full artistic maturity, even greatness. Only Duke Ellington, with his
own deep interest in the spirituality inherent in jazz, which he
explored in compositions like "Come Sunday," "David Danced Before
the Lord," and "In the Beginning, God," could rival her in the realm of
sacred jazz.

There are, in fact, some intriguing parallels between the two composers in this musical arena. Mary did not think it mere coincidence
that Ellington put on his first sacred concert in the fall of 1965, shortly
after she'd given him her recording of *St. Martin de Porres,* or that he
presented his second sacred concert in 1968, the same year Mary
wrote her second mass. Both composers became absorbed in the
Bible; both wrote three long sacred works, and they wrote them
around the same times. (Ellington created three sacred concerts—in

1965, 1968, and 1973. And although he was commissioned to write liturgical music, in the end he chose not to do so, preferring to concertize.)

————

MARY'S MISSION TO write a jazz mass really took shape in the spring of 1967, when Bishop Wright hired her to teach music at a Catholic high school for girls in Pittsburgh. Mary was euphoric at the opportunity to prepare a sacred jazz concert with the school's choir. "The Bishop of Pittsburgh will have 1,000 kids to sing the Mass I finish in the Cathedral here, in July!!" she wrote O'Brien with high enthusiasm.

As so often, though, Mary's optimism hit a wall, and her spirits soon dipped when she began working at the school. Seton High's principal expected her to teach music to 400 girls, and, many complained, was so prejudiced that Bishop Wright replaced her (with a black administrator), and directed that Mary's music class be reduced to a manageable twenty-five. Then Mary tackled the curriculum. Although she noted with approval that the teenagers had a talented choir director in their Sister Gracia, they seemed bored and restless. "I was teaching them theory and the kids just sat there and glared at me," Mary said later. "I couldn't stand that, so finally I said, 'Let's do it how it is.' I wrote a bop blues and the kids went wild." Mary's mood soared again. "After that, they couldn't wait to get to class. I was teaching them to sing like Billie Holiday—teaching them the sounds the way she made them. They loved it. They were scatting like Ella!" She began adapting "religious" pieces like "Praise the Lord" and some secular but soulful tunes like "O.W." for her planned mass with the choir. "I had lost my inspiration, but I was truly inspired by the girls. For the first time in a while I really felt like writing, so I began composing during the class. I'd tell the kids to take a break and I'd write eight bars of the Mass. They'd sing it right off." To which she added, "I wrote that mass in a week."

Not exactly. She actually had to simplify a good deal of material— for example, there were three versions of "Praise the Lord" written for that mass, each progressively less complex harmonically, to suit the abilities of her amateur choir, as was the case with "O.W.," which served as a processional. As she was to do in the next two masses she wrote, Mary was responding to the pragmatic needs of the choirs she worked with, and perhaps as well to her own limited experience in directing choirs.

Although she was inspired with fresh ideas by working with the girls in class, much of the work of rewriting was done at her sister Mamie's house in East Liberty where, as was always her habit, Mary stayed while she was in Pittsburgh. It was an atmosphere that she later described pungently in a letter to Peter O'Brien as the "most hell you can imagine—all that noise."

Can't seem to write in New York, but listen to this. There's eight of us where I live. In the house, kids are running up and down the stairs, TV on in the room to the left and to the right. Records are being played by the boys downstairs. Yet I stay up til 4 a.m. frequently, writing for the kids—something else, huh? I am teaching them to sing the arrangements I'm writing for them, including the "Gloria" ("Glory to God"), "Kyrie" ("Lord Have Mercy"), and "O.W.," arranged for entrance music.

At last, after one postponement when Bishop Wright was called to China on a mission, at the end of July 1967, Mary was able to hear her mass celebrated in Pittsburgh's beautiful St. Paul's Cathedral, with a choir of thirteen, some probably drawn from CYO summer-camp attendees. (It was recorded by Mary herself, on a home tape recorder.) She had tried, Mary said, to capture in the music "*the way I feel when I'm praying.*" This first quietly serene mass (simply titled *Mass*), composed for piano and voice, flowed lyrically out of the African-American experience, its jazz influence residing primarily in the naturalistic phrasing of the vocal lines and masterful piano accents that gently swing the piece. Mary's liturgical work stirred attention of church authorities sufficiently to ask her to appear on a Catholic television program about the history of salvation, where she was part of a company that included Dr. Tom Dooley and U Thant.

But Mary was far from satisfied with her first effort. "It was long, drawn out, like a symphony, like the kind of thing they have in churches," she later said dismissively. Like so many of her earlier compositions, it would be revamped, overhauled and added to, and then would flow into her next mass, titled *Mass for the Lenten Season*.

IN CONTRAST TO the serenity and rich sonority of her spiritual music, Mary's private life continued in disarray. While working on *Mass,* she

wrote O'Brien grimly from Pittsburgh, "You know I'm going through
the worst period of my life. God knows what He's doing, but I don't.
Wish I could leave His business alone, stop complaining, find a rocking chair and sit in it, ha!" But at least her teaching stint in Pittsburgh
had given her a respite from the problems of her second Bel Canto
Thrift Shop, which from the beginning was as impractical a business
venture as the first—more a place to socialize than to do business. Into
the storefront she moved an old piano and a drum set donated by
Dizzy Gillespie, invited her friends to stop by and play cards and talk,
and threw parties for friends on their uppers, like Eartha Kitt and
Hazel Scott. (Scott had divorced Powell and married an Italian 15
years younger than herself. Father Woods performed the ceremony
and Mary was maid of honor. But Scott's second marriage was a failure
as well, and soon her glamorous career in Europe foundered. Once
back in New York, however, she promptly reestablished herself.) Mary,
who could ill afford it, constantly gave merchandise away yet still
expected the shop to allow her to fund her own needs, modest though
they were, plus those of others. Typical of Mary's attitude was a 1966
letter to the landlord, in which she pleads with him to reduce the
shop's rent from $125 to $75 a month: "I'm away making money to
run the store. The store is closed when I have to go away until such
time I can find someone capable of taking care of it. Last year I gave
away close to $3,000." Needless to say, this argument did not impress
her landlord. And business continued to worsen. "She was not tough
enough to run a business," says Peter O'Brien.

Meanwhile, Mary's silent partner, Joe Wells, watched his investment being run into the ground, while Mary responded to his worried
queries with wildly impractical suggestions. Why didn't "they" buy up
the whole block, she asked at one point, and set up stores serving the
community? Mary may have been "Madame Queen" to Wells, but he
was out of patience. He brought in his wife Ann to manage the store,
dump the Salvation Army goods, and expand the section called "Votre
Boutique" featuring African-American designers. Mary defended her
castoffs, but Ann Wells held firm. Finally, in the winter of 1968, the
store was closed for good, with the Wellses demanding that Mary pay
her share of rent and electric bills.

Mary felt betrayed. "It seemed as if God had deserted me and I
wondered what I had done. I was off the beam for quite a while," she

confided in a letter to Joyce Breach. Ann Wells was a "witch," and her husband worse: in Mary's view, they had taken everything she had built up, while she had lost money and hope. "She had a lot of paranoia, she didn't trust people," thinks Elaine Lorillard. "On the other hand, if people gave her money or lent it to her, they didn't or shouldn't have expected to get it back. I didn't."

With the shuttering of the shop, all hope of funding the Bel Canto Foundation ended. But for Mary the dream of having a foundation that could provide both outreach *and* a basic living for her, so that she would not have to depend on nightclub work, only went dormant. Within a few years she was mulling over plans to apply for foundation grants for outreach projects.

———

IN PRACTICAL TERMS, the closing of Bel Canto Thrift Shop confronted Mary with a pressing need to find an income. She decided to try her hand again at writing arrangements for the few big bands that still survived. In particular she wanted to arrange for Duke Ellington, regarding him as both the best composer and bandleader in jazz. In August of 1967 she stopped by to chat with him during an engagement at the Rainbow Room, and there, she said, "He asked me, again, if I would do some things." Soon after, she wrote him the following letter:

8/21/67

Dearest Duke:
Received a call from Inez Cavanaugh last night. Seems that many of your ardent fans would like me to write for your band. I have already started a few things and hope to get them to you before you leave New York.

Was reluctant, due to the fact I am trying madly to do something about my compositions that I have in Cecilia Publishing company. I asked [Tempo Music—Ellington's Music publishing company] for the return of "You Know Baby" because I have spent a great deal of loot trying to do something about it and at last it was used in a Frankie Sinatra film a few months ago. I called Ruth [Ellington] several times to help with the exploitation. You do realize that this is unfair for the artist to do all the work.

First I had the Foundation to help musicians. I dropped all this to get back to music. Lost a great deal of money in a partnership store after deciding to return to music. In fact, my partner actually took the store from me (had invested over $15,000 of my salary to keep the foundation going). Have been teaching jazz in Pittsburgh at Seton High School. Wrote the Mass and Bishop Wright celebrated the Mass with teenagers singing it. Had wanted you to hear to do a big Mass here or Pittsburgh. Came to New York the first of August.

Well to make a long story short, I have earned very little in the past year and to be able to arrange for a band without a goodsized advance of money would put me in really bad shape.

I love writing for you because you are my favorite but, I will have to receive some kind of compensation. I have bills to pay. If I had money I'd write for you and not charge you anything.

Am making up "You Know Baby" (two arrangements of it, due to the fact that you have a Rock and Roll singer). It's a natural for a hit if you're lucky to get it through all this "muck and mud (smile)." Unfortunately nothing happened with the record I recorded, mainly because one cannot understand the singer's words, his diction was very bad. The kids in Pittsburgh and Fordham liked both the "Chief" and "You Know Baby."

If you can possibly do so, I'd like an advance of between $2500–3000 so that I can do as many things as possible for the band. This will enable me to pay up bills and devote the next three months to writing.

As usual, I'd like to concentrate on "ol standards and originals."

May God Bless you . . . Love
P.S. Please call immediately.

In the mid-forties, when for a time he couldn't play any works registered with ASCAP, Ellington had needed her. Now he didn't, and was charming but noncommittal. Bassist Brian Torff recalls Mary's stories about Ellington's use of charm: "She would write arrangements for him, then go to him to get paid and he would say something like, 'Well, Mary, what a lovely dress you have on!' " Mary was nothing if not determined and continued to pursue the idea of writing for Ellington for at least another year, even as she was writing arrangements for the Count Basie and Woody Herman orchestras.

One of the pieces she arranged for Ellington, her "Scratchin' in the Gravel," now called "Truth," was magnificent, taken at a dirge-like tempo before a majestic finale, with lead alto solos tailored for Johnny Hodges. "That's her crusading thing again," remarks O'Brien. "The idea was this is the truth about jazz—the blues." There were as well the new rock-and-roll and ballad versions of "You Know, Baby," and rock and jazz versions of "Chief Natoma from Tacoma," the piece Mary had written and produced on a 45 for teenagers.

Both versions of "Chief" wound up on Ellington suites: the "rock" version in the center section of the long suite *The River,* and the "jazz" version in the "Loco Madi" (short for "location Madison") movement of the *UWIS Suite.* Though the tempo is changed in the latter, and there is an inimitable Ellington treatment at the end of the movement, Mary's "Chief" melody can be clearly heard. Mary was never credited nor paid.

It is more than likely that Mary's "Chief"s were folded into the two suites unintentionally. After all, Ellington was a composer who, as his long-term friend, Patricia Willard, remarks, said that he did not often go out to hear others play: he had become aware that he was too likely later to unwittingly "compose" something he'd heard. Mary knew nothing of how her material had been used, never heard the suites, though there was a close call: while team-teaching with her at Duke University in the late seventies, O'Brien recalls listening to *The River* for the first time with students right before Mary arrived in the classroom. "When I realized what I was hearing, I took the needle off the record before she entered. She would have been furious. There would have been some shit flying—she would have gotten on a bus for New York and raised hell."

———

MARY'S SECOND MASS took shape when Father Robert Kelly approached her about writing one for the six weeks of Lent in 1968. Kelly, a priest at St. Thomas the Apostle Church in Harlem, was in charge of a project to commission works by African-American composers in the New York Catholic Diocese. She agreed with alacrity. This second work she described as "a quiet piece," and in large part it is: the music's appeal lies in its delicate, pensive sensibility, dabbed with the blues, a properly contemplative but subtly swinging mass. The "jazz" aspect of the mass was contained in her arrangements for saxophone (Harold Ousley), flute (Roger Glenn), guitar (Ted Dunbar or Grant Green), bass (Major Holley and others)—but with the unfortunate addition of Robbie Mickles on drums, playing a loud, rock-oriented beat (which Mary may have hoped would "reach the kids"). Again Mary used singer Honi Gordon, whose golden tones, at once earthy and ethereal, lifted the amateurish mixed choir, for whom Mary's long, sinuous boppish melody lines and jazz-inflected stops and pauses were familiar territory. The younger, more pliable voices handled their parts better, but even they, many noted, were a struggle to train.

Again Mary approached Moe Asch. Wouldn't he record this mass, she pleaded? By sheer word of mouth, she told him, the Lenten jazz service had packed the church for four Sundays. But again Asch declined. There was no one else to go to, and to date Mary's *Mass for the Lenten Season* has not been recorded, although it has been performed several times, including once at Dorothy Day's Tivoli Farm that summer for a Pax Christi meeting, and in 1969 at a concert in Rome. Like its predecessor, it lives on in certain rearranged and revised sections of her third and most famous mass.

On April 4, 1968, Martin Luther King, Jr., was assassinated. At the request of a priest from a nearby school in Harlem, Mary wrote two songs in tribute to the civil rights leader afterward. Composing them virtually on the spot, she drew their titles from his sermons. The stately "If You're Around When I Meet My Day" and the exuberant "I Have a Dream" were performed by a children's choir on Palm Sunday that year. Mary, who had taken care to write music that captured King's voice and inflections, admitted that she was "shaking with fear" at the task, but she was pleased with the results, and as usual hoped that Moe Asch might produce an album, including the new songs. In vain.

Then Mary, to use her phrase, "picked up her cross" and went on, her life kept in balance by prayer and music, which by then utterly interconnected for her. "I'm praying through my fingers when I play," she said often. It was the kind of prayer that reached out and sought to heal. "I think the entire world is kind of upset and I don't think people know very much what to do with themselves," she observed. "I make it by sticking with my work and thinking that everything's going to be okay—which I think it will be."

Chapter Seventeen
Zoning
1968–1977

WITH HER SECOND mass completed, Mary determined to begin another. Both her first and second had been "quiet," so as not, she explained, "to detract from prayers when the beat becomes more important than union with God." But her third was aimed at her favorite target—young people. And she intended it not only to swing, but to *rock* teenagers into the fold.

She needed financial support to write the lengthy new work. Reasoning that the time was ripe for papal support of a jazz mass, she set her sights on the Vatican, enlisting Peter O'Brien's help in contacting the Jesuit curia in Rome, and plying Brother Mario with letters and plans. Once she had Vatican approval, she felt, a stipend to compose the work would surely follow.

Meanwhile, she had to earn a living. In Copenhagen, Baron Timme Rosenkrantz was opening a new jazz club. From there, Mary reasoned, it would be easy enough to get to Rome and the papal officials she hoped would fund her third mass. So she agreed to debut at "Timme's Club." And she had the baron's word as well that she would find plenty of work on the other side of the big pond.

Traveling to Scandinavia on a German steamer (she still feared flying), Mary arrived in Copenhagen in the middle of August to find Timme's Club far from ready to open, although she was booked for the following week. Rosenkrantz found her a room, but it was a distance from the city. Being isolated and broke in an expensive city took a toll on her; Mary's spirits fell and her health worsened. In letters home she complained of a raft of disorders: an infected eye, back pain, a sluggish digestive system, and the possibility that she'd contracted mumps or chicken pox (she had not). Mary's weight had been creeping up; she now tipped the scales at 200 pounds. She joked about her struggles with diets, but hated being obese. A physician-friend, music-lover Dr. Sam Atkinson, notes that Mary "was powerfully built and extremely durable, as great musicians are," yet her health was never very good from that time on. Most ominous, as she mentioned in a letter to Joyce Breach, "I had a slight discharge from carrying luggage, etc," and immediately began a new diet, a "grape cure" for cancer. "I used the grape juice and I healed it," she added. It would be exactly ten years later that her bladder cancer, in an advanced state, became manifest.

Living on credit, she spent time window-shopping, tempted by beautifully crafted Danish silver, furs, and clothing. But mostly Mary sat waiting and stewing. She was worried about the war in Vietnam, about the Black Power movement, about hippies, drugs, and the recently elected President Richard Nixon—and she worried about Peter O'Brien. "Mary was forever counseling me not to get hung up on my family. I didn't give a damn about my family! I guess she couldn't imagine that. She was absolutely the opposite of that." She also worried about his career plans and associations outside of the sheltering wing of the seminary. He was making plans to go out to the University of California at Berkeley to pursue a doctorate in theater arts. Mary wrote: "I'd say no to going to San Francisco—it's tricky out there." It was a typically veiled reference to the sexually free-wheeling life, including the gay scene, which had burst into the open there. Says O'Brien, "Years before, in 1964, Mary Lou finds out that I'm going down to the Bon Soir, a club in the Village, and has her first major hissy in regard to me and my sexual purity. She thought anything could happen down there because the Bon Soir was very gay, number one. *I* didn't know this; they were perfectly nice to me, wonderful; and it was a great show. But Mary wanted Father Woods to straighten me out, so she arranges this meeting and Woods says, 'Stay away from those people—you can't trust them. They'll do things, say things.' I paid no attention. I had no notion that the world was evil and was never disrespected by anybody. She had this idea about me. Maybe she saw even then that I'd better watch out. And she was right, as it turned out. I used to resent that because my life was so goddamned straight it was crazy at that point. I certainly did go off the deep end—but it was after she died."

Mary, maternal, wise, prescient, overbearing, wrote letter after letter of advice to O'Brien throughout his life. In 1968, it was: "You've gotta get closer to God before you go anywhere with anybody. Listen, get on your knees and cry the way I've been doing here. I was a mental wreck when I came here. Stood in the middle of my room and asked God to help me."

While Mary was waiting for Timme's Club to open—it finally did, about two months behind schedule—she put the finishing touches on big-band arrangements for Ellington, Basie, and Herman, also amending them for performances by the excellent Danish National Jazz Orchestra, heard on radio programs produced by Baron Timme.

She was less happy about the beautifully decorated but tiny Timme's Club ("small as a bathroom"). The place was the swan song of the amiable but hard-drinking baron and his equally hard-drinking but less amiable companion, Inez Cavanaugh. In October, Mary wrote to Brother Mario in Rome to complain: "Inez is nice one night and yells at me and the waiters the next night—I cussed her out a couple of times and she cooled it for several days. She went too far, then too I'd heard that everybody hated her so I made her focus her attention on me so she'd be loved again, but it started tonight again. Guess I'll have to put a tack on her seat. . . . But one thing I can say," she added, "when angered or pestered, I play good."

Mary's nerves worsened. When the Gillespies arrived for a tour, Mary confessed she felt depressed and anxious for her future. "There's not enough work for jazz people," she said flatly. Nevertheless, Mary canceled an upcoming Continental tour. "I'm too nervous and then, too, the promoters are making all the money," she explained. Both she and Teddy Wilson, who followed her at Timme's, turned down offers to return to the club, rattled by Cavanaugh's scenes. "He [Wilson] almost ran amuck running to the kitchen after playing," Mary wrote in a letter to Brother Mario. "On his second set I grabbed his hand and told him to sit quietly next to me, to play ballads 'cause he was racing on the piano so fast the bassist couldn't keep up with him." Wilson was given Mary's room at the boardinghouse attached to the club, to which she had moved, and Mary, she wrote, "was asked to go, with nowhere to live." But then her luck turned: a friendly priest found her a room with the Benedictine sisters at the serene old St. Lioba Cloister in the heart of Copenhagen. Her room was sunny, clean, inexpensive, filled with fresh flowers and fruit. "I'm rehearsing, eating and praying. The Holy Spirit came to my heart so strongly New Year's Eve while I was in Church I had to go outside for two or three minutes and cool off. I thought my heart would burst!" she wrote, festooning a letter to Joyce Breach with her trademark sketches of smiling faces and lips. "I'm so happy I could kiss a mule!" she added, even though she was reduced to playing one-nighters: "Like the good ol' Andy Kirk days, horrors! Old cars and the musicians are sort of boring and the piano bad. But I didn't insult anyone or become angered, I just played, whammed and banged, etc. I sounded like a nickelodeon, put on an act and aped the action going down."

Mary focused on Rome, planning to leave Denmark for Italy in January. She buzzed with plans; maybe Father Bob Ledogar would be able "to get me a salary to do the Lenten Mass in upstate New York. And it would be nice to do it in Rome at Lent, huh?"

She read Thomas Merton's autobiography, *The Seven Storey Mountain,* in the fall, identifying closely with Merton—his ardent conversion, and, perhaps more important, his combination of mysticism and earthy practicality. (Merton would have been amused at her bedside reading: beside her missal and his book lay the Sunday comics, sent over from New York, piles of crossword puzzles, and copies of *True Detective* and other lurid crime rags, to which Mary was addicted.) Merton was a champion of universal civil rights and insisted, as Mary wrote in a letter to Joyce Breach, on "the white man's taking responsibility for wrongs to the black man. He wrote some eight freedom songs in 1965 along with a church composer. My life is parallel to Merton's but I think I suffered more when I was 3 and 16," she added, a rare mention of her painful childhood.

Inspired by Merton's memoir, Mary set to work on her own book again (and indeed her first sentences mirror Merton's opening passage). She now had a title to frame her philosophy: *Zoning the History of Jazz. Zoning,* also the title a few years later of one of her outstanding LPs, had a specific, musical-spiritual connotation for Mary: "It means getting rid of the elements that destroy music and putting them in their right place," explains O'Brien. Although Mary did eventually type up some eighty pages of a new draft of *Zoning*, she did it piecemeal and never completed the project.

As the Christmas season approached, she planned to go to Rome, but she was delayed by the sudden illness in Copenhagen of her old friend Mae Mezzrow, who was alone and without funds. As she tended to her, Mary jotted a warning to herself in her diary, "Have to watch my budget or I'll give all of it away. Have to use my common sense, something I wasn't born with." Taking a gig in a hotel restaurant, she plunged into depression. "Felt a breeze (bad vibes)," she noted. "Played very badly, piano keys slick, rhythm section bad, sabotage, miserable feeling after I played. Sick people, poor Mae and Inez, God have mercy on their souls, show them the light. I can't make it but with God's help, yes. Pick up my cross and make it. At 58 the old bones are pretty tired, have difficulty with my back, pains, gas, etc. Much blood from hemorrhoids, coughing. Everything is offered up. But then, sometimes the Holy Spirit comes."

At last she was ready to quit Copenhagen for Rome. Rosenkrantz and the convent sisters saw her off at the train station with packets of sandwiches—and money. It was the last time she saw the baron. The following year, Timme Rosenkrantz collapsed and died in a New York hotel room. He was fifty-eight. Inez Cavanaugh, still attractive, left Copenhagen without a word of goodbye to anyone. Brother Mario met her in Rome, through friends: "Inez wanted some money to get back to New York but she was indirect and casual about it. She didn't talk about the music world, just about hard times and how she wanted to get back to work." "I met her not long after that in New York," adds Peter O'Brien. "She was like a skeleton and looked horrible. And then she disappeared."

MARY ARRIVED IN Rome inauspiciously. It was a cold and rainy January and, after having to change trains five times, she had slept past her destination, arriving hours late and exhausted. Disappointed too, when she was met not by Brother Mario but a seminarian, who took her to her room. But after she rested she felt better temporarily. "Went out to dinner with Mario, drank wine and beer and got dizzy and couldn't walk, next day sick, but made it to church in time for the Pope's blessing. Rome OK, nothing exciting. Would like to be here in the spring."

Rejoining Brother Mario improved her mood. "We used to have great spiritual talks," he reminisced. "She loved talking about God and the experiences she went through and she'd want your sincere opinion about things, although my experiences were so different and some of the deep things I couldn't relate to—her visions and premonitions." Through him, she met influential Romans she hoped would help with her mass project. One, Rembert Weakland, was not only the Abbot-General of the Benedictine Order but a pianist himself who had taken advanced studies at Juilliard.

But even Weakland and other highly placed clerics were unable to persuade the Vicariate—the ecclesiastical authority for the city—to lift a sudden injunction on Mary's presentation of her *Mass for the Lenten Season* (also called at that time *Jazz for the Soul*) at a church service on February 2, in honor of the forthcoming first anniversary of Dr. King's death. Instead, it was ruled, she would have to play the mass at a recital. According to an Associated Press report: "Cardinal Angelo Dell' Acqua, vicar general for Rome, was asked about cancellation of Mary Lou Williams' jazz Mass for the slain civil rights leader, Dr. Martin Luther King Jr. The Cardinal disclosed that he cancelled the jazz Mass at the Pontifical Latin American College and substituted a recital after the Mass. He said it had been his policy to 'compromise' by permitting jazz Masses as long as they don't involve a drummer. Mary Lou's group had a bongo drummer." A "spokesman" for the local church added that they had had some beat music and folk masses, but they needed to "rethink" Mary's performance.

Although Mary told a reporter at the time that she was "not upset" over the Vicariate's ruling, her diary reports otherwise. She walked the streets during an icy rainstorm for hours that day, trying to decide what to do: "O Lord, am I supposed to move on, go home? What shall I do?" In the end, she blamed herself for "pushing too hard," and made up her mind to accept the decision gracefully. By the day of her recital, soon after, she was tremendously excited, not least by a visit she paid to a convent with Brother Mario. "Holy spirit strong, can't cool myself. Mario took me to see the sights, but of all, the poor little Sisters are the greatest—I can truthfully say I'm jealous of them, tears, feeling of

Jesus' presence." Later that day, she presented the *Mass for the Lenten Season* to a packed house in a seminary chapel. After the concert came the crash. On February 10, she was "blue again, always cold and my teeth are going bad." Worse, a strike in Rome made a coming paid concert—money she badly needed—impossible to schedule. There was no work for her in Rome, she wrote Joyce Breach: "No nightclubs here. It's all folk music. The loot I have will not sustain me for two or three months. . . . In working for God (don't think I'm nuts), one does not charge a fee. And they can't give me a salary."

She persevered, playing a sprinkling of concerts in other Italian cities. As the mass was by then usually celebrated in the vernacular, she also tried to get the text for the Lenten season translated into Italian for the Vatican to review. The deepening depression she regularly wrote home about—feeling "off," eating and drinking too much, and constantly "trying to adjust"—was nowhere in evidence in live broadcasts taped in the studios of Vatican Radio, which had a worldwide network. Rather, she sounded in a warm and inspired mood in a solo set of standards and originals. She also prepared new arrangements of her King songs and pieces from the Lenten mass for a chorus of some twenty seminarians (which included, she wrote happily in a letter to Breach, a few blacks), plus flute and bass. No drums or bongos, however.

"Could be the concert will end up in the lap of the Pope," she wrote ebulliently to O'Brien, adding: "The students sang their butts off, except the bass player who couldn't swing to save his soul." She attempted to press O'Brien into service. Would he take copies of the tapes of the Vatican concerts around to radio stations? Could he "maneuver" a performance at St. Patrick's Cathedral for her? That would make the Pope sit up and listen, she continued, ignoring the doubts of "handsome soul brother Mario" and Abbot Weakland, who thought her plans farfetched. "If I send you the money, will you go to New York and see Cardinal Cooke? and write to Bishop Wright in Pittsburgh to help us get to the Pope?" After O'Brien protested to Mary that he was just a student and could hardly be expected to track down these eminent churchmen, Mary backed off, but the push-and-pull of their relationship a few years later as manager and artist was already set then.

Finally, Mary did see Pope Paul in a semiprivate audience. "He grasped my hand and said, 'Thanks for the work you are doing with my brothers,' and gave me a blessing and rosary beads, and I blurted out that I'd like to do a concert for him. He almost blushed and smiled like a little boy, but nothing said." Wrote Abbot Weakland afterwards to O'Brien, "It might be just what he [the pope] needs if she doesn't play too many blues. But chances of working that out are less than nil."

Waiting for a signal or a sign, Mary struggled through March, finding occasional work—"little gigs around Rome where I didn't know myself; I composed as I played. The Italians are starved for jazz, love it." With her choir of seminarians, she played selections from the Lenten mass along with other originals and standards in a concert on March 12 in an ancient Jesuit church, for an organization called the Approdo Romano. "They were beat-out nobilities," Mary wrote (somewhat inaccurately), "who tried to understand the scene but I'm afraid it didn't reach them . . . until I started playing a funky blues beat," she added.

At the end of March, she got a break. "Guess what," she wrote exuberantly to O'Brien, "a big-shot priest asked if I'd write another Mass for the peace of the world. He'd pay me—what! ha! and will use his influence to get it to the Pope." Monsignor Joseph Gremillion was indeed an influential priest: secretary of the Pontifical Commission on Justice and Peace. Having obtained her commission—to write a votive, or devotional, mass that Gremillion suggested be titled *Mass* [*or Music*] *for Peace*—Mary was ready to go home. She booked passage on the ship *Michelangelo,* sailing for New York on April 17.

She was upbeat and full of plans: the mass; her book (again); and work—for cables were piling up from Joe Glaser about an attractive job offer in New York at a new club, Plaza Nine, that was opening in the Plaza Hotel. It was to be an unlimited run at a good salary with a sextet of her choice. Mary waffled with the kind of maddening hesitation that had put off managers and agents for decades and would infuriate Peter O'Brien when he became her manager a couple of years later. Although the job offer was, on paper, the best she'd had in many years, Mary was convinced that the New York media were generally against her. Her reluctance had another source, however; she simply hated the prospect of working long-term in the corrupting atmosphere of a nightclub, especially now that she had her papal commission to write a mass, as she confided to O'Brien.

So Mary turned down the Plaza Nine offer. But by then Joe Glaser, lying in a hospital bed, was too ill to react. When he died a month later, at the age of seventy-two, Mary sincerely mourned him. While for some he was crude and overbearing, she preferred to remember Glaser's kindnesses, writing that she considered him to be "the most charitable," the highest praise she could give.

————

MEANWHILE, DURING THE summer of 1969, Mary began work on *Music for Peace.* If the first mass had been written in the "worst hell imaginable," her personal life two years later was mired even deeper in that same region of hell. In May, Roland Mayfield drove Mary's mother and her sister Mamie from Pittsburgh for a visit to New York. Never did Mary write more candidly about family than she did in her journal then; nor did she spare herself:

> Mamie had to fool Mom to get her over here. Been on my knees cleaning for days. Mom wanted to leave. I got nervous and started my prayers. Wonder why Mom gets mad when I mention church. Had her to go to confession. Later, went to Gimbel's to shop for Mom, wanted to make her look good.
>
> Mom and her snuff and gin. I am old, fat and tired.

The next day, an agonizingly sad, troubled passage about a disastrous picnic in a park with the entire lot of them:

> I became very nasty after drinking, started confusion, lost my watch. Fought sister Grace, wanted to punch her in the mouth for throwing a lighted cigarette in Robert's face. She's fast as a cobra, poor Robert is a nervous wreck. I felt so sorry for him. I got so drunk I don't know how I drove home with Robert.
>
> Please forgive me God for not being more charitable. Must get the weight off, am choking in the throat. Grace doesn't want Mom or any of them to her house. Poor Mom.

Eventually, her mother returned to Pittsburgh and, with relief and resolve, Mary turned to the sanctuary of writing *Music for Peace.* Certainly, early, undated music manuscript pages show a far denser composition than the final version of *Music for Peace,* which was recast into jazz-rock or gospel idioms—"young-thinking," as Mary liked to call it. Having struggled so long with amateur choirs, was it then that she made the crucial decision to streamline and simplify her writing? For help, she enlisted her friend the arranger Bob Banks, who was at ease with rock rhythms.

Peter O'Brien recalls stopping by Mary's apartment to find Mary and Banks "absolutely gleeful together at their work. I never saw her so content, so happy, so relaxed, as when she was working on her mass with Bob Banks." (In addition to his contribution as a collaborator, Banks also recommended the gospel singers who appear on the 1971 recording of the mass.) Yet when the mass debuted—on July 15, 1969—at a memorial service for the recently slain Kenyan leader Tom M'boya, at Holy Family Church near the United Nations, it was a work in progress, still "quiet."

As usual, Mary needed money to pay bills as she concentrated on composing, so she pushed aside her fear of flying to travel to London for a lucrative gig at Jazz Expo '69. It was the first time she'd been back in England since the 1950s, and it was her old lover, Jack Higgins, who arranged the trip. She got mostly excellent reviews, and one evening, she dropped in at Ronnie Scott's jazz club to play a set during an engagement by Cecil Taylor, the powerful avant-garde pianist, with whom she would have a dual concert in the seventies (though some would see it as a "duel" concert).

Back in New York, Mary set to self-producing *Music for Peace,* for which she tapped the efforts of many people, above all Father Ed Flanagan, then a Maryknoll priest and today a Boston-based psychotherapist. Flanagan had met Mary while riding the subway just weeks before she met Peter O'Brien, in 1964. "I was a seminarian and had my collar on and she introduced herself to me, and invited me to drop by the Hickory House and hear her, which I did." After working in Korea for four years, Flanagan had returned to New York to study filmmaking. As part of a course, he had to make a film and, after reconnecting with Mary, persuaded her to allow him to make one about her outreach. The result is a rare glimpse of Mary in those still-reclusive years at home and working with kids.

As for *Music for Peace,* "I put up six grand of my own money for it," Flanagan recalls (worth far more today), and in his words, "ran interference" for Mary at the recording sessions. Later, when he tried to get his money back, Mary responded curtly that he had not sufficiently promoted the record: "You need to do a mission for the record, fast and furious, placards, buttons, throwaways and 100 large posters. In business one has to do business in a business way." She concluded by snapping, "You see, I'd starve if I waited for you to do it." Mary ran out of money to pay contributors at midpoint. "I was left to finish the arrangements alone," she wrote candidly in liner notes to the album. "Was I ever weary, and my brain just seemed to stop with all the troubles and aggravating sounds that seeped through." Her faithful old friend David Stone Martin was glad to contribute the cover art, a powerful line drawing of prayerful hands. Others, including Flanagan, contributed to the composition.

Friends recall stacks of records piled everywhere in her apartment, and in the trunk of her car. She sold hundreds of copies at performances and through mail-order, but that was peanuts, not enough to break even. The old familiar story.

Yet *Music for Peace* was building a reputation far beyond its record sales. In its full shape, the piece was premiered as a concert at St. Paul's Chapel, Columbia University, in April 1970. Says Barry Ulanov, "Her jazz setting of religious material, the Mass, the toughest of all and the most central of all, is not just good, it's secure. You feel with most composers it's gimmicky, a novelty, not really quite appropriate. But Mary knew and felt the music and she knew how to notate it. I hear the Mass as a complete success—and I'm not that easy of a critic, I don't like that many things. It works."

Indeed, *Music for Peace* was a succès d'estime. But Mary could not rest until it was performed as part of the church service proper. In 1970 she wrote to Brother Mario in Rome: "They all still think that jazz is pagan music." She was more determined than ever to place jazz at the very heart of New York's Catholic life—in St. Patrick's Cathedral. Again she urged O'Brien to approach Cardinal Cooke about the venture; again he demurred. Finally, at least as Mary liked to tell it, she "ran into" the Cardinal while with O'Brien at Fordham University. "So Peter hid behind a tree and I went chasing across the campus shouting, 'Cardinal Cooke! Cardinal Cooke!' I told him I'd written a Mass and I'd like to do it at St. Patrick's. He said 'fine.' I said, 'It's kind of noisy and loud.' 'That's what we need,' he said. He thought it would be a wonderful thing for young people." But it would be four more years before *Music for Peace*—known after 1971 as *Mary Lou's Mass*—was heard in St. Patrick's. In the meanwhile, Mary presented it at churches, universities, and other schools around the country, rewriting the sung parts to fit the capabilities of singers and streamlining the score to make it more accessible and economical for local ensembles to perform.

Not everyone was happy about *Mary Lou's Mass.* "NO JAZZ" read the pickets outside St. Francis Xavier Church in Kansas City, in May of 1973, when Mary arrived to perform it. How ironic, given that Kansas City was the city that had nurtured some of the most legendary figures in jazz, including Mary herself, and the city that honored Mary that same year by naming a street after her: Mary Lou Williams Lane (near Tenth Street and Paseo). But inside the church, a different spirit prevailed, with hundreds of enthusiasts jamming the pews to hear jazz in church.

———

IN THE SUMMER of 1971, O'Brien was pushing to have one of the major dance companies choreograph *Mary Lou's Mass.* In particular, he had his eye on Alvin Ailey's American Dance Theater. "Mary warned me, 'Don't aim so high.' But there had never been a jazz mass done in a big way in dance, and I thought the climate was right— Ellington's sacred concerts and Leonard Bernstein's own mass had opened the way. Mary advised me to go to Brother John Sellers: 'That's how you get to Ailey.' " Born a Holy Roller, Sellers was a blues singer from Mississippi and a fortune-teller who sang in Ailey's *Blues Suite,* and in the *Mingus Dances* for the Joffrey Ballet. He became a strong advocate for *Music for Peace.* Ailey himself loved jazz, and Mary's mass was rooted in the spiritual tradition he'd grown up in. He also loved Mary's long connection with music and dance—her early vaudeville days, the ten-cents-a-dance "jitney" dances, the swing-era ballrooms, and Mary's recollections of earlier greats like Seymour James, Bill Robinson, Bill Bailey, Pearl Primus, and Baby Lawrence.

For Ailey, Mary expanded the mass, and Peter O'Brien resequenced the parts—the "common," or unchanging, elements, and the "proper," those that pertain to the day in question in the proper church order. The collaboration premiered on December 9, 1971.

A rare instance of Mary photographed with her back to the piano.
Note the "caged bird" and the religious icon behind her, her form-fitting
dress yet formidably serious presence, her closed eyes but highly vulnerable
expression. Taken in Mary's apartment in 1958. *(Photograph by Dennis Stock.*
Copyright © Dennis Stock/Magnum Photos, Inc.)

Mary and close friend Dizzy Gillespie in the spring of 1979,
after she had moved to North Carolina.

Mary in her element: teaching children circa 1968.

Mary running her second thrift shop, circa 1965. The Bel Canto Foundation shop was uptown on Amsterdam Avenue.

Peter Francis O'Brien as a young
seminarian, photographed just before
he met Mary, in February 1964.
*(Photograph by Carl Van Vechten, with the
permission of the Van Vechten Trust)*

Mary in the mid-1970s, still happy with
Father O'Brien, S.J.

Mary's confessor,
Father Anthony Woods, S.J.

Mary's close friend the Franciscan
Brother Mario (Grady Hancock),
in the 1960s.

Mary kneeling at prayer in church in 1964.

(Copyright © Tom Caffrey/Globe Photos, Inc.)

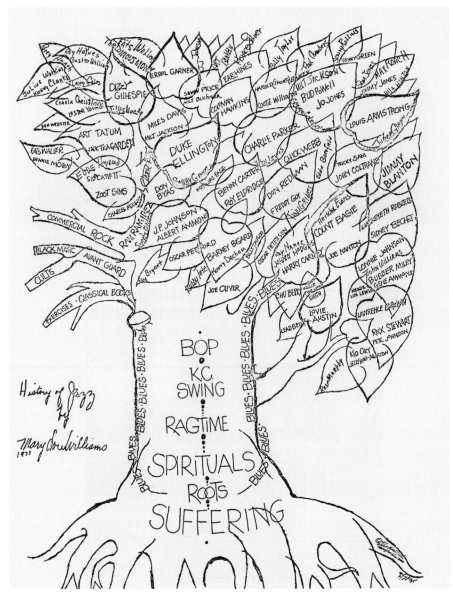

The "jazz tree," a work by Mary and David Stone Martin.

Mary teaching jazz as artist-in-residence at Duke University, Durham,
North Carolina, circa 1978.

Mary convalescing at Duke University Hospital after her
major surgery in January 1980.

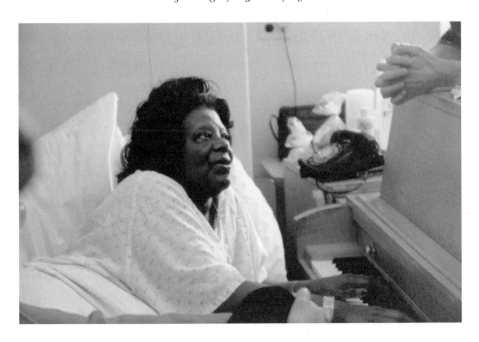

Mary performing at the Cookery Restaurant, New York, 1973.
(Photograph by Ken Abé. Copyright © Ken Abé.)

Mary played one work with her trio in a brief prelude to the dances, for which the trio was joined by an ensemble of other musicians, including vocalists.

Expectations were high; Judith Jamison was singled out for her solo in the "Lord's Prayer," in particular. Clive Barnes spoke of the piece's "spiritual exaltation, its concern with the special ecstasy of grace," and another reviewer enthused over its "timeless richness of ritual and of music rooted deep in the Negro spiritual"; yet the New York critics were in general agreement that it did not approach the power of Ailey's previous *Revelations,* which had been firmly anchored in Negro religious music, whereas *Mary Lou's Mass* contained jazz elements in addition to her interpretations of spirituals and blues. Nor were Mary and Alvin Ailey completely satisfied with the *Mass.* Ailey, had worked very fast on the choreography—wrapping it up, as O'Brien recalls, in just about three weeks.

Unhappy with what she called the stiff quality of Howard Roberts's conducting of her typically difficult voicings, Mary insisted on taking over the direction of the choir as well as the musicians, guiding the singers with her head from the piano in the pit. "But she didn't know what to do when things went wrong—once when some scenery fell, and again when Judith Jamison got her toe stuck in the hem of a dress," explains O'Brien. "Then, one night, Mary became distracted when the bass player, Suggs, wasn't playing as she wanted. She missed a chorus of the music—just left it out. The dancers could not improvise and they had to stumble through. Ailey stormed out of the theatre into the night when the curtain fell. Of course Ailey *always* stormed out into the night, but that night he was furious. After that he said, 'Howard conducts.' " The *Mass* passed out of Ailey's company's repertoire in 1973.

A recording of the Ailey version of *Mary Lou's Mass* had seemed a natural. Actually, the record was all Mary's idea, a re-release of *Music for Peace,* along with several new pieces commissioned by the choreographer. For a while, it seemed there would be no record at all: Ed Flanagan, who had never been paid back his loan for *Music for Peace,* held on to the original tapes from that album as collateral. Feeling betrayed, Mary lashed out at Flanagan, who presently "had a change of heart," as he recalls. "I decided it was my duty to give her the tapes for her new album because I thought she was a saint. I met her in midtown

Manhattan one noon with two huge shopping bags full of tapes. She pulled up in a cab to get them and drove off. And after that, we were friendly again."

————

MEANWHILE, THERE WERE continuing problems with her nephew. Robbie's behavior, always erratic, was now getting him in deeper trouble as he entered his teens. Mary feared and blamed the company he kept, and longed to get him far away from New York's mean streets. After a fresh crisis, she enlisted Brother Mario's help: Could he find a school run by the brothers in Rome willing to take Robbie? Brother Mario did, and ever-loyal Joyce Breach paid his airfare and drove him to the airport.

Mary's letters to Mario at that time reflect her frantic concern: "Will Robbie know how to get back and forth from school? Half the time Grace kept him out of school, be careful of him crossing the streets, everybody's sad about him, he was mistreated all his life and was becoming bitter. He has asthma, is afraid of the dark, can't sleep alone, nervous, constipated, lives on candy."

Within a month, Robbie was creating new problems: "Mario tell me the truth, Does he vibrate bad to you? Is he obedient? Is he sassy? I'm so upset I can't think, this thing will put me in a bad way financially. I feel so sad, I feel like crying. I had no place to send him here. . . . Mario I have to know the bad things in order to correct myself and others I'm helping. There's an epidemic of children using dope and several 13 and 14 year old boys have died. Can you keep him there until May? School's over by June. Please get Robbie settled and find me a one-bedroom apartment in Rome with a foldout bed in the living room for Robbie."

She proposed that Mario set up concerts for her—on Vatican Radio again, in Rome, all over Europe. "I'll live there until Robbie is schooled and I'll be with you half the time. . . . I'll make us a lot of money, just wait and see," she wrote him. But within weeks Brother Mario was reporting that Robbie had flunked entrance exams to one school, and he could not find another that would admit the boy. Soon Robbie was back in New York.

And though neither spoke of it, the Robbie experience apparently strained the relationship between friar and musician. Mary no longer wrote of her plans for a house together, no longer plied him with letters festooned with her pencil drawings of smiling lips, or her little-girl coquettishness ("you're so sweet. Make sure you write me every day"). No longer did she confide all her doings to him.

There was a new (religious) man in her life.

————

MARY'S RELATIONSHIP WITH Peter O'Brien initially provided the good times she loved and missed in her relationship with Brother Mario. Yet it turned out to be as emotionally difficult as any grand passion she'd had in her busy life.

The arts, especially the performance arts, continued to fascinate O'Brien, who still dreamed of being involved with the theater. In June of 1970, he enrolled in a summer school program at UC Berkeley, with the long-term goal of obtaining a doctorate in theater arts. In the meantime, he'd kept up his relationships with the artists he met in New York, including a phone conversation with Mary that turned out to be pivotal to their relationship. "I called Mary from San Francisco, which was all rock and flower children. I told her about the lack of jazz there and said she should come out and play."

Mary still had deep reservations about taking on performance commitments. Friends had been urging her to do so for some time, but she continued to hesitate: there were the ongoing problems with Robbie, the memories of her decades of struggle over pay and conditions on the nightclub circuit. And, crucially, who was to represent her? She had tried, without success, many times, to take care of the business end of her music now that Joe Glaser had passed on. Yet the young priest's zeal, loyalty, crackling energy, and, most important, the empathy between them, satisfied enormous needs in both. As she talked with him, perhaps Mary sensed that her dream of playing spiritual jazz as a healing mission could best be fulfilled by having an articulate, energetic priest as her manager. Wouldn't he also be able to help her tap into the huge network of Catholic schools and colleges as performance venues to get her mass out everywhere?

When his summer course at Berkeley was over and O'Brien returned to New York to complete his studies, Mary asked him to be her manager. It was as quick, as moving, and as serious as a proposal of marriage. "I remember it was in her Cadillac," he recalls, "parked on 102nd Street and Riverside Drive late at night, before I went upstairs to where I lived. Mary said: 'I'll go out if you come with me.' And I decided my ministry should be Mary Lou and saving jazz. I said yes." Although there was no precedent for such an occupation (even the "jazz priest," Father Norman O'Connor, had been restricted to acting as an m.c. at jazz concerts and a d.j. on radio shows), O'Brien saw no conflict between being a priest and managing a jazz musician. "I was full-time with her and full-time with the Jesuits," he points out. "The Jesuits are very flexible and I was authorized to travel and help her with her career. This would have been much more difficult for me in any other organization within the Church." Actually, while managing Mary, O'Brien also worked from 1972 to 1977 as one of a number of parish priests on the huge staff at the important St. Ignatius Loyola Church on Park Avenue (the same church where Mary had been baptized). And he was paid in both capacities, although he and Mary never had a written contract and his income as her personal manager was negligible. Was he also Mary's religious advisor? "Certainly not!" he emphasizes. "If anything, she was my spiritual director, truly."

Mary and O'Brien, who has a smooth, oratorical style, began conducting workshops on jazz history at the Jesuits' own Fordham University and at other colleges, with O'Brien presenting the remarks Mary had developed over the decades about the evolution of jazz, while Mary illustrated with examples at the piano. Often, they combined her popular jazz history "lesson" with performances by local choirs of *Mary Lou's Mass,* for very quickly Mary had achieved that dream and was called on to produce her namesake mass around the country in the seventies.

———

EVEN BEFORE HE became her manager in '70, O'Brien facilitated a career move for Mary that had important repercussions for her. The year before, as editorial advisor for Fordham Prep's literary magazine, he took his student editors down to Greenwich Village to interview a legendary show-business press agent, Ivan Black, who had represented Café Society in the 1940s. Through Black, O'Brien met Barney Josephson, at Josephson's new restaurant, the Cookery. "Mary came with me;

she was looking for a place to play jazz on a regular basis, because she had decided that she could build on that. And she said to Barney, 'Why don't you put a piano over there for me to play?"

There were by then precious few places to hear jazz in New York City, Mary reminded Josephson. "We have to do something to help bring jazz back," she told him. (*"We?"* he responded.) But realizing there were few risks, Josephson agreed to rent a piano for a few months. He could only pay her scale, he said—the union minimum. O'Brien, who had been doing publicity for Mary even then, learned a good deal from that experience. "I thought everybody was as nice as pie then. But after Mary paid her bass player (New York cabaret law forbade a drummer), she took in $450 a week. And this for working five sets a night, six nights a week—he wanted her to do *six* sets, but Mary said, 'Man, I play with my whole body.' "

In the summer of 1971, after O'Brien had come aboard officially as her manager, Mary tried to negotiate a raise for herself, pointing out the increase in business she'd brought to the club. She made a vintage Mary Lou complaint to Josephson, writing, "My sister, poor Grace, makes almost as much as me, wrapping meat for the Food Union!" The comparison failed to move Josephson.

"But Mary was playing there to reestablish herself, and it worked," says O'Brien. "There was a lot of publicity. We were a smash hit and lots of musicians came in, people like Charles Mingus and Cecil Taylor. I was furious at myself for not cracking the whip about money, but after that I negotiated raises every year."

The Cookery became Mary's "room," and she played long engagements there until 1978. She considered her success at the Cookery a vindication of jazz and her mission to keep the heritage alive. It was no coincidence, she told Josephson, that rock clubs in the neighborhood closed after she began to play at the Cookery. "She says to me," Josephson said, " 'Since we put jazz in your restaurant, you and I with the help of the Lord Jesus Christ'—crossing herself—'we closed Fillmore East, Fillmore West, the Electric Circus'!"

———————

AS FOR RECORDINGS, by 1971—despite the glowing reviews in the press, lines of people wanting to get in the Cookery, and new job offers—there was, sadly, not a single record album featuring Mary in print. "I was putting down 78's to show examples. Nothing! I badly wanted her to do a record," says O'Brien.

That at last came about through John Hammond, who with his wife, Esme, often dropped into the Cookery to hear Mary. By 1971 the coolness between Mary and Hammond had subsided. He urged producer Hank O'Neal to record Mary for the debut of his fledgling record company, Chiaroscuro. O'Neal agreed, and Mary cut a solo piano album. *From the Heart* includes as poignant and expressive a version of her "Cloudy" as she ever recorded and a carefully constructed "Little Joe from Chicago" that one musician, Joel Simpson, who has transcribed a number of Mary's important arrangements, aptly calls "solid food for the soul." Around the same time, Mary also finished her jazz history project, melding narration and piano examples of the various styles of jazz, for Moe Asch at Folkways. The record was not released until the late seventies, however, when O'Brien agreed to make necessary cuts. "We had to do a huge number of edits—more than 150—on the tape she'd made, and those were the days when you used razor blades," he recalls. The resulting *History of Jazz* is quintessential Mary. If it has a home-made feel, it is also intimate, totally unselfconscious, a deeply felt tour through the eras of jazz. And although some jazz "critics" at the time carped at Mary's exclusion of then-popular styles—fusion, jazz-rock, and "free" jazz—her decision was solid: a quarter-century later they sound as dated and ephemeral as, say, bellbottoms and flower children, and as out of place, while Mary's music remains.

Another superbly sparkling set was captured on tape one afternoon that same year at the Overseas Press Club, when Mary played powerfully alongside Dizzy Gillespie and Bobby Hackett on trumpets, George Duvivier on bass, and Grady Tate on drums. The recording, titled *Giants,* was nominated for a Grammy, and reviews were ecstatic. Dan Morgenstern, in *Downbeat,* was practically hyperventilating: "This is one of the truly great jazz records of all time. Mary Lou Williams, a most remarkable musician, is not only the ideal accompanist to the heady work of the trumpeters, but contributes solos that maintain the level of inspiration. She swings like a demon, turns the changes inside out, and makes some musical statements that rank with the greatest jazz piano playing on record. The senior member of this gathering, she thinks and plays like a youngster, but with a dimension of wisdom

beyond the grasp of youth." It had been a shamefully long time since
Mary was recorded with musicians of this caliber.

Mary's renditions of Scott Joplin music at a concert recorded with
other performers in New York, called *An Evening with Scott Joplin,* document her continued love of earlier styles of jazz piano. Her playing of
Joplin's work did not adhere to the notated version, causing inevitable
controversy among ragtime "purists." But her admirers found her playing charming and graceful, true to the spirit of the music, if not the
letter.

THE EARLY SEVENTIES marked the beginning of Mary's comeback.
"She'd had in mind working with the church, making religious
records," remarks O'Brien. "But all that changed overnight." Despite
the well-received performances of *Mary Lou's Mass,* it was Mary the jazz
musician the audience demanded. Though he was a priest, he was also
Mary's manager, and O'Brien prodded her to respond to that increasing demand. Besides the Cookery gig and the recordings, engagements at Blues Alley in Washington and the London House in
Chicago, and an appearance at the Newport Jazz Festival, helped to
reestablish her as a presence. "But Newport was an appearance and
nothing more—that was the year that all hell broke loose," recalls
O'Brien. Hippies had crashed the festival, demanding to be let in free.
"I remember that Mary was the next artist scheduled and I was talking
to the stage manager about where to place the piano and then everything started to fly, broken chairs and so on. That riot stopped the concert. When it became clear she couldn't go on, Mary asked George
Wein, standing nearby, 'Do I get my money?' 'Yes, Mary, you get your
money,' Wein said, not annoyed, just even-voiced."

It was the last year that the Newport Festival was held in its namesake city. In 1972, Newport changed its venue to New York, and Mary
played there the next two years. Indeed, in 1973, she had one of her
strongest performances at Philharmonic Hall, though sadly, it was not
recorded. In a lineup that included Gil Evans's orchestra, the Sonny
Rollins quartet, and a solo Keith Jarrett, Mary, with her favorite bassist,
Buster Williams, and Billy Hart on drums, stood out as the star of the
evening, inspiring listeners to describe her as "hair-raisingly good,"
"awe-inspiring."

Now she was being discovered by a new generation of fans. At the Monterey Jazz Festival in September of '71, she and Jay McShann were hailed as the "rediscoveries of the year," and she received a standing ovation. The recognition that was coming Mary's way—"her return is a major event in the jazz world," wrote John S. Wilson in the *New York Times*—had little effect on Mary. When she played, she took her music seriously and brooked no nonsense or competition from the audience. One evening, her friend Jean Bach (who later produced the film *A Great Day in Harlem*) came to the club, and Bella Abzug, at the height of her fame as a feminist politician, came in and sat down. "She was a neighbor of mine and so we were talking," Bach recalls, "and Bella was not a quiet woman. And Mary says something like, 'I have two more songs to play here, then you can talk.' "

Her private life remained problematic; she had been in debt and on the doorstep of poverty for a long time. Often she continued to find it hard to pay her bills. One afternoon at Gimbel's her credit card was not honored when she tried to charge stockings and a blouse. (She had been proud to have charge cards with Saks and Gimbel's since the 1940s, at times when credit was far from usual for black Americans.) Mary went home, cried in humiliation, and wrote an angry letter to the store; eventually her account was reinstated. Her neighborhood, meanwhile, had deteriorated badly. The once-elegant Hamilton Terrace, on Sugar Hill, had long since bade goodbye to the doorman and was down-at-heel. Mary petitioned to have her already low rent reduced further, citing years of neglect. And then her apartment was robbed yet again; but although the thieves went so far as to rip out an entire window frame, she refused to consider moving. Instead she paid a retired cop from the neighborhood to sit with a gun in case they came back. "It was her home and she wanted to be there," says O'Brien. Clearly, though, she did have misgivings. At times, he recalls, "She would still talk about living in a convent. I'd tell her, oh no—same turmoil as out here. There's no escaping it."

———

THAT BUSY YEAR of 1971, which marked O'Brien's maiden voyage as manager, also marked the beginning of a relationship increasingly fraught with tension, one that made heavy demands on both of them. "When I celebrated my first mass in June of '71, she felt I was not paying attention to her, and she got all hurt," says O'Brien. "This went on all the time. For example, I wanted to use the church to put on concerts by other artists, too, and Mary said, 'You're paying attention to everybody but me.' She thought I would be pulled away from her and would leave her out. It continued for years. Another time, for Palm Sunday in 1973, we presented *Mary Lou's Mass* at St. Ignatius Loyola. This was my debut—make a big splash on the home turf. I worked for weeks on this and it was an enormous amount of work. We had six musicians and a choir. I said the mass and preached the sermon and ran the whole thing. The place was packed and it was a huge success. Then afterwards, she comes up to me with a shopping bag full of receipts and things about her income tax and says, 'Take these down to Gemma,' her friend who helped with her bookkeeping. Not 'Thank God,' not 'It was great,' but putting me down. Undoubtedly, that's how she was treated when she started—rough, not acknowledged. The same kind of thing happened other times, too, but they never counted in her mind, because she's Mary Lou Williams.

"There were so many good times, though. I would have walked away if she were a phony. But she was real. However, I made her do what she didn't want to do—go out in public. I put her back in the professional world she didn't want to be in. So it's a very different and a harder Mary Lou after 1970. She's blaming me, getting angry at me for getting her back out there when she just wanted to be off in church. Later on, maybe a lot of people thought 'that priest' got her to do these masses and things. No! They were her idea. I supported her, yes, but I didn't give her a lot of encouragement about the masses—I wanted piano records, but she would not be deterred from what she wanted to do, and wasn't going to have her creativity messed up by anybody, including me."

Professionally, there is no question that Mary appreciated what O'Brien was doing for her. In a letter to recently made friends, Dr. Sam and Mrs. Marge Atkinson, in the summer of 1972, she wrote: "Poor Peter is working so very hard for me. I feel sorry for him. He's thorough in his work and seems to enjoy it. He loves me so much—which is what the world needs. He's so dedicated."

Many people viewed the relationship between a young white man of the cloth and a black woman thirty years older with frank suspicion. A black priest once confronted O'Brien directly: "What are you doing around this old black woman?" John Williams echoed the query: "I often wondered, why her and Peter? He was right with her, night and day."

"Some people said that Peter and Mary Lou had an affair," confides Elaine Lorillard. And Delilah Jackson adds, "People were saying that he was in love with Mary." But those who knew them well actively deny it. "Was Mary in love with Peter?" asks Joyce Breach rhetorically. "Forget that. No: she thought that she was saving him." Yet, the relationship resonated very much like an affair. "Part of the problem for me was getting lost in the relationship—that codependency bag," O'Brien explains. "I went to the Cookery every night, for example. She wanted me right there, all the time. I didn't live in the same house, but it was round the clock. It was a different kind of relationship, one that had everything to do with who the two of us were and trying to become. To her, love meant exclusivity. I was supposed to be absolutely devoted. Love meant I wouldn't go away, I wouldn't have anybody else in my life. I wouldn't be apart. Whatever she imagined love would be. But no sex.

"After a while, I paid no attention to that. I finally resorted to getting a private phone number that Mary knew nothing about; or she would have been calling me 24 hours a day. I was interested in all the arts, I was not limited to the jazz world and that was threatening to Mary Lou. If I got friendly with someone in the Cookery, she got mad. I was not allowed an opinion on any subject. If people ended up liking me, she got mad. I was not supposed to have a life. I tried to preserve some kind of separateness, but—and this is the point—she wouldn't have thought of that as healthy."

Further complications arose when this quasi-marriage became a classic triangle, as Mary increasingly devoted herself to Robbie, whose behavior had worsened since Brother Mario sent him back from Rome. Mary helped place Robbie in various group homes, including Lincoln Hall in Westchester County, and a Catholic facility for troubled youngsters in Vermont, where the priest in charge wrote to her gently but firmly to stop sending the boy money: it would be better for Robbie to get a job and earn it himself. Mary's letters to Robbie were the appeals of a desperate mother. "I got fed up one night and said: 'Why don't you just adopt him?' " O'Brien recalls. "She told me, 'You don't know nothin'.' But she was really devoted to him and terrified that something would go wrong with him." As it did. Later in the seventies, Robbie—severely asthmatic, prone to rages, and by then a chronic drug user—had a dope party at Hamilton Terrace while Mary was out on tour. She returned to complaints from the neighbors and an apartment in shambles, and wrote Robbie a letter full of raw hurt, begging him to stop hanging around with his friends: "I was happy when you left your job in Harlem. Why? Dumb niggers on the job who thought themselves smart were influencing you too much, even in clothing and wine. Only Harlem and dumb ignorant people wear the clothes they think are hip and the slang and other things are degrading."

Her sorrow and disappointment over Robbie's self-destructiveness were her constant companions. "I had hopes," the letter continues, "that you would be able to team with me someday for success. Robert I've always loved you and worry about you."

The letter was returned unopened.

Mary's continued loyalty to Robbie enraged O'Brien, who recalls an instance when he had finalized arrangements for an important concert at Trinity Church in Manhattan. "But she had to take Robbie, who was terrified, to the dentist and just refused to sign the contracts," he says. "And I went out of my mind—the anger was so great I felt that something bad would happen."

During an engagement in Canada, it did most unexpectedly. In 1973, Mary was booked at a Toronto nightclub for several weeks, and scheduled also to perform *Mary Lou's Mass* at the venerable St. Basil's Church. According to O'Brien, after the performance he and Mary had stayed up talking most of the night, not unusual for two night people. "I was in her hotel room, in my suit. I hadn't gone to my room yet. She was in her nightgown, but that didn't seem untoward to me. There were all kinds of domestic situations we were in. And then—a horrific moment. She asked, 'Why do you stay here?' in a little-girl voice, so sad. It was a terrible moment—it was all indirect, all expectations, very threatening, although I didn't even know what she meant for sure but I thought she meant the feelings she had for me. Then she fell on the pillow, crying, and said, 'I just have to let it wear off.' It was bad. I just left, I certainly wasn't going to go over and hold her."

Was Mary's question a painful declaration of passion that he then spurned, as O'Brien implies? Or was it something else altogether, perhaps even a figment of his imagination, as many who knew Mary suggest emphatically? Others simply deride the notion that Mary, then in her early sixties, could have passionate sexual feelings for a priest who was thirty years younger than she. Of course, older women, and especially highly creative older women, have been known to fall in love with much younger men—why not? Louise Nevelson adored her companion Arnold Glimcher, about forty years her junior, and artist Georgia O'Keeffe was very old when she fell in love with a youthful Juan Hamilton.

As an explanation, O'Brien offers this: "For ten years, I was consistently there, available. I was *really there*. And although I was relatively inexperienced, the religious thing for me was a defense, a great bypass. And she had recently found out something about me that told her yes: here's Peter, available." His career as the personal representative of a major artistic personality coincided with his own coming-of-age. "I was only twenty-three years old when I met her, fairly innocent, very conventional in a way, all during that time. That was the period in the early and mid-seventies when there was all that liberation, including sexual, and we used to argue heavily. There was tremendous jealousy. It was terrifying, and preposterous too. My own attitudes and opinions and behavior—certain things Mary'd found out about me—could be looked upon as a betrayal of her. She discovered something about me, that I'm no longer little Peter her son but a man, a sexual person too."

Indeed, a few years later, a distressed Mary wrote, but never mailed, a series of frank letters to him that indeed seem to address her discovery of his loss of innocence as well as the "terrible moment" of 1973. In a letter dated September 3, 1977, she wrote:

> It would be a great loss if you do not do something about yourself. I'm very sorry about some things I have to say to you at times, but nobody was born freaked up [that is, given to sexual proclivities outside the norm].
>
> *Think: I never cared for younger men.* Got away from love affairs 30 [sic] years ago. Musicians almost drove me mad. But I could deal with men by avoiding such things. *All of a sudden I'm mixed up.* Think hard, Peter. You never realized this. My entire soul was in danger! *Why? I was confessing what you felt for someone else, just terrible! But I continued to pray, allowing it to melt away.*

In her letter, Mary seems to be describing, in her hermetic, mystical way, a transference—a kind of visitation—of an unwelcome physical passion, but, crucially, the passionate feelings that *O'Brien*, as she had learned, felt for another: "I was confessing what you felt for someone else." If so, this would have been as "terrible" for Mary as for O'Brien, above all because of her deeply sincere belief in the sanctity of a priest's vows of chastity, and her shock if she thought that he had violated them. But that may not have been all that disturbed her. On another level, Mary—who had taken a self-imposed "vow" of celibacy upon her conversion in the 1950s—might have been reminded by an eruption of unwanted passion that she still had sexual feelings. Although she had seemed to close the book on this side of her nature after her passionate embrace of religion, aspects of her sensual female nature continued, all right. Why would she, who had been slim and beautiful, have come to despise herself to some extent physically? "I am old, fat and tired," she wrote.

But if the scene between Mary and O'Brien in the Toronto hotel room was in part between a man, albeit a priest, and a woman who could still feel desire and be humiliated by rejection, there is another, more fundamental, layer of interpretation possible. For Mary asked the question key to any real relationship: *"Why do you stay here?"* What are your motives? What needs keep you, a man of thirty, with *me*, a woman of sixty?

O'Brien provides at least part of the answer in a candid self-assessment: "When I met Mary," he says, "I was all over the place pursuing certain artists. But Mary was the one that paid off for me. From an outsider, I became an insider and a mover in the world I wanted to be in." Was she, Mary might have feared, only being used again?

"It took awhile, about six months, I guess, for us to renegotiate our relationship after that night in Toronto. The goal was to salvage the real relationship and not the fantasy. But I had to renegotiate my independent position gradually and she had to negotiate her independence, too. But after Toronto, I was no longer going to get my personal life mixed up with how we were going to work.

"On one level, she was trying like mad to protect me—like Woods had done. She wanted me right there but I paid no attention to that. And in many ways, she was absolutely right. It was a rough world."

AS EVER, WORK provided the best release for Mary in a difficult time. Nineteen seventy-one was an extremely busy and important year professionally. With minimal financial investment, she managed to produce piecemeal for Mary Records one of her most brilliant projects of original music, the album she titled *Zoning*. In four separate sessions—two in January and one each in February and March—Mary recorded with different combinations new compositions such as the playful "Rosa Mae" (lyric added later by Gracie Glassman). This number, she recalled, was "written for the kids (with bassist Larry Gales). It had a little bass figure of rock so I could win the kids over and show them the little dances to the rhythms of jazz because I'm still playing the blues and jazz on top of it." As for "Medi II," a.k.a. "Busy, Busy, Busy," Erica Kaplan notes: "Because of the simplicity and proportion of the harmonic phrasing, it gives the effect of a blues. [But] the composition's slow half step harmonic oscillation creates a modal type effect and she demonstrates her absorption of the developments of saxophonist John Coltrane. The net result gives 'Busy Busy Busy' the feeling of a cross between a blues and a modal piece."

An interesting experiment was Mary's addition of a second piano (along with Bob Cranshaw on Fender bass, and Mickey Roker on drums) on "Intermission," and especially "Zoning Fungus II." "Zita Carno could play a fly dot," Mary said of this versatile pianist. (Carno played for the New Jersey Symphony, for Bugs Bunny cartoons *and* wrote transcriptions of John Coltrane's music as well.) Mary wrote Carno's part and much of her own in the somewhat atonal and scalar "Zoning Fungus II," which resolves into a blues infused with longing, a far different kind of "free" playing from the two-piano performance that Mary would give a few years later with Cecil Taylor. Pianist Hilton Ruiz says of "Fungus II": "Everything that she does here relates to something that's going to happen over there. Everything." Even at its most atonal, there is a certain strange beauty, the beauty of an ice goddess—shades of the "frozen chords" of Kansas City jam sessions of the 1930s. Critical response to *Zoning* was positive (twenty years later, a remastered compact disc with additional material has been issued). One reviewer extolled the "joyful, lifting pulse that she uses most effectively with the trio in which Cranshaw is on the bass and Roker on drums." "She had a lot of fun putting this *Zoning* thing together," confirms O'Brien. "She was dead serious. But I can see her coming around the bend in her apartment, in a housecoat. She's got one hand held up high, this long trail of music paper coming down, a pencil in the other hand, and she's smiling."

But there was also the usual emotional letdown after a sustained creative push. "She was hurt and furious about the liner notes I wrote for *Zoning*," says O'Brien of his thoughtful and highly respectful writing for the LP, "and I never knew why. However, I think she was looking for spectacular treatment, as in the olden days—great stuff to happen. And she wasn't getting that. The big record companies were absolutely distant, and for the eleven years I tried, I was never successful in getting a major company per se interested in Mary Lou. Norman Granz did finally record her in 1977 and 1978, but his label, Pablo, only paid about $2,000 each time, that's all. Maybe that's why Mary let me have it."

Part of her "fury" may also have been in response to the collapse of Peter O'Brien in late winter due to a serious bout of hepatitis for which he had to be hospitalized. This capped a disappointing engagement at the Cafe Carlyle in January and February, when she substituted for vacationing entertainer Bobby Short at the posh East Side club. "I thought, here's a steady job for her—it would mean return engagements," says Elaine Lorillard. "Then I don't know what happened. I remember she had to have a certain piano." "Oh, *yes*, Mary Lou Williams," says Bobby Short. "She used to hate to come on after me," he adds, laughing. "I pounded that piano, you know, broke strings and so on." Worse, the audience was the kind Mary disliked playing for, nostalgically calling for boogie-woogies and Café Society repertoire; "cornball" was her term for them. "That was a red flag," says O'Brien. "She would become uptight and uncooperative—*evil* is the term black people use and it's the right one." Critics as well felt she was miscast. "Seeing her in such genteel surroundings is like being served steak at a garden party," commented Whitney Balliett in *The New Yorker*.

When Marian McPartland, whom Mary viewed not so much as a rival as an interloper, was asked to sub the following year at the Carlyle, Mary took it as a snub. Though McPartland was a keen admirer of Mary's brilliance, Mary was envious of the successful career the well-spoken, socially adept Englishwoman had built in America, writing frankly to Joyce Breach from Rome a few years before: "She wants to be the Queen of the ivories. Me, I don't care—I pray for her. Anything I do she tries to ape me, ha! I never liked being in her company 'cause I always felt a breeze but this is not reason for me not to pray for her. Her idea is to top me—imitating etc., to reach the top. Now, Barbara Carroll (white) plays better jazz than Marian—it's more soulful.

"We [African-Americans] are the only people nobody wants, and now you can see why many become bitter. They never have a chance to receive credit for all they create through their suffering."

At times, Mary would balk when McPartland came into the Cookery to hear her, complaining that she would steal her arrangements and style. When McPartland began what is now a long-established successful radio program called "Piano Jazz" in the fall of 1978, she invited Mary to be her first guest, and the taped encounter shows Mary's prickliness as she fairly bulldozes over her smooth hostess—but it is also a fair sampling of Mary's later brilliance, with a furiously fast "Morning Glory," a lightly seasoned "Rosa Mae" (with rare vocals by Mary), and a brilliant "I Can't Get Started." The two most famous female jazz musicians did make peace after 1978, when Mary's cancer became public knowledge. McPartland recalls that Mary softened a good deal toward her; and Mary was especially appreciative of a lovely medal of Saint Cecilia, the patron saint of music, that McPartland sent her as a gift.

————

O'BRIEN RECOVERED FROM hepatitis, and Mary's career rolled on. In May, invited by Ruth Ellington, she performed a homage to Duke Ellington at his grand funeral at the Cathedral of St. John the Divine. Unlike other performers, she didn't select a composition by the maestro but played the beautiful ballad "Holy Ghost." "She got into trouble for that," says O'Brien, "but she replied, 'I counted it as a prayer for Duke. I put Duke Ellington chords in there.' "

In 1975, Mary returned to the Cookery. She also performed a luminous version of *Mary Lou's Mass* at a Composers' Showcase at the Whitney Museum (a series that was—mostly—taped, though not issued on recordings). It was one of her most accomplished *Masses*, with Milton Suggs on bass, Jerry Griffin on drums, Tony Waters on congas, and a vocal choir that included Carline Ray.

It was in 1975, too, that Monsignor James Rigney, rector of St. Patrick's Cathedral, gave approval for *Mary Lou's Mass* to be performed there. Rigney wanted to involve schoolchildren in services at the cathedral, and the work Mary described as a "Mass for the Young— or the Young Thinking" was deemed just the thing. "It's going to swing," she told the press firmly before the performance. Regarding the choir of forty students drawn from area Catholic boys' and girls' schools, she noted: "*They* don't have to swing. All they have to do is sing their lines. The bass and drums and me—we'll swing them." With Mary was Buster Williams on bass and Jerry Griffin on drums.

On a cold Tuesday afternoon in February, more than 3,000 people came to witness the *Mass.* The audience overflowed into the aisles, a respectful audience, quiet until the end, when they burst into applause after "Praise the Lord," the concluding hymn. "Miss Williams," reported the *Times,* "threw kisses."

But the aftermath of the mass was anything but upbeat. O'Brien had attended to the thousand and one details that surround such an event, working feverishly on publicity, not to mention writing and delivering the homily. But after the service, when he unvested and sought Mary, what should have been a celebratory moment collapsed. "I wanted to go out and wind down. I was exhausted—I'd been at the church for hours beforehand, preparing. And all of a sudden, there's Mary, with her neighbor Edith and Robbie, who's glowering. And she said, 'Let's go around the corner and get some Chinese food.' And I erupted: 'No, Mary, *no!*' I thought, what a way to end the day! And Mary turned away. Then I finished up at the church and I left."

Mary was also disappointed by the lack of response on the part of the music industry after the performance at St. Patrick's, just as her recent, highly accomplished and self-produced creative work, *Zoning,* had not accorded her widespread recognition. "She got furious at *me* later," says O'Brien. "I should have that mass going on all around the world, she told me. She had thought that George Wein and all those powerful people were going to immediately take her to the top after she was at St. Patrick's."

With no recording contract, despite her achievement at St. Patrick's, Mary had to take what was offered, and she readily agreed to do a trio album for the Danish Steeplechase label. The money was low but the company gave her free rein, and the result (recorded on July 8, 1975) was *Free Spirits,* a contemplative, somewhat subdued set of tunes saturated in the blues, prominently featuring Buster Williams. It is a benchmark album: Mary was at the zenith of her mature powers, absolutely confident, every note honed and placed with precision (despite the fact that she was suffering muscle strain in her left arm, wrapped in a thick Ace bandage during the recording). As usual, Mary mined her own material, recent and ancient, including "Gloria," which on *Free Spirits* features a more rock-oriented beat, a more sub-servient bass, and a more sinuous piano than the "Gloria" of a year before on *Zoning,* which had been gutsier and more intense.

Six months later, Mary recorded again for Chiaroscuro. The self-descriptive *Live at the Cookery* was made, with a young and green Brian Torff on bass being covered like a blanket by Mary's piano. (Like others, Torff went on to a fine career after being launched by Mary.) "I could not believe," writes Torff, "that one could record an album in such a noisy club. Right behind where I stood (at Mary's left hand) was a bin where the waiters would throw dirty dishes while we played." Per-haps that is why Mary, who plays louder than on *Free Spirits,* also seems to swing more vigorously; that and the fact that she was breaking in a new bass player: when she was not playing with a favorite, like Buster Williams, her playing tended to sacrifice delicacy for strength.

Torff had once auditioned for Mary and been turned down, but when Milton Suggs left, she hired him to work at the Cookery in Sep-tember. Torff worked with Mary throughout the winter of 1976. Rehearsals, held at Mary's apartment, he remembers, were casual but memorable. Mary was going through a rough period with Robbie at the time, of which Torff was unaware. "I would show up in the after-noon and usually she greeted me at the door in a housecoat and slip-pers," recalls Torff. "She'd sit down at that great old piano all scarred with cigarette burns, she'd pull something out, and just start playing. She was not a master of tact and she always seemed tired; there were circles under her eyes. But I saw her help many people—including me."

In fact, Mary had continued to help many up-and-coming pianists; since the sixties, Cedar Walton, Horace Parlan, and Andrew Hill, among others, had benefited from her advice. Teenaged Hilton Ruiz became a favorite protégé: "She offered to teach me for free, and I went to her house in Harlem every day." Lessons, he remembers, would sometimes go on for hours, with Mary cooking dinner while shouting instructions from the kitchen. "I was in awe of her; I was

scared. She was serious, but she also had a great sense of humor."
Torff, too, was in awe. "I would be scared stiff on the job," he recalls.
"She'd tell me to play the changes—but she'd play *different changes* on
the second chorus. She was tough on me, soul on ice, and she admonished me for all my mistakes. I realized with her that I was not prepared—I didn't know the older repertoire and the bop standards, and
she told me to go out and buy bop records—which she pronounced
'rekeds.' But I learned and I think looking back that she had taken me
on out of her generosity—teaching and guiding me. We played colleges, schools, nightclubs—the Copley Plaza Hotel for three weeks in
Boston, where Mary also performed her *Mass* at a church and did
workshops for children at a school in Roxbury. That was a poor, tough
neighborhood—I can remember seeing dirt in the piano keys that
Mary Lou played; but she suddenly improvised a piano solo so compelling and beautiful that the hair stood up on the back of my neck.

"Her power of concentration was incredible. I can even remember
her falling asleep once in the middle of a song. We were playing and I
heard this soft, snoring sound. I looked over and there was Mary Lou,
head down, fingers moving, but playing the piano in her sleep. When I
hit the wrong note on my bass, Mary woke up!" Mary called her dozing
on the job "being hypnotized."

While working steadily in the 1970s and commanding a higher
salary than before, Mary nevertheless continued to live simply and fru-
gally. When she finished working at the Cookery, for example, she'd
usually drive home alone, in her Cadillac supplied by Roland Mayfield
(still a friend), and according to Torff, "she'd often sleep on the front
seat until six or seven A.M., when she could legally park it. Then she'd
go upstairs to her apartment." When she wasn't driving, Mary would
often take the subway downtown to the Cookery, wearing a cloth coat
in cold weather and carrying her luxurious, full-length fur in a shopping bag. When she got off the train in the Village, she'd dress in the
fur and put the cloth coat in the bag. On her days off, rather than
going out to fancy parties or restaurants, she preferred to relax by playing cards with friends or visiting relatives. Grace had stabilized and
Mary often went to the Bronx to picnic in the park with the Mick-
leses on food she prepared herself—fried chicken, chitlins, black-eyed
peas, greens, and sweet potato pie. She was similarly low-key when she
visited family in Pittsburgh. Recalls a favorite grandniece, Karen

Rollins, "After she'd unpacked and settled in, she'd take me with her to Highland Park. We'd walk around, then go to Isley's ice cream shop and get pineapple sherbet. She never wore her talent as a badge. It was never discussed. And no one in the family really respected her talent. Now, finally, the younger ones are beginning to realize who she was."

––––––––––

MANY PEOPLE WONDERED why Mary chose to perform in a a dual-piano concert at Carnegie Hall with Cecil Taylor, perhaps the ultimate avant-garde pianist. She had repeatedly made her negative feelings clear about the avant-garde in jazz, with its rejection of established harmonic and tonal patterns. In an essay that became part of her liner notes for *Embraced,* the album resulting from her concert with Taylor, she described the avant-garde as being filled with "hate, bitterness, hysteria, black magic, confusion, discontent, empty studies, musical exercises by various European composers, sounds of the earth, no ears, not even relative pitch and Afro galore" (although she hastened to add, "I'm crazy about African styles in dress").

Yet something in Taylor's music appealed to her, as did John Coltrane's late playing; or, rather, she accepted both musicians' work because they could still, if they wanted to, play "within the tradition." And although tradition—the heritage of suffering embodied in spirituals and the blues—was sacred to her, Mary had always pushed herself to experiment and master new styles. And by the mid-seventies, she was eager to reposition herself on the cutting edge. She was not, she wrote in her diary, "corny" (her word for passé and hidebound); she had "changed with the times." Still, by then she had felt at least a twinge at being passed over. So much had happened since her reemergence in the sixties—rock, soul, long hair, Afros.

Hair had always been a potent symbol in the black community: "good" hair meant straight hair, "bad" hair meant frizzy, African hair. Mary, of course, belonged to the generation for whom straightening, or pressing, hair was as important to good grooming as brushing teeth. "In 1971, when Mary was at the London House in Chicago, Earl Hines was at another club. And he had these lacquered, glossy toupees, funny colors sometimes too," recalls O'Brien. "Everybody's hair from her era was pressed; Erroll Garner had conked hair. Duke. Louis Armstrong wore a stocking in his dressing room. And of course Mary."

In her little yellow kitchen, she spent hours transforming her hair into a smooth, glossy bouffant. "Once I came into Mary Lou's apartment and I almost fell apart," recalls O'Brien. "She'd washed her hair and it was up like a bush around her head: huge, frizzy hair, straight up and out. And I started laughing, and she said, 'What's the matter with you? Ain't you never seen anybody's hair?' And I had not; I had no notion that that was the way it was." But the sixties was also the period of "naturals," dashikis, Black Power, all of which Mary viewed with suspicion. "Mary's at the London House and the young bass player said something derogatory about Earl Hines's hair—his wig—and Mary went ape-shit," recalls O'Brien. "The anger was fierce and she wouldn't speak: nothing. Not even on the stand. Three days like that. It was violent. God knows what that remark unleashed in Mary. No, *she* didn't have an Afro." On the other hand, in one of her playful moods she could go out and buy the biggest Afro wig she could find and come in with it on one night at the Cookery. She and O'Brien fell about laughing.

She didn't find too much to laugh about in the radical movements then in fashion on the fringe, sensing the possibility of violence behind the Black Muslims and Black Panthers. She also felt, especially after her dealings with Joe Wells soured, that she could not trust her "own people" in business. As she wrote in a letter in 1969: "I'm a little afraid of my own race. The black Americans at one time were the sweetest. Now they are killing off one another. It's dangerous to be black! I never allow them to get too close." It's not surprising, then, that she wouldn't join in the movement among many black intellectuals to celebrate the African heritage in African-American life. Some critics saw this as a result of deep shame about her origins. And Mary stuck her finger right into the wound, so to speak, when she declared in an essay:

> We were sold into slavery by our African chiefs. I was born in the U.S.A. This new mixture of Afro and everything else does only one thing—it destroys two arts—you have neither Afro nor jazz. It seems that before changing to another country's musical heritage, I should try to persevere and fight here at home through my music of love and peace and bring this heritage forward. Perhaps if all black Americans went to Africa, we would

be treated worse. We would perhaps be rejected by the native Africans and (who knows) even put into concentration camps.

When she played with African musicians at a jam session, Mary added, they could not play jazz rhythms—they simply did not understand them.

This insistence in her writings and speech on the *Americanness* of jazz—that is, on the importance of the complexity of influences that gave rise to the African-American aesthetic called jazz—ran counter to the then politically correct rhetoric in hip black America. It was bound to inflame people, and it did. In the late 1970s, Mary became artist-in-residence at Duke University. "When I first got to Duke the black students all sat by themselves in the cafeteria, all studied together. I would tell them you are too young to know, you haven't seen racism, but they wouldn't listen to me for the first year." Nor would they deign to take her Introduction to Jazz course to which white students were flocking. "And I would tell them, 'Because they know what's happening, you dumb son of a b——. Send your Al Capone [leader] to me.' And I had to prove to them that they were the Toms."

To illustrate her philosophy, her vision of jazz as cultural alchemy, Mary asked David Stone Martin to draw her a "tree of jazz." Central to that vision is the role of slavery, and the release from its torment the slaves sought in music. The roots of Mary's great old "tree" are the spirituals, European forms married to the African-based blues, both of which are depicted climbing up the sturdy trunk, to branch out—into ragtime, swing, and bop—while the "leaves" of the tree are the individual players who contributed important sounds. With only three exceptions—Mary's friends Zoot Sims, Benny Goodman, and Jack Teagarden—all of the leaves are named for black musicians. Importantly, the tree also contains dead branches, what Mary called the soulless exercises: commercial rock, black magic, avant-garde, cults, and, simply, "exercises." The withered leaves on the dead branches represent the musicians who turned away from the spiritual heart, the soul, of the music (spirituals and the blues).

"*Community* is the word she used all the time in relation to jazz," explains O'Brien. "And the spiritual feeling in the blues that arises out of suffering. That was a big thing with her. Some people don't like this. But to her, that's where the depth came from."

One critic who took decided umbrage with Mary's views, Chuck Berg, lambasted her for her arrogance in *Downbeat* (December 1978): "She claims that all of jazz is divided into her four parts [and that] there is 'nothing new in jazz since bop,' and that 'jazz is America's only art form.' Such narrow, misguided and incomprehensible pronouncements can perhaps best be dealt with in socio-psychoanalytic terms. [They] do little to benefit their author [and] reveal a similar sense of confusion in the music." This was not her only bad press: she received a particularly mean-spirited review from a critic in the *New Statesman* when she was appearing at Ronnie Scott's club in London that same year. After ceding reluctant praise for her "tortuously inventive" "Mack the Knife," he descended to unchivalrous comments about Mary's appearance, describing her as "fairly mountainous in striped pink chiffon with heavily chipped nail varnish."

This kind of panning was most unusual. Brother Mario's is a far more representative voice: "She communicated that hope that one day jazz would come back in full force—the music of love, that soulful feeling that blacks had forgotten." Adds Barry Ulanov, "If you hear in her music what I hear in her music—almost a kind of prayer, even before it becomes overtly religious—you hear that she's saying: 'This is how it is with me.' She knew what she wanted to do. She had an indomitable will about her." After all, hope, rebirth, redemption, were at the core of Mary's religion, and her religion was at the center of her life.

It was, then, in the spirit of reconciliation between the two "camps" of jazz (avant-garde versus everything that came before) that Mary conceived the idea of doing a concert with that lion of "out" players, Cecil Taylor. He had won her over with his admiration for her playing. Actually, he'd been listening to and appreciating Mary's music for a long time; he first caught her at the Savoy Club in Boston while a conservatory student in that city in 1951. "She was playing like Erroll Garner, but her music had a lot of range," Taylor said in a rare interview. Almost two decades passed before Mary, in turn, listened to Taylor— during his engagement at Ronnie Scott's in 1969. Then, in 1975, Taylor really began listening to Mary, dropping by the Cookery often. When Taylor told her, "No one's playing anything but you," Mary's reaction was, at first, "Here's somebody else putting me on." And each time he came into the club, as Mary remembered it, he'd move closer to the piano, until, she said, "He sat down one night at the end of the gig and played, but a little too long," clearing out the club. But he kept showing up to listen, and eventually Mary broached the idea of doing a concert together. (It was Taylor who came up with the title, *Embraced.* In response, Mary drew a picture of three concentric circles, symbolizing, as she saw it, her music, his, and the music of their interplay.)

Organizing the April 17, 1977, event fell to Mary, who followed her usual game plan. Friends received photocopied requests: "Help save this precious music and keep me out of Bellevue! Smile! Send checks for your tickets or donations." Despite such efforts, made at her own expense, and O'Brien's publicity, the house at Carnegie Hall was not filled, and the concert just about broke even.

But it would be a hall peopled with partisans of the two pianists, among whom speculation ran high about what sort of jazz would emerge from the meeting of two such strong musicians—for if Taylor was a *lion* at the piano, Mary was a *lioness.* To *Village Voice* jazz writer Gary Giddins the concert promised to be "doubly innovative for bringing together two great keyboard artists in a program of duets, and for dramatizing the enduring values in the jazz-piano tradition." But hints of a possible musical fiasco were also in the air. Rehearsals revealed frayed nerves and disparate purposes. Cecil Taylor had never shown any desire to play predetermined music from a written score, although Mary claimed that for the first half of the concert he'd agreed to play the new dual-piano arrangements of spirituals she'd written, using her "history of jazz" approach. Then, after an intermission, they would use "rhythm patterns as a shell," in Mary's words. "When Cecil is doing his things, I'll start moving in his direction. I'll play free and then I'll jump back to swinging." But in the hours before the concert began Taylor fumed. Not only had she written a part for him—a "free" player of the first rank—but she had not consulted him about the rhythm section— her own—that was to accompany them for the first half. To Mary, of course, this seemed fair: she got the first half, and he got the second half of the concert. But as Taylor told a journalist, Mary "wanted him to play her music but [she] refused to perform his music the way he wanted it heard. We are not certain exactly how the concert will be structured," Taylor warned.

Clashed would be a more accurate title than *Embraced* for the music that ensued; the concert confirmed gloomy predictions. Reviewers tended to write about it more as a contest than a collaboration: "The result was at best a tug of war in which Mr. Taylor managed to remain dominant," wrote the *New York Times*. On "Back to the Blues," to take one example, Taylor plunges deep into his favorite nether musical regions. It takes Mary's strongest playing, the signature crash and crush of her left hand at full throttle, to tug the piece back from outer space. When, as Gary Giddins described Taylor, "the predatory avant-gardist" overreached Mary's "spare, bluesy minstrations," she called in the rhythm section—as if she were calling in the troops.

Listeners—at least those in Mary's camp—saw little of the "love" she had urged Taylor to play after the difficult first half. Backstage, fur flew. "I slammed the door on him hard," says Peter O'Brien, "and saxophonist Paul Jeffrey, who was listening backstage, had to be physically restrained from punching him. Mary came off the stage and said to me, 'Oh man, I played my ass off.' And she *did*, but I made her go back out there." Her adrenaline up, Mary played brilliant encores—"A Night in Tunisia," "Bags' Groove," and "I Can't Get Started," the last a frequent source of inspiration for Mary.

Perhaps the best review, though never published, came from Nica de Koenigswarter, in a letter she shot off to Mary after the concert, written in the Jazz Baroness's beautiful hand and careful multicolored underlinings:

> Rather than an 'embrace,' it seemed to one like a confrontation between heaven and hell, with you (heaven) emerging gloriously triumphant!!! I know it wasn't meant to be that way, but this is the way it seemed. I also know what a sweet cat C.T. is and what beautiful things he writes, in words, that is, but the funny part is that he looks just like the Devil when he plays as well as sounding like it, as far as I am concerned, sheets of nothingness, apparently seductive to some. Anyway I loved Mickey Roker and Bob Cranshaw for seeming like Guardian Angels, coming to your defense and it was worth it all to hear you bring it back to music.
>
> Love you, Nica

Two years later, Mary could joke a little about the concert. "When I was coming along, it wasn't enough just to play. You had to have some tricks—I used to play with a sheet over the piano keys. So when Cecil started playing like that and kept on going, I started to get up from the stool, turn around and hit the piano with my butt—chung, choonk! That woulda got them!" She revealed her hurt only to her fellow artist in a letter after the fiasco:

> Cecil! Please listen if you can. Why did you come to me so often when I was at the Cookery? Why did you consent to do a concert? You felt I was a sincere friend. In the battlefield, the enemy (Satan) does not want artists to create or be together as friends.
>
> Cecil, the spirituals were the most important factor of the concert (strength), to achieve success playing from the heart, inspiring new concepts for the second half. I wrote you concerning the first half. You will have a chance to listen to the original tapes and will agree that being angry you created monotony, corruption, and noise. Please forgive me for saying so. Why destroy your great talent clowning, etc? Applause is false. I do not believe in compliments or glory, my inspiration comes from sincere love. I was not seeking glory for myself when I asked you to do the concert. I am hoping you will reimburse me for 30 tickets—would you like to see the receipts?
>
> I still love you, Mary

Within six months of the concert with Taylor, Mary was back at Carnegie Hall for another concert with another difficult musician, as a "special guest" in January of 1978 in a forty-year "reunion" concert at Carnegie Hall. Billed as "An Evening with Benny Goodman," the concert attempted to re-create the spirit of the famous 1938 concert where Goodman had been dubbed "King of Swing." But the 1978 event was a disappointment, underrehearsed, ragged, with Goodman off balance. Mary played gamely and took a sparkling solo on "Lady Be Good," but the gig was just a gig to her, a way to pay bills. (When Goodman approached her afterwards about doing a record together of Fats Waller tunes, she declined).

After going from playing with way-out Cecil Taylor to comping for Benny Goodman—a breathtaking musical leap few pianists would attempt—Mary could declare with satisfaction, "Now I can really say I played all of it."

Chapter Eighteen
Artist-in-Residence
1977–1981

IN THE 1970S, a number of black musicians began to obtain positions at universities around the country. Mary was approached in 1975 by Max Roach about teaching at the University of Massachusetts, where he was ensconced, but they couldn't come to terms. The following year, Duke University, just a cut below the "Ivys" and set in the thriving Raleigh–Durham–Chapel Hill "Research Triangle" of North Carolina, began an active search for more black faculty under the presidency of the late Terry Sanford, a liberal presence in southern politics who had been governor of North Carolina and a U.S. senator. Frank Tirro, a saxophonist and jazz scholar then heading the music department at Duke, was especially eager to build up the jazz department, but at first Mary was not on his short list. "The possibility," as Tirro puts it, "of securing such an artist as Mary Lou Williams seemed remote." But her name kept coming up, and to Duke's delight, she expressed interest when contacted. Tirro invited her down to tour the campus, and in May, Mary boarded a Trailways bus for Durham, O'Brien in tow.

She found a small city, southern and bucolic but also sophisticated and prosperous, with an established black middle class—worlds apart from the Durham Mary had visited with the Clouds of Joy in the 1930s, when segregation, "the shame of America," as Senator Sanford put it, was in full force. Back then Mary had stayed in Haiti (pronounced "Hay-*tie*"), the black section of town, near the railroad tracks. "Haiti was very famous," noted Sanford. "There were black hotels and every kind of store. There was some kind of opera house. Durham was much more hospitable to blacks than Atlanta—they were voting here in the 1920s, certainly not the case in the rest of the South—because they were a much more dominant part of the community. The oldest black-owned insurance company in America is in Durham. But you still had a very segregated society in Haiti, where white people would only venture down to clubs and stuff."

Haiti is all gone now, just fields of weeds—a victim of urban renewal. "They ran a highway through there," remembered Sanford. "Typical. The cheapest land. There were some very substantial black businesses there, and they were given an area and some shops across the highway, but it never has worked out."

Mary liked Durham's gentle-mannered people, the manageable size of the city, the easy social interaction between the races, telling an interviewer later, "Nowadays, whites down here will say, 'Yes, ma'am,' 'No, ma'am.' And they come to my house and help me." And she liked Duke University—the venerable-looking campus, the brick buildings graced by large trees and squared by big, comfortable-looking houses—with its well-equipped music building and excellent auditorium. As artist-in-residence, she would teach two courses: Introduction to Jazz, and Jazz Improvisation, as well as direct Duke's jazz ensemble—and she would receive, for the first time ever in her career, an assured regular salary with full benefits.

Within weeks, Mary made her decision to go, signing a contract for the 1977–78 academic year, then signing on for three more years in the second semester. She was delighted: "Ha ha ha—look at me! A high school dropout. Now I'm a college professor," she wrote gleefully to John Williams. Sanford and Tirro were delighted too: "Tirro said to me, 'This is a three-time winner: black, female, and jazz,'" recalls O'Brien. Sanford explained, "We just put her on the faculty roll as an indefinite appointment when it was clear she wanted to stay; the contract was technical."

Although Mary became extremely popular and beloved as a teacher, it took a little time for Duke to grasp what an asset she was. "When she came, she didn't arrive with a great splash," says Paul Vick, then head of the Alumni Office. "People began to realize who she was by seeing her, by this infectious enthusiasm for life and for the

music. You couldn't be around her and not be affected. She capti-
vated people."

Mary immediately decided to buy a house, and by the end of the
summer, with O'Brien's help, she had found what she wanted at a
good price—a largish, well-maintained raised ranch at 1205 Shepherd
Street. It was not a fashionable address, but the neighborhood was
integrated in race and class. Through her front windows she faced an
elementary school; from the back, through her kitchen picture window, a sloping backyard with shade trees and rhododendrons blazing
with color in the spring. Inside, a staircase led to a large second floor
with five bedrooms—large enough, she planned, to accommodate
houseguests and to provide rooms for Robbie and O'Brien. For herself, she chose a corner bedroom—not the largest—where, following
her old road-gypsy habits, she did most of her work from her bed—
writing music and letters, eating, watching television.

Downstairs there was a snug den where Mary gave private lessons
on her battered old Baldwin, and across the hall was her rather formal
living room, with a grand piano (loaned by Baldwin Piano's Raleigh
office), deep blue velvet couches, and antiques she bought from local
stores. The heart of the house, though, was the large, informal kitchen.

Mary didn't care that she wasn't in the stylish part of town. "Mary
didn't mingle much either with the fancy black middle class in
Durham," says O'Brien, "or with the neighbors. She didn't want to meet
them; she thought that was bad luck, they'd get all involved in her life."

On the surface, her life in Durham was simple and serene. When in
town, she liked to shop daily for food. "She had her fish store, her meat
store, her store for produce. She would make a vegetable pie and she
carried a bag of vitamin pills from a nutritionist who prescribed for
her. Despite her weight, Mary ate healthy food." She relaxed by playing
cards or telling jokes. Joyce Breach had a special card table made up
for her and sent it down to Durham, and when one of her sisters or
friends was there, they would set it up in the kitchen or den and play
for hours.

But moving from New York to Durham, from the freelance life to
artist-in-residence, from North to South, was no simple adjustment.
Mary was restless and blue at first, pining for her old life and friends.
"Wish I could find some poker players down here," she wrote Joyce.
But once she began teaching, the feeling lifted. Twice a week she

taught her two classes, and rehearsed a select ensemble of fifteen or twenty student musicians for whom she wrote fresh arrangements. (There were some unusual combinations, dependent on the talent at hand: one semester there were seven trumpets and no trombones.) Word of mouth filled her classes quickly, and by her second year she had moved into a larger space. Hundreds were turned away.

Her teaching methods were those she'd honed since the fifties. She taught from the piano bench, playing—and calling out, sometimes singing—illustrations of jazz styles, coaching students to imitate the phrasing of Bessie Smith, Billie Holiday, Dizzy Gillespie, and so on. She wanted the students to become active participants in the learning process, getting inside the music. And she lectured: "Rock puts you in a box and makes you stiff as a 90-year-old man. Jazz is love. You have to lay into it and let it flow," she told her classes. When her students clapped and sang out the lines of the spirituals, of the Fats Waller and Art Tatum records she played, they were following the old, time-honored methods of African-American music-making. Her classes, mostly white (but more and more black students enrolled as time went on), loved it; alumni recall her with affection. "We'd spend three or four classes learning a song," recalls a former student, John Dear. "She'd have us singing and talking about the song; bebop and blues. She'd perform one or two songs every class. Just getting a feel for it." The impact she had on private students was even more powerful, for her goal was to teach them how to become their own teacher, emphasizing the strong left hand of the old masters. "I'll write out a tune that they like, such as 'Over the Rainbow,' or 'Night in Tunisia,' " she said. "I'll give them eight bars each time they come to me. After four weeks, I make them apply all the chords that I've given them to other tunes—in that way guiding them, teaching them how to become their own teacher. . . . We're living in a technical society, and people think that if they go to school and learn it, they'll be able to play it right. Sure, you can play like a typewriter, but it'll make your audience nervous to listen to it. It's nothing that's written down in a book, you know." Technique was the jumping-off point, the servant of the muse. A jazz pianist needed, she added, to establish the authority of his or her presence, to create a mood from the first note: "Willie the Lion said . . . 'Play that note, get the mood going, hold it, and you've got the audience.' "

It was the same message she'd been spreading for decades, but the university brought her a different kind of student. Marsha Vick, who soon became a friend, was one such, a white college student (though older, in her thirties). Says Marsha, "I didn't know much about jazz, but I had always listened to it and I'd played the piano—pop music. I was really interested in taking private lessons. She agreed to that and I went to her house, and I took with me this arrangement of 'Sunny' I had. I put it up there on the piano and I started. And she said, 'Oh, don't do it like this.' And she started playing it. She tried to show me the various chords. She told me after that first lesson that I was playing 'the way the cats used to play,' and I later realized that was a great compliment, though I never really learned to improvise. For a student jazz ensemble, she made me play. She brought in Buster Williams for this concert in February 1979. I was scared to death, but he was very polite, and she'd say, 'Steady now! Steady now.' And she said if I went up there and played like a lamb, nobody would listen to me. I had to play like a lion." Later, I played little jobs on my own. At one, for a Christmas party for President Sanford, she arranged 'Jingle Bells' for me.

"Mary's ears were amazing. She called me once when Eubie Blake was on television and said, 'That old man's on TV, he's playing all in sevenths.' And once I took her somewhere in my car, a Volvo. It had a certain sound to it. She said, 'Your car is running in E.' "

John Dear was studying classical piano, with dreams of becoming a rock star when Mary came to Duke. "I went to her class and I couldn't figure jazz out. None of it made sense to me from the background I had. So I asked to take private lessons and she accepted me. She'd play for me and talk about what she was doing on the keyboard. I remember the width of her hands—great stretch—and I remember her playing with flat fingers, punching into the piano. She used to say, 'Hug the keys.' It's the complete opposite of what I was learning in classical music, which was that everything flows together to create a whole. *This*—jazz—was all confrontation between the left hand and the right hand.

"I always remember her entrance into the room in class, a big class. She was a presence. She'd be late and we'd be hanging around. She'd come in looking around, slowly taking it in. Everything would stop. She'd sit at the piano and just start playing. Powerful."

The administration was thrilled to have her. "It turned out to be a very happy arrangement to have her here," said Sanford. "I got to where, as I was describing the various achievements and assets of Duke to alumni groups, I would add Mary Lou as one of our irreplaceable assets. She was a spirit, a presence, on the campus that was very important." Soon, Mary even managed to win over the black students who styled themselves as radicals, by sitting and talking with them at their cafeteria tables at lunchtime. "If they're not careful, they're going to love this music," she said slyly and she made a point of hiring local black talent when she performed in the area. Eventually, she became so respected that when, after her death, a black student center was opened, it was named in her memory.

———

AS MARY WAS adjusting to her new role at Duke, her relationship with Father Peter O'Brien took a sharp downturn. Although the university had hired Mary alone, O'Brien left his job as a parish priest at St. Ignatius Loyola in order to continue to manage her career and to assist her with teaching at Duke. "It was when we taught that the relationship really got bad," says O'Brien. "I could have let her just do the teaching, but I was looking for an identity, and after all, I had been a teacher. So, I took half an hour or 45 minutes to teach. But the very idea of doing this for so little money was enraging.

"My Provincial Superior in New York had been reluctant to do so, but he released me for one year from my job as a priest at St. Ignatius, to go to Durham with her. A lot of it had to do with Mary's big impact as a convert, with the *Masses*. My boss, the pastor at St. Ignatius, said to me, 'I'm going to need your room, Peter, right away.' I had no financial support, and no assignment now as a priest—and I'd have to pay my own health insurance. I was on my own—with her. However, Mary had fantasies of the Catholic Church somehow taking care of me. She said to me, '*You got your Mammy and Pappy, you got the Church; I have nobody, I just have myself.*' Well, this situation led to catastrophe between Mary and me.

"Mary wanted me to live in her house and get $50 a week! She wanted to clip my wings. In New York, I'd had a foot in two worlds and I could always retreat to one or the other. I moved in, but I don't think I lasted a day and a half before my rage came up so hard. I went and packed up my shit again, and I sailed out of the house. She was sitting on the third step and she said, 'When are you going to New York?' That was sad. She thought I was leaving altogether and she was hurt terribly."

O'Brien, however, simply moved across town, taking a room in the rectory of Holy Cross Church, a small, attractive Jesuit mission church of stone built originally for African-American Catholics in the 1930s, when segregation was still in force. There he stayed for about a year. But he was still as involved with Mary's career as ever. "For that whole year, I lived on $135 a week, plus 10% commission on her concerts. That was not enough to pay rent and buy food, but she didn't understand and, of course, business details were never clear between us. But what bothered me was she treated me halfway like a lousy agent. I was scraping by and I felt she was using me. She bought all kinds of things—a new Cadillac, antiques, an $800 rug. She'd saved—it was her money—but I got very angry. She had a good thing going and she didn't have to pay me much. On the other hand, if I'd gotten sick or were stuck, there's no question that she would have taken care of me. Completely generous but stingy. A complicated, double thing, a way of controlling and making sure, because *she'd* been so done in."

O'Brien's worsening psychic and emotional health, the rants and rages, took a terrible toll on both the priest and the player. "I was in very bad shape during my era with Mary, mentally and emotionally," he affirms. "There was anger, fury, frustration. Mary would say, 'Why would you mistreat me?' That was a word she used a lot. And I admit the mistreatment, with regret. I wrecked Mary's peace of mind."

This is painfully clear in a letter she wrote to O'Brien late in 1977 but never mailed to him:

> This year I've given Robert, Bobbie and you plenty of money (and others in the past) yet I scraped enough together to save a bird-turd. If I didn't love God, I could be very lonely. But loving God means treating people right. You have lied to me a few times.
>
> Your mind does a lot of wrong things. I get a little tired of continuing to show you through experience. And how can you accuse me of cheating you when you work me to death traveling to make up a loss *I* can't see.
>
> I have had crosses all my life. Father Woods helped me, he taught me how to live with them and stop complaining, then they became more bearable. Peter, everybody is sexually something—but learn how to control this. That is, balance it off some way, not allowing it to enter the work.
>
> My mind is so confused, half the time I can't do music and it's not the age, because I finally pull out of it. I do not have any

peace at all except when I lie in bed, go to sleep, wake up fresh and suffer again. I can't get out of bed half the time, trying to think how to maneuver out of hell.

I have a job to teach and you have no job. I say I can give you $200 per week and I discover later this is all I have to live on. As a personal manager you ok'd the job without calculation! A personal manager saves his act from peril, people, saves him money, looks out for appearances, gets work, keeps wolves away, static, makes everything easy for his act to perform and write music and play. I've spent a great deal of loot having you with me but did you appreciate this? I felt something would grow out of it, but never! We do not have a goal and we are not together in mind and soul, and to be successful, togetherness is the key word.

You do a lot of hard work without a goal. One has to have a goal or his work is aimless. So I go along, reach upstairs and say, Well here I go again, so please offer it up for the good of souls, etc.

God has helped you through me, Peter, and I do not have an ego. Everybody knows about your mental condition. Yet I'm sick: I don't know how long I'll be able to take it.

Robert is a different kind of annoyance. My first love (work) is involved with you. So I'll put it this way: I'll continue to offer up mistakes, suffering, etc. You were never treated as badly as I was. Well, we could have been put together for your aid. 'Cause as you know you were kinda off mentally. Stop fighting God and let things melt away. Stop disliking people. Stop taking over other folks' friends, find your own. Your work is to clear the way for my work, so we can help the poor and pay our bills.

What are you doing about the vow of poverty and what are you doing about your vows? Tell me I'm lying and I'll show you. Stop allowing the bad spirit to split your mind in two places.

By the end of that year O'Brien was seeing a psychiatrist regularly, if secretively. Mary also occasionally visited a Harlem psychiatrist she respected, a Dr. Miller, who treated her fear of flying and other anxieties, and she corresponded with Dr. Chester Pierce, at Yale. At Thanksgiving, she wrote confidingly to Joyce, "Down here I feel crazy or senile. It's really terrific but I can't get myself together."

Always, there was her faith to help her. And her music. Personal upheavals had not the slightest effect on the power of Mary's music-making then; quite the contrary. "As long as you keep working, you'll be all right," she was fond of saying. The music that she made from 1977 until her death in 1981 was charged with a vitality and maturity as never before, and a serene acceptance of her position—one writer called her "quiet queen" of jazz. Not that she disguised her conflicts and pain, but her dark side was transformed, lending tremendous vitality to her playing. She constructed her solos, said one reviewer, "like small dramas of the spirit in search of light."

She ranged the continent—always by train—to Buffalo in upstate New York, to San Francisco and Vancouver, and back to New York for the summer. And she persuaded Norman Granz of Pablo Records to let her record an album of the blues. "I returned to my first love," she said. *My Mama Pinned a Rose on Me* is mostly blues, sixteen brilliantly phrased versions, seven of them piano solos, recorded in two sessions on one day. The shadow was there, a brooding, somewhat somber but stately return to her past: Miss Ginnie and Fletcher Burley shuffle-dancing barefoot in their alley shack, then all dressed up, ready to go sport.

On the first side of *My Mama Pinned a Rose on Me* are: "The Blues," a slow and soulful entrance (with swooping vocal introduction by Durham singer Cynthia Tyson); "N.G. Blues" (dedicated to Norman Granz), a modern blues notable for its modal patterns and crisp attack; "Dirge Blues," written after the assassination of President Kennedy; "Blues for Peter"; "Baby Bear Boogie," quintessential Mary, with fast-working chords and riffs from the right hand and a steady boogie-woogie rhythm from the left; and "My Mama Pinned a Rose on Me," a favorite that she had previously recorded. As a lagniappe, there was Mary's pleasant voice turning in a lyric in memory of her stepfather, Fletcher Burley.

On side two, Mary was joined by the rich-toned Buster Williams, and on "J.B.'s Waltz," and "The Blues," by vocalist Tyson. "Rhythmic Pattern," with Buster Williams walking a strong bass, and Mary improvising over the changes to "I Got Rhythm," one of her favorite exercises, is the sole uptempo tune on the second side. There is also an outstanding version of "What's Your Story, Morning Glory?"

Mary had arrived at a transcendent level of artistry, and the Duke community came to realize they had greatness in their midst. Her students presented ambitious programs. She created new arrangements of her compositions. CBS filmed "A Christmas Special with Mary Lou Williams at Duke University" that aired nationwide on Christmas Eve, 1977.

Above all, earlier that December, there was her inaugural concert, accompanied by Buster Williams and Roy Haynes. It was a sensational concert. But it was sandwiched between violent quarrels with O'Brien. "Before the concert," he relates, "I was backstage getting it all set up, and she came in, dressed beautifully with a long blue dress on and a mink coat. And when she saw that the place was packed to the teeth— the kids were hanging on the rafters and everybody who was important in Durham was there—she said to me, 'Go out to the house and get those records because I'm not makin' any money on this!' Oh my God, the rage in me from that. If I had been more mature, I would have said, 'Mary, go sit in your dressing room and calm down.' But I went and got the shit. She couldn't have made more than $300 total from me selling those records. And that's not the worst. A faculty man was there setting up all these mikes out there to record the concert, and she has him take the mikes off the drums! And so the tape of that sensational concert is fucked up because there's no mike on the drums! That relates to her own lack of confidence, the invasion of rock and all this loud stuff.

"I called her up the next morning, early. She said, 'I thought the concert came out pretty good.' Well, I cussed her up and down. I told her she put me through shit. I said everything. Then I went to New York and I disappeared for several days."

"Why did she put up with this from him?" muses Joyce Breach, who had known Mary well since the late fifties. "It was because she thought she could make him well. She believed in miracles. It was that simple. She wrote me in a letter in '78: 'I'm going to pray for Peter—the demons have him again today.' " And Mary continued to esteem the vocation of the priesthood, the special position of the clergy. Back in 1971 Mary had written of O'Brien, in a letter to Barney Josephson: "As much as I know about the cruel world, I put myself in his hands. A Jesuit priest is the highest form of religion." This despite what she knew of O'Brien's, and other priests', failings. In the 1960s, before she had met Peter O'Brien, Mary had seen a number of clergymen tested on the spiritual firing line, several of whom had left the priesthood (thus placing themselves, in Mary's view, in mortal sin). "Pray for the priests," she wrote, "they're in great danger of the man [Satan] using them—in fact all God's servants are in danger." All the more reason, then, to pray, counsel, and prod O'Brien into a healthier life in the late 1970s.

Despite the problems, Mary was clear in the late seventies about the benefits that O'Brien brought her as her manager. "He opens things up and contacts people. He will not let anybody say no to him," said Mary tellingly. Gary Giddins notes, "He could be very irritating; tenacious. He was constantly at me to go to her concerts. And so, I *went*." But Mary's loyalty continued to be tested with scenes and verbal battles. Mary wrote to Breach: "Joyce, Peter is out of it. One year down here and he'll be cuckoo. He's very grouchy and, well, nowhere, changeable—guess he's turning into a werewolf. God forbid—smile— what a lovable person before now. And I'm tired."

At about this time, Mary had also turned to the late Antonio and Martha Salemme for some kind of solace or advice. Antonio Salemme was an artist who had sculpted a legendary life-size figure of Paul Robeson in the thirties; O'Brien had sought him out to immortalize Mary, which he did, in several bronzes and a portrait in oils.

Remembers Martha Salemme, the sculptor's widow: "She called us and said, 'I don't know, Peter's very ill, he's not behaving the way he usually does. He wants money and he's supposed to have taken a vow of poverty.' And she wanted us to observe him and then to tell him he was not well, that he should see a psychiatrist—her Dr. Miller in New York."

Martha Salemme got upset at O'Brien herself. "Nobody should use that language—too rough." Others remarked on ugly scenes. Father O'Connor at nearby Holy Cross Rectory, tired of the loud, angry phone calls O'Brien made to Mary that he was forced to overhear on the one rectory telephone, asked O'Brien to get a private phone while he roomed there. And, says Phyl Garland, who went to Durham in the late seventies to work on an in-depth story about Mary for *Ebony*, "He seemed like a nice charming young Jesuit when I first met him years before. Then I was working with her in her house in Durham when Mary Lou got a phone call from Peter, and Mary said in a fierce, pained way I'd never heard in her before, 'No son of a bitch has ever talked to me like this before!' And she was furious. And I could hear *him* being furious in the background."

Sometimes the anger was in the form of indirect cuts. "He would say little asides about her that were uncomplimentary," recalls John Graziano, a friend of Mary's who was a hairdresser. "Once when she asked me to comb her hair before a job, he asked, 'Did you see the bald spot?' "

But O'Brien was also doing a great deal of work for Mary by then, arranging bookings (that summer, she played in Nice, Montreux, The Hague, London), and attending to the myriad details her performances entailed. Her career had taken off, but for all the work he was doing, O'Brien felt underpaid. "I finally demanded more money and all hell broke loose," he recalls. "We really had it out—it was vicious." After that, he got up to 20% commission on the larger jobs.

O'Brien also felt that his work with Mary at Duke was unappreciated. The university had turned down his proposal to be put on staff as a teaching assistant and paid a modest salary, along with health insurance and a university-owned apartment. In the fall of 1978, he asked Mary to press his suit. At first Mary refused to speak to President Sanford directly, but after a rapturous reception to her performance at a university fund-raiser, attended primarily by prominent CEOs, she felt comfortable enough to broach the matter of O'Brien's stipend with the president. "I expected her playing to be a pleasant interlude at a fund-raising dinner; the usual thing," recalled President Sanford. "I was totally unprepared for the applause she got before she played a note and then the rapt attention she got—as if she brought tumbling from them childhood memories of happiness—not the music alone, perhaps not the music at all, but the aura that accompanied her performance. Here were grown, tough men with tears in their eyes as Mary Lou Williams finished." After that, Sanford was ready to give Mary just about anything she wanted, including a raise for herself, and readily agreed when her friends Marsha and Paul Vick found a way to pay O'Brien and give him housing. "We at the Alumni Affairs Office wondered if Mary would go around the country and perform at concerts at four alumni meetings a year, in order to bring in the younger alumni," notes Paul Vick. "And she was happy to do it to advocate jazz. We decided to pay Peter, whose role became vital as a manager, a small stipend against Mary's doing those four concerts a year."

"So 1978, that second year at Duke," adds O'Brien, "saw a truce between Mary and me, although things were never the same."

Now began the busiest years of Mary's professional life, as she wove club dates and performances of the *Mass* around her class schedule. In spite of the "truce" with O'Brien, she felt more comfortable when she was at leisure with old friends and family. She especially valued her visits to Washington, D.C., where she could visit with Brother Mario. Her old friend had been reassigned from Italy to a post at Howard University's Newman Center, a meeting-place for college Catholics. "I'd give her my room at the Newman Center and I'd take a foldout cot in the library," recalls Brother Mario. "Sometimes she'd be puffing on a cigarette in bed, writing music. There'd be students here and they wouldn't know jazz, but with her air, she drew people to her and she made friends with them. She'd never let an opportunity go by to let them know about their heritage. These young dynamic black students at Howard were the future leaders. She would go shopping for the food and bring it here, and she'd cook a little, some kind of pasta perhaps. Always made way too much. She was never a burden. On one of her trips, I remember she went to the National Theater to see the Pope, who was visiting the White House. She wore a special dress, dark blue, slippers too, and took a copy of her *Mass* to give to the Pope, but he was out of reach.

"We seldom went out after her concerts. She enjoyed just coming back and relaxing, sitting with me for a couple of hours and talking." Even when the President of the United States, then Jimmy Carter, sent her an engraved, signed invitation to a jazz party on the White House lawn in June, she had to be prodded. Why should she just go sit at some party? she asked grumpily. But she did, and played "Somewhere over the Rainbow."

Several months before that, in March, she'd had a bittersweet triumph as the featured performer at the first Women's Jazz Festival in Kansas City. That she was not of one mind philosophically or politically with the festival's organizers she made perfectly clear, both in the perfunctoriness of her performance and in her shoot-from-the-hip remarks at a press conference before the festival: "As for being a woman, I never thought much about that one way or the other. All I've ever thought about is music," adding, "I'm very feminine, but I think like a man. I've been working around them all my life. I can deal better with men than women, and I've never heard objectionable remarks from men about being a woman musician." After the Women's Jazz Festival, she sent a letter trembling with anger to festival spokesman

Leonard Feather, who had spoken pointedly about Mary's "all-but anti-feminist posture," while championing Marian McPartland, in an article about the festival that was picked up by the wire services and reprinted in newspapers across the country.

"So many things you've done to me," she wrote. "Was it because I asked for my compositions or what I know? *I've* worked all my life on my own merits. I'm out here trying to help poor souls which means nothing to you. You're on your way to getting hurt through your awful methods. Don't push me too far. I have a strong Taurus streak still, worse than ten ferocious lions."

Mary did her best playing either with highly talented players—as she did in Europe that summer with Stan Getz and Jo Jones at a jam session in Nice, and in duet with John Lewis—or playing solo, as she did at Montreux. "The old lady," she wrote happily to Joyce Breach, "is wailing with foreign sounds, I'm playing my buns off." In Montreux she made the last recording to be released before her death, titled *Solo Recital at Montreux,* for Granz's Pablo label. It is an album representative of her repertoire, with a massively developed "Little Joe from Chicago," a tender "Morning Glory," and a "Honeysuckle Rose" with a rather sly "fungus-y" beginning—tunes she had played hundreds, maybe thousands of times, yet they sound fresh, at once modern, mellow, and majestic.

AFTER HER SISTER Mamie died in the mid-1970s, Mary declared that she wasn't going back to Pittsburgh ever again: the city held too many painful memories for her, including those of Mamie's lingering death, which Mary had witnessed. Mary paid for the funeral, and played the organ at the funeral service, where she, who seldom cried, broke down. Instead, she tried to reassemble the family at her house in Durham for the holidays, paying for their airline tickets at Thanksgiving in 1978. But it would be the last time she had the clan gathered with her at holiday time.

At Christmas in 1978, Mary, as usual, cleaned her house from top to bottom (she would not hire a cleaner) and bought a small fir tree, under which she set out her model train sets. She would have spent the holiday alone (neither Peter, Robbie, nor any other relatives were around), if Marsha Vick, who'd begun taking private lessons, hadn't dropped in for a friendly holiday visit. Marsha and (to a lesser extent) her husband, Paul, had become good friends of hers. When Paul Vick decided to run for city councilman, Mary dusted off her old "Ballot Box Boogie," written in the early forties for FDR, now dubbing it "The Paul Vick Boogie." (Vick won.) "From the time we were married, until we met Mary, I never heard Marsha play," says Paul. "Then with Mary, Marsha was playing and transposing music—just this amazing change in her, that was all due to Mary, that amazing ability Mary had to bring things out in people." Marsha gave Mary some heirloom Christmas ornaments for her tree. Touched, Mary offered her a drink. "But she was sort of blue. We both had a drink of whiskey and neither of us drank."

Mary fought the blueness by going to church. Her favorite place to worship was the little stone church of Holy Cross. Says Father Frank O'Connor, then the parish priest, "It was a friendly place and the parishioners didn't press her. On home football days, the men of the parish would sell barbecued ribs and chicken, and they had a fair once a year. She enjoyed that.

"She liked Saturday evening mass; she'd sit in the back. Her friend Jane Lynch, who taught classical piano at Duke, played the piano for the services. And I recall her putting on her jazz mass at Holy Cross where she used our choir as the singers. And I think she liked that because most of the choir were black people and they had a better sense of what the music was like. I remember at the choir practice, it didn't take long before she had them ready. She took a couple of chords apart and showed how there was a kind of pain in the music. She'd play each note separately and say, 'Did you hear the cry in it?' It was just a parish mass that she did the music for."

———

ALTHOUGH HE NOW had his independence, an income, and a psychiatrist, O'Brien felt little relief from the anger that seized him in his relationship with Mary. "Then my analyst moved from Durham to Richmond. I used to say I had a blood disease I had to go treat up in Richmond. I did not trust her in terms of my own mental health. I could never let her know I was seeing him."

As head of the alumni office, Paul Vick had many dealings with O'Brien in setting up the concert series Mary had agreed to do for the

university. "Peter was this very hyper person. You spent a lot of time trying to calm him. But Peter was useful to her. His concern was the
finances, how to get the money. But even though he was the manager,
she took care of him—like a mother taking care of her child. And he
did what *she* wanted, how she wanted it done." And if Mary was too
often strict and overbearing in O'Brien's opinion, she could also be
contrite, as she was after yet another confrontation when she accused
him of skimming her performance fees. She wrote later,

> Dear Peter:
> I have something to say to you concerning my unexcused
> behavior. You are truly an inspiration to me and my endeav-
> ors. . . .

In a chilling prediction of her own failing health, she added,
"There is something in my system that is poisoning my spirits and I
don't know what is." She felt a sense of foreboding and was afraid. Mary
clearly had not been feeling well for years, suffering from complications of obesity and occupational hazards such as finger and arm strains
and back pain, a recent hearing loss in her left ear, and occasional dis-
charges of blood. But lately her sense of unwellness, along with the
pain in her back, had gradually worsened. She'd been suffering back
pain since the late 1960s, visiting various physicians for temporary
relief. Joyce Breach remembers accompanying her to a chiropractor in
1970. As she recalls, "He told me—but privately, not to her—that it
wasn't her back, but that something else was seriously wrong."

As a musician, Mary was bothered most of all by her hearing loss,
probably gradually incurred while at the Cookery, where the large
amplifier for the bass player had been placed on a shelf close to her
left side. Among the first things she did when she moved to Durham
was to visit the North Carolina Eye and Ear Hospital (then MacPher-
son Hospital), where she learned that the deafness in her ear was quite
advanced and irreversible. During Christmas of 1978, when she was
feeling low, Mary became ill enough to ask Marsha Vick to take her to
the University Hospital clinic. There she was told she had a bad cold
and sent home. But it was not long after that, in February of '79, that
she saw the first unmistakable sign that something far more serious was
wrong—the persistent presence of blood in her urine. Terribly upset,

she called Marian Turner, the secretary of the music department at Duke and another recent friend, for a reference to a doctor. Turner sent her to her internist, a Dr. Brown, who had the sad task of making the diagnosis: bladder cancer.

Dr. Brown urged her to check into the hospital immediately, to determine the stage of her disease, but Mary said no, she had commitments to honor first; she would deal with the bad news in her own way. She took a bus to Washington, D.C., where she visited briefly with Brother Mario and played various engagements. Back in Durham, she went into the hospital on March 27 for a transurethral biopsy as well as a bladder-scraping procedure—what a doctor describes as like "peeling the skin of an apple"—and was at the piano bench the very next day, performing her *Mass* at the Durham Academy. Throughout 1979, Mary continued to concertize heavily. She who hated to fly even took the very long flight to Brazil for the São Paulo Jazz Festival. In May, she performed *Mary Lou's Mass* again in New York, at St. Patrick's Cathedral on the occasion of its one-hundredth anniversary, with Buster Williams on bass and a choir from Fordham Prep along with several Duke students—and even played for a Duke alumni reception afterwards at a suite at the Carlyle, where she was supplied with her favorite Baldwin baby grand and persuaded shy Marsha Vick to perform at her Fats Wallerish best. Present also was Mary's old friend, the journalist "Popsy" Whitaker, who wrote an important and affectionate sketch of an ebullient Mary for *The New Yorker.* For Whitaker, Mary spun her fantasy (though real for her as long as she was performing) of being part of a big, happy, jazz-loving family back at Duke. "We're all happy," she said. "Peter plays records . . . I play piano for them, sometimes I dance for them." The kids were so "eager," she added, that she no longer felt "so troubled." And as he listened to her play at the Carlyle that afternoon, Whitaker noted later with satisfaction that Mary had achieved an "air of quiet confidence—even of majesty . . . a Mary Lou Williams fully realized." Mary's playing, though buoyant as well as brilliant, was only a temporary surge of vitality, however, tied to her fantastic hope that she could beat the cancer, as a note she wrote to Joyce Breach from a Corpus Christi jazz festival appearance in July of '79 makes clear: "Got news about my illness. Can get medicine (Laetrile) in Dallas, Texas—will cost $3000. I'm working hard, raising loot now! A miracle happened elsewhere in me."

Then, back in Durham before school began, to bad news: routine follow-up tests at Duke Medical Center showed that the tumor had returned. Again she was hospitalized and had the bladder scraping a second time on August 27, 1979. She viewed it as a routine procedure, however, was back home shortly afterwards, and again rebounded vigorously. Off she went to Washington in early September, where she performed her "history" and the *Mass* with the Howard University Chorale at Ford's Theater. The next evening she began a week's stint at Blues Alley, and played for a cocktail reception of Duke alumni. Recalls Marsha Vick, "She was glowing, masterful—the music went way beyond even the best I'd heard from her. She told me later that Suggs and Walker [Milton Suggs and Hugh Walker, bass and drums] were together with her like never before, and that she had felt more like playing than she had in 10 years." When bassist Charles Mingus stopped in to hear her at Blues Alley (Ella Fitzgerald was another guest), he was knocked out and pressed Mary to go out with him on a concert tour for Norman Granz. But Mary said no. With rare exceptions, she had always liked best to work as a soloist or with her own combo.

In fact, though, the results of her transurethral biopsy were not good: Mary had grade-III bladder cancer, an advanced stage of the disease. After an engagement in Chicago at Rick's Café Américain, where she played with her usual vigor, even exuberance, she faced a third scraping in December of 1979. By then, she seemed to sense that her condition, far from getting better, was worsening. In Chicago, she wrote to Breach in a tone that suggests a kind of flat acceptance of her fate:

> I'm supposed to go into the hospital when I get back to Durham. I lost my hair and lost the use of my left wrist and was peeing blood three weeks ago. Doctors found a growth on my bladder. I prayed so hard that I think it has melted away, ah. Oh, yes, I also have the gout in my knees and wrists. I ran into a cut freak at the hospital and I am thinking about not going into the hospital. Just opened at the club here, kinda nice. I tie my wrist up to play. Marsha got a raise for me so that I could continue to pay Peter.
>
> Love, Mary

But although advanced bladder cancer does not respond well to chemotherapy or radiation, Mary still showed tremendous recuperative powers. "She sprang back and really went to work—she had her strength and lots of work," says Peter O'Brien.

————

UNHAPPILY, MARY'S RELATIONSHIP with O'Brien had not improved appreciably, as shown in another letter she wrote but did not mail him (there were several) after she was released from the hospital. It reveals the depth of her pained anger:

Peter,
You're living above your means. I begged you to give me receipts for anything you did. There were no calculations. You've gotta talk to somebody like Dr. Miller to settle you to your good side which is tremendous. I always confuse you, you never understand me. . . . Try and put yourself in my place. Peter, I think you have a grudge somewhere because you're telling lies. You see things in a very mixed-up way. . . . Right now I'm sad and lonely but not for long. God will help me, I'm sure of this. How someone can take the abuse I go through—but this is proof of God's love and nobody can tell me anything else, you see.

When you accused me of stealing and abusing kindness, I began thinking—what have I done wrong? I tried to teach you the business. I'm still thinking for you when I write Norman [Granz] and others. I have taught you and give you ideas to go on your own to make millions because you're white. But now you're throwing your money away, spend it all with nothing saved for a rainy day. Your not having any money ever, means I have to take work, overworking with bad health. You've almost made me lose my mind from your accusations. I'm almost hating you, but will never allow this to happen. I never would have taken such amateurish dealings from anyone as I do with you, if I hadn't thought they needed help.

Now my mind is in a mess. I can't be around anybody long. Seems you have very strong powers and it ain't too good at times. Man, I'm a creative artist. The mind has to be clear at all

times. Being alone I can ward off distraction better. . . . You
have done quite a few bad things to me and acted as if you knew
it all. You listened to jealous sounds and returned attacking me.
Recently I've felt like going into retirement. But I snap back.
Have they got you believing that jazz isn't needed? I'm tired of
talking, man.

O'Brien was not her only trial during this most difficult time. After
Mamie's death, having assumed the mantle of matriarch of the family,
Mary took on the rehabilitation of her nephews Clifford and Robbie.
As Helen Floyd bluntly puts it, "Motherhood kicked her right in the
ass." The problem children she had worried about were now problem
adults, in some cases with problem children of their own. Robbie's
nephew, Clifford (Grace's grandson), who was a few years older than
Robbie, visited Mary in Durham, bringing his small son; Mary talked,
pleaded, prayed over, and got angry at Clifford, trying to get him to
stop using drugs. "Mary was terrified that her nephews, especially Robbie and Clifford, would get on dope and die," explains O'Brien. "She
certainly said that, almost crying one day." Robbie, who wrote polite
letters to Mary one day and abusive, name-caliing rants the next
(though invariably asking for money), finally joined the army.

In a letter to Robbie (this one returned unopened) she felt obliged
to defend the "expense" of her penny-ante card-playing hobby:

> I play cards with friends to keep my spirits up. I have a lot to do
> before I die. But my health is very bad and I'm weak. I didn't
> want to tell you but I had to, I'm going into the hospital here.
>
> Robert, I am a friend, not an enemy. You are not supposed
> to treat me badly. I try to help you. I do not have the loot to do
> what you want done all the time and you do not have to
> threaten me, all you have to do is ask or talk to me. Is anyone
> using you to harm me? I told you that black people are danger-
> ous to their own kind. Did you know or care that I'm sick? Don't
> allow fears to anger you.
>
> I love you, Mary

As Robbie's behavior became even more erratic, and as Mary's illness progressed, "she didn't want Robbie in Durham," says Brother

Mario flatly. Still, she always carried his photo in her wallet, and kept his room in her house waiting, complete with the old drum set Dizzy Gillespie had given him as a teenager.

Mary made other plans for the future she still hoped to have, flying in her sister Geraldine and niece Helen from Pittsburgh for company and paying them to help care for her as she weakened, even to accompany her on her travels. "She wanted to go visit Peru, where St. Martin de Porres was from," recalls Helen Floyd.

As for O'Brien, she devised a plan she thought would give him his independence, while keeping him near. "There was an empty lot next door to her house. After she got sick, she wanted to buy it and build a separate unit there for me," he says. "She thought maybe I would come around if I was completely alone. She very rarely ever cried, but when I said I absolutely will not do that, she cried in her car, I remember. I was harsh in my refusal and she took it as hatred and rejection of her and she didn't understand that I was terrified of being crushed. Although after that, she understood more." But one thing he did not seem to consider: some of her tears may have flowed from her sorrow and fear for the way he was conducting his life.

In the midst of all this, Mary played on. Of a concert in May with Milton Suggs, opposite the Ellington Orchestra led by Mercer Ellington at Lincoln Center in New York, the *Times* critic John S. Wilson rhapsodized that her "personalized history of jazz [was] a tour de force [with] a crispness and emotional richness that raised it from a series of brief examples to a developed whole." She continued her high level of performance all summer: at Notre Dame in mid-June, Wolf Trap in Virginia, the Corpus Christi Jazz Festival for the Fourth of July, and the Knickerbocker Saloon (in Manhattan) in July and August. "No matter what she plays she swings," commented Wilson.

Mary had left Barney Josephson's employ for the nearby Knickerbocker, the Cookery's main rival. "Barney Josephson had a fit when I told him we were leaving the Cookery, like you were supposed to be his slave forever," says O'Brien. Mary told Andy Kirk, says Delilah Jackson, who was visiting Kirk at his home when Mary stopped by, that she had borrowed $1,000 from Josephson and then gave notice. "And he said, 'Wait a minute, how can you borrow money from me and then quit?' I answered him, 'Barney, I *have* to quit to get a job to make enough money to pay you back!' " This is pure, pungent Mary.

As the holiday season approached in 1979, Mary's favorite, Thanksgiving, was a happier one than the year before. She made turkey, candied yams, and all the trimmings for dinner, inviting Brother Mario, Marsha Vick, and several of her students. "It was very casual, sitting in the kitchen," Brother Mario recalls. "We played cards and Mary showed Marsha various techniques on the piano. The next day we drove around, did a lot of shopping, went to a market and her favorite antiques store." It was the last holiday she would experience without intense physical pain.

In early December, she went to the University of Richmond to concertize. D. A. Handy, artist-in-residence there who had a background in classical music, had arranged the concert and panicked when Mary's preferred Baldwin piano was dropped while being moved and could not be replaced. "I called Mary, offering to search high and low for something else," recalls Handy. "But Mary didn't even blink when she got there, she just waved me away. She didn't even want to test it! She said that she had learned in her early years how to play in all the keys and on all kinds of beat-up, out-of-tune pianos. She just sat down and played."

Mary knew she had more hospitalization ahead as Christmas approached, but she wanted to see friends and family in New York first, so she took a Trailways bus up north. She shopped, saw family and friends, and tended to her New York apartment. But in a few days, complaining that she felt dizzy, weak, and nauseated with intermittent but severe back pain, she returned to Durham and Duke University Medical Center for a third scraping of the bladder. This time, the news was worse: the cancer had spread into her body, and the doctors wanted to remove her bladder and uterus.

During her hospitalization for this major surgery, on January 10, 1980, Marsha Vick and Peter O'Brien visited her daily. She joked with the nurses. "One day she said she was in such pain that she closed her eyes and said to the nurses, 'Goodbye!' " recalls Vick. "It scared them. But she was very frightened at the prospect of a serious operation. To pass the time, she either slept or played cards; she taught me to play many games, from poker to crazy eights."

O'Brien had fought against accepting the severity of her condition, even when she grew weaker as the time for her radical surgery approached. "I thought it was still manageable cancer. Mary was in bed and said 'Bring me the bedpan,' but I told her, 'Stand up—if you don't, it's all over!' So she said 'All right,' and stood up to go to the bathroom. The urology surgeon was convinced they'd got all the malignancy out. But then the oncologist, Dr. Paulson, came to talk to us. He said she needed chemo and so on. The diagnosis suddenly knocked the shit out of me."

Although she was now seventy years old, was enduring chronic pain, and had undergone major surgery, Mary continued to show resilience. As soon as she could, she had a piano wheeled into her room and would play for the doctors, nurses, patients, friends, and students who came by. Joyce Breach flew in, bearing a huge bouquet of Mary's favorite red roses, and recalls that Mary wouldn't be seen until she had her teeth in and her makeup and wig on. Home by the end of January, Mary was helped in her recuperation by her sister Geraldine Garnett, who came down from Pittsburgh to care for her, at Mary's expense. Mary pressed ahead with plans. Some fell through, like her wish for a jazz festival at Duke. But one thing she decided she could no longer put off was a long-germinating idea for an extended composition: orchestrating her "history of jazz" for a Duke concert band called the Wind Symphony. Confusingly, she often referred to the project as the *Wind Symphony*.

She wrote Joyce: "I didn't realize that my operation was so heavy. Now I'm feeling better—almost ready to get going. A few days before you arrived I had begun to feel sorry for myself, was in tears etc., but am ok thanks to friends. I shall always remember you all. I'll be ok now, anxious to get back to the Wind symphony. I feel very thankful and great inside—please believe me."

She set to work, but now had to deal with mounting pain as the cancer spread to her spine (though Mary stubbornly called it "arthritis"); medication with all kinds of side effects; having to use an ostomy bag; and the clear knowledge that her days were numbered. Despite many good days, her mood often dipped sharply. "She was in more and more pain from her back," recalls Marsha Vick years later, who attended Mary faithfully during her illness. "Once she told me the pain was so bad she thought about suicide. On bad days, she said she couldn't get any more inspiration, and would complain about 'cornball' music. And once she played a concert where her back was killing her, but then, she said, she started playing and the pain went away." Vick jotted in her diary, "She relies on God for all things, to keep her going. She feels that God has given her the talent and will make her able to play as long as He wants."

———

GIVEN THE DECLINING state of her health, her musical coherence in the summer of 1980 is nothing short of miraculous. (Of course, Mary *did* believe in miracles.) After a performance in June at Duke for an alumni reunion that drew more than a thousand people, she played to a packed audience at the Spoleto Festival in Charleston. "Just listening to her doesn't even hint that she might be 70," remarked a reviewer. After repeating the previous year's superlative performance in New York at the Knickerbocker, she performed *Mary Lou's Mass* in Newark, at Seton Hall.

Then back to Duke, where she managed to play at a reception for Beverly Sills on September 10. Afterwards, she went to her birthplace, Atlanta, where despite the severe pain that now radiated down her right leg as the cancer spread, she prepared the Clark College Jazz Orchestra for a performance of her music (including a luminous "Gloria") at the Atlanta Free Jazz Festival. While in town, she also received an award from the NAACP and visited with her half-brother Willis Scruggs.

In October, she flew with O'Brien to Canada to perform solo and in tandem with Oscar Peterson on a television show he hosted in Toronto. "Actually she went there," says O'Brien, "because she wanted to buy a fur coat to replace the one that had been stolen some time before in Chicago. It cost a lot less to buy one in Canada, and even less because she avoided paying customs duties when she reentered the States. She just folded up that new mink and sat on it!"

But Mary appeared noticeably drawn from her illness now, and playing was often an extreme effort. Almost too exhausted that fall to play at a reception for Princess Grace of Monaco at Duke, she nevertheless made an appearance, and she played a concert in October in Tallahassee, Florida, with Milton Suggs. Saxophonist Ricky Ford, who deeply admired her music, met her for the first time there, and performed an atonal version he'd arranged of her "Whistle Blues." But the pain escalated, and the Florida concert was her last professional performance; and back at Duke, October 23 was her last full day of teaching. By November she was in such bad shape that her doctors insisted she check back into Duke Medical Center for a month of tests and radiation treatments.

"Mary was going to postpone going into the hospital again, partly because she had other things she wanted to do and partly because of Robbie, who had turned up again," says Peter O'Brien. "She said, 'If I'm not there at the house, he'll get two girls in here, one will get him upstairs and the other will clean me out.' We argued, and at last she consented to go in the hospital."

As Mary began to pack to go into the hospital, she called Robbie in, informing him she was giving him a hundred dollars and a bus ticket back to New York. Later she told Marsha Vick of the painful scene that followed. Robbie went berserk, smashing up his drum set and screaming. At last, Robbie stormed out of the house, shouting at her, "You're an old woman going to die soon!"

"So we locked up the house and put the alarm on, and Mary called the police to protect it while she was away," continues O'Brien. "A black policeman, very nice, came. He asked what to do if Robbie came back and tried to get in the house. And she said in a low, matter-of-fact voice, 'Treat him the same as you would treat anybody else.' Then we went to a Chinese restaurant nearby. And she cried, not loud, but openly." All her life, Mary had witnessed the destruction of people she loved in their dark dance with drink or drugs or rage: her mother, her sister, and musicians, both lovers and friends. The list went on and on. Although many of the members of her own family were leading normal, productive lives, her brother Howard, nine years her junior and a promising artist, died a heroin addict in the 1970s. Her nephew Clifford died of an overdose a few years later. But no unraveling ever hurt Mary as much as Robbie's. She had prayed that music would redeem him, that he might become a professional drummer. But that was not to happen.

————

MUSIC MEANT LIFE to Mary, and even while she was in the hospital undergoing a regimen of radiation treatments, she struggled to continue with her music. In November 1980, though too weak to dress without help, she made the trip to the Catholic Cathedral in Raleigh, where she had agreed to play the *Mass* with a half-dozen of her college students singing. But that would be the last time she performed it. Released from the hospital shortly before Thanksgiving, "She couldn't even eat the turkey wing she loved so much for Thanksgiving dinner," notes O'Brien. "The radiation had just knocked her out." And the pain, for the cancer had spread to her liver: her life from then on revolved around pain management. In January of 1981, she was in and out of Duke Medical Center for a series of chemotherapy treatments, each time staying overnight in the chemo ward to recover from the nausea and exhaustion induced by the drugs.

On January 27, after her last chemotherapy treatment, Mary attempted to teach at least one class—she knew she couldn't handle a full day as before. Marsha Vick took notes on Mary's last time at Introduction to Jazz:

> The students sat quietly waiting for her, and as she came through the door of the room, wheeled in and wearing a beautiful blue dress and lavender shoes, they burst into applause. She was helped out of the wheelchair onto the piano bench and began the class on unison singing of "Rosa Mae." She critiqued their phrasing and rhythm as pointedly as ever, stopping to comment as they sang: "Put something on that note," "Make a noise on that one," and "there: almost." In the middle of her solo on "Rosa Mae," she motioned to Peter nearby. "I need to sit in the chair." And Peter and two students jumped up and moved her from the bench back to the wheelchair, from which she continued to play. The class resumed singing and when they finished, she clapped for them. Next she set them to work on "The Lord Says," from *Mary Lou's Mass.* "This is the jazz gospel," she told them. She tried to help a male student to sing falsetto. "Clear your throat—I'll cover you." Then, "I need someone to scat on the end—do you scat?" At the end of the piece, she laughed and everyone clapped. And you could feel the love in the room.

When Mary gamely tried to reenter the classroom a week later, she lasted only a few minutes before she was wheeled out of the room, nauseated and gray with exhaustion. O'Brien finished out her second semester classes.

The excruciating pain that Mary now suffered constantly was the spark that ignited a long-simmering feud between Peter O'Brien and Joyce Breach. Both were desperate actors in the last act of Mary's life. "I was looking for a miracle with Mary and the doctors couldn't give me one," says O'Brien. "I was pushing too hard, maybe I thought there were other medical things that could be done. But the doctors told me no, *no*." For her part, Breach, who flew down early in '81 from New York, was shocked at Mary's condition, and could not accept the cruel reality of Mary's physical anguish. Mary was receiving the American version of the so-called Brompton's cocktail, the strongest pain medicine then available for terminal cancer patients in America, a mixture of morphine, alcohol, and cocaine. The British version also contained heroin. Says O'Brien, "Joyce was questioning me the same way I questioned all the doctors, but she was accusing *me* of doing the wrong thing. I let her have it. She had money. I said, 'Why don't you fly Mary to London and get heroin for her then? That'll obliterate all the pain.'"

But Marsha Vick and Breach (who, although she had lost most of her money by then, was quietly supplementing the salaries of Mary's attendants and providing other touches of comfort) were both angry over what they saw as O'Brien's inattentiveness to Mary's needs as she lay dying. "I was upset with Peter because I didn't think he was paying close enough attention to her condition," says Vick. "Before the time he had nurses in around the clock, he and I would fill in when the nurse was not there. He started off spending the nights there, but then he couldn't take it and he'd call me and I'd come over and sit with her. This was really not a good arrangement because I was not a nurse and she was bedridden. And he kept trying to get her up out of bed, thinking that if we could get her up walking around, she'd be better. There was a circle around the five bedrooms upstairs, but she really was not able to do that. And she couldn't eat. *I* would make up the juices for her, carrots and apples and so forth, in her blender; then, fortunately, Geraldine came and she stayed for weeks on end, taking care of Mary."

Friends and family came to visit her one last time. Another sister, Dorothy Rollins, spelled Geraldine, as did Helen Floyd and Edythe Beltz, Mary's Hamilton Terrace neighbor, a professional nurse. When Dizzy Gillespie dropped in, Mary invited the Vicks also. "We got there, Mary was sitting propped up in bed, Dizzy's on the other bed, there's like six or eight different little paper cartons of Chinese food, and they were laughing and talking," remembers Paul Vick. "This was a time when she was not doing well, but there was a great spark between them. That great, rolling laugh of hers. She told Marsha, 'You know Lorraine made him come.' "

Mary had a last hurrah, hosting a party at her house on Valentine's Day. Her house was packed with friends and students, plenty of food and drink, and a big cake with her favorite pink icing. At the party, her last piano performance was filmed for *Music on My Mind,* a documentary of her life (although it does not appear in the final version). She dressed—with assistance—in a new, dressy skirt and blouse that fit her much-slimmer figure, and almost managed to descend the stairs from her bedroom. But the effort proved too much for her: she fainted and had to be carried to the piano bench. "Peter and I were both in tears," wrote Marsha Vick. "It had been a long, painful slide down those stairs."

That Mary managed to rise from her bed that day, let alone play the piano coherently, was a stunning testament to her willpower and love of music. Not only did she play several songs, old favorites and new, but the playing revived her. Afterwards, she was carried upstairs on a kitchen chair, and prepared for bed. "We visited," wrote Marsha in her journal, "and she seemed fine, but she didn't want me to go."

The next day she had weakened so much that an ambulance was called to take her to the hospital. A frequent side effect of her disease, severe depression, had set in, and she began taking mood elevators, which gave her more good days—days when she talked of her composition plans, of playing a concert for the Duke alumni in Pittsburgh, of eating "home cookin'" again. She requested a bowl of hot chili, made to her own recipe, but could eat only juices now. Still, her wit returned in flashes. Watching pianists play during a tribute to Duke Ellington on television one night, she turned to tell Marsha Vick, "Billy Taylor just missed a beat."

She was as motherly as ever, guiding Marsha Vick's nascent career as a piano player at local gigs. Advising her not to undersell herself in negotiating a salary, Mary challenged her: "Aren't you worth it?" And from her sickbed, when Marsha couldn't find a bass player for a job, Mary called around town and landed one for her.

Above all, Mary found it wonderfully therapeutic to focus her mind on her *History of Jazz for Wind Symphony* project. Brian Torff describes the unfinished project as an "interesting combination of African-American blues and band music mixed with dissonant chords." She had been turning over the new work in her mind for some time. With obvious relish, she explained, "I'm experimenting again with voicing and sounds, writing the blues for the oboe to play. And the bassoon," adding, "If I can't get anything new then it's just a waste of time to me." Most of the piece remained in outline form, but the several minutes of composition she managed to get down on paper are an important musical statement on what, at the last, was of most value to her. She sketched out five parts. According to O'Brien, the dense chords and long lines of the introduction, titled "Suffering," were supposed to depict the lashing of a slavemaster; it was followed by two spirituals, a ragtime, and a blues. One imagines Mary, ill and aware that she was at the end of her life, reaching back as never before to memories from early childhood for the shape of the *Wind Symphony:* remembering the stories of the cruelties of slave times that she had heard as a little girl; the dimly recalled visits to Grandpa Riser's storefront church where Virginia Riser may have danced for coins before the draped altar; the blues she heard when her stepdaddy Fletcher smuggled her into gambling dens. "The ragtime section of the piece," says O'Brien, "focused on clarinets, which was as far as she got with that. And she also wrote seven or eight bars of a single melody line of the blues for the bassoon, but that writing ended in midstream, not yet orchestrated. That was the last note of music that she wrote."

The unwritten sections were to represent various jazz eras—swing, bop (possibly an arrangement of her 1940s piece "Knowledge," which she was then revising for an octet), the postbop modern era—and a finale. As part of her research for the post-bop, avant-garde, section, she resorted to a favorite pastime—watching horror movies. "She asked me to take her to *Alien,*" recalls Marsha Vick, "and I was scared to death. But she just sat there and said, 'Oh, don't pay attention to all that,' and taped it on her recorder."

In the 1930s Mary had turned to Andy Kirk to learn how to read and notate her arrangements, and in the 1940s classically trained Milt Orent had provided technical assistance on *Zodiac.* For the *Wind Symphony* project, she sought help from two music professors at Duke (both now retired), Paul Bryan, conductor of the Wind Symphony, and Robert E. Ward, an opera specialist.

Comments Ward, "Mary Lou was very ill by that time but she was avid for any help to complete her piece before the end of her life. Most jazz musicians live within their limitations, but interestingly, she was trying to stretch beyond that. She asked me to look at the score as she was doing it and I helped her with information about certain instruments: once she was outside the realm of improvisatory jazz, she had only the most rudimentary knowledge, but she aspired to those larger forms. She was very certain in her knowledge of the instruments she knew, but she didn't realize the sound and range of others she was unfamiliar with, like the English horn. And the cello. For example, in the upper register it sounds higher than it is due to the intensity of the sound. So, I helped her to orchestrate."

Lead sheets and fragments, including the introduction of the work, were then given to conductor Paul Bryan. "Whatever I had in hand, I tried to score for the Wind Symphony. I went over to see her and we talked about it a few times, but there was not very much connection, as she was pretty far gone by that time. To complete the work would have taken a whole lot of energy, which at that time she no longer had. If she'd started sooner, chances are she'd have found a way to get from one thing to another to make it more of an extended composition. Kind of frustrating to realize that she didn't get to that place, because it could have been pretty darn good." By that time, Mary no longer had the strength to play the piano, but was buoyed by her composition in progress even as her health deteriorated rapidly. In a phone conversation, Barbara Carroll recalled that Mary enthused about the piece, "Baby, it sounds like Stravinsky!"

Bryan conducted the sole rehearsal of Mary's new composition, consisting of a little more than six and a half minutes of music, on February 16, 1981, with Mary's long-time bassist, Milton Suggs, and a rehearsal pianist. Fortunately the session was recorded. And bits of the piece can be heard in the documentary film about her.

IN APRIL, WHEN the rhododendrons in her backyard were awash in pinks and whites, Mary began a suffering descent toward death. Father O'Connor of Holy Cross Church came often to give her communion.

Then Brother Mario came down from Washington to see her. "That was the saddest visit I ever spent with her. She was so highly drugged that she slept most of the time and she didn't have her wig on or her teeth. But although she was dying, she was still very strong, I thought. I felt that she didn't really want to talk about it—we were communicating nonverbally. I remember holding her hand and that's when I became emotional. She woke up at one point and she said, 'Oh, you're still here,' and fell asleep." Peter O'Brien had by then moved into her house to spell the round-the-clock practical nurses; Marsha Vick was at the house every day. On May 8, Mary's seventy-first birthday, they celebrated with a cake, and two days later, Duke's president, Terry Sanford, came from the college's graduation ceremonies—still in cap and gown—to present Mary with the Trinity Award, given to the best-loved faculty member. "Mary looked beautiful with a new short hairdo and makeup," wrote Marsha in her diary of the event, "and when I called her later, she said, 'That touched me more than any award I've gotten since I've been playin'.' "

Two days later, she was drifting in and out of lucidity, sometimes thinking she must get up and prepare for a concert. She was hospitalized again, and felt she'd lost her grip. "She talks about death matter-of-factly, with no sadness," Vick had jotted in her diary. But as the disease tightened its vise of pain ever more cruelly, Mary became frightened. In the hospital, she grabbed Vick's hand. "I used to be able to handle anything, but no more," she told her. *"I don't want to die."*

Father John Dear, who'd taken private piano lessons a couple of years before, was working as a hospital volunteer then. "I was in the hospital every day and I'd see Mary Lou. I asked her about her interest in faith and her life. She said love is the meaning of life, that's what faith is all about. She was warmly welcoming. But at the end of March, she didn't want to see me. She rolled over and wouldn't see any visitors; she said she just wanted to die." Yet as the end loomed, Mary did rally. "There were no complaints, no self-pity, and no anger. She was spiritually coherent, even great, as she was dying," observes O'Brien.

A hospice volunteer, Helen Keese, began to come to Shepherd Street several times a week in April. "My job was not medical at all," explains Keese, "but to go buy things such as food that were needed, to check with the nurse, to stay an hour or so, and then leave—and to help with the dying, touching and talking even when she was comatose, to help ease the soul." Hospice was then new in America; Keese's husband, Father Peter Keese, an Episcopalian priest, had introduced it to North Carolina. "At first she didn't like or perhaps understand what I was doing there," Helen Keese continues, "but after a month or so, we had a rapport for several weeks before she died, although I never had any meaningful conversations with Mary Lou. By the time she couldn't talk, we were friends. She was alert and lucid until the end. I didn't know her music until then, but I went out and bought a record and I loved it—afterwards, I told her how much I enjoyed it and asked if I could kiss her forehead. Mary Lou consented."

"THE MORNING OF her death, May 28, 1981, I told my husband, 'I think Mary Lou's going to die today and I'll stay till she dies.' And I did," says Keese. Jerry Burley, Mary's brother, had come to visit her the day before and left for New York in the morning. O'Brien had left the house around noon, after calling Marsha to tell her that no one expected Mary to live much longer and that he couldn't stand to be there any longer. "At the very end," he says, "she told me she could hear the music, but she couldn't reach the keys anymore."

Mary was alone in her house, with just the nurse and Helen Keese. "Things get quite still before someone dies," says Keese. "And it *was* very quiet. She hadn't eaten or drunk anything for several days and she was on that Brompton's cocktail. Her favorite nurse, Ruth, had her arm around Mary Lou, and then she walked out of the room. I kept on talking and holding her hand and then she died. It was during the 3–11 P.M. shift, around 10:00 P.M."

"The worst moment was coming to her house with Marsha after she'd died," says O'Brien. "I stood by the side of the bed and Marsha leaned over and kissed Mary on the forehead."

They finished the obituary and, in the middle of the night, O'Brien delivered it to the wire services; then he flew to New York the next day with Mary's body. The undertakers met him at the airport. Determined to have her look in death as she had in life, he insisted that her hair, makeup, and clothes look natural. Her wig was styled in the smoothed-back pompadour she favored, and she was dressed in a long dark skirt and dressy blouse for the viewing on May 30 and 31.

The next day, June 1, a crowd packed St. Ignatius Loyola Church for the first of two funerals. It was a quarter of a century after Mary had been baptized in the same church. Musicians, friends, and fans flocked to pay their respects. Hazel Scott and Benny Goodman sat near the front. Sarah Vaughan sent flowers in the shape of a piano. "Lorraine Gillespie never comes out, but she was there, and I had to calm her down," recalls O'Brien. Brother Mario read from scripture, and O'Brien said the mass and gave the sermon. There were quantities of musical tributes, among them Dizzy Gillespie's "Con Alma," Buster Williams's "I Love You," Hilton Ruiz's "Medi II," Ellis Larkins's "Willow Weep for Me," and others.

After the funeral in Manhattan, Jerry Burley accompanied her casket to Pittsburgh for a Mass of Christian Burial on June 2, at Saints Peter and Paul Catholic Church in East Liberty. Again, the church was filled with family, friends, dignitaries, and musicians. Afterwards, Mary was interred in Calvary Cemetery in a peaceful, hilly section of Pittsburgh, close to other family members, in a plot that has been kept neatly weeded and supplied with fresh flowers. It was a fitting place of burial. Mary had liked hills. With a view spreading out before her, she had often taken out music paper and pencil and composed.

Jazz critic Gary Giddins, who was asked to deliver the eulogy at the funeral in Manhattan, had confronted the basic reality of sexism in jazz, which Mary had preferred to deflect in life. Giddins noted, "When she later attributed her acceptance among the giants of the era to 'that mannish thing in my playing,' she was confronting a basic truth about jazz: that it was a driven, competitive music, and that its clubbish milieu and traditional celebration of masculine bravura made it difficult for women to participate as equals." He went on: "She didn't—couldn't—completely succeed, but she made a crucial difference." This assertion—that jazz was a macho preserve that largely excluded women, and that Mary as a woman player was not completely successful in overcoming the layers of resistance—was bound to rile some who were present. (In fact, it probably would have riled Mary.) But for others, especially the younger generation of jazz lovers, Giddins spoke a poignant truth by acknowledging the tremendous hurdles that a black American female artist of high caliber had to surmount.

Chapter Nineteen
The Mary Lou Williams
Foundation

IN JANUARY 1980, soon after her major surgery, Mary, facing her mortality, made plans to update her will and revive her dream of helping others after she'd gone by founding a nonprofit organization. It was a dream she'd deferred since her unsuccessful Bel Canto Foundation in the 1960s. She had hoped too optimistically then for specific goals to be achieved: to divert some of her income to help fund her Cecilia Music Publishing Company and Mary Records, as well as to help support her ailing mother and her nephew Robbie's music education, and to have enough left over to give to then-Bishop Wright in Pittsburgh for his youth ministry—"especially," she designated, "for blacks and native Americans." She'd had a tough time just maintaining herself, let alone funding a flurry of worthy projects. But by 1980, things had changed; her mother had died, Robbie wanted little to do with her, and she was reasonably prosperous.

Although she kept her own counsel, Mary seems to have considered several possibilities for setting up her new foundation. She sought the advice of her old friend the pianist Billy Taylor, who had spearheaded the Jazzmobile, a very successful nonprofit organization in New York. She tiptoed around the topic of O'Brien's involvement. "She did say she wanted to talk about Peter someday," Taylor recalls, adding, "but she never did." Similarly with her close friend Joyce Breach: "She said over the phone the next time she saw me that she wanted to talk about Peter, but I never pressed her about it. Nor did I

tell Mary how I felt about Peter," adds Breach, "because I didn't want
to hurt her." In the end, when Mary incorporated the Mary Lou
Williams Foundation, she chose Peter O'Brien as director, but she also
asked Joyce Breach. The two were soon at loggerheads.

Mary, according to the minutes taken by Marian Turner at a bedside meeting to plan the foundation in the winter of 1981, "wanted
Duke University to be considered. She also made special reference
that some place be chosen not already involved in jazz—a fresh beginning may ensure more enthusiasm for her own purpose." Duke's president, the late Terry Sanford, was eager to cooperate. "There was
enough money in the estate that with the university's management
policies, the endowment could have been grown to a reasonable
amount," adds Paul Vick. "And there are the resources at Duke to catalogue her material. But to do this, *Duke* would have had to manage the
assets—it couldn't be done as a structure to support Peter. But Peter
wouldn't let anybody else in—control of the foundation became central to his life." The head librarian at Duke, Dr. John Druesdeou, adds,
"We really tried to get Father O'Brien to leave her papers here. However, he took everything."

O'Brien remembers things quite differently, emphasizing that no
one "at the top" approached him from the university about any such
arrangements. He soon began to set his sights elsewhere; eventually,
Mary's archive came to be housed at the Institute of Jazz Studies,
founded by Marshall Stearns and long overseen by Dan Morgenstern,
at Rutgers University's Newark campus. An important and prestigious
institution, yes; but hardly "a place . . . not already involved in jazz."

Mary was quite clear about her goals for her foundation, as stated
in the certificate of incorporation, dated February 25, 1980:

> To conduct activities which are exclusively charitable, literary
> and educational . . . including the advancement of public
> knowledge of the art of jazz music by teaching the same in all its
> forms to children between the ages of 6 and 12, individually
> and/or in groups, enabling them to perform before audiences,
> and giving them the opportunity to hear jazz in concert and
> studio performance.

In May, while Mary was in New York, she met O'Brien and Breach
at the Greenwich Village apartment of the late Gloria Josephson, a

lawyer (and Barney Josephson's former wife), to discuss plans for the foundation at some length. It was a poignant gathering: during the meeting, Mary turned to Gloria Josephson, who was to die of cancer not long after Mary, and said sotto voce, "I have cancer too." Josephson, recalls O'Brien, replied simply, "Yes, I know."

With her foundation now in order, as she thought, Mary delayed finalizing her will until the last stage of her illness. In March 1981 she summoned O'Brien and Marian Turner, as coexecutors of her estate, to her bedside and signed her last will and testament. Her nephew Robbie and her half-brother Jerry Burley were each left $1,000; everything else was left in trust to the Mary Lou Williams Foundation. Once again, according to the minutes of the meeting, she spoke specifically of her wish for the foundation. It was to be "a means of accomplishing after my death an objective that was very dear to me during my life," an organization set up "to aid the musical education of boys and girls between the ages of 6 and 12 in Black American music." Also, she emphasized, "the financial status of both the youngsters who will study music and the musicians chosen to teach through the Foundation should be considered when offering scholarships or making appointments."

Although she was still able to articulate her vision for her foundation, Mary was too distracted by pain, too groggy from medication, to handle her personal affairs in the months before her death and had come to depend on others completely—Marian Turner, Marsha Vick, her sisters and niece who flew in periodically at her expense to help the nurses, and Peter O'Brien. She gave powers of attorney to Turner and O'Brien to write checks for household expenses and the like. Once she died, the melancholy job of putting her affairs in order fell to her coexecutors, although Mrs. Turner was content to remain largely on the sidelines. "For me," remembers O'Brien, "there was a tremendously unhappy undertow all the time during that period when she was declining and dying and I was taking care of the house and all her business. Afterward, it was terrible for months—that huge house full of clothes and stuff that I had to go through."

There was, as mentioned in the previous chapter, a long-simmering resentment of O'Brien on the part of those closest to Mary after she became ill. Only a month before she died, Marsha Vick recorded in her diary that Mary told her she "was upset by the way Peter talks to me." The hospice worker Helen Keese, who was there to the very end of Mary's life, observes that "Peter was a man much given to great enthusiasm, hyperbole, and anger. He'd get upset when things didn't go right. I think he was scared of the dying process and the circumstances agonized him. Then he could speak rather roughly."

With Mary gone, this resentment toward O'Brien by many of her friends and family members exploded into acrimony. The flash point came when O'Brien barred anyone from entering the Shepherd Street house without his approval—in fact, no one was allowed in except Helen Floyd, who was summoned to help him sort and inventory Mary's belongings. Accusations of highhandedness and insensitivity, and also mistrust of his motives, followed. "We who were friends of Mary's had to buy back things we'd given her," says Vick. "I didn't resent that—because it was part of the estate. But no one could *get* to the things for the longest time, because Peter wouldn't let you in the house. Only he had access. We had to wait and wait and write him and implore him."

Says Reeny Burley, Jerry's widow, "I think Mary trusted him. But no one in the family knows to this day what happened to her things—all her jewelry and so on. Everything was sold after she died—it all had a price on it. Marsha Vick bought Mary's old car eventually, I remember. And then Peter completely ignored the family. Just cut them dead."

Many friends felt the same. "We weren't important or useful to him, so he passed over us after she died," says John Graziano, who'd been a good friend of Mary's in the 1970s. Adds Bernice Daniels, whose friendship went back to the 1940s, "I liked Peter. We used to joke and carry on. We drove down to North Carolina together, laughing about these little towns. Then, when Mary was sick, she told me she wanted me and Joyce on the board of her foundation. But after this show-biz lawyer, Gloria Josephson, set the thing up, then Peter wouldn't talk to me. I wasn't on the board, so he just cut me out." And bassist and vocalist Carline Ray, another friend of Mary's, says, "Peter could be very articulate about her life and times, but he just clamped down on everything she owned after she died, and I find that a very underhanded way for a Catholic priest to act."

O'Brien was also a priest in a peculiar position—dependent on himself for his livelihood, rather than having the support of a parish or of his Jesuit brotherhood at large. He eked out a living as a supply priest and cast about for a way to continue his role at Duke as spokesman for Mary Lou Williams. "The university continued to pay the stipend for him for a while when Mary was ill, and during the spring of '81 when she was sick, he was teaching the course," says Paul Vick. "But it was *Mary* who was the employee of Duke: everything was geared to Mary." O'Brien's was a peculiar and also a lonely position, surely. "After Mary died, I was one of his few friends around here in Durham for a little while," says Marsha Vick. "Well, I sort of put up with him, had him to dinner a lot, and my boys in high school entertained him. He'd come over to our house and just sit there."

"Peter," remembers Paul Vick, "kept trying to find a way of becoming an employee at Duke. When there was an opening for director of the Office of Student Activities, he applied for that." And Marsha adds, "At a university, you have to deal with academic affairs. They would have been crazy to hire him. He was always in this fog, and when things went wrong, it was always somebody else's fault. He wanted it all taken care of and he didn't want to deal with it." The directorship went to someone else, but O'Brien did manage to line up a teaching job in the fall of 1981—one course, called "Introduction to Jazz"—through Duke's Office of Continuing Education.

All of the assets in Mary's estate had been immediately transferred by the clerk of the court into the foundation, to pay, O'Brien said, "for expenses for stationery and things like that." O'Brien was also receiving from the foundation a salary of $300 a week plus expenses and 25 percent of his apartment rent (for six months, at which point it was supposed to be reviewed). Mary had left only a modest, if respectable, sum to fund her vision; her assets included her house, a life insurance policy, and valuables such as her car, jewelry, furs, and so on, all of which would yield roughly $200,000, according to a professional estimate that summer. (Contributions to the foundation from her wide circle of friends added more.) As the summer wore on, Marsha Vick and Joyce Breach began to have misgivings about oversight of the foundation expense account, and Breach successfully pressed for a policy of check cosigning as a way to control expenditures. "Because he was always writing checks," Breach says flatly. And when O'Brien moved back to New York in 1982, remembers Jerry's widow, Reeny, he would frequently come to their apartment for Jerry's cosignature. Gary Giddins, another board member, recalls, "He'd come over to my office at the *Village Voice* all the time to have me cosign checks. It was convenient for him to go there. But they were not *big* checks, just constant small money." Nevertheless, it could all add up. (The check-cosigning policy ended in 1987, when O'Brien moved from New York City.)

Marsha Vick approached Marian Turner about her concern that the estate's assets might be frittered away. Turner, who was supposed to examine the accounts once a month, reassured Vick that O'Brien's expenses were legitimate, but Vick was not convinced. She and her husband and especially Breach, who had a forceful personality, became increasingly estranged from O'Brien. As he remembers it, though, he and Breach had "got along perfectly" until Mary became ill, when their relationship deteriorated. "We had a good time together, going out. I just thought she was a wealthy friend of Mary's, you know. I did think it was a big mistake for Mary to appoint Joyce to the board, yes. I thought that Joyce would be useful only as a source of funds for the foundation."

By August, Marsha Vick was having sleepless nights over what she feared was O'Brien's lax stewardship of Mary's estate. "Turner feels that O'Brien can't do anything without the approval of the Board, so she feels safe. But she's a yes-man. Joyce, you're a fighter. You're our only hope!" she wrote to Breach. The fight came at the end of that month, when a newly appointed full board of directors of the foundation met in New York—O'Brien, Breach, Turner, Gary Giddins, and Dan Morgenstern, with Gloria Josephson attending as attorney-advisor. Breach was furious at the outcome of the meeting: O'Brien, over her objections, was given what she viewed as continued carte blanche with finances. (According to the minutes of a board meeting in December 1982, the board pledged to "discuss financial matters in particular and in depth." If such a meeting did occur, records of it have not been found.)

In Breach's view, the new board made a second mistake when it discussed amending the foundation's charter to preserve its assets rather than fulfilling its original mandate. "*She* wanted scholarships for kids so they could create and grow," says Breach. "But Peter was too busy to attend to what she wanted." After the meeting, she submitted her resignation in a letter that, as she says drily, "my lawyer made me tone down":

It is my belief that ultimately Mary Lou's wishes for her foundation will not be realized. At the last board meeting held, Monday August 31, 1981, New York City, it was made eminently clear to me that the foundation would be run without controls. Considering the above, I could not in all good conscience to Mary Lou serve as a member of a board that refuses to institute and maintain proper procedures.

In response, O'Brien wrote a brief note accepting her resignation with almost palpable relief. Giddins also wrote; he was "surprised and saddened" by her resignation, "and what puzzles me is why you don't think Mary Lou's wishes will be realized. I have the feeling you know something I don't and I'd be grateful to know where you think the trouble lies." But Breach did not answer; she would have nothing more to do with the foundation.

A year later, O'Brien had finished disposing of Mary's household goods, and he still had no firm commitment of a job with the university. Then, during that summer, he says, "I was told to come back to New York by the Jesuits. I'd had an agreement with them for one 'clear year,' as we call it, in 1977, and the next year I should have been evaluated, but through an oversight, I wasn't until 1982."

Back in New York, he worked at Fordham University's Lincoln Center campus, becoming director of the Campus Ministry. At first, he also made ambitious plans for the foundation. In 1983, he started a "Mary Lou Williams Children's Jazz Chorus, with 25 students under the directorship of singer Carmen Lundy," according to a press release. The chorus, an expensive undertaking, soon folded, although the New York Boys' Choir, drawn from Harlem schools, did perform *Mary Lou's Mass* that December, and kept parts of it in repertoire. O'Brien also promoted a series of fund-raising concerts for the foundation, often featuring name artists like Dizzy Gillespie, but they failed to make money. "It became too expensive to do these things," O'Brien says in retrospect, "and we were spending our capital fast."

Meanwhile, O'Brien's grief over the end of what he termed his "profound but needy relationship" with Mary, along with his inner demons, proved a steadily deteriorating mix in his life. "He did have personal problems after she died—heavy, big-time problems," says Giddins. O'Brien adds, "When I was with Mary in the seventies, I'd go out all night and drink a club soda. I knew nothing about the world of uptown—it wasn't dangerous yet." *Nite life* was what Mary called the domain of the mostly illicit activities of Harlem after-hours clubs where O'Brien's safe, club-soda drinking days were now over. And his disregard for many of the conventions, his moods swings and angry fits, continued to exacerbate the tensions between him and many of Mary's friends and family.

Then, as the summer of 1987 approached, O'Brien left New York for Minnesota and what he hoped would be a fresh start. "I moved there for personal reasons," he says. "There I had a different job, working in hospitals and at parishes. I also continued to do foundation work, though. But in Minnesota I didn't find musicians to work on the *Mass* or other projects involving children's choirs." Meanwhile, the finances of the foundation dwindled. "Then, in 1989, I went to New York for a meeting of the board of directors to discuss the foundation in depth. It was really dissipating its money at that point, and we needed to build it up. It was decided that the Mary Lou Williams Foundation was to become a *memorial* foundation; because Mary Lou's mission was to preserve jazz."

With the new resolution to memorialize Mary and her music, the need to sort, order, catalogue, transcribe, transfer tape, and untangle copyrights—nearly a half century's worth of music—as well as to preserve her other documents, would of necessity override the foundation's original purpose of teaching jazz to talented underprivileged children. That would have to wait.

Now in recovery, O'Brien set to work. "I moved to Syracuse in the summer of '91, and with that mission in mind—and with the help of Gray Weingarten, Mary's old friend, a librarian who lived there—I got Mary's music manuscripts in order along with her many personal photographs. A mountain of work." Having moved back to the New York area in 1994, O'Brien has remained active, both as a priest, directing spiritual retreats based on the philosophy of the twelve-step programs, and as head of the foundation. "The board of the foundation has only met irregularly for the past several years," he concedes, " but all the legal necessaries are fulfilled. Everything is up to date." And now, as he says, "It is her music that provides the income to fund other projects; income from the important copyrights that are finally in order now." Much of the work the foundation has accomplished is costly—for example, the commissioning of precise transcriptions of many of her compositions that had not been available before, pieces such as the radiant 1968 big-band version of "Aries" (a.k.a. "Knowledge"); the "Variations on Stardust" written for Harold Baker and the Ellington band in 1943; "Waltz Boogie," a masterwork; and her bass clarinet version of "Oo-bla-dee."

Marian Turner points out, "People might have thought there was a large legacy—and there wasn't. Producing the transcriptions and, before that, getting her music transferred from acetates onto the modern equipment—all of that costs a great deal. So does organizing her music and putting on concerts, like an important one with the American Jazz Orchestra." While alienated from O'Brien, especially by what they consider the harsh and arrogant way with which he treated Mary at times, his detractors do not dispute that his efforts on her behalf have been prodigious. Acknowledges Mary's friend Louis Ruffulo, "Despite his personal life, Peter did work like hell for her at the beginning and even at the end, as long as she lived, to do the best he possibly could for her."

Is the Mary Lou Williams Foundation fulfilling its mandate? Opinions remain divided. "The money was to be spent on talent, for children, for scholarships," insists her friend Bernice Daniels. Others point out what O'Brien has accomplished in preserving Mary's musical heritage, and O'Brien himself talks of the difficulty and expense of finding suitable students, adding that since the foundation has become more flush, it has recently been able to make grants for children's jazz programming in New Jersey.

It should be abundantly clear by this point that Mary was a tenacious dreamer of dreams, a spinner of gold from flax, a most impractical person who lived her dream against great odds. In short, an artist. She had a grand vision—to rescue poor, musically gifted children from dreariness and defeat in the same way that music had provided a way out of poverty and despair for "the little piano girl of East Liberty." Yet to fulfill this vision she left only a modest legacy. And at the time of her death, a great deal of her own music was falling into obscurity. One could well argue, as O'Brien does, that Mary's vision is better served by using that legacy to preserve her music, which in turn can act as a beacon for young musicians. Certainly it would be a terrible waste and shame to lose the luminous body of work that she produced, music that can be a standard bearer for creative musical minds to come.

Without question, through his hard work O'Brien has ensured that

Mary Lou Williams's music will not prove to have been ephemeral but will remain an accessible part of America's legacy. He is frequently a guiding hand and a contributor to the growing number of events that celebrate her—symposia, carefully crafted concerts (including, since 1995, an annual Mary Lou Williams Jazz Festival at the Kennedy Center in Washington, D.C.), museum exhibits, panel discussions, radio broadcasts, previously unreleased recordings, and so on. His presence at such events lends depth and a breadth of understanding of Mary Lou Williams the musician and Mary the human being.

Some artists learn their trade and then carry on with little variation for the rest of their lives. Others—and we know these are rare—are passionately engaged in self-discovery, in metamorphosis, in an often surprising, sometimes dangerous journey. Mary was this rare kind of artist.

Unpredictable, increasingly uninterested in placating the marketplace, such artists as Mary Lou Williams predictably confuse, anger, and even alienate that part of their audience yearning for the known quantity—for jazz fans, it is the hummable tune, the predictable variations. Yet to those who esteem the great tightrope adventure of art, Mary provides proof, as her music and her motives changed and deepened, that there is no one so interesting as the person who completely engages her soul in her work. As Peter O'Brien puts it, "She would have something to say, and then she was finished. And she had to wait until the creative thing came again."

Or as Mary herself said, looking back at the end, "I did it, didn't I? Through muck and mud."

Acknowledgments

IN THE JOURNEY that turned an idea into this book, I was guided by the good counsel and knowledge of extraordinary people. I wish to thank them all. First, Mary Lou Williams's personal manager, Father Peter F. O'Brien, S.J., who shared so many hours and insights with me, meticulously chronicling his unparalleled trove of memories of Mary Lou Williams's music and life. He also gave me unrestricted access to her large archive of papers, including letters, diaries, photos, and transcripts of interviews he made after her death with many of her friends and family. These include those with: Dr. Sam and Mrs. Marge Atkinson; Howard Burley; Father John Dear, S.J.; Father Vincent O'Keefe, S.J.; Father Frank O'Connor, S.J.; Doc Cheatham; Brother Mario (Grady Hancock); Conchita "Niki" Nikitani; Buttercup Powell; Irving "Mouse" Randolph and Henrietta Randolph; Anna Mae Riser; Willis Scruggs; Hilton Ruiz; Martha Salemme; John Williams (bassist); and Claude "Fiddler" Williams (also interviewed by Chuck Haddix for the Oral History Project for the Smithsonian Institution). For all Peter O'Brien's help, I am deeply grateful.

Mary's family also opened their doors to me. (A family reunion dinner in Pittsburgh one hot summer day ranks among the best barbecue I've tasted.) For sharing their store of memories and memorabilia about their beloved Mary, who may have moved to New York and then Durham, North Carolina, but never completely left Pittsburgh, thanks to: her sisters Geraldine Garnett and Marge Burley, her nieces Helen Floyd, Dorothy Rollins, and Bobbie Ann Ferguson, and her grand-niece Karen Rollins. In Philadelphia, to Geraldine Stokes Williams, who pieced together a family genealogy. To Mary's sister-in-law Ruth "Reeny" Burley in New York, widow of Mary's brother Jerry. In Columbus, Ohio, the late John Williams, Mary's first husband, assisted by his friend Andy Klein, gave me more great barbecue, recalling at ninety years old, with crystal-clear accuracy, dates and events from the 1920s on.

Mary had many champions, and a talent for keeping friends. In no particular order, I wish to thank them for their generosity. To M. Gray Weingarten, a long-time friend of Mary's who provided valuable nuggets from the Golden Age of Jazz and helped put order to the music as well. To Joyce Breach, Mary's confidante and great fan for many decades, for exuberant talk, unflagging support, and beautiful Mary memorabilia. To Marsha Vick and her husband, Paul Vick, in Durham, North Carolina, who gave me southern hospitality, memories of Mary's years while artist-in-residence at Duke University, and especially to Marsha for sharing the journal she kept during Mary's last year and a half of life. To Johnnie Gary, whose candor and humor about Café Society days lit up the 1940s. To Lorraine Gillespie, Mary's close friend and fellow convert to Catholicism, who laid aside her usual reticence to talk about Mary. To Barry Ulanov, Mary's friend both musically and spiritually, for a highly insightful conversation. To Bernice Daniels, for her memories spanning many decades, and also for her astringent humor. To Elaine Lorillard, a steadfast admirer of Mary's music and a free-spirited commentator on her life. To Jean Bach, another great lady, for the same. To Gemma Biggi for filling in the later Village period. To the Blisses—father Herbert, Mary's attorney, and sons John and Matthew, who came of age in the 1970s hearing Mary play at the Cookery. To John Graziano and to Louis Ruffulo, for their candor—and thanks as well, John, for the photos. Also thank you to Chris Albertson, Gary Giddins, David Hadju, Phil Schaap, Lewis Porter, Jim C. Hall, Chuck Pickeral, Phil Schaap, Loren Schoenberg, D. Antoinette Handy, Eileen Egan, Lance Carter, Edward Flanagan, Delilah Jackson, Patricia Willard, Dr. Frank Kessler, Phyl Garland, Helen Keese, and others too numerous to include here.

Many musicians were Mary's friends as well as admirers and gave generously of their time, particularly in sharing memories about the music. Many thanks to: pianists Marian McPartland and Dr. Billy Taylor; saxophonist Harold Arnold for filling in details about Mary's band with "Shorty" Baker in the mid-1940s; vocalist Al Hibbler, who was in the Ellington band in 1943 along with Mary. And for insight into her European sojourn in the 1950s, thanks to: vocalist Annie Ross, drummer Gérard "Dave" Pochonet, and pianist Aaron Bridgers. Also thanks to bassists Carline Ray and Brian Torff, both of whom played with Mary often. And to pianists Bob Rodriguez and Joel Simpson, who helped me with technical questions.

I was given invaluable help by everyone at the Institute of Jazz Studies at Rutgers University's Newark campus, where the Mary Lou Williams Archive is housed. Thanks especially to director Dan Morgenstern, music librarian Vincent Pelote, and archivist Tad Hershorn. At Duke University in Durham, university personnel were gracious, and thanks in particular to: Mrs. Marian Turner, retired secretary of the Music Department and Mary's friend at the end of her life, and to Robert E. Ward and Paul Bryan, both of whom were with the Music Department when Mary was alive, for helping to elucidate Mary's progress on her last major, unfinished composition. Thanks to the Ellington Archive at the Smithsonian Institution, above all to Annie Kuebler for her patient and meticulous work in identifying

Mary's manuscripts there. To Suzanne Egglestone, Public Services Librarian at Yale University, for help with the Benny Goodman Papers. Last but not least, my appreciation to Phyllis Keaton, library director of the Brewster Public Library, and the library staff, for cheerfully locating carloads of books for me.

So many people contribute, immeasurably so, to the written "life" of a fabulous person such as Mary Lou Williams. Yet at some point, the writer has to go it alone, and then it can seem at once an exhilarating challenge and a lonesome job, as taxing on muscle and nerve as running a marathon or scaling a cliff. For their understanding, forbearance, and support of me during the "Mary Lou" years, I owe a particular thank-you to my friends, to all in my family, my sisters, brothers, and in-laws, and especially to my mother, Marilyn Decamp Dahl, for their understanding, forbearance, and support. To my stepson Tim and my daughter Katrina, my chief cheerleaders, and above all, to my husband, A. J. Vogl, for his good and wise counsel and selfless wielding of the red pencil. Finally, thanks to my faithful friend and agent, Susan Zeckendorf, and to the people of Pantheon, especially to the peerless Bob Gottlieb, who shepherded this book home.

Sources and Notes

MARY LOU WILLIAMS'S own writings and voluminous personal papers, a group of lengthy published interviews, and many oral interviews of family, friends, and musicians conducted by the author or others, and used with their permission, constitute the main sources for this book (see Acknowledgments).

Mary Lou Williams wrote a series of eleven autobiographical articles, called *Mary Lou Williams: My Life with the Kings of Jazz*, edited by Max Jones, that appeared in *Melody Maker* magazine from April to June of 1954. They have been reprinted since in various books and are identified in the notes as: M/M.

She also wrote an incomplete autobiography she called *Zoning the History of Jazz*, plus many other fragments and sections of drafts in her notebooks, all of which are identified in the notes as: ZONE.

Some important interviews quoted from (followed by their identifying abbreviations) include:

Whitney Balliett, "Out Here Again," *The New Yorker*, May 4, 1964 (OHA).

Stan Britt, a 1978 interview, "First Lady of Jazz," *Jazz Journal*, September 1, 1981 (BRITT).

D. Antoinette Handy, "Conversation with Mary Lou Williams," *The Black Perspective in Music*, vol. 8, n. 2 (Fall 1980) (HANDY).

Will Moyles, radio interview, "The Essence of Jazz," Buffalo, N.Y., February 18, 1977 (MOYLES).

Martha Oneppo, Yale University Oral History American Music Series, March 16–17, 1981 (YALE).

John S. Wilson's interview for the National Endowment of the Arts/Institute of Jazz Studies (WILSON/IJS).

1. *My Mama Pinned a Rose on Me*

p. 8   **"My mama pinned . . ."**   Lyric to "The Blues," on *My Mama Pinned a Rose on Me*, Pablo CD 2310-819.

p. 9   **"You see these things . . ."**   WILSON/IJS.

p. 9   **"I was born . . ."**   ZONE.

p. 10   **"Both my great-grandparents . . ."**   Arnold Shaw, *The Street That Never Slept* (New York: Coward, McCann & Geoghegan, 1971), pp. 223–24.

p. 14   **"I've had a lot . . ."**   OHA.

p. 15   **So separate was . . .**   Correspondence with the author, March 3, 1995.

p. 17   **"I must have frightened . . ."**   ZONE (M/M April 3, 1954).

p. 17   **"I never left the piano . . ."**   Owen Coyle, "Mary Lou Williams and the Jazz Crusade," *The Mississippi Rag*, 3(1976):16.

p. 17   **"My half-brother would . . ."**   Lynn Gilbert and Gaylen Moore, *Particular Passions* (New York: Clarkson N. Potter, 1981), p. 79.

2. *The Little Piano Girl of East Liberty*

p. 20   **"Almost everywhere white labor . . ."**   John Hope Franklin, *From Slavery to Freedom*, ed. Alfred A. Moss (New York: McGraw-Hill, 1998), p. 493.

p. 23   **Her very first professional gig . . .**   Naomi Jolles, *New York Post*, December 11, 1944.

p. 23   **"I was out booking my gigs . . ."**   MLW quoted in Joanne Burke's documentary film, *Music on My Mind*, released 1981.

p. 25   **"And he sometimes took me . . ."**   ZONE (M/M).

p. 26   **"He told me always to play the left hand louder . . ."**   WILSON/IJS.

p. 26   **"None of the original pianists . . ."**   David Jasen and Trebor Jay Tichenor, *Rags and Ragtime* (New York: Seabury Press, 1978), p. 6.

p. 27   **"You don't get the feeling . . ."**   WILSON/IJS.

p. 27   **"I had to see things for myself . . ."**   Gilbert and Moore, *Particular Passions*, p. 85.

p. 29   **"You can imagine my surprise . . ."**   BRITT.

p. 29   **"During the summer . . ."**   WILSON/IJS.

p. 31   **After graduating from . . .**   Located by Lance Carter, Activities Director, Westinghouse High School, Pittsburgh, Pa., 1996.

p. 32   **Mary was suitably impressed . . .**   HANDY.

p. 32   **If Mary had completed . . .**   Per David Hadju, transcription of talk by Billy Strayhorn to the Duke Ellington Society in 1962.

p. 33   **"They gave me $10 . . ."**   Earl Hines to Barry Ulanov in Frank Joseph, "We Got Jazz!" *Pittsburgh Magazine*, October 1979.

p. 35   **But black musicians . . .**   Leonore R. Elkus, ed., *Famous Men and Women of Pittsburgh* (Pittsburgh: History and Landmarks Foundation, 1981).

3. *Hits 'n Bits*

p. 39   **"It was terrible . . ."**   YALE.

p. 45   **"I was playing saxophone . . ."**   Interview by Peter O'Brien, 1995.

p. 46   **"My husband would say . . ."**   WILSON/IJS.

p. 47   **"You come out with . . ."**   Coyle, *Mississippi Rag.*

p. 51   **"There was a musician friend . . ."**   MOYLES.

p. 52   **"Almost immediately I was stopped . . ."**   M/M.

p. 55   **Gunther Schuller agrees . . .**   Gunther Schuller, *The Swing Era* (New York: Oxford University Press, 1991), pp. 351–52.

p. 56   **"I played the entire show . . ."**   M/M.

p. 62   **"Holder's boys rehearsed . . ."**   M/M.

4. *Nite Life*

p. 65   **"To get around that . . ."**   Frank Driggs, "My Story, by Andy Kirk," *Jazz Review,* February 1959.

p. 65   **"This was the most . . ."**   WILSON/IJS.

p. 69   **"We didn't even know . . ."**   Andy Kirk as told to Amy Lee, *Twenty Years on Wheels* (Ann Arbor: University of Michigan Press, 1990), p. 60.

p. 71   **"No other city . . ."**   Dave Dexter, liner notes, *The Best of Andy Kirk,* MCA 2-4105.

p. 71   **"In Kansas City it was like . . ."**   Kirk, *Twenty Years on Wheels.*

p. 72   **"It was the first time . . ."**   Gary Giddins, "Mary Lou Williams 1910–1981," *Village Voice,* June 10, 1998.

p. 73   **They auditioned us . . .**   Kirk, *Twenty Years on Wheels,* pp. 70–71.

p. 74   **"But the boys . . ."**   M/M.

p. 76   **"The next night . . ."**   ZONE (early draft only).

p. 77   **"Don Redman was my model . . ."**   OHA.

p. 78   **A reviewer lauds . . .**   Dick Raichelson, *The Territories, Volume One,* Arcadia LP 2006.

p. 81   **"I told her . . ."**   Kirk to Chip Deffaa, *In the Mainstream* (Metuchen, N.J.: Scarecrow Press, 1992), p. 87.

p. 82   **"She had a set of ears . . ."**   Kirk to Dick Sudhalter, Mary Lou Williams obituary, *New York Post.*

5. *Walkin' and Swingin'*

p. 85   **"When Kirk came backstage . . ."**   YALE.

p. 85   **"I just loved it . . ."**   Ibid.

p. 86   **"The word went round . . ."**   M/M.

p. 87   **"I didn't hang around . . ."**   Count Basie as told to Albert Murray, *Good Morning Blues* (New York: Random House, 1985), p. 110.

SOURCES AND NOTES 387

p. 87   "When we arrived . . ."   Pete Johnson, *Jazz Journal,* August 1959.

p. 88   "If they were looking . . ."   Count Basie, *Good Morning Blues,* p. 149.

p. 88   "At set's end . . ."   Dave Dexter, *Billboard* magazine, June 13, 1981.

p. 88   "She had a good ear . . ."   Kirk, *Twenty Years on Wheels,* p. 73.

p. 90   "Actor Dick Powell . . ."   *Seventeen* magazine, 1947, article in MLW papers.

p. 94   "Ben Webster was the type of guy . . ."   WILSON/IJS.

p. 94   "I needed a fourth saxophone . . ."   Interview on KUON-TV, Nebraska Educational Television, 1980.

6. *Silk Stockings*

p. 98   "By 1937 and thereafter . . ."   Schuller, *The Swing Era*, p. 353.

p. 99   "If I passed out an arrangement . . ."   YALE.

p. 99   "odd, beautifully constructed . . ."   OHA.

p. 100   "frequent unison playing . . ."   Erica Kaplan, "The Lady Who Swings the Band," Jazz Research Papers #9 (1989).

p. 100   "Built on jam sessionlike riffs . . ."   Liner notes, Decca CD GRD-2-641, *Black Legends of Jazz.*

p. 103   "When we first began to hit . . ."   WILSON/IJS.

p. 104   "Joe Glaser was the most . . ."   Max Gordon, *Live at the Village Vanguard* (New York: St. Martin's Press, 1980), pp. 78–83.

p. 105   "I didn't like Joe . . ."   Kirk to Deffaa, *In the Mainstream,* p. 82.

p. 106   "There was nothing you could do . . ."   Ibid.

p. 106   "When I used to play 'Froggy Bottom,' . . ."   Mary to Eric Townley, *Mississippi Rag,* January 1980.

p. 106   "Andy Kirk said to me . . ."   YALE.

p. 106   "I was very high strung . . ."   Quoted in John S. Wilson, Mary Lou Williams obituary, *New York Times,* May 30, 1981.

p. 107   "Arranger Mary Lou Williams . . ."   Schuller, *The Swing Era,* p. 353.

p. 107   "little that is really unexpected . . ."   Albert McCarthy, *Big Band Jazz* (London: Royce Publications, 1974), p. 244.

p. 107   "I did 20 things . . ."   MOYLES.

p. 108   "letters like lyrical talking notes . . ."   Ibid.

p. 109   "The studios have always typed . . ."   Morroe Berger, Edward Berger, and James Patrick, *Benny Carter: A Life in American Music,* vol. 1 (Metuchen, N.J.: Scarecrow Press, 1982), p. 276.

p. 109   "I was writing . . ."   MOYLES.

p. 109   "Whenever musicians listened . . ."   M/M.

p. 110   "Usually, we'd play five or six arrangements . . ."   Benny Goodman, quoted in Gary Giddins, *Village Voice,* June 10, 1981.

p. 115   "I was one of the first . . ."   M/M.

p. 116   "I learned how to accompany . . ."   Jimmy Rowles, quoted in Whitney Balliett, *Night Creature* (New York: Oxford University Press, 1981), pp. 153–54.

7. Why Go On Pretending?

p. 117   **"We arrived in most places . . ."**   M/M.

p. 121   **"June [Richmond] . . . was the cause . . ."**   Kirk, *Twenty Years on Wheels,* p. 110.

8. Trumpets No End

p. 126   **"We rehearsed the new outfit . . ."**   M/M.

p. 127   **"Then," Mary went on . . .**   WILSON/IJS.

p. 130   **"This particular time . . ."**   YALE.

p. 131   **she was paid $100 . . .**   Payroll records in the Ellington Archive of the Smithsonian Institution in Washington, D.C.

p. 131   **"Duke," Mary reminisced . . .**   BRITT.

p. 131   **His way of writing voicings . . .**   MOYLES.

p. 131   **"Sometimes there was a mistake . . ."**   Gilbert and Moore, *Particular Passions,* p. 86.

p. 132   **"Mary Lou Williams is perpetually . . ."**   Duke Ellington, *Music Is My Mistress* (Garden City, N.Y.: Doubleday & Co., 1973), p. 169.

p. 133   **"Harold called me . . ."**   MOYLES.

p. 134   **Mary performed for . . .**   Jolles, *New York Post,* December 11, 1944.

p. 134   **"I moved around . . ."**   M/M.

9. Café Society Blues

p. 137   **"our first political nightclub . . ."**   Helen Lawrenson, *Whistling Girl* (Garden City, N.Y.: Doubleday & Co., 1978), pp. 86, 89.

p. 139   **"The way they are treating my people . . ."**   Quoted in Mary L. Dudziak, "Josephine Baker, Racial Protest, and the Cold War," *Journal of American History,* September 1994.

p. 139   **"My friends thought . . ."**   Wambly Bald, "A Gamble on Race Equality That Paid Off," *New York Post,* November 4, 1946.

p. 140   **"Not only were Reds . . ."**   David W. Stowe, *Swing Changes: Big Band Jazz in New Deal America* (Cambridge: Harvard University Press, 1994), p. 67.

p. 142   **"On my way down to the club . . ."**   WILSON/IJS.

p. 143   **"Mary Lou was very self-effacing . . ."**   Phyl Garland, "The Lady Lives Jazz," *Ebony,* October 1979.

p. 144   **"Hammond himself said . . ."**   James Lincoln Collier, *Benny Goodman and the Swing Era* (New York: Oxford University Press, 1989), pp. 99–100.

p. 145   **Another review of Mary . . .**   Jolles, *New York Post,* 1944.

p. 148   **"full of joys . . ."**   Eric Thacker, *The Essential Jazz Records,* 1984.

p. 151 **"was the first visual artist . . ."** Obituary for David Stone Martin, *New York Times,* 1992.

p. 151 **Martin went on to illustrate . . .** Manek Daver, *David Stone Martin, Jazz Graphics* (Tokyo, Japan: Graphic-Sha Publishing Co., 1991).

p. 152 **"I can't keep husbands . . ."** *New York Post* article, 1945, clipping from MLW files.

10. *The Zodiac Suite*

p. 159 **"I wrote 'Scorpio,' . . ."** Dan Morgenstern, liner notes, *Signs of the Zodiac,* Folkways LP FTS 32844.

p. 160 **"many pedal-point ostinatos . . ."** Andrew Homzy, liner notes, *The Zodiac Suite,* Vintage Jazz Classics CD 1035.

p. 164 **It was at this point . . .** Carter Harman, unidentified newspaper article about Mary's long appearance at the Village Vanguard, fall of 1949, in MLW papers.

p. 165 **"Stylistically the suite . . ."** Richard Thompson, "Mary Lou Williams: Zodiac Suite, a Critical Analysis," undated academic paper archived at Institute of Jazz Studies, Rutgers University, Newark, N.J.

p. 166 **"The long, drawn-out strings . . ."** M/M.

p. 167 **"This is the way music . . ."** Barry Ulanov, unidentified review in MLW papers.

p. 167 **"Fortunately," agreed another . . .** *Record Review,* no byline or date, in MLW papers.

p. 167 **"when she turns to composing . . ."** Colin McPhee, "The Torrid Zone," *Modern Music* 23 (Winter 1946).

p. 168 **"As pure instrumental music . . ."** Homzy, liner notes to *The Zodiac Suite,* VJC-1035.

p. 168 **With the exception of "Capricorn" . . .** Thompson, "Mary Lou Williams: Zodiac."

p. 172 **"Being determined . . ."** M/M.

p. 172 **"I said, 'Oh my goodness' . . ."** WILSON/IJS.

p. 173 **The next day, June 22 . . .** Program notes to Carnegie Hall concert, in MLW papers.

p. 175 **"My Carnegie Hall recording . . ."** Carbon copy, letter to Bernard Stollman, her then attorney, August 6, 1961.

p. 176 **"One of my greatest ambitions . . ."** Mary Lou Williams, "Music and Progress," *Jazz Record,* November 1947.

11. *Kool*

p. 177 **"If we are to make . . ."** Mary Lou Williams, "Music and Progress," *Jazz Record,* November 1947.

p. 178 **"We forget how . . ."** Eric Lott, "Double V, Double-Time, Bebop's Politics of Style," *Jazz Among the Discourses*, ed. Krin Gabbard (Durham, N.C.: Duke University Press, 1995), p. 245.

p. 179 **"an enormous variety of . . ."** Erica Kaplan, National Association of Jazz Education Research Papers #9.

p. 182 **"her bop recordings . . ."** Gary Giddins, "Mary Lou and That Mannish Thing," *Village Voice,* June 20, 1975.

p. 182 **"All the bop musicians . . ."** WILSON/IJS.

p. 183 **"'Leeches' would scribble . . ."** M/M.

p. 183 **"When a woman is on the scene . . ."** Leslie Gourse, *Madame Jazz* (New York: Oxford University Press, 1995), p. 28.

p. 183 **But little did Josephson know . . .** Chip Deffaa, *In the Mainstream*, p. 36.

p. 185 **Mary herself never tried heroin . . .** See *Variety*, February 24, 1965.

p. 185 **"After finishing work . . ."** MLW notebooks, edited version in M/M.

p. 187 **"Everything went along . . ."** MLW diary.

p. 187 **"She made them [Powell and Monk] . . ."** Ira Gitler, *Swing to Bop: An Oral History of the Transition of Jazz in the 1940s* (New York: Oxford University Press, 1987), p. 103.

p. 189 **"If you touch someone . . ."** MOYLES.

p. 190 **"When Bud came to me . . ."** BRITT.

p. 190 **"Whatever people may tell you . . ."** M/M.

p. 190 **"There's no precedent . . ."** WILSON/IJS.

p. 190 **"Thelonious is a nice guy . . ."** YALE.

p. 191 **"In the forties," notes Whitney Balliett . . .** OHA.

p. 192 **"Nowhere does Mary Lou . . ."** Gitler, *Swing to Bop*, p. 105.

p. 193 **"I had Monk write . . ."** MOYLES.

12. *Benny's Bop*

p. 195 **"Charlie and I used to play . . ."** M/M.

p. 196 **"that Benny is building . . ."** D. Russell Connor, *Benny Goodman: Listen to His Legacy* (Metuchen, N.J.: Scarecrow Press, 1988), p. 178.

p. 196 **"jarred his ear. . . ."** George Simon, "Benny Blows Bop," *Metronome*, August 1948.

p. 196 **"Benny had scoffed . . ."** Ross Firestone, *Swing, Swing, Swing: The Life and Times of Benny Goodman* (New York: W. W. Norton, 1993), p. 339.

p. 196 **"Eventually Williams persuaded . . ."** Collier, *Benny Goodman and the Swing Era*, p. 326.

p. 198 **"of course, very enthusiastic . . ."** Simon, *Metronome*, August 1948.

p. 200 **Negotiations to end the recording ban . . .** Loren Schoenberg, liner notes to *Complete Capitol Small Groups of Benny Goodman, 1944–55*, Mosaic CD MD4148.

p. 201   **"receiving a last-minute . . ."**   Ibid.

p. 202   **"It is unbelievable . . ."**   Excerpt from Joe Glaser letter in MLW papers.

13. *Walkin' Out the Door*

p. 204   **"No other pianist male or female . . ."**   Barry Ulanov, unidentified review, circa 1949, in MLW papers.

p. 204   **"A brilliant musician . . ."**   Sharon Pease, "MLW Still Rated Top Femme Pianist," *Downbeat*, November 2, 1951.

p. 204   **"How many Negro performers . . ."**   Unidentified newspaper article, 1957, in MLW papers.

p. 205   **"It seems no one can sing it . . ."**   Ibid.

p. 208   **Apparently he had other talents . . .**   M/M, May 22, 1954.

p. 211   **"I realize she has been . . ."**   Carbon copy of letter in MLW papers.

p. 211   **The Vanguard engagement . . .**   Review in *Time*, September 12, 1949.

p. 211   **"When she comes on . . ."**   Review in *International Musician*, 1949, clip in MLW papers.

p. 211   **"I always had bop ideas . . ."**   Quoted by Carter Harman, unidentified newspaper clip in MLW papers.

p. 219   **"a terrific engagement . . ."**   WILSON/IJS.

14. *Chez Mary Lou*

p. 225   **"nothing less than a revelation . . ."**   Max Jones, M/M, December 19, 1953.

p. 227   **she "was bitterly disappointed . . ."**   Undated clipping from *New Musical Express,* in MLW papers.

p. 229   **"As Mary Lou has . . ."**   Jones, M/M, September 26, 1953.

p. 235   **"Actually I'm the only . . ."**   "Mary Lou Still Learning, Teaching and Progressing," clip from unidentified Chicago newspaper, December 12, 1952, in MLW papers.

p. 236   **"But," adds Aaron Bridgers . . .**   Pianist Aaron Bridgers, correspondence with the author, 1996, from Paris.

p. 236   **"Le Boeuf sur le Toit seemed . . ."**   Chris Goddard, *Jazz Away from Home* (London: Paddington Press, 1979), p. 117.

p. 236   **"It's a place where . . ."**   WILSON/IJS.

p. 236   **"a remarkable pianist . . ."**   Unidentified clip in MLW papers.

p. 237   **"That offbeat can . . ."**   Helen and Stanley Dance, M/M, January 10, 1953.

p. 237   **"I didn't feel that way at all . . ."**   MOYLES.

p. 238   **"The poor lil drummer . . ."**   Mary Lou Williams, "What I Learned from God about Jazz," *Sepia*, April 1958.

p. 239   **"Quite amazing," she added . . .**   Carbon copy of a letter to Stuart Sprague, August 1955. Sprague was then her attorney.

p. 239   **"I was in my hotel room . . ."**   Ibid.

p. 241   **"I'm sure that I was on my way . . ."**   Mary Lou Williams, "What I Learned . . ." *Sepia*, April 1958.

p. 241   **"Life looked mean and ugly . . ."**   Carbon copy of a letter addressed simply to "Dan," one of several long missives circa 1957–58.

p. 241   **"I'd pray and thank God . . ."**   Ibid.

p. 242   **"gained some spiritual strength . . ."**   Mary Lou Williams, "What I Learned . . ." *Sepia*, April 1958.

15. *Praying Through My Fingertips*

p. 246   **"She's back in America . . ."**   *Downbeat*, April 20, 1955.

p. 246   **"This collection makes up . . ."**   Peter Russell, *Jazz Journal*, December 1959.

p. 248   **"I cooked for them . . ."**   *People*, May 12, 1980.

p. 254   **As for the Gillespies, . . .**   Ibid.

p. 254   **"Birdland's vibrations are . . ."**   Carbon copy of letter to Maxwell Cohen in MLW papers.

p. 259   **"She has the beauty . . ."**   Father Woods, quoted in Marian McPartland, "Into the Sun," *Downbeat*, August 27, 1964. Reprinted in McPartland, *All in Good Time* (New York: Oxford University Press, 1987), and in Frank Alkyer and John McDonough, eds., *Downbeat: Sixty Years of Jazz* (Milwaukee: Hal Leonard Corp., 1995).

p. 263   **Though Mary made a strong showing . . .**   Gary Giddins, liner notes to *Masters of the Jazz Piano*, Verve 2-2514.

16. *Black Christ of the Andes*

p. 271   **"It's the suffering . . ."**   *Newsweek*, December 20, 1971.

p. 273   **"If anyone is capable . . ."**   F. Anthony Woods, unidentified newspaper clip in MLW files.

p. 275   **"The tenors and basses . . ."**   Gayle Murcheson, "Black Christ of the Andes: St. Martin de Porres," research paper read at Sonneck Society Convention, Worcester, Mass., April 1994.

p. 276   **"St. Martin was neither fish nor fowl . . ."**   Fran Goulart, *Sounds and Fury*, December 1965.

p. 277   **Like Woods, Crowley, and other priests . . .**   William D. Miller, *Dorothy Day: A Biography* (New York: Harper & Row, 1982), p. 479.

p. 279   **If the rhythm section . . .**   Marian McPartland, "Into the Sun," in *All in Good Time*, and in Alkyer and McDonough, *Downbeat*.

p. 280   **"We've got to think . . ."**   HANDY.

p. 280   **"I said, 'No . . .' "**   Ibid.

p. 282   **"It's like Father Woods said. . . ."**   Pittsburgh newspaper, unidentified, MLW clipping file.

p. 282   **"Miss Williams has a pair of brilliant solos . . ."**   *High Fidelity,* October 1966.

p. 284   **"My piano faced the door. . . ."**   YALE.

p. 284   **"He kept looking up at me . . ."**   HANDY.

p. 288   **She had, of course, long been . . .**   Mary Lou Williams, "Music Can Help Youth," *People's Voice,* June 1, 1946.

p. 290   **"From Suffering came the Negro spirituals . . ."**   Mary Lou Williams program notes for "New Concepts in Jazz," concert at Philharmonic Hall, Lincoln Center, New York, November 1962.

p. 292   **"I had lost my inspiration . . ."**   John S. Wilson, "Mary Lou Takes Her Jazz Mass to Church," *New York Times,* February 9, 1975.

p. 293   **"It was long, drawn out . . ."**   John S. Wilson, *New York Times,* February 18, 1975.

p. 295   **"He asked me, again . . ."**   BRITT.

p. 295   **"8/21/67 . . . Dearest Duke: . . ."**   Carbon copy of letter to Duke Ellington in MLW files.

p. 296   **"She would write arrangements . . ."**   Brian Q. Torff, "Mary Lou Williams: A Woman's Life in Jazz," in James R. Heintze, ed., *Profiles in American Music Since 1950* (New York and London: Garland Publishing Co., 1999).

p. 297   **There were as well . . .**   Ruth and Duke Ellington Collections, Duke Ellington Archive, Smithsonian Institution, Washington, D.C.

p. 297   **Though the tempo . . .**   The two "Chief" lead sheets by Mary in the rock and jazz versions, and the corresponding parts in Ellington's *The River* and *UWIS Suite,* have been analyzed by Peter O'Brien and the author, and by Annie Kiebler at the Duke Ellington Archive at the Smithsonian Institution. An incomplete score in Mary's hand is also at the Ellington Archive, in the "Loco" and "Madi" files for the third movement of *UWIS.*

17. *Zoning*

p. 304   **"Cardinal Angelo Dell'Acqua . . ."**   Associated Press release, February 3, 1969, in MLW papers.

p. 309   **"So Peter hid behind a tree . . ."**   John S. Wilson, *New York Times,* February 9, 1975.

p. 324   **"written for the kids . . ."**   MOYLES.

p. 324   **As for "Medi II," . . .**   Erica Kaplan, Jazz Research Papers #9.

p. 324   **"joyful, lifting pulse . . ."**   John S. Wilson, *High Fidelity,* November 1974.

p. 327   **"*They* don't have to swing. . . ."**   John S. Wilson, *New York Times,* February 9, 1975.

p. 328   **"I could not believe . . ."**   Brian Torff, "Mary Lou Williams," *Profiles in American Music.*

p. 331   **"We were sold into slavery . . ."**   Mary Lou Williams, "Has the Black American Musician Lost His Creativeness and Heritage in Jazz?" unpublished essay, circa 1970.

p. 332   **"When I first got to Duke . . ."**   Jacqueline Trescott, *Washington Post*, September 24, 1979.

p. 333   **"She was playing like Erroll Garner . . ."**   A. B. Spellman, *Four Lives in the Bebop Business* (New York: Pantheon Books, 1966), p. 56.

p. 333   **"He sat down one night . . ."**   BRITT.

p. 334   **"doubly innovative . . ."**   Gary Giddins, "Search for a Common Language," *New York Magazine*, April 18, 1977; revised version in *Riding on a Blue Note* (New York: Oxford University Press, 1981).

p. 334   **"When Cecil is doing his things . . ."**   Ibid.

p. 334   Mary **"wanted him to play . . ."**   Hollie West, *Washington Post*, April 18, 1977.

p. 335   **"The result was . . ."**   John S. Wilson, *New York Times*, April 19, 1977.

p. 335   **"When I was coming along . . ."**   Phyl Garland, "The Lady Lives Jazz."

p. 336   **"Cecil! Please listen . . ."**   Carbon copy of letter from MLW to Cecil Taylor, dated July 29, 1977, in MLW files.

18. *Artist-in-Residence*

p. 337   **"The possibility," as Tirro . . .**   Frank Tirro, *Summer Chronicle* (Duke University newspaper), May 19, 1977.

p. 338   **"Nowadays, whites down here . . ."**   BRITT.

p. 340   **"Rock puts you in a box . . ."**   MLW, "From Duke Ellington to Duke University, Mary Lou Williams Tells the World: Jazz Is Love," *People*, May 12, 1980.

p. 340   **"I'll write out a tune . . ."**   HANDY.

p. 340   **"We're living in a . . ."**   Quoted in Catherine O'Neill, "Swingers with a Mission," *Books and Arts*, December 7, 1979.

p. 340   **"Willie the Lion said . . ."**   Quoted from a 1977 interview in Len Lyons, *The Great Jazz Pianists* (New York: William Morrow, 1985), p. 345.

p. 345   **She constructed her solos . . .**   Jeff Simon, *Buffalo Evening News*, February 17, 1977.

p. 350   **"So many things you've done . . ."**   Carbon copy of letter to Leonard Feather, spring 1978.

p. 353   **"We're all happy . . ."**   Quoted in Rogers E.M. "Popsy" Whitaker (unsigned), "Talk of the Town," *The New Yorker*, May 14, 1979.

p. 353   an **"air of quiet confidence . . ."**   Ibid.

p. 354   the results of her . . . **biopsy . . .**   Per MLW's medical records, Duke University Medical Center, March 21, 1979, through May 15, 1981.

p. 355   **"You're living above your means . . ."**   MLW letter and cc in MLW files.

p. 362   **"The students sat quietly waiting . . ."**   Marsha Vick, log of conversations with and commentary on MLW, 1979–1981.

p. 369   **"When she later attributed . . ."**   Gary Giddins, MLW eulogy reprinted in *Village Voice,* June 10, 1981.

19. *The Mary Lou Williams Foundation*

p. 372   **"a means of accomplishing after my death . . ."**   Quoted in Marian Turner, minutes to Mary Lou Williams Foundation planning meeting, March 1981, in MLW papers.

p. 374   **a teaching job in the fall of 1981 . . .**   Susan Brioli, "Father O'Brien Will Teach Jazz of Mary Lou Williams," *Durham Sun,* September 17, 1981.

p. 374   **O'Brien was also receiving . . .**   Per Mary Lou Williams Foundation meeting minutes of June 1981, in MLW papers.

p. 376   **his "profound but needy relationship . . ."**   O'Brien letters in MLW papers.

A Selective Bibliography

Mary Lou Williams's Writings

PUBLISHED

Mary Lou Williams: My Life with the Kings of Jazz. Edited by Max Jones. Eleven auto-
biographical articles published in *Melody Maker* magazine, April–June 1954.
Most reprinted in Nat Shapiro and Nat Hentoff, eds. *Hear Me Talkin' to Ya* (New
York: Holt, Rinehart & Winston, 1955); Max Jones, *Talking Jazz* (New York:
W. W. Norton & Co., 1988); and Robert Gottlieb, ed. *Reading Jazz* (New York:
Pantheon Books, 1996).

"Music Can Help Youth." *People's Voice,* June 1, 1946.

"Music and Progress." *Jazz Record,* November 1947.

"What I Learned from God About Jazz." *Sepia,* April 1958.

Untitled essay on the origin and roots of jazz, in program notes for "New Concepts
in Jazz" concert at Philharmonic Hall, Lincoln Center, New York, November
1962.

UNPUBLISHED

Zoning the History of Jazz. Incomplete autobiography in several drafts.

"Why I Wrote the *Zodiac Suite.*" Circa 1945.

"Has the Black American Musician Lost His Creativeness and Heritage in Jazz?"
Circa 1970.

Writings Involving Mary Lou Williams

Balliett, Whitney. "Out Here Again." *The New Yorker,* May 4, 1964. Reprinted in Balliett, *Such Sweet Thunder* (New York: Bobbs-Merrill, 1966), and in *American
Musicians II: 72 Portraits in Jazz* (New York: Oxford University Press, 1996).

Briscoe, James R., ed. *Contemporary Anthology of Music by Women*. Bloomington: Indiana University Press, 1997. See companion CD, p. 412.

Britt, Stan. "First Lady of Jazz." *Jazz Journal*, September 1, 1981.

Dahl, Linda. *Stormy Weather: The Music and Lives of a Century of Jazzwomen*. New York: Pantheon Books, 1984. New York: Limelight Editions, 1989.

Fledderus, France. "The Function of Oral Tradition in Mary Lou's Mass by Mary Lou Williams." Master's music thesis, University of North Texas, 1996.

"From Duke Ellington to Duke University, Mary Lou Williams Tells the World: Jazz Is Love." *People*, May 12, 1980.

Garland, Phyl. "The Lady Lives Jazz." *Ebony*, October 1979.

Giddins, Gary. "Search for a Common Language." *Riding on a Blue Note*. New York: Oxford University Press, 1981.

———. "Mary Lou and That Mannish Thing." *Village Voice*, June 20, 1975.

———. "Mary Lou Williams 1910–1981." *Village Voice*, June 10, 1981.

Gilbert, Lynn, and Gaylen Moore. *Particular Passions*. New York: Clarkson N. Potter, 1981.

Gitler, Ira. *Swing to Bop: An Oral History of the Transition of Jazz in the 1940s*. New York: Oxford University Press, 1987.

Goldsmith, Peter D. *Making People's Music: Moe Asch and Folkways Records*. Washington, D.C.: Smithsonian Institution Press, 1998.

Hall, James C. "The Stewardship of Mary Lou Williams," in "There Is No Deed but Memory: African-American Antimodernism and the American Sixties." Ph.D. dissertation, University of Iowa (American Studies Program), 1992.

Handy, D. Antoinette. "Conversation with Mary Lou Williams." *The Black Perspective in Music* 8, n. 2 (Fall 1980).

Holmes, L. D., and J. W. Thomson. *Jazz Greats: Getting Better with Age*. New York: Holmes & Meier Publishers, 1986.

Kaplan, Erica. "The Lady Who Swings the Band." Jazz Research Papers #9 (1989).

Kernodle, Dr. Tammy L. "Anything You Are Shows Up in Your Music: Mary Lou Williams and the Sanctification of Jazz." Ph.D. dissertation, Ohio State University, 1997.

Kirk, Andy, as told to Amy Lee. *Twenty Years on Wheels*. Ann Arbor: University of Michigan Press, 1990.

Kufrin, Joan. *Uncommon Women*. Santa Barbara, Calif.: New Century Publishers, 1981.

Lyons, Len. *The Great Jazz Pianists*. New York: William Morrow & Co., 1985.

McPartland, Marian. "Into the Sun." *Downbeat*, August 27, 1964. Reprinted in McPartland, *All In Good Time* (New York: Oxford University Press, 1987); and in Frank Alkyer, ed., *Downbeat: 60 Years of Jazz* (Milwaukee: Hal Leonard Corp., 1995).

Murcheson, Gayle. "Black Christ of the Andes: St. Martin de Porres." Research paper read at Sonneck Society Convention, Worcester, Mass., April 1994.

Norvell, Derek. Untitled thesis on Mary Lou Williams, jazz, and spirituality. *Thesis* magazine (City University of New York), Spring 1992.

O'Brien, Peter, S.J. "Mary Lou Williams." Extensive essay, liner notes for Folkways Records Album no. 2966, reissue of Asch 1944–47, August 19, 1977.

Pickeral, Charles W. "The Masses of Mary Lou Williams: The Evolution of a Liturgical Style." Ph.D. dissertation, Texas Tech University, 1998; Ann Arbor UMI, 1998.

Placksin, Sally. *American Women in Jazz.* New York: Wideview Books, 1982.

Porter, Lewis. "You Can't Get Up There Timidly: Jazzwomen Part II." *Music Educators' Journal,* October 1984.

Schuller, Gunther. *The Swing Era: The Development of Jazz, 1930–1945.* New York: Oxford University Press, 1989.

Shaw, Arnold. *The Street That Never Slept.* New York: Coward, McCann & Geoghegan, 1971.

Thompson, Richard. "Mary Lou Williams: Zodiac Suite: A Critical Analysis." Undated paper, Institute of Jazz Studies, Rutgers University, Newark, N.J.

Torff, Brian Q. "Mary Lou Williams: A Woman's Life in Jazz." In *Profiles in American Music Since 1950,* edited by James R. Heintze. New York and London: Garland Publishing Co., 1999.

Ulanov, Barry. *A History of Jazz in America.* New York: Viking Press, 1952.

Unterbrink, Mary. *Jazz Women at the Keyboard.* Jefferson, N.C.: McFarland Press, 1983.

Whitaker, Rogers E. M. "Popsy" (unsigned). "Talk of the Town." *The New Yorker,* May 14, 1979.

Winter, Nina. *Interview with the Muse: Remarkable Women Speak on Creativity and Power.* Berkeley, Calif.: Moon Books, 1978.

Yampolsky, Carol Jane. "The Solo Piano Music of Three American Composers: Armando 'Chick' Corea, William 'Billy' Taylor, Mary Lou Williams: A Performance-Tape Project." DMA dissertation, University of Maryland, 1986.

Audio and Video

Burke, Joanne. *Music on my Mind.* Documentary film, 1981. Distributed through Women Make Movies, New York.

Flanagan, Edward. *I Have A Dream.* Documentary film, New York University Motion Picture Workshop, 1968.

Moyles, Will. Radio interview. "The Essence of Jazz." Buffalo, N.Y., February 18, 1977.

Oneppo, Martha. Interview for Yale University Oral History American Music Series, March 16–17, 1981.

Wilson, John S. Interview for the National Endowment of the Arts/Institute of Jazz Studies.

Reference Works

Carr, Ian; Digby Fairweather; and Brian Priestly. *The Rough Guide to Jazz.* New York: Viking Penguin, 1995.

Case, Brian, and Stan Britt. *The Illustrated Encyclopedia of Jazz*. New York: Harmony Books, 1978.

Cook, Richard, and Brian Morton, eds. *The Penguin Guide to Jazz on CD, LP and Cassette*. New York: Penguin Books, 1994.

Erlewine, Michael; Vladimir Bodganov; Chris Woodstra; and Scott Yanow, eds. *All Music Guide to Jazz*, 3rd ed. San Francisco: Miller Freeman Books, 1998.

Esquire Editors. *Esquire's World of Jazz*. Edited by George Simon. New York: Thomas Crowell, 1975.

Feather, Leonard. *The Encyclopedia of Jazz*. New York: Horizon Press, 1955, 1960, 1965.

————. *The Encyclopedia Yearbook of Jazz*. New York: Horizon Press, 1956.

Holtje, Steve, and Nancy Ann Lee, eds. *Music Hound Jazz: The Essential Album Guide*. Detroit: Visible Ink Press, 1998.

Kernfeld, Barry, ed. *The New Grove Dictionary of Jazz*. New York: St. Martin's Press, 1996.

A Selective Mary Lou Williams
Discography: 1927 to Present

"THERE SHOULD HAVE been fifty Moe Asches to record Mary," says Barry Ulanov about the legendary record producer, "but there was only one, and he only had a limited amount of money. It's to the eternal disgrace of the record companies that she was not recorded widely."

Mary was not easy to market after the 1940s. "Nobody can put a style on me," she said repeatedly. Admirers agreed. "She was an elusive pianist, a styleless pianist," noted Popsy Whitaker in *The New Yorker*, "a catalyst, a refractor, a mirror." Yet her very achievements in incorporating the successive styles of jazz earned her admiration but also made her harder to place. Her very *elusiveness* as a stylist, many critics seemed to imply, placed her just this side of greatness in the jazz pantheon. Happily, today's listeners can much more readily judge for themselves, because far more of Mary's music is currently available than ever before, including a number of previously unreleased recordings.

This selective discography is intended to be user-friendly rather than scholar-oriented and all-inclusive. In chronological order (according to date of recording, starting with the earliest), everything that is available on compact disc is listed first, followed by a *selective* list of vinyl (LP, EP, 78, 45) and tape (issued and unissued), where no CD exists of a performance. Finally, there are appendices of several other important sources of the work of Mary Lou Williams.

ABBREVIATIONS

arr	arranger	b-cl	bass-clarinet
as	alto saxophone	bgs	bongos
b	bass	bj	banjo
bars	baritone saxophone	bsn	bassoon
bb	brass bass (sousaphone/tuba)	cel	celeste

cgs	congas	o	oboe
cl	clarinet	or	organ
cond	conductor	p	piano
d	drums	sop	soprano saxophone
dir	director	t	trumpet
el-g	electric guitar	tb	trombone
f	flute	ts	tenor saxophone
flgh	fluegel horn	v	vocal
frh	French horn	vbs	vibraphone
g	guitar	vln	violin
MLW	Mary Lou Williams	wbd	washboard

Recordings by Mary Lou Williams on CDs

recorded: Chicago, ca. January 1927
Jeanette James and Her Synco Jazzers: MLW (as Mary Leo Burley) (p); Jeanette
  James (v); Henry McCord (t); Bradley Bullett (tb); John Williams (as, bars);
  Jo Williams (bj); Robert Price (d).
Midnight Stomp • The Bumps
Classics 630. Originally issued on Paramount.

_____

recorded: Chicago, February 1927
John Williams' Synco Jazzers: same personnel as above except Jeanette James out.
Down in Gallion • Goose Grease
Classics 630. Originally issued on Paramount.

_____

recorded: Chicago, ca. March 7, 1927
Personnel same as above.
Pee Wee Blues • Now Cut Loose
Classics 630. Originally issued on Gennett.

_____

recorded: Kansas City, ca. November 7, 1929
Andy Kirk and His Twelve Clouds of Joy: MLW (p, arr); Andy Kirk (bars, bb, dir);
  Gene Prince (t); Harry Lawson (t, v); Allen Durham (tb); John Harrington
  (cl, as); John Williams (as, bars); Lawrence Freeman (ts); Claude Williams
  (vln); William Dirvin (bj, g); Edward "Crackshot" McNeil (d).
Mess-A-Stomp • Blue Clarinet Stomp
Classics 655. Originally issued on Brunswick.

_____

recorded: Kansas City, ca. November 8, 1929
Personnel same as above.
Cloudy
Classics 655. Originally issued on Brunswick.

_____

recorded: Kansas City, ca. November 9, 1929
Personnel same as above.
Casey Jones Special
Classics 655. Originally issued on Brunswick.

─────────────

recorded: Kansas City, ca. November 9, 1929 and November 11, 1929
John Williams and His Memphis Stompers: same personnel as above.
Somepin' Slow and Low • Lotta Sax Appeal
Classics 655. Originally issued on Vocalion.

─────────────

recorded: Kansas City, ca. November 11, 1929
Andy Kirk and His Twelve Clouds of Joy: same personnel as above.
Corky Stomp • Froggy Bottom
Classics 655. Originally issued on Brunswick.

─────────────

recorded: Chicago, ca. April 24, 1930
MLW (p solos).
Nite Life* • Drag 'Em
Classics 630. *Also Decca 639. Originally issued on Brunswick.

─────────────

[Note: MLW does not take part in the Andy Kirk session of April 29, 1930.]
recorded: Chicago, April 30, 1930
Andy Kirk and His Twelve Clouds of Joy: same personnel as November 11, 1929,
    except Edgar Battle replaces Gene Prince (t).
Snag It • Sweet and Hot • Mary's Idea
Classics 655. Originally issued on Brunswick.

─────────────

recorded: Chicago, May 1, 1930
Andy Kirk and His Twelve Clouds of Joy: same personnel as above, except Billy
    Massey is added (v).
Once or Twice
Classics 655. Originally issued on Brunswick.

─────────────

recorded: Chicago, July 15, 1930
Seven Little Clouds of Joy: MLW (p); Harry Lawson (t); Floyd Brady (tb); John
    Harrington (as); Andy Kirk (bb); William Dirvin (bj); Edward "Crackshot"
    McNeil (d).
Gettin' Off a Mess
Classics 655. Originally issued on Brunswick.

─────────────

recorded: Chicago, October 9, 1930
Andy Kirk and His Twelve Clouds of Joy: same personnel as May 1, 1930.
Dallas Blues • Travelin' That Rocky Road • Honey, Just for You • You Rascal You
Classics 655. Originally issued on Brunswick.

─────────────

recorded: New York, December 15, 1930
Andy Kirk and His Twelve Clouds of Joy: same personnel as above, except Dick
    Robertson (v) is added.
Saturday • Sophomore
Classics 655. Originally issued on Brunswick.

––––––––––

recorded: Camden, New Jersey, March 2, 1931
Blanche Calloway and Her Joy Boys: MLW (p, arr); Blanche Calloway (v, dir);
    Harry Lawson and Edgar Battle (t); Clarence Smith (t, v); Floyd Brady (tb);
    John Harrington (cl, as); John Williams (as, bars); Lawrence Freeman (ts);
    William Dirvin (bj); Andy Kirk (bb); Ben Thigpen (d); Billy Massey (v).
Casey Jones Blues • There's Rhythm in the River • I Need Lovin'
Classics 655. Originally issued on Victor.

––––––––––

recorded: New York, March 2, 1936
Andy Kirk and His Twelve Clouds of Joy: MLW (p, arr); Andy Kirk (dir); Harry
    Lawson and Paul King (t); Earl Thompson (t, arr); Ted Donnelly (tb); John
    Harrington (cl, as, bars); John Williams (as, bars); Dick Wilson (ts); Ted
    Robinson (g); Booker Collins (b); Ben Thigpen (d).
Walkin' and Swingin' (take A)* • Walkin' and Swingin' (take C) • Moten
    Swing*** • Lotta Sax Appeal†**
*EMI 797 906-2. **Decca 622; Classics 573. ***Decca 622; Classics 573; EMI 797 906-2. †Classics 573;
    EMI 797 906-2. Originally issued on Decca (US) and Columbia (UK).

––––––––––

recorded: New York, March 3, 1936
Andy Kirk and His Twelve Clouds of Joy: same personnel as above, except Pha
    Terrell (v) added on "All the Jive Is Gone."
Git • All the Jive Is Gone
Classics 573; EMI 797 906-2. Originally issued on Decca (US) and Columbia (UK).

––––––––––

recorded: New York, March 4, 1936
Andy Kirk and His Twelve Clouds of Joy: same personnel as above.
Froggy Bottom* • Bearcat Shuffle* • Steppin' Pretty
Classics 573; EMI 797 906-2. *Also Decca 622. Originally issued on Decca (US) and Columbia (UK).

––––––––––

recorded: New York, March 7, 1936
Andy Kirk and His Twelve Clouds of Joy: same personnel as above.
Christopher Columbus • Corky
Classics 573; EMI 797 906-2. Originally issued on Decca (US) and Columbia (UK).

––––––––––

recorded: New York, March 7, 1936
MLW (p, leader & composer); Booker Collins (b); Ben Thigpen (d).
**Corny Rhythm • Overhand,* a.k.a. New Froggy Bottom • Isabelle • Swingin' for
    Joy • Clean Pickin'**
Classics 630; EMI 253 625-2. *Also AJA 5073. Originally issued on Decca.

––––––––––

recorded: New York, March 11, 1936
Andy Kirk and His Twelve Clouds of Joy: same personnel as on March 7, 1936.
I'se a Muggin' • Until the Real Thing Comes Along
Classics 573; EMI 797 906-2. Originally issued on Decca.

---

recorded: New York, March 31, 1936
Andy Kirk and His Twelve Clouds of Joy: same personnel as above.
Puddin' Head Serenade (take A)
Classics 573; EMI 797 906-2. Originally issued on Decca.

---

recorded: New York, April 2, 1936
Andy Kirk and His Twelve Clouds of Joy: same personnel as above.
Until the Real Thing Comes Along
Decca 642; Classics 573. Originally issued on Decca.

---

recorded: New York, April 3, 1936
Andy Kirk and His Twelve Clouds of Joy: same personnel as above.
Blue Illusion • Cloudy
Classics 573; EMI 797 906-2. Originally issued on Decca.

---

recorded: New York, April 7, 1936
Andy Kirk and His Twelve Clouds of Joy: same personnel as above.
Give Her a Pint
Classics 573; EMI 797 906-2. Originally issued on Decca.

---

recorded: New York, April 9, 1936
MLW (p, cel & leader); Ted Robinson (g); Booker Collins (b); Ben Thigpen (d).
Mary's Special
Classics 630; EMI 797 906-2. Originally issued on Decca.

---

recorded: New York, April 10, 1936
Andy Kirk and His Twelve Clouds of Joy: same personnel as on March 2, 1936.
Puddin' Head Serenade (Take C)
Decca 622; Classics 573. Originally issued on Decca.

---

recorded: New York, December 9, 1936
Andy Kirk and His Twelve Clouds of Joy: same personnel as above, except Harry
   Mills (v) added.
**Fifty-Second Street • The Lady Who Swings the Band* • What Will I Tell My
   Heart? • Dedicated to You**
Classics 573. *Also Decca 622. Originally issued on Decca.

---

recorded: New York, February 15, 1937
Andy Kirk and His Clouds of Joy: MLW (p, arr); Andy Kirk (dir); Harry Lawson

and Paul King (t); Earl Thompson (t, arr); Ted Donnelly (tb); Henry Wells
(tb & v); Earl Miller (as): John Harrington (cl, as, bars); John Williams (as,
bars); Dick Wilson (ts); Ted Robinson (g); Booker Collins (b); Ben Thigpen
(d); Leslie Johnakins, Claude Hopkins (arr).

Wednesday Night Hop* • Skies Are Blue* • Downstream • (Keep It) In the
Groove*****

*Classics 573. **Classics 581. ***Decca 2-641; Classics 581. Originally issued on Decca.

---

recorded: New York, April 17, 1937
Andy Kirk and His Clouds of Joy: same personnel as above.

**Worried over You • Foolin' Myself • I'm Glad for Your Sake • I'll Get Along Some-
how**

Classics 581. Originally issued on Decca.

---

recorded: New York, July 26, 1937
Andy Kirk and His Clouds of Joy: same personnel as above.

**A Mellow Bit of Rhythm* • In My Wildest Dreams • Better Luck Next Time • With
Love in My Heart**

Classics 581. *Also Decca 622. Originally issued on Decca.

---

recorded: New York, July 27, 1937
Andy Kirk and His Clouds of Joy: same personnel as above.

**What's Mine Is Yours • Why Can't We Do It Again? • The Key to My Heart • I Went
to a Gypsy**

Classics 583. Originally issued on Decca.

---

recorded: New York, December 13, 1937
Andy Kirk and His Clouds of Joy: same personnel as above, except Clarence Trice
(t) replaces Paul King.

Lover, Come Back to Me • Poor Butterfly • The Big Dipper • Bear Down*

Classics 583. *Also Decca 622. Originally issued on Decca.

---

recorded: New York, February 8, 1938
Andy Kirk and His Clouds of Joy: same personnel as above.

I Surrender Dear • Twinklin'* • It Must Be True • I'll Get By

Classics 583. *Also Decca 622. Originally issued on Decca.

---

recorded: New York, ca. February 8 or 10, 1938
Andy Kirk and His Twelve Clouds of Joy: same personnel as above.

Little Joe from Chicago

Classics 583. Originally issued on Decca.

---

recorded: New York, September 9, 1938
Andy Kirk and His Clouds of Joy: same personnel as above.

Bless You, My Dear • How Can We Be Wrong? • Messa Stomp*

Classics 598. *Also Decca 622. Originally issued on Decca.

---

recorded: New York, September 12, 1938
Andy Kirk and His Clouds of Joy: same personnel as above.

Toadie Toddle • I Won't Tell a Soul • What Would People Say? • How Much Do You Mean to Me?

Classics 598. Originally issued on Decca.

---

recorded: New York, September 14, 1938
MLW (p solos).

The Pearls* • Mr. Freddie Blues** • Sweet (Patootie) Patunia • The Rocks

Classics 630. *Also AJA 5073. **Also Hallmark 304062. Originally issued on Decca.

---

recorded: New York, October 24, 1938
Andy Kirk and His Clouds of Joy: same personnel as on September 12, 1938.

Jump Jack Jump • Breeze • Ghost of Love • What a Life

Classics 598. Originally issued on Decca.

---

recorded: New York, October 25, 1938
Andy Kirk and His Clouds of Joy: same personnel as above.

Sittin' Around and Dreamin' • What's Your Story, Morning Glory?*

Classics 598. *Also Decca 622. Originally issued on Decca.

---

recorded: New York, December 5, 1938
Andy Kirk and His Clouds of Joy: same personnel as above, except O'Neil Spencer (v) added.

Honey • September in the Rain • Clouds • Julius Caesar • Dunkin' a Doughnut*

Classics 598. *Also Decca 2-629. Originally issued on Decca.

---

recorded: New York, December 6, 1938
Andy Kirk and His Clouds of Joy: same personnel as above.

Goodbye • Mary's Idea* • But It Didn't Mean a Thing • Say It Again

Classics 598. *Also Decca 622. Originally on Decca.

---

recorded: New York, March 1939
Mildred Bailey and Her Oxford Greys: MLW (p); Mildred Bailey (leader, v); John Williams (b); Floyd Smith (g); Eddie Dougherty (d).

There'll Be Some Changes Made • Gulf Coast Blues

Topaz Jazz 1007. Originally issued on Columbia.

---

recorded: New York, March 16, 1939
Andy Kirk and His Clouds of Joy: same personnel as September 12, 1938, except Don Byas (ts) and Floyd Smith (g, el-g) replace John Williams and Ted Brinson; and June Richmond (v) added.

You Set Me on Fire • I'll Never Learn • Close to Five* • Floyd's Guitar Blues

Classics 640. *Also Decca 622. Originally issued on Decca.

———————

recorded: New York, March 23, 1939

Andy Kirk and His Clouds of Joy: MLW (p & arr); Andy Kirk (leader); Clarence
    Trice, Earl Thompson, Harry Lawson (t); Ted Donnelly (tb); Henry Wells (tb,
    v); John Harrington (cl, as, bars); Earl Miller (as); Dick Wilson, Don Byas (ts);
    Floyd Smith (g, el-g); Booker Collins (b); Ben Thigpen (d); June Richmond,
    Pha Terrell (v).

**Then I'll Be Happy • S'posin' • I'll Never Fail You • Why Don't I Get Wise to
    Myself?**

Classics 640. Originally issued on Decca.

———————

recorded: New York, October 12, 1939

MLW (p solos).

Little Joe from Chicago* • Margie**

*Classics 630. **Classics 655; Topaz 7234. Originally issued on Columbia.

———————

recorded: New York, November 15, 1939

Andy Kirk and His Clouds of Joy: same personnel as March 23, 1939.

**I'm Getting Nowhere with You • I Don't Stand a Ghost of a Chance • Please Don't
    Talk about Me When I'm Gone • Big Jim Blues***

Classics 640. *Also ASV 51408. Originally issued on Decca.

———————

recorded: New York, January 2, 1940

Andy Kirk and His Clouds of Joy. Same personnel as above, except Fred Robinson
    (tb) replaces Henry Wells.

Wham • Love Is the Thing • Why Go On Pretending? • It Always Will Be You

Classics 640. Originally issued on Decca.

———————

recorded: New York, January 26, 1940

Six Men and a Girl: MLW (leader, p, arr); Earl Thompson (t); Earl Buddy Miller
    (cl, as); Dick Wilson (ts); Floyd Smith (el-g); Booker Collins (b); Ben Thig-
    pen (d).

Mary Lou Williams Blues • Tea for Two • Scratchin' in the Gravel • Zonky

Classics 630; Savoy Jazz 2DS1202. Originally issued on Varsity.

———————

recorded: New York, June 25, 1940

Andy Kirk and His Clouds of Joy: MLW (p, arr); Andy Kirk (leader); Harold
    Baker, Clarence Trice, Harry Lawson (t); Ted Donnelly, Fred Robinson (tb);
    John Harrington (cl, as, bars); Rudy Powell (cl, as); Dick Wilson (ts); Edward
    Inge (cl, ts); Floyd Smith (g, el-g); Booker Collins (b); Ben Thigpen (d); June
    Richmond, Pha Terrell (v).

Fine and Mellow • Scratchin' in the Gravel* • Fifteen Minute Intermission • Take Those Blues Away

Classics 640. *Also Decca 622. Originally issued on Decca.

—————

recorded: New York, July 8, 1940
Andy Kirk and His Clouds of Joy: same personnel as above.
Now I Lay Me Down to Dream* • No Greater Love* • Midnight Stroll** • Little Miss**
*Classics 640. **Classics 681. Originally issued on Decca.

—————

recorded: New York, November 7, 1940
Andy Kirk and His Clouds of Joy: same personnel as above, except Henry Wells (tb, v) replaces Fred Robinson.
The Count* • Twelfth Street Rag* • When I Saw You
Classics 681. *Also Decca 622. Originally issued on Decca.

—————

recorded: New York, November 18, 1940
Mary Lou Williams and her Kansas City Seven: MLW (leader, p, arr); Harold Baker (t); Ted Donnelly (tb); William Inge (cl); Dick Wilson (ts); Booker Collins (b); Ben Thigpen (d).
Baby Dear • Harmony Blues
Decca 622; Classics 630. Originally issued on Decca.

—————

recorded: New York, November 18, 1940
Andy Kirk and His Clouds of Joy: same personnel as November 7, 1940.
If I Feel This Way Tomorrow • Or Have I?
Classics 681. Originally issued on Decca.

—————

recorded: New York, January 3, 1941
Andy Kirk and His Clouds of Joy: same personnel as above.
Cuban Boogie Woogie • A Dream Dropped In • Is It a Sin? • Ring Dem Bells*
Classics 681. *Also Decca 622. Originally issued on Decca.

—————

recorded: New York, July 17, 1941
Andy Kirk and His Clouds of Joy: same personnel as above, except Earl Miller (as) replaces Powell.
Big Time Crip • 47th Street Jive • I'm Misunderstood • No Answer
Classics 681. Originally issued on Decca.

—————

recorded: New York, February 1944
MLW (p solos).
Blue Skies • Caravan • Yesterdays
Classics 814. Originally recorded for Asch but not released.

—————

recorded: New York, March 7, 1944
MLW (leader, p); Al Lucas (b); Jack Parker (d).

Roll 'Em • Eighth Avenue Express • Limehouse Blues • Froggy Bottom • Marcheta • Medley (Cloudy/What's Your Story, Morning Glory?/Ghost of Love) • Yankee Doodle Blues • Taurus Mood • People Will Say We're in Love

Solo Art SACD-43. Originally on World Broadcasting Systems.

---

recorded: New York, March 12, 1944

Mary Lou and Her Chosen Five: MLW (p, leader); Frankie Newton (t); Vic Dickenson, (tb); Edmond Hall (cl); Al Lucas (b); Jack Parker (d).

Lullaby of the Leaves • Little Joe from Chicago • Roll 'Em • Satchel Mouth Baby (and alt. take) • Yesterday's Kisses

Classics 824. Originally issued on Asch.

---

recorded: New York, April 19, 1944

MLW (p solos).

Mary's Boogie • Drag 'Em • St. Louis Blues

Classics 814. Originally issued on Asch.

---

recorded: New York, prob. May–June 1944

MLW (leader, p), with Nora Lee King (v).

Until My Baby Comes Back Home

Classics 814. Originally issued on Asch.

---

recorded: New York, June 5, 1944

MLW (leader, p, arr); Dick Vance (t); Vic Dickenson (tb); Claude Greene (cl); Don Byas (ts); Al Lucas (b); Jack Parker (d).

Stardust, Part 1 • Man O'Mine • Gjon Mili Jam Session • Stardust, Part 2

Collectables 5612; Classics 814. Originally issued on Asch.

---

recorded: New York, August 10, 1944

MLW (p, leader, arr); Bill Coleman (t, v); Al Hall (b).

Russian Lullaby • Blue Skies • Persian Rug • Night and Day • You Know, Baby (v-B.C.) • I Found a New Baby

Classics 814. Originally on Asch.

---

recorded: New York, November 24, 1944

Mildred Bailey with Paul Baron's Orchestra: MLW (p, arr); Charlie Shavers (t); Trummy Young (tb); Remo Palmieri (g); Al Hall (b); Specs Powell (d); (Bailey out).

Roll 'Em • Gjon Mili Jam Session

Classics 814. Originally issued on V-Disc (375-B).

---

recorded: New York, December 11, 1944

MLW (p, leader, arr); Bill Coleman (t); Jimmy Butts (b); Eddie Dougherty (d); Josh White (v).

The Minute Man • Froggy Bottom
Classics 1021. Originally on Asch 2001.

_____

recorded: New York, December 15, 1944
MLW (p, arr, leader); Coleman Hawkins (ts); Bill Coleman (t); Eddie Robinson
  (b); Denzil Best (d).
Lady Be Good
Collectables 5612, Classics 1021. Originally issued on Asch.

_____

recorded: New York, December 15, 1944
Same personnel as above, except Joe Evans (as) and Claude Greene (cl) added.
Song in My Soul • This and That
Collectables 5610, Classics 1021. Originally issued on Asch.

_____

recorded: New York, unknown date in 1944
MLW (p, leader); Bill Coleman (t); Al Hall (b).
Carcinoma
Collectables 5612, Classics 1021. Originally issued on Asch.

_____

recorded: New York, June 29, 1945
MLW (p, leader, arr); Al Lucas (b); Jack Parker (d).
**Aries (2 takes)* • Taurus • Gemini* • Cancer (2 takes)* • Leo • Virgo (2 takes)* •
Libra (p solo) • Scorpio (2 takes)* • Sagittarius (p solo) • Capricorn (p solo) •
Aquarius (p solo; 2 takes)* • Pisces • Stars, a.k.a. Libra** • Moon, a.k.a.
Cancer****
Zodiac Suite, Smithsonian/Folkways 40801, Classics 1021. Originally issued on Asch. *Previously unissued
  take. **Different takes. Originally issued on Selmer (France) Y7134.

_____

recorded: New York (Town Hall), December 30, 1945
MLW Chamber Ensemble: MLW (composer, leader, arr, p); Milton Orent (cond,
  co-arr); Ben Webster (ts); Edmond Hall (cl); Eddie Barefield (cl, bsn); Irving
  Randolph (t); Henderson Chambers (tb, frh & vln); Al Hall (b); J.C. Heard
  (d); Hope Foye (v); unknown strings and flute.
**Aries • Taurus • Gemini • Cancer • Leo • Virgo • Libra • Scorpio • Sagittarius •
Capricorn • Aquarius • Pisces (v-H.F.) • A Potpourri (What's Your Story,
Morning Glory?/Cloudy/Ghost of Love/Froggy Bottom) • Lonely Moments •
Gjon Mili Jam Session • Roll 'Em**
Zodiac Suite, Jazz Classics JZCL-6002. Previously issued on Vintage Jazz Classics VJC-1305.

_____

recorded: New York, July 24, 1946
MLW (leader, p, arr); Marjorie Hyams (vbs); Mary Osborne (g, v); June Roten-
  berg (b); Rose Gottesman (d).
Boogie Misterioso* • Harmony Grits** • Conversation/Jump Caprice
Bluebird BMG 6755-2-RB. *Also Bluebird 2192. **Also Rhino 70722. Originally issued on Victor.

_____

recorded: New York, October 7, 1946
MLW (leader, p); June Rotenberg (b); Bridget O'Flynn (d).
Hesitation Boogie
Bluebird BMG 6755-2-RB. Originally issued on Camden.

---

recorded: New York, ca. late 1947
MLW (leader, p, arr); Mary Osborne (g); June Rotenberg (b); Bridget O'Flynn (d).
Just You, Just Me • Just an Idea, a.k.a. Mary's Idea
Mercury/Verve 314 525 609-2. Originally issued on Mercury.

---

recorded: New York, July 1948
Benny Goodman and bop combo: MLW (p, arr); Benny Goodman (leader, cl);
   Wardell Gray (ts); Billy Bauer (g); Clyde Lombardi (b); Mel Zelnick (d).
**Benny's Bop, a.k.a. Wardell's Riff* • (There's a) Small Hotel • Mary's Idea
(3 takes)* • Bye Bye Blues (2 takes)* • (There's a) Small Hotel (3 takes)* •
Blue Views* • I Can't Give You Anything But Love***
Hep 36. *Originally issued on V-Disc 880-A. Recorded from AFSC (Armed Forces Radio Services)
   broadcasts and previously unissued recordings.

---

recorded: New York, March 7, 1951
MLW (leader, p, arr); Carl Pruitt (b); Bill Clarke (d).
In the Purple Grotto
Atlantic 781 707-2. Originally issued on Atlantic.

---

recorded: London, January 22–23, 1953
MLW (leader, p & arr); Ken Napper (b); Allan Ganley (d); Tony Scott (bgs).
**Koolbongo • For You • Don't Blame Me • Lady Bird • Titoros (2 takes) • They
Can't Take That Away from Me (2 takes) • 'Round about Midnight (2 takes) •
Perdido**
Vogue 74321115162. Originally issued on Vogue.

---

recorded: London, June 26, 1953
MLW (leader, p, arr); Ray Dempsey (g); Rupert Nurse (b); Tony Kinsey (d).
**Melody Maker • (New) Musical Express, a.k.a. N.M.E. • Sometimes I'm Happy •
Monk's Tune, a.k.a. Monk's Mood**
Hallmark 303062, 391172 (multiple-CD that includes 303062). Originally issued on Esquire.

---

recorded: Paris, December 2–3, 1953
MLW (leader, p, arr); Don Byas (ts); Alvin "Buddy" Banks (b); Gérard Pochonet
   (d).
**O.W. • Mary's Waltz • Just You, Just Me • Lullaby of the Leaves • Moonglow • Why
• N.M.E., a.k.a. New Musical Express • Chicka Boom Blues, a.k.a. Blues**
Vogue BM 720. (CD includes 2 selections from other sessions not on LP: "Yesterdays" and "'Round
   Midnight.") Originally issued on Vogue.

---

recorded: London, unknown date in 1953
MLW (leader, p, arr); Lennie Bush (b); Tony Kinsey (d); Tony Scott (bgs).
**Azure Te • Twilight • Flying Home • Nickles • Yesterdays (2 takes) • The Man I
Love (2 takes) • Just One of Those Things (2 takes) • Why**
Vogue 74321115162. Originally issued on Vogue.

---

recorded: Paris, March 1954
MLW (leader, p, arr); Buddy Banks (b); Jean-Louis Viale (d).
Nicole
Smithsonian RD 039. Originally issued on Blue Star.

---

recorded: New York, March 1955
MLW (leader, p, arr); Wendell Marshall (b); Osie Johnson (d).
**Jericho • Sweet Sue • Talk of the Town • Amy • I Love Him • Roll 'Em • Taurus • I
Love You • Lullaby of the Leaves • Easy Blues • Mama, Pin a Rose on Me •
Fandangle**
Mary Lou Williams—Lady Piano, Blackbird CD (no number). Originally issued on Jazztone LP as *A Keyboard History*

---

recorded: Newport, July 6, 1957
MLW with Dizzy Gillespie and His Orchestra: MLW (composer, p); Dizzy Gillespie
(leader, t); Melba Liston (arr); Paul West (b); Charli Persip (d).
Virgo • Libra • Aries • Carioca
Verve 314 513 754-2. Originally on Verve LP MGV 8244.

---

issue, in CD compilation, of music recorded in New York 1970 and 1972
MLW (p, composer, arr, leader); for other personnel, see pp. 423–24.
Our Father
In 3-CD set, *Contemporary Anthology of Music by Women*, compiled by James R. Briscoe, Indiana University
Press, 1999. Previously issued on LPs *Music for Peace*, 1970 (Mary Records, no number), and *Mary
Lou's Mass*, 1971 (Mary Records 104).

---

recorded: New York (Overseas Press Club), January 31, 1971 ·
All-Star Group: MLW (p); Dizzy Gillespie and Bobby Hackett (ts); George
Duvivier (b); Grady Tate (d).
Autumn Leaves
Giants of Jazz 53 180. Originally on Perception LP.

---

recorded: New York, May–June 1971
MLW (p solos).
**Nite Life • Cloudy • Little Joe from Chicago • What's Your Story, Morning Glory?
• The Scarlet Creeper • Scratchin' in the Gravel • Offertory • Blues for John
(Hammond) • Marnier Mood • Gemma • For the Figs • Anima Christi***

(2 takes) • Chief* • Nite Life Variations* (A Swinging Meditation/A Full-bodied Portrait/A Modern Improvisation) • What's Your Story, Morning Glory? #2* • The Scarlet Creeper #2* • Scratchin' in the Gravel #2* • Little Joe from Chicago #2*

Chiaroscuro CR(D)103.Originally on Chiaroscuro LP. *Previously unissued.

---

recorded: New York (New York Public Library for the Performing Arts), October 22, 1971
MLW (p. solos).

Elite Syncopations • Pleasant Moments • Pineapple Rag • My Mama Pinned a Rose on Me/Fandangle

Chiaroscuro CR(D)103. Previously issued on Nonesuch.

---

recorded: New York, probably 1971
MLW (narration).

Jazzspeak

Chiaroscuro CR(D)103. Previously unissued.

---

recorded: New York (Newport Jazz Festival), July 3, 1972
MLW (p); Dizzy Gillespie (t); Benny Green (tb); Stan Getz (ts); Milt Jackson (vbs); unknown others.

Bags' Groove • Night in Tunisia

Atlantic REP 4381-WZ. Originally issued on Atlantic.

---

recorded: New York, June 1, 1973
Buddy Tate and His Buddies: MLW (p); Buddy Tate, (leader, ts); Illinois Jacquet (ts); Roy Eldridge (t); Steve Jordan (g); Milt Hinton (b); Gus Johnson (d).

Rockaway • Medi II • Paris Nights • When I'm Blue • Sunday

Chiaroscuro CR(D)123. Originally issued on Chiaroscuro.

---

recorded: New York, January 17, February, and March 18, 1974
MLW (leader, p, arr, producer); Zita Carno (p); Bob Cranshaw, Milton Suggs (b); Mickey Roker (d); Tony Waters (cgs).

Holy Ghost (MLW, B.C.) • Medi I (MLW, B.C.) • Syl-O-Gism* (MLW, B.C., M.R.) • Medi II (MLW, M.R.) • Rosa Mae (MLW, M.R.) • Olinga (MLW, M.R.) • Intermission** (MLW, B.C., M.R., Z.C.) • Zoning Fungus II (MLW, B.C., M.R., Z.C.) • Gloria* (MLW, B.C., M.R.) • Gloria (MLW, M.S., T.W.) • Praise the Lord (MLW, M.S., T.W.) • Play It Momma (MLW, M.S., T.W.) • Ghost of Love (MLW)

Smithsonian/Folkways 40811. Originally issued on Mary Records. *Previously unissued. **Full-length version not included on original LP issue.

---

recorded: New York, July 8, 1975
MLW (p); Buster Williams (b); Mickey Roker (d).

Dat Dere • Baby Man #2* • Baby Man • All Blues • Temptation • Pale Blue • Free Spirits #2* • Free Spirits • Blues for Timme • Ode to Saint Cecilia* • Surrey with the Fringe on Top* • Gloria*

Free Spirits, SteepleChase 31043. Previously issued on SteepleChase LP. *Previously unissued.

---

recorded: New York (The Cookery Restaurant), November 1975
MLW (p; arr); Brian Torff (b).

Praise the Lord • Blues for Peter • I Can't Get Started • Roll 'Em • The Jeep Is Jumping • My Funny Valentine • Waltz Boogie • The Surrey with the Fringe on the Top • The Man I Love* • All Blues* • Mack the Knife* • A Grand Night for Swinging

Live at the Cookery, Chiaroscuro CR(D)146. Previously issued on Chiaroscuro LP. *Previously unissued.

---

recorded: New York (Carnegie Hall), April 17, 1977
MLW (p, co-leader), Cecil Taylor (p, co-leader); Bob Cranshaw (b); Mickey Roker (d).

The Lord Is Heavy (MLW, C.T.) • Fandangle (MLW, C.T.) • The Blues Never Left Me (MLW, C.T.) • K.C. 12th Street (MLW, C.T.) • Good Ole Boogie (MLW, C.T.) • Basic Chords (MLW, C.T.) • Ayizan (MLW, C.T.) • Chorus Sud (MLW, C.T.) • Back to the Blues (MLW, C.T.) • I Can't Get Started (MLW, B.C., M.R.)

Pablo Live PACD 2620-108-2. Originally issued on Pablo.

---

recorded: New York (Carnegie Hall), January 18, 1978
Benny Goodman and various. MLW (p); Benny Goodman (leader, cl); unknown others.

Roll 'Em • King Porter Stomp • That's A-Plenty • How High the Moon • Moonglow • Lady Be Good • Seven Come Eleven • Someone to Watch over Me • Please Don't Talk about Me • Medley • Sing Sing Sing

London 820-349-2. Originally issued on London LP.

---

recorded: Montreux, Switzerland, July 16, 1978
MLW (p solos).

Medley (The Lord Is Heavy/Fandangle/Old Fashioned Slow Blues/For the Figs/Baby Bear Boogie/Roll 'Em) • Over the Rainbow • Offertory Meditation • Tea for Two • Concerto Alone at Montreux • Little Joe from Chicago • The Man I Love • What's Your Story, Morning Glory? • Honeysuckle Rose

Pablo OJCCD-962-2. Originally issued on Pablo LP.

---

recorded: New York, October 8, 1978
MLW (p); Marian McPartland (radio narrator, host, p); Ronnie Boykins (b).

Space Playing Blues (MLW, R.B.) • Baby Man (MLW, R.B.) • What's Your Story, Morning Glory? (MLW, R.B.) • Scratchin' in the Gravel (MLW, M.McP.) • Medi II (MLW, R.B.) • Rosa Mae (MLW, R.B.) • Caravan (MLW, R.B.) • I Can't Get Started (MLW, R.B.) • The Jeep Is Jumpin' (MLW, R.B.) • Exit Playing (MLW, M.McP., R.B.)

Jazz Alliance TJA-12019. Debut NPR radio program, "Marian McPartland's Piano Jazz, with guest Mary Lou Williams."

_____

recorded: *Chicago (Rick's Café Américain), November 14, 1979*
MLW (p, leader, arr); Milton Suggs (b); Drashear Khalid (d).
Autumn Leaves • I Can't Get Started • You Can't Take That Away from Me • Satin Doll • The Jeep Is Jumping • St. James Infirmary • Surrey with the Fringe on Top • My Funny Valentine • Mack the Knife • 'Round Midnight • What's Your Story, Morning Glory? • Without a Song • Caravan • A Grand Nite for Swinging
Storyville 8285.

_____

Recordings by Mary Lou Williams on LPs, 78s, 45s, EPs, Tapes, Unissued

recorded: *Chicago, January 1927*
MLW (as Mary Leo Burley, p); Jeanette James (leader, v); Henry McCord (tp); Bradley Bullett (tb); John Williams (as, bars); Jo Williams (bj); Robert Price (d).
Downhearted Mama • What's That Thing?
Originally issued on Paramount. On Historical LP, ASC-5829, volume 2.

_____

recorded: *Chicago, March 1 and 3, 1927*
(As "Duke Jackson and Serenaders") MLW (p); John Williams (leader, as, bar); Henry McCord (t); Bradley Bullett (tb); Jo Williams (bj); Robert Price (d).
My! My! My! • Kansas City Yellow Front
Recorded for Gennett, unissued.

_____

recorded: *Chicago, May 20 or 21, 1927*
Same personnel as above.
Tiger Rag • San • Someday, Sweetheart
Recorded for Gennett, unissued.

_____

recorded: *New York, March 1939*
Mildred Bailey and Her Oxford Greys: MLW (p); Mildred Bailey (leader, v); John Williams (b); Floyd Smith (g); Eddie Dougherty (d).
Prisoner of Love • Barrelhouse Blues • Arkansas Blues • You Don't Know My Mind Blues • There'll Be Some Changes Made* • Gulf Coast Blues*
On Columbia LP C3L22. *Also on CD.

_____

recorded: *Cleveland, January 29–February 6, 1937*
MLW (p, arr); Andy Kirk (leader); Harry Lawson, Paul King, Earl Thompson (t); Ted Donnelly (tb); John Harrington (as, cl); John Williams (as, bars); Dick Wilson (ts); Ted Brinson (g); Booker Collins (b); Ben Thigpen (d, v); Pha Terrell (v).

**Until the Real Thing Comes Along • Swingtime in the Rockies • Froggy Bottom •
What Will I Tell My Heart • There, I Love You Coast to Coast • Make Believe
Ballroom • Sepia Jazz • Dear Old Southland • Yours Truly • Medley from
Golddiggers of 1937 (Boo Hoo/One, Two, Button Your Shoe/Trouble Don't
Like Music/One in a Million) • Trust in Me • All the Jive Is Gone • Never
Slept a Wink Last Night • You're Slightly Terrific • Organ Grinder's Swing •
Until the Real Thing Comes Along**
Jazz Society AA503.

---

recorded: Cleveland, Ohio, ca. January 29–February 6, 1937
Andy Kirk and His Clouds of Joy. Same personnel as above.
**You Turned the Tables on Me • Good Night My Love • You Do the Darnest
Things, Baby • Spring Holiday • When I'm with You • I Went to the Gypsy •
Piano Introduction of Untitled Blues • In the Chapel in the Moonlight •
Honeysuckle Rose • Walkin' and Swingin' • Dedicated to You • Untitled
blues—MLW solo • King Porter Stomp • Liza**
Tape from aircheck; in MLW collection.

---

recorded: New York (Cotton Club), May 5, 1940
Andy Kirk and His Clouds of Joy, inc. MLW (p, arr).
The Sheik of Araby • Marcheta • The Riff
Everybody's LP EV 3006. Live broadcasts.

---

recorded: New York, probably November 24, 1944
Mildred Bailey with Paul Baron's Orchestra: MLW (p, arr); Charlie Shavers (t);
Trummy Young (tb); Remo Palmieri (g); Al Hall (b); Specs Powell (d); (Bailey out).
Just a Blue Riff • It Takes One Deep Breath
V-Disc 881-B.

---

recorded: New York (Carnegie Hall), June 22, 1945
MLW (composer, co-arr, leader, p); Milt Orent (co-arr); Carnegie Pops Orchestra.
**Sagittarius • Aquarius • Scorpio • Boogie-woogie Jazz for Orchestra • The Man I
Love (solo p)**
Tape in MLW collection.

---

recorded: New York (WNEW radio broadcast), August 5 and 12, 1945
MLW (composer, leader, p); probably Bill Coleman (t); A. Hall (b); Specs Powell
(d).
Sleep • Gjon Mili Jam Session
Jazz Panorama LP 11.

---

recorded: New York, 1946
MLW (p solos).

How High the Moon • The Man I Love • Cloudy/What's Your Story? • Blue Skies • These Foolish Things • Lonely Moments

Originally issued on Asch/Disc 78s and Folkways LP.

---

recorded: New York, February 16, 1946

MLW and Her "Girl Stars": MLW (leader, p, arr); Marjorie Hyams (vbs); Mary Osborne (g): "Bea" (Billy) Taylor (b); Bridget O'Flynn (d).

Blues at Mary Lou's/Cafe Society Blues • DDT • DDT (alt. take)* • Rhumba Rebop • (S)he's Funny That Way • Timme Time

Originally issued on Continental 78s 6021 and 6032. *On Masterseal 78 75.

---

recorded: New York, July 24, 1946

MLW (leader, p); Marjorie Hyams (vbs); Mary Osborne (g, v); June Rotenberg (b); Rose Gottesman (d).

Fifth Dimension* • Humoresque** • It Must Be True***

*Camden Cal 384. **RCA (F) 741106. ***Unissued.

---

recorded: New York, October 7, 1946

MLW (leader & p); June Rotenberg (b); Bridget O'Flynn (d).

Waltz Boogie

Camden LP 384; CAL 306.

---

recorded: New York, 1947

MLW Ensemble, a.k.a. Milton Orent–Frank Roth Orchestra: MLW (composer, arr, cond); Irving Kustin, Leon Schwartz, Edward Sadowski (t); Martin Glaser, Allan Feldman, Maurice Lopez, Orlando Wright (reeds); Frank Roth or MLW (p); Milt Orent (b); Jack Parker (d).

Lonely Moments • Whistle Blues

LP Folkways FA 2966. Originally issued for Asch/Disc.

---

recorded: New York (Carnegie Hall), April 5, 1947

Charlie Ventura and his Sextet. Personnel: MLW (p); Charlie Ventura (leader, ts); Charlie Shavers (t); Bill Harris (tb); Marjorie Hyams (vbs); Bill Dearango (g); Curly Russell (b); Dave Tough (d).

Just You, Just Me

LP Verve MGV-8132.

---

recorded: New York, 1947

MLW and group: MLW (leader, p); Kenny Dorham (t); Johnny Smith (g); Grachan Moncur (b).

Mary Lou • Kool

Folkways LP FA 2966. Originally on Asch/Disc.

---

recorded: White Plains, New York, June 26 and July 3, 1948

Benny Goodman "bop" combo: MLW (p, arr); Benny Goodman (leader, cl); Stan

Hasselgard (cl); Wardell Gray (ts); Red Rodney (t); Billy Bauer (g); Clyde
Lombardi (b); Mel Zelnick (d).

Mary's Idea • Mel's Idea • Swedish Pastry • Indiana

LP Dan VC 5003. Originally a radio broadcast, "The Benny Goodman Show," for WNEW Radio in New
York City. Tape in MLW collection contains extensive playlist.

_____

recorded: New York, March 18, 1949

MLW and group: MLW (composer, leader, p); Idrees Sulieman (t); Martin Glaser
(b-cl); Allen Feldman (cl, as); Mundell Lowe (g); George Duvivier (b); Denzil
Best (d); Kenny "Pancho" Hagood (v) on "Oo-bla-dee" and "Shorty Boo."

Tisherome* • Knowledge* • In the Land of Oo-bla-dee • Shorty Boo

King LP 295-85; King EP 279; King 78 15013. *Also King LP 540. Also issued on LP JS (F) 612,
Vogue (E)V21247.

_____

recorded: New York, January, 1950

MLW (leader, p, or); Mundell Lowe (g); George Duvivier (b); Denzil Best (d).

**Bye Bye Blues (MLW, p & or)* • Moonglow (MLW, p & or) • Willow Weep for
Me** • I'm in the Mood for Love*****

King LP 295-85; King EP 280. *Also King 78 4349. **Also King LP 540; King 78 4349. ***Also King LP
540. All titles also released on Parlophone (E)GEP8567.

_____

recorded: New York, March 7, 1951

Mary Lou Williams trio. Personnel: MLW (leader, p, arr); Carl Pruitt (b); Bill
Clarke (d).

**In the Purple Grotto • Opus Z • Surrey with the Fringe • Pagliacci* • From This
Moment On* • S'Wonderful • You're the Cream in My Coffee • Mary's Waltz •
Would I Love You** • My First Date with You****

Atlantic 114; Atlantic 1271. *Also on Blue Star 78 236. **Unissued.

_____

recorded: New York, 1951

MLW (p solos).

**Yesterdays • It Ain't Necessarily So • Why Evade the Truth, a.k.a. Monk's Mood •
Mary's Waltz • It's the Talk of the Town • Stompin' at the Savoy • Why • Cara-
van • Crazy Rhythm • Scorpio • The Man I Love • People Will Say We're in
Love • The Man I Love • For You • Reprise**

Unissued Circle LP (*Mary Lou at Midnight*).

_____

recorded: New York, June 20, 1951

MLW (leader, p, arr); Billy Taylor (b); Al Walker (d); Sabu Louis Martinez, Willie
"Bobo" Correa (bgs); Correa (v).

Sheik of Araby* • Lover Come Back • When Dreams Come True** • Bobo** •
Kool** • Handy Eyes, a.k.a. St. Louis Blues* • Tisherome** • 'Sposin'*****

*Circle LP 412; Circle 78 3008. **Circle LP 412. ***Circle 78 3009; unissued Circle LP 412 (*Piano
Contempo: Modern Piano Jazz*). Also on Blue Star 242.

_____

recorded: New York, June 15, 1951
MLW (leader, p, arr); Skippy Williams (b-cl); Billy Taylor (b); Al Walker (d);
    Willie de la Guerra (bgs); Dave Lambert, Norma Carion, Bill Crow, others (v).
Walkin' (Out the Door)* • De Function, a.k.a. The Great MacBeth** • Cloudy** •
    I Won't Let It Bother Me**
*Circle 78 3008. **Unissued. Rehearsal in MLW tape collection.

---

recorded: New York, ca. June 15, 1951
MLW (leader, p, arr); Art Phipps (b); Bill Clarke (d); Dave Lambert Singers.
Yes, We Have No Bananas* • Caravan* • Lonely Moments** • Untitled**
*Circle 78 3013. **Unissued. Rehearsal in MLW tape collection.

---

recorded: New York, July 11, 1952
MLW (leader, p, arr); Harold Baker (t); Vic Dickerson (tb); Morris Lane (ts);
    Nevell John (g); Eddie Safranski (b); Don Lamond (d).
C-Jam Blues • Downbeat • Out of Nowhere
Brunswick 54000.

---

recorded: U.S., May-De Recording Studio, August 7, 1952
MLW (p solo).
Take the Wagon
Unissued test recording.

---

recorded: London, March 20, 1953
MLW (leader, p); Jack Fallon (b); Gerry McLaughlin (d).
Laughing Rag • Rag of Rags
London Records 78 1174.

---

recorded: London, 1953
MLW
Ca Ra Van, a.k.a. Caravan • Easy Blues
Unissued test recording.

---

recorded: London, 1953
MLW
Nicknames • We Three
Unissued recording for Brinson Records.

---

recorded: Paris, March 1954
MLW (leader, p, arr); Buddy Banks (b); Jean-Louis Viale (d).
There's a Small Hotel • En Ce Temps Là • Lover • Between the Devil and the Deep
    Blue Sea • Carioca • Tire tire l'aiguille • Autumn in New York • Nicole
Blue Star LP F BLP6841.

---

recorded: Paris, 1954

MLW in various combinations: MLW (leader, p, arr); Nelson Williams (t); Ray
    Lawrence (ts); Buddy Banks (b); Kansas Fields or Jacques David (d); Beryl
    Bryden (v, wbd).

**Swingin' for the Guys • Club Français Blues (p solo) • Freight Train • Memories of
    You • Leg 'n Lou • Avalon • Gravel, a.k.a. Scratchin' in the Gravel • Rock Me •
    (I Made You) Love Paris (p solo) • Nancy Is in Love with the Colonel**

Club Français du Disque LP (F) J12.

————————

recorded: Paris, 1954

MLW (p); unidentified male and female vocalists.

Untitled • Untitled • You Know, Baby • Blue Monday

"Paris Material" tape in MLW collection.

————————

recorded: Paris, circa 1954

MLW (p solos).

O.W. • Nicole • N.M.E. • Just You, Just Me

Tape of radio broadcast in MLW collection.

————————

recorded: Baden Baden, Germany, November 29, 1954

MLW (p); the Kurt Edelhagen All Stars (big band).

Perdido • The Man I Love • Yesterdays • St. Louis Blues • Untitled Blues

Tape in MLW collection.

————————

recorded: Paris, circa 1954

MLW (p); Lucienne Delforge (p); Marjorie Dunton (radio host); François
    Valorbe (poet).

Radio broadcast tape in MLW collection. Also includes interview and improvised response by MLW to a
    surrealist poem dedicated to her.

————————

recorded: New York, 1957

MLW (p, leader, composer); Melba Liston (arr); unidentified (fl; b-cl; b; d)

Waltz Boogie • Untitled • Morning Glory

Unissued material recorded by Roulette Records, tape of test pressing in MLW collection.

————————

recorded: Toronto (Town Tavern), circa late 1957

MLW (p, leader); Tommy Potter (b); Denzil Best (d, bgs).

**Untitled blues • Easy Blues • Fine and Dandy/The Devil and the Deep Blue Sea •
    Chunkalunka (Jug) • Grand Night for Swinging • The Man I Love**

Aircheck of radio program, "Live Jazz from the Town," in MLW collection.

————————

recorded: West Point, New York, April 27, 1958

MLW (p, leader); Ali Muhammad (b); Ray Mosca (d); West Point Jazz Band.

**Untitled Original Blues • The Man I Love • I Can't Get Started • Caravan • Sweet
    Sue • St. Louis Blues/Duke's Place (MLW trio & West Point Jazz Band)**

Tape of concert in MLW collection.

————————

recorded: Philadelphia, 1958
MLW (leader, p, arr); Bruce Lawrence (b); Jack Parker (d).
I Got Rhythm* • Night and Day* • Chunkalunka (Jug) parts I & II**
*Sue 45 715. **Sue 45 724.

---

recorded: Place unknown, circa 1960
MLW (leader, p, arr); Chris White (b); Rudy Collins (d).
My Blue Heaven • Yesterdays
Il Grandi di Jazz GDJ60.

---

recorded: New York, October 10, 1962
MLW (p); Milt Hinton (b); Howard Roberts (v cond, with the Ray Charles
    Singers).
Black Christ of the Andes, a.k.a. St. Martin de Porres • The Devil
MLW (p); Theodore Cromwell (b); George Chamble (d).
Miss D.D.
MLW (p); Melba Liston (arr, cond); Budd Johnson (b-cl, ts); Grant Green (g);
    Larry Gales (b); Percy Brice (d); Jimmy Mitchell (v); The George Gordon
    Singers (v group).
Anima Christi • Praise the Lord
MLW (p); Ben Tucker (b); Percy Brice (d).
It Ain't Necessarily So
MLW (solo p).
A Fungus Amungus
Mary 101; Folkways FJ 2843.

---

recorded: November 19, 1963
MLW (p); Percy Heath (b); Tim Kennedy (d).
Grand Night for Swinging* • My Blue Heaven* • Dirge Blues
Mary LP 101; Folkways FJ 2843. *Also Mary 45 631. Originally issued on Mary Records LP M101, *Mary
    Lou Williams Presents St. Martin de Porres*, a.k.a. *Black Christ of the Andes*. See also Mary EP3626, *Jazz for
    the Soul.*

---

recorded: New York, October 1963
MLW (p, leader, arr); Percy Heath (b); Tim Kennedy (d).
Unissued Mary Records sessions tapes.

---

recorded: Pittsburgh, June 20, 1965
MLW (leader, p, arr); Larry Gales (b); Ben Riley (d). Also MLW with Earl Hines
    (p) and/or Willie "The Lion" Smith (p); Billy Taylor (p) George Wein (p);
    Larry Gayles (b); Ben Riley (d).
45 Degree Angle (trio) • Joycie (trio) • Rosetta (with pianists)
RCA LSP 3499.

---

recorded: New York, 1966

MLW (leader, p, arr); Melba Liston (arr); Leon Thomas (v); unidentified rhythm.

Chief Natoma from Tacoma • You Know, Baby • Joe • Pittsburgh

2 Mary Records 45s. No numbers available.

---

recorded: New York (Carnegie Hall), January 1967

MLW (p, arr); Bob Banks (cond, co-arr); Clemens J. McNaspy, S.J. (narrator); Bill Salters (b); Percy Brice (d); Ralph MacDonald (cgs); Julius Watkins (flgh); Honi Gordon, Leon Thomas (v. soloists); Interfaith Chorus and Instrumental Ensemble.

History of Jazz (solo p & narration by Fr. McNaspy) • Thank You, Jesus • Our Father • Praise the Lord • Joycie

Praise the Lord in Many Voices, Avant Garde LP AVS 103.

---

recorded: Pittsburgh, June 1967

MLW (p, leader, composer); Seton High School for Girls Choir (soprano and alto).

O.W. • Praise the Lord • Lord Have Mercy, a.k.a. Kyrie • Glory to God, a.k.a. Gloria • The Creed, a.k.a. I Believe, a.k.a. Credo • Holy Holy Holy, a.k.a. Sanctus Benedictus • Our Father, a.k.a. Pater Noster • Lamb of God, a.k.a. Agnus Dei • Act of Contrition • Thank You, Jesus

Tape of rehearsal of first jazz mass in MLW collection.

---

recorded: New York (St. Thomas the Apostle Church), March 1968

MLW (leader, p, composer); Honi Gordon (v); choir (mixed: male-female, adult-child); Harold Ousley (s); Roger Glenn (f); Ted Dunbar or Grant Green (g); Major Holley (b); Robbie Mickles (d).

O.W. • Clean My Heart O Lord • Kyrie, a.k.a. Lord Have Mercy • The Lord Is My Light • Offertory • Holy Holy Holy • Amanuensis • Amen • Lamb of God • Martha Said to Jesus • Return of the Prodigal Son (Harold Ousley, composer)

Unreleased tape of performance and rehearsals of MLW's second mass, *Mass for the Lenten Season,* in MLW collection. (The *Mass* was performed each Sunday during Lent of 1968.)

---

recorded: Copenhagen, Denmark, fall 1968

MLW, the Danish National Jazz Orchestra, and combo: MLW (leader, p, arr); Niels-Henning Ørsted Pedersen (b); Svend Asmussen (vln); Timme Rosenkrantz (narrator); Inez Cavanaugh (v).

Aries (not from *Zodiac Suite* but a reworked "Thank You, Jesus") • You Know, Baby (IC, v) • Scratchin' in the Gravel, a.k.a. Truth • Chunkalunka • OW!, a.k.a. O.W. • N.M.E., a.k.a. New Musical Express • Mary's Blues • My Blue Heaven • Yesterdays • It's a Grand Night for Swinging • Autumn Leaves • Caravan

Unreleased tape of airchecks of broadcasts on Danish radio, in MLW collection.

---

recorded: Rome, February 1969
MLW (leader, p, arr); Maltoni Quarto (fl); Maurizio Majorana (b); orchestra and choir of Roman Catholic seminarians.
I Have a Dream • Tell Them Not to Talk Too Long • Selections from *Mass for the Lenten Season*, a.k.a. *Jazz for the Soul* • Extemporaneous
Unreleased tape of airchecks of performances for Vatican Radio, in MLW collection.

---

recorded: New York (Holy Family Church), July 15, 1969
MLW (leader, p, arr); Leon Thomas (v); unidentified (b); probably Roger Glenn (f).
People in Trouble • The Lord Says • Kyrie • In His Day • Peace I Leave with You • Alleluia • Turn Aside • Our Father • Blessed Are the Peacemakers • Spring (Leon Thomas, v) • Exit (solo p, improv.)
Tape of early version of *Music for Peace*, in MLW collection.

---

recorded: New York, 1970
MLW, solo piano and narration.
Medi • Medi I (MLW voiceover) • Anima Christi Suite • Medi I • Who Stole the Lock of the Henhouse Door • Medi I • My Mama Pinned a Rose on Me • Night Life, a.k.a. Nite Life • Hesitation Boogie • Old Blues • New Blues • Medi I
The History of Jazz, Folkways LP FJ 2869, issued in 1978.

---

recorded: New York, 1970
MLW (p, composer, arr, leader); Edward Flanagan (producer); various musicians (see below).
Ensemble #1: MLW (composer, p, arr); Bob Banks (co-arr); David Amram (frh, f); Carline Ray (b, v); Al Harewood (d); Leon Atkinson (g); Randy Peyton, Christine Spencer, Eileen Gilbert (v).
Ensemble #2: MLW (composer, leader, p); Chris White (b); David Parker (d); Roger Glenn (f); Sonny Henry (g); Abdul Rahman (cgs); Carl Hall, Milton Grayson, James Bailey (v).
Ensemble #3: same as #2, plus Eileen Gilbert, Randy Peyton, Carline Ray, Christine Spencer (v).
Ensemble #4: same as #1, plus Carl Hall, Randy Peyton (v).
O.W. (#1) • The Lord Says (#2) • Kyrie, a.k.a. Lord Have Mercy (#3) • Gloria (#1) • In His Day (#4) • Peace I Leave with You/Alleluia (#1) • Turn Aside (#1) • Holy, Holy, Holy (#3) • Creed, a.k.a. Credo (#1) • Our Father (#1) • People in Trouble (#2) • Lazarus (MLW p, leader, composer, arr; Leon Atkinson g; Carline Ray b, v) • The World, a.k.a. One (#1) • Praise the Lord (#2)
Issued as Mary LP (no number), *Music for Peace*.

---

recorded: New York, 1970, and January 1972
MLW (p, leader, composer, arr), various artists. Makeup of ensembles as above.
Praise the Lord (#2)* • Old Time Spiritual (MLW p, leader, composer, arr; Milton

Suggs b; David Parker d; Ralph MacDonald cgs; Roger Glenn f) • The Lord
Says (Ensemble #2, M.G. v solo)* • Act of Contrition (MLW p, leader, com-
poser, arr; Milton Suggs b; Honi Gordon v) • Kyrie, a.k.a. Lord Have Mercy
(Ensemble #3)* • Gloria (Ensemble #1)* • In His Day (Ensemble #4)* •
Lazarus (MLW p; Leon Atkinson g; Carline Ray b, v)* • Credo (Ensemble
#1)* • Medi I (and Medi II, in a medley) (MLW p, leader, composer, arr;
Milton Suggs b; David Parker d; Ralph MacDonald cgs; Roger Glenn f) • Holy
Holy Holy (Ensemble #3)* • Our Father (Ensemble #1)* • Lamb of God
(MLW p, leader, composer, arr; Milton Suggs b; Roger Glenn f; Honi Gordon
solo v, screams; chorus conducted by Howard Roberts) • People in Trouble
(Ensemble #2)* • One (a.k.a. The World) (Ensemble #1)* • Praise the Lord
(Come Holy Spirit) (MLW p, leader, composer, arr; Milton Suggs b; David
Parker d; Ralph MacDonald cgs; Leon Atkinson g; Julius Watkins frh; Peter
Whitehead v; chorus conducted by Howard Roberts)

Issued in 1975 as *Mary Lou's Mass,* Mary Records 102. *Included also on *Music for Peace,* Mary LP (no
number).

---

recorded: New York, 1970
MLW (p, leader, arr); Sonny Henry (g); Leon Thomas (v); unidentified rhythm.
Let's Do the Froggy Bottom* • Jesus Is the Best* • Credo • Willis****
Mary Records 45 MA5. **Mary Records 45 MA6.

---

recorded: New York (Overseas Press Club), January 31, 1971
All-star group: MLW (p); Dizzy Gillespie and Bobby Hackett (t); George Duvivier
(b); Grady Tate (d).
**Love for Sale • Autumn Leaves* • Caravan • Jitterbug Waltz • Willow Weep for Me
• Birks' Works • My Man**
Released as *Giants,* Perception LP 19. Also on Giants of Jazz CD 53 180.

---

recorded: New York, October 17, 1972
MLW (interviewee, narrator); Thomas More Society (producer).
Phonotape: *Jazz and the Spirit.*

---

recorded: Durham, North Carolina, December 1977
MLW (p), with chorus.
**Christmas Celebration Interlude • Silent Night • Deck the Halls • Jingle Bells • O
Come All Ye Faithful • Shoo be doo be doo, Santa Claus/It's Old Saint Nick**

---

recorded: New York, December 27, 1977
MLW (p, composer, arr); Buster Williams (b); Cynthia Tyson (v).

PIANO SOLOS

**The Blues • N.G. Blues • Dirge Blues • Baby Bear Blues • Turtle Speed Blues •
Blues for Peter • My Mama Pinned a Rose on Me**

TRIO

Prelude to Prism • Prism • What's Your Story, Morning Glory? • Prelude to Love Roots • Love Roots • Rhythmic Patterns • J.B.'s Waltz • The Blues • No Title Blues •

My Mama Pinned a Rose on Me, Pablo LP 2310-819.

---

recorded: Durham, North Carolina (Baldwin Auditorium, Duke University), December 12, 1977
MLW (leader, p); Buster Williams (b); Roy Haynes (d).
Spiritual II • Fandangle • Old Fashioned Slow Blues • Nite Life • Baby Bear Boogie/Roll 'Em • On Green Dolphin Street • I Can't Get Started • Naturally • Olinga • I Love You • Caravan • A Grand Night for Swinging • Baby Man • Gloria • Somewhere Over the Rainbow • Surrey With the Fringe on Top • 45° Angle • Bags' Groove (incomplete)
Concert tape in MLW collection.

Selected Reissues/Compilations on CD Containing Work by Mary Lou Williams

Jazz Archives 15900   *Mary Lou Williams' Story*
Suiza JZCD 35   *Greatest Lady Piano Player in Jazz*
Topaz LC7234   *Mary Lou Williams—Key Moments*
Giants of Jazz 53180   *First Lady of the Piano 1952–1971*
Collectables COL 5612   *Mary Lou Williams and Orchestra/ Meade Lux Lewis*
Pro Arte CDD 3408   *Andy Kirk—Moten Swing*
Living Era AJA 5108 (E)   *Andy Kirk: The Twelve Clouds of Joy with Mary Lou Williams*
Black & Blue CD 59 2402(F)   *Kansas City Bounce*
Disky DCD 8004   *Kansas City and the Southwest*
LaserLight 17 171   *Jazz Piano Anthology: The Magic Touch, volume 4*

It is beyond the scope of this discography to mention the many LP reissues of recordings made by Mary Lou Williams, especially from the Clouds of Joy era, and her work as a soloist and leader in the 1940s. Several interesting LP's are:

Stash 109, 111 (a collection of female pianists); and Stash 113, *Jazz Women: A Feminist Retrospective*
MCA 1308, *Instrumentally Speaking*
Folkways FJ 2852, *Piano Greats*

Selected Appearances by Mary Lou Williams on Video

I Have a Dream (1968)   Documentary film of MLW by New York University Motion Picture Workshop, produced by Edward Flanagan.

Segment on *Mr. Roger's Neighborhood* (1973)   Program No. 1313.

Segment on *Sesame Street*, Children's Television Workshop(1970s, undated).

Mary Lou's Mass (1976)   Documentary film of *Mass* and performance at the Cookery, produced by Thomas C. Guy, Jr.

"A Christmas Special with Mary Lou Williams at Duke University" (1977) Taped on December 5 and aired on Christmas Eve 1977, this program includes MLW with bassist Freeman Ledbetter, and with Duke University students, singing her arrangements of Christmas carols.

Live performance for ETV-Nebraska (1980)   Valuable documentation of one of her last filmed public performances; with Milton Suggs (bass), and Hugh Walker (drums). Portions excerpted for the 1983 TV program "Swinging the Blues," hosted by Dr. Billy Taylor.

Music on My Mind (1981)   Documentary study of MLW by Joanne Burke. Distributed through Women Make Movies, New York.

See also Mary Lou Williams Archive at Institute of Jazz Studies for more listings.

Selected Available Recordings on CD of Mary Lou Williams Compositions Performed by Other Artists

(Various tunes)

Dave Douglas (t, leader, arr, composer) and combo (personnel not known), *Soul on Soul: Celebrating Mary Lou Williams*, RCA Victor, forthcoming late 1999

Marian McPartland (p), *Marian McPartland Plays the Music of Mary Lou Williams*, Concord Jazz 4605

Roll 'Em

Shirley Scott (o), Impulse GRP 147

Diva Big Band, Diva Ltd. CD-079602

Pretty-eyed Baby

Roy Eldridge, Dizzy Gillespie (leaders, t, vcl), Verve Clef 314521647-2, October 29, 1954

Satchel Mouth Baby

Nat Cole (trio) (v, p, leader), Classic Jazz 8477, 1944

Nat Cole (trio) (v, p, leader), Four Star "Master Series," FS-40047

Little Joe from Chicago

Nat Cole (trio) (v, p, leader), Four Star "Master Series," FS-40047

Nat Cole, Delta Music LaserLight 15 746, Volume 1

What's Your Story, Morning Glory?

Ella Fitzgerald (v), Verve 517535-2, 1958

Jimmie Lunceford Orchestra, Living Era AJA 5091, 1940
The American Jazz Orchestra, Music Masters Jazz 65072-2, 1991
Anita O'Day (v), Verve Polygram 837939-2, 1959
Milt Jackson (vib) Original Jazz Classics 404-2, 1963

———

Black Coffee
Sarah Vaughan (v), Columbia C2K 44165 (after MLW's *Morning Glory*)

———

In the Land of Oo-bla-dee
Dizzy Gillespie Orchestra, RCA/BMG 09026-68499-2, 1949
Benny Goodman septet, Capitol 32086, and Mosaic MD4-148, 1949 (also MLW,
     arr.)

———

Walkin' Out the Door
Nat Cole (trio) (p), Capitol Jazz CDP 0777 7 89545 2
Honi Gordon (v), Prestige PR 7230

———

Why
Honi Gordon (v), Prestige PR 7230

———

Lonely Moments
George Shearing (p), Verve 314 529 900-2, 1951
Benny Goodman Orch. (leader, cl), Capitol 32086, 1948 (also MLW, arr.)

———

Whistle Blues
Benny Goodman Orch. (leader, cl), Capitol 32086, 1948 (also MLW, arr.)

———

Walkin' and Swingin'
Jim Galloway Big Band, Sackville (C) 3222, 1993

———

Steppin' Pretty
Jim Galloway Big Band, Sackville (C) 3222, 1993

———

Koolbongo
Billy Taylor (p), Original Jazz Classics (Fantasy) OJCCD-1830-2, 1959

———

Swingin' Til the Guys Come Home
Lambert, Hendricks and Bavan (v), Bluebird 6282-2-R11, 1962

———

Mary's Idea
Benny Goodman combo, Dragon (Sweden) 183, 1948

———

Lullaby of the Leaves
Geri Allen (p), Somethin' Else CDP 72438 300028 25 (arr. only by MLW)

———

Recordings of Mary Lou Williams Arrangements by the Duke Ellington Orchestra or by Small Ensembles of Ellington Personnel

Trumpets No End   The best-known arrangement by Mary for the Ellington Orchestra is "Trumpets No End," a.k.a. "Trumpet No End," an arrangement of "Blue Skies." It first appeared on record on November 8, 1943; there were many later recordings, from 1944 to 1953. CD Circle 101 includes five takes of "Trumpet(s) No End."

Sweet Georgia Brown   Mary's arrangement of "Sweet Georgia Brown," recorded in June 1943, is available on CD Jazz Archives 15 8432, *Kansas City Legends*. In the band on the date was a young Dizzy Gillespie, subbing for Mary's then-husband Harold Baker.

Chief (Natoma from Tacoma)   Mary's composition, in a new arrangement, is on CD SAJA Records 791045-2, *Duke Ellington, The Private Collection, Volume 5, The Suites, New York 1968 and 1970*, in *The River*. A second arrangement of "Chief" is on CD Pablo OJCCD-446-2, *The Ellington Suites*, in the *UWis Suite*.

Chopsticks   Mary Lou Williams is coarranger with Duke Ellington on this January 1945 recording, on Circle CD-103.

Variations on Stardust   Recorded at Carnegie Hall concert December 11, 1943, on LP Ember (E)EMBD2001.

Ghost of Love   Ben Webster (ts); Billy Strayhorn (p); Al Hibbler (v); unidentified rhythm. IAJRC 30

A Selection of Mary Lou Williams Compositions Recorded by Other Artists on LPs

Cloudy   Red Garland (p), Moodsville LP MVPL10 (Japan), 1960

Steppin' Pretty   Buck Clayton (t), Riverside R-353/9353

The Devil (Is a Woman)   Ada Moore (v), Debut Records 15

Strange Fascination   Ada Moore (v), Debut Records 15

Walkin' and Swingin'   (1) Gene Krupa and Orchestra, Ajax 110, 1938; (2) Les Brown and Orchestra, Decca 3167, 1940

A Mellow Bit of Rhythm   (1) Les Brown and Orchestra, Decca 3167; (2) Red Norvo, Big Band Archives LP 2201, 1944

Lonely Moments   (1) Gene Sedric and Orchestra, Harmonia H1806, 1946; (2) Edmond Hall and Café Society Orchestra (cl), Continental 6026 1946

Little Joe from Chicago   Wingy Manone (t), Bluebird B-7622, 1938

(In the Land of) Oo Bla Dee   (1) Junior Mance (p), Jazzland JLP 30, 1960; (2) Les Brown and Orchestra, Hindsight HSR 132

Scorpio   Oscar Pettiford octet (b), Bethlehem BC-P33, 1955

What's Your Story Morning Glory?   Glenn Miller Orchestra, BB B10832/reissue RCA (F) LFMI-7516, 1940

Messa Stomp   Dreamland Syncopators, Keith Nichols (leader), Stomp Off Records LP SOS 1150

WNEW Half-hour Weekly Program, "The Mary Lou Williams Piano Workshop": 1945

Tapes in Mary Lou Williams collection.

4/11/45   With Al Lucas (b), Jack Parker (d), and Joe Carroll (v). Mary played *and sang* her composition "You Know, Baby." On "Put Another Nickel In," she provided bop accompaniment to Joe Carroll's vocals. Other tunes included "Sheik of Araby," "I Found a New Baby," "Lullaby of the Leaves," "Roll 'Em," "Dark Eyes," and, "Froggy Bottom."

4/18/45   With Lucas and Parker. Mary opened with an untitled and improvised theme, followed by "St. Louis Blues," "Sweet Lorraine," "I Know That You Know," "Limehouse Blues," "In My Solitude," "Blue Skies," "Mary Lou's Boogie," and "Honeysuckle Rose."

4/25/45   With Lucas and Parker. Mary played her theme, then "Marcheta," a medley of "Morning Glory"/"Cloudy"/"Ghost of Love," "Limehouse Blues," "Beloved Comrade" (Josh White, vocals), "You Know Baby," "Froggy Bottom," "When Dreams Come True," and "I Got Rhythm."

5/2/45   With Lucas, Parker, Betty Leeds (ts). Opened with the theme, then "Blue Skies," "Sweet Georgia Brown" (with Leeds), "I Know That You Know," "Gjon Mili Jam Session," "The Man I Love" (with Leeds), "St. Louis Blues," "Honeysuckle Rose," and "I Got Rhythm."

6/17/45   With Al Hall (b), Bill Coleman (t), Elwood Smith (v). The theme, "I Got Rhythm," "Persian Rug," "Let My People Go" (with Elwood Smith), "Blue Skies," "Lady Be Good," "Night and Day," "Oh No John" (with Smith), "I Know That You Know," "Mary Lou's Boogie" (Mary and Hall only), "I Got Rhythm" (quartet).

6/24/45   With Johnny Williams (b), Art Trappier (d), Edmond Hall (cl). Opened with the theme, "Limehouse Blues," "Rose Room" (with Edmond Hall), "Gjon Mili Jam Session" (with Hall), several bars of possibly "Salt Peanuts," "After You've Gone" (with Hall), "In My Solitude," "Marcheta," "Roll 'Em" (with Hall), "Honeysuckle Rose" (with Hall).

7/1/45   Same personnel as above. Theme, "St. Louis Blues," "Carcinoma" (with Hall), "I Never Knew" (with Hall), "Stardust" (introduced but not on the tape), "I Know That You Know" (with Hall).

7/8/45   With Dose or Mose Dickens (b), Wally Bishop (d), Gene Sedric (cl). Theme, "Lonely Moments"—misintroduced as "Lovely Moments"—(with

Sedric), "Man of Mine" (with Sedric), unidentified tune (with Sedric), "You Know, Baby" (with Sedric and v by Mary), "After You've Gone" (with Sedric).

7/15/45 Same personnel as above. Theme, "Twinklin'" (with Sedric), "Sometimes I'm Happy" (with Sedric; interrupted by World War II news bulletin), "I've Got a Song in My Soul" (new MLW comp). Again a news bulletin interruption. "Lonely Moments" (with Sedric), "It Had to Be You" (v by Dickens with Sedric), "When Dreams Come True," "The Man I Love" (with Sedric), "The Sheik of Araby" (with Sedric).

7/22/45 With Curley Russell (b), Charlie Simon (d), Sylvia Syms (v). Theme, "When Dreams Come True," "Song in My Soul" (with Sylvia Syms), "Dark Eyes," "Mean to Me" (with Sims), "Marcheta," Gershwin Medley (piano solo), "I Got Rhythm," "St. Louis Blues," "Honeysuckle Rose," theme.

7/29/45 With Josh White (v and g), Bunny White (v). Theme, "Honeysuckle Rose" (piano solo), "Tea for Two" (piano solo), "I Want You, I Need You" (v and g by Josh White only), "Waltzing Matilda" (B. White, v), "Mary Lou's Boogie" (piano solo), "Lord Randall" (B. White, v), "Free and Equal Blues" (by Josh White), theme, piano solo.

8/5/45 Personnel unclear; probably Al Hall (b), Specs Powell (d), Bill Coleman (t). "When Dreams Come True" and "Lonely Moments" introduced, but only the last chorus is on the tape, "Roll 'Em." "Sleep" on LP (see p. 416).

8/12/45 Same personnel, also Ann Hathaway (v). "Gjon Mili Jam Session" (on LP: see p. 416), "Persian Rug," news interruption, "Let My People Go" (Bill Coleman, v), "How High the Moon," "The Man I Love," "Ghost of Love" (Ann Hathaway, v).

On the WNEW program, Mary played the following signs of the Zodiac:

4/4/45	Gemini
4/11/45	Cancer
4/18/45	Leo
4/25/45	Virgo
5/2/45	Libra
6/17/45	Capricorn (piano solo)
6/24/45	Aquarius—incomplete sketch.
7/1/45	Pisces
7/8/45	Scorpio
7/22/45	Aquarius
7/29/45	Sagittarius
8/5/45	Pisces

WOR RADIO

9/7/45   Interview and performance before a studio audience, Mary with Al Lucas (b), Jack Parker (d). "Waltz Boogie" and "Fifth Dimension."

Mary also performed frequently on radio in the 1940s, early 1950s, and mid-1960s (WABC, *circa* 1964).

Compositions and Arrangements
by Mary Lou Williams

1. Mary Lou Williams's Compositions and Co-compositions for Andy Kirk and the Clouds of Joy

1936

Walkin' and Swingin'
Lotta Sax Appeal
Git
Froggy Bottom (rearranged version)
Bearcat Shuffle
Steppin' Pretty
Corky
Cloudy (rearranged version)

1937

In the Groove
A Mellow Bit of Rhythm

1938

Twinklin'
Little Joe from Chicago
Messa Stomp (rearranged version)
Toadie Toddle
Ghost of Love
What's Your Story, Morning Glory?

Dunkin' a Doughnut
Mary's Idea (rearranged version)

1939

Close to Five
Big Jim Blues

1940

Why Go on Pretending
Scratchin' in the Gravel

1941

Big Time Crip

2. *Selected Arrangements by Mary Lou Williams for Other Big Bands*

For Benny Goodman: "The Count," "Messa Stomp," "Toadie Toddle" (and see below)

For Cab Calloway: "Ghost of Love," "Toadie Toddle"

For Louis Armstrong: "Messa Stomp," "Walkin' and Swingin'," "A Mellow Bit of Rhythm," "Cloudy"

For Bob Crosby: "Steppin' Pretty," "Ghost of Love"

For Tommy Dorsey: "Little Joe from Chicago"

For Red Norvo: "A Mellow Bit of Rhythm," "Messa Stomp"

For Glen Gray and the Casa Loma Orchestra: "Walkin' and Swingin'," "What's Your Story, Morning Glory?"

For The Sweethearts of Rhythm: "St. Louis Blues"

3. *Selected Compositions and Arrangements by Mary Lou Williams for Benny Goodman*

Most of the material that Mary Lou Williams arranged for Benny Goodman in the 1930s and 1940s, including many incomplete scores, is contained in the Benny Goodman Archive at Yale University; other material is at the Library of the Performing Arts, at Lincoln Center in New York.

Benny's Bop   MLW composer, arranger

Benny's Boogie   MLW arranger

Blue Views (1948)   MLW arranger

Bye Bye Blues (1948)   MLW arranger

Camel Hop

Conversation (1947)   MLW arranger

The Count (late 1930s)

Donna Lee (1948)   MLW arranger

(In the Land of) Oo-bla-dee   MLW composer, arranger

Knowledge (1949)

Kool (1948)   MLW composer and arranger

Lonely Moments (1946)   MLW composer and arranger

Lonely Moments (1947)   MLW arranger (new version)

Mary's Idea, a.k.a. Just an Idea (1946)   MLW composer and arranger

Mary's Idea (1948)   MLW arranger (new version)

Messa Stomp (late 1930s)

Out of This World (1941)   MLW arranger

Riffs (1937)   MLW composer and arranger

Roll 'Em (1937)   MLW composer, arranger

Shafi (1977)   MLW co-composer (with Shafi Hadid), arranger

Shorty Boo (1949)

Stealin' Apples (1948)   MLW arranger

(Sweet) Georgia Brown (late 1930s)

(There's a) Small Hotel   MLW arranger

Tisherome (1949)

Toadie Toddle (late 1930s)

Untitled (1948)   MLW arranger

Walkin' (Out the Door)   MLW and Lindsay Steele co-composers, MLW arranger

Whistle Blues (1946)   MLW and Milt Orent co-composers, MLW arranger

Whistle Blues (1947)   MLW arranger (new version)

You Do Something to Me (1940)   MLW arranger

You Turned the Tables on Me (1948)   MLW arranger

You Were Meant for Me (1948)   MLW arranger

4. *Compositions and/or Arrangements by Mary Lou Williams for the Ellington Orchestra, 1940s through 1960s*

Between the Devil and the Deep Blue Sea   MLW arranger

Blue Love   MLW arranger, possibly composer

Blue Skies/Trumpet(s) No End   MLW arrangement (Ellington archive) (recorded)

Body and Soul   MLW arranger

Canteen Bounce   MLW arranger

Chief (Natoma from Tacoma)   MLW arranger (recorded)

Chopsticks   MLW and Ellington coarrangers (recorded)

Conversation   MLW arranger

The Count   MLW arranger

Don't Play the Mambo   MLW arranger

Everything but You   MLW arranger (recorded)

Fill the Cup   MLW arranger

Flamingo   MLW arranger

Ghost of Love   MLW composer and arranger (recorded)

Giddap Mule   MLW arranger

Gone with the Blues   MLW arranger

Gone with the Wind   MLW arranger

He Should'a Flipped When He Flopp'd   MLW arranger (recorded)

Honeysuckle Rose   MLW arranger

I Love Coffee, a.k.a. Java Jive   MLW arranger

Joe   MLW and Milt Orent co-composers, MLW arranger

Knowledge   MLW composer and arranger

Little Joe from Chicago   MLW composer and arranger

Lonely Moments   MLW composer and arranger

Lotsa Mama   MLW co-composer
with Bob Russell (lyric), MLW
arranger
Mister Good Blues   MLW arranger
Move It Over   MLW arranger
My Blue Heaven   MLW arranger
My Gal Sal   MLW arranger
(New) Musical Express, a.k.a. N.M.E.
MLW composer and arranger
Ogeechee River Lullaby   MLW
arranger
Otto, Make That Riff Staccato   MLW
arranger (recorded)
O.W.   MLW composer and arranger
Perdido   MLW arranger
Scorpio (from *Zodiac Suite*)   MLW
composer and arranger
Scratchin' in the Gravel, a.k.a. Truth
MLW composer and arranger
Seventy-one   MLW composer and
arranger
Shiny Stockings   MLW arranger
Shorty Boo Blues   MLW composer and
arranger
Sleepy Valley   MLW arranger
Somebody Stole My Gal   MLW
arranger
Something to Live For   MLW arranger
Spring's Swing   MLW arranger
Star Dust, a.k.a. Mary Lou Williams's
Stardust   MLW arranger
(Sweet) Georgia Brown   MLW
arranger (recorded)
We'd Be the Same   MLW arranger
You Know, Baby ("rock-'n-roll" version)
MLW composer and arranger

5. *Selected Compositions by Mary Lou Williams*

Act of Contrition
The Adding Machine
Amy
Angel Love (*with M. D. Foster*)
Anima Christi, a.k.a. Anima Cristi Suite

Aquarius
Aries, a.k.a. Aries Mood
Babs
Baby Bear Boogie
Back to the Blues
Ballot Box Boogie (in the Key of
Franklin D.) (*with Bob Russell*)
Basic Chords: Bop Changes on the Blues
Bearcut Shuffle
Big Jim Blues (*with Harry Lawson*)
Big Time Crip (*with Henry Wells*)
Black Christ of the Andes, a.k.a. (Hymn
in Honor of) St. Martin de Porres
(*with Anthony Woods*)
Blue Pastel, a.k.a. (In the) Purple
Grotto, a.k.a. Mary's Blues
The Blues (*with Cynthia Tyson*)
Blues for Club Français, a.k.a. Club
Français Blues
Blues for John
Blues for Peter
The Blues Never Left Me
Bobo
Bobo and Doodles
Boogie Misterioso, a.k.a. Flunga Dunga
Breeze
Camel Hop
Cancer
Cancer Mood, a.k.a. Carcinoma
Capricorn
Cee E. Larkins
Chant of the Jitterbugs (*with Sharon
Pease*)
Chicka Boom Blues
Chief Natoma from Tacoma (*with Milton Orent*)
Chili Sauce
Christmas Celebration Interlude
(medley)
Chunka Lunka
Clean Pickin'
Close to Five
Cloudy
The Colonel's in Love with Nancy,
a.k.a. The Colonel Loves Nancy

Conversation, a.k.a. Jump Caprice

Cootchie

Corky, a.k.a. Corky Stomp (*with Andy Kirk*)

Corny Rhythm

Deuces Wild

The Devil, a.k.a. Devil (*with Ada Moore*)

Dirge Blues, a.k.a. Don't Cry, Baby

Don't Do This—Don't Do That—That's How She's Treatin' Me (*with Frank Lewis*)

Drag 'Em

Du

The Duke and the Count

Dunkin' a Doughnut

Easy Blues, a.k.a. Easy

8th Avenue Express

Elijah (Under the Juniper Tree) (*with Ray M. Carr and Milton Orent*)

Exit Playing

Fandangle

Fannie

The Feller from Savannah

Fifth Dimension

Flying Solo (*with Paula Stone*)

For the Figs

Froggy Bottom (*with John Williams*)

Froggy Bottom (*with lyric,* 1938; and 1944 variation on melody)

A Fungus Amungus

Gemini

Gemma

Gerrard Street (*with Albon Timothy*)

Gettin' Off a Mess

Ghost of Love (*with Sharon Pease and Jack Lawrence*)

Gjon Mili Jam Session

Gloria (*with Robert Ledogar*)

Glory to God

Good Ole Boogie

Gootchie

Hesitation Boogie

Holy Ghost (*with Larry Gales*)

Holy Holy Holy

I Can't Go On This Way (*with Cecil Doty*)

I Don't Know

I Have a Dream (*after words of the Rev. Martin Luther King, Jr.*)

I Love Him, a.k.a. I Love You

I Never Know

(I Went to a) Gypsy (*with Dick Brooks*)

(I) Won't Let it Bother Me

I'd Still Love You (*with Morris Minton*)

If I Thought You Cared (*with Henry Wells*)

If You're Around

I'm Fooling Myself

I'm Happy, I Guess (*with Ada Moore*)

I'm Not Complaining

In His Day

In the Land of Oo-bla-dee (*with Milton Orent*)

Isabelle

Jazz (Close Your Eyes and Listen with the Ears of Your Heart) (*with Gracie Glassman*)

J.B.'s Waltz (*with Milton Suggs*)

Jesus Is the Best (*with Tom Virga*)

Joe (*with Milton Orent*)

Joycie, a.k.a. Joyce, a.k.a. Watchers

K.C. 12th Street: Kansas City Swing

(Keep It) in the Groove (*with Dick Wilson*)

Knowledge, a.k.a. Elevation

Kool

Koolbongo a.k.a. Koolbonga

Lamb of God

Lazarus, a.k.a. Beggar Man

Laudle Leedle (*with Leon Thomas*)

Lazy Ginger

The Left Side Is the Right Side (*with Milton Orent and Stuart Sprague*)

Leo

Let's Do the Froggy Bottom (*with Juanita Fleming*)

Libra, a.k.a. Libra Mood

Little Joe from Chicago (*with Henry Wells*)

The Little Scotch Tailor (*with Frank Lewis*)

Little Willie & Stack O' Lee

Lonely Moments

Lord Have Mercy

Lord Have Mercy (*with George Tucker*)

The Lord Is Heavy, a.ka. Spiritual II and Spiritual III

The Lord Says

Lotta Sax Appeal (*with John Williams*)

Love

Love Lies (*with Milton Orent*)

Love Roots

Man O'Mine, a.k.a. Sweet Juice

Marnier Mood

Mary Lou Williams Blues

Mary's Boogie

Mary's Idea, a.k.a. Just an Idea

Mary's Waltz (*with Herbie Nichols*)

Mass for the Lenten Season, a.k.a. Praise the Lord

Medi

Medi II, a.k.a. Busy Busy Busy (New York) (*with Gracie Glassman*)

A Mellow Bit of Rhythm (*with Herman Walder*)

Melody Maker

Messa Stomp (*revised 1938*)

Midnite Blues

Miss D.D.

Misty Blues

Mr. Kennedy (*with Paul Oakes*)

Mu

My Brother Jim (*with Robert Scott and Paul Oakes*)

My Dreamer

My Favorite Memory (*with Sharon Pease*)

My Horoscope (*with Milton Orent*)

My Last Affair

My Mama Pinned a Rose on Me

N.G. Blues

Nickels

Nicknames

Nicole

Nirees (*with Idrees Sulieman*)

Nite Life, a.k.a. Night Life

N.M.E., a.k.a. Express, a.k.a. Musical Express, a.k.a. New Musical Express

No Title Blues

Nursery Rhyme No. 2 (Mary's Lamb)

Ode to Saint Cecilia

Offertory Meditation

Old Time Spiritual

Out of My Dreaming (*with Vic Dickenson and Tobie Kaye*)

Overhand

Overture

O.W.

Pater Noster, a.k.a. Our Father

People in Trouble

Pisces

Pittsburgh (*with Milton Orent*)

Play It, Momma

Po-ta-be, a.k.a. Po-tabe (*with Melba Liston*)

Praise the Lord

Prelude to Prism

Pretty-eyed Baby, a.k.a. Piccola Baby (*with William Johnson and Leo "Snub" Mosley*)

The Pussy's in the Well (Nursery Rhyme 1)

Rhythmic Pattern

Riffs

The Rocks

Roll 'Em

Rosa Mae (*with Larry Gales and Gracie Glassman*)

Sagittarius

Satchel Mouth Baby

The Scarlet Creeper

Scorpio

Scratchin' in the Gravel, a.k.a. Truth

Selas

Shafi (*with Shafi Hadid*)

She Went Up and Down on a Merry Go Round (*with Frank Lewis*)

Shoo be doo be doo, Santa Claus (*with Cynthia Tyson*)

Shorty Boo (*with Milton Orent*)

Show Business

Song in My Soul

Space Playing Blues

Special Freight

Steppin' Pretty (*with B. Kaempfert and H. Rehbein*)

Strange Fascination (*with Ada Moore*)

Strictly on the Know (*with Paula Stone*)

Sweet (Patootie) Patunia

Swingin' for Joy

Swingin' Til the Guys Come Home (*with Oscar Pettiford*)

Syl-O-Gism (*with Larry Gales*)

Take the Heat off Me

Take the Wagon

Taurus, a.k.a. Taurus Mood, a.k.a. Study in the Blues

Tell Him Not to Talk Too Long (*after words of the Rev. Martin Luther King, Jr.*)

Tell Me How Long Will the Train Be Gone? (*with Paula Stone*)

Terry Sanford (*with Cynthia Tyson*)

Thank You, Jesus

Theme from the Third World (*with Herbie Nichols*)

There's a Thing in My Heart (*with Joseph Mangiapane*)

This Is the Way to My Heart

The Time Is Now (*with Paula Stone*)

Timme Time

Timme's Blues, a.k.a. Blues for Timme

Tisherome

Toadie Toddle (*with Sharon Pease*)

Turtle Speed Blues

Twilight

Twinklin'

Virgo

Votive Mass for Peace, a.k.a. Mass for Peace

Waiting (*with Don Mickles*)

Walkin', a.k.a. Walkin' Out the Door (*with Lindsay Steele*)

Walkin' and Swingin'

Waltz Boogie, a.k.a. Dunga

Wanderland (*with Don Mickles and Manny Fernandez*)

We Three

We're in Harmony

What I Really Like Is Loving You (*with Paula Stone*)

What's Your Story, Morning Glory? (*with Paul F. Webster and Jack Lawrence*)

Whistle, a.k.a. Whistle Blues (*with Milton Orent*)

Whose Little Who Are You? a.k.a. Whose Little Boy Are You? (*with Ada Moore*)

Why?

Why Go On Pretending? (*with Roy Jacobs*)

Willis

Yankee Doodle Blues (*with lyric by Bob Russell*)

Yarm (*with George Tucker*)

Yatcha Dubue

Yesterday's Kisses

You Are My Little One (*with Paula Stone*)

You Know Baby (*with Frank Lewis*)

You Locked the Door (*with Vic Dickenson and Tobie Kaye*)

Zoning, a.k.a. Intermission (*with Milton Suggs*)

Zoning Fungus II, a.k.a. Fungus Number 2

Index

ILLUSTRATION CREDITS

The photographs in this book are reproduced courtesy of the following:

Geraldine Burley Garnett: Fletcher and Julius Burley

Helen Floyd and Geraldine Burley Garnett: with Mamie Floyd and her children

John Williams: John Williams with saxophone; Mary Lou Williams with Margaret Warren and Arletta Harris; the Clouds of Joy

W. Eugene Smith Archive, Center for Creative Photography, The University of Arizona. Copyright © The Heirs of W. Eugene Smith, Courtesy of Black Star, Inc., New York: listening to playback at recording session (begins second photo section)

Photograph by Bob Parent. Copyright © Bob Parent Archive: with Oscar Pettiford at Child's Paramount Theatre

Photograph by William P. Gottlieb. Copyright © William P. Gottlieb. From the Collection of The Library of Congress: at jazz "salon," 63 Hamilton Terrace; with Jack Teagarden

M. Gray Weingarten: Lindsay Steele

Photograph by Art Kane. Copyright © The Estate of Art Kane: with Ronnie Free, Mose Allison, Lester Young, Charlie Rouse, Oscar Pettiford

Photograph by Dennis Stock. Copyright © Dennis Stock/Magnum Photos, Inc.: in apartment, 1958, with back to piano (begins third photo section)

Copyright © 1984 by Malcolm G. Moore, Jr. Courtesy of Joyce Breach: with Dizzy Gillespie

Photograph by Carl Van Vechten, with permission of The Van Vechten Trust: Peter O'Brien as a young seminarian

Copyright © Tom Caffrey/Globe Photos, Inc.: kneeling at prayer in church

Duke University Library: teaching jazz at Duke University

Photograph by Louis M. Ruffulo: convalescing at Duke University Hospital

Photograph by Ken Abé. Copyright © Ken Abé: performing at the Cookery Restaurant

All other photographs are courtesy of the Mary Lou Williams Collection at the Institute of Jazz Studies

ABOUT THE AUTHOR

LINDA DAHL has written the acclaimed *Stormy Weather: The Music and Lives of a Century of Jazzwomen,* and many shorter pieces about music and musicians. She lives with her husband, daughter, dog, and cat in upstate New York.